JANUARY MOON

JANUARY MOON

The Northern Cheyenne Breakout from Fort Robinson, 1878–1879

JEROME A. GREENE

University of Oklahoma Press : Norman

"Fort Robinson," from *Sure Signs: New and Selected Poems*, by Ted Kooser, © 1980. Reprinted with permission of the University of Pittsburgh Press.

Library of Congress Cataloging-in-Publication Data

Names: Greene, Jerome A., author.
Title: January Moon : The Northern Cheyenne Breakout from Fort Robinson, 1878–1879 / Jerome A. Greene.
Description: Norman : University of Oklahoma Press, [2020] | Includes bibliographical references and index. | Summary: "Draws from extensive research and fieldwork to explore the desperate flight of Chief Dull Knife's Northern Cheyenne Indians from imprisonment at Fort Robinson, Nebraska, their near annihilation, the survivors' dreadful experiences in the aftermath, and the present-day Cheyenne tribal events commemorating the breakout"—Provided by publisher.
Identifiers: LCCN 2019046216 | ISBN 978-0-8061-6478-6 (hardcover)
Subjects: LCSH: Cheyenne Indians—Nebraska—Government relations. | Massacres—Nebraska—Fort Robinson—History—19th century. | Indians of North America—Wars—1866–1895.
Classification: LCC E99.C53 G75 2020 | DDC 323.1197/353078293—dc23
LC record available at https://lccn.loc.gov/2019046216

The paper in this book meets the guidelines for permanence and durability of the Committee on Production Guidelines for Book Longevity of the Council on Library Resources, Inc. ∞

2 3 4 5 6 7 8 9 10

To the Northern Cheyennes and the Crazy Dogs,
and to the memory of Steve Brady, 1956–2014,
educator and warrior for his people

Fort Robinson

When I visited Fort Robinson,
where Dull Knife and his Northern Cheyenne
were held captive that terrible winter,
the grounds crew was killing the magpies.

Two men were going from tree to tree
with sticks and ladders, poking the young birds
down from their nests and beating them to death
as they hopped about in the grass.

Under each tree where the men had worked
were twisted clots of matted feathers,
and above each tree a magpie circled
crazily calling in all her voices.

We didn't get out of the car.
My little boy hid in the back and cried
as we drove away, into those ragged buttes
the Cheyenne climbed that winter, fleeing.

—Ted Kooser

Contents

Illustrations

Figures

Maps

Preface and Acknowledgments

This book is a product of my long personal and professional interest in the history of Fort Robinson, Nebraska, during the period of the Indian conflicts of the mid-nineteenth to late nineteenth century. The post's initial years coincided with several intriguing yet altogether tragic facets of the American experience in the West, perhaps none more appallingly heartrending than the U.S. Army's incarceration of Chief Dull Knife's Northern Cheyenne Indians at Fort Robinson after their attempt to leave the Indian Territory (in modern Oklahoma) and return to their homes on the northern plains. While the entire episode evokes nearly universal consternation over the policies and practices of the United States government with regard to Indian matters, the experiences of the Northern Cheyennes at Fort Robinson proved especially harrowing as events played out. The descendants of those people survive today, which has more to do with their ancestors' spirit and tenacity as well as their own commitment to fairness and right than with the federal incentive and military comportment that largely fostered the events of 1878–79.

This study further embraces a special interest of mine: the history of America's military presence in the greater West during the late nineteenth century, especially the U.S. Army's interaction with regional Native peoples. The allure of these events is reflected in part by my previous studies of the Sand Creek Massacre, Washita, the Sioux and Nez Percé wars, Wounded Knee, and other related subjects. The decade of the 1870s was fraught with army-Indian combat in the West, much of it grounded in the Native American tribes' resistance to government regulation and attempted domination of their lives. The Northern Cheyennes' decision to forego their untenable experience on the southern plains and strike out for their home country in the north was in keeping with similar movements by other Native peoples who despairingly chose to break away, including the Navajos, Lakotas, Nez Percés, Poncas, and Utes as they resisted uncertain futures on government reserves. I was drawn to the present study by what I felt was the need for a holistic treatment of the Fort Robinson breakout based on a panoply of sources, many of them new or hitherto underutilized, as well as by the appeal of visiting sites where the events played out.

The study, of course, required the use of evidence from Northern Cheyenne participants, because such testimony is vital to comprehending what happened at Fort Robinson. Fortunately, numerous such first-person accounts survive, as referenced herein, and were mined for pertinent data. I hope that other Northern Cheyenne tribal reminiscences, if they are still extant among descendant families, may yield still more vital information to enhance our comprehension of these events and enthusiastically encourage such a pursuit. Additional facets of the story emerged in my study of period maps and locational information, which assisted my subsequent ground-truthing of elements of the onerous landscape that Northern Cheyenne men, women, and children, as well as the pursuing troops, navigated in the days immediately following the initial escape from the post. I was fortunate, too, in obtaining important data explaining the army's removal of some Northern Cheyenne victims' remains more than a year after their burial at Antelope Creek, as well as material describing their appropriate return home generations later.

A profoundly essential primary source for what happened at Fort Robinson in 1878 and 1879 in regard to the army and the Northern Cheyennes is "Proceedings of a Board of Officers." This document, generated immediately after the military response to the breakout, has provided essential data. Despite passing references in earlier studies, however, it has not previously been employed sufficiently to broaden our knowledge of events. The "Proceedings" offer a bureaucratically sanctioned foundational record for what happened and consequently present the army's perspective on events. As in the case of many other government-generated documents (including some cited herein), its tenor and conclusions must be judiciously considered. That said, its contents proved of inestimable benefit to my work.

I would particularly like to acknowledge Father Peter J. Powell, whose voluminous and definitive studies reflect his lifelong commitment to learning and sharing the Northern Cheyenne perspective on these and other events. I am grateful for his insightful and meaningful work. In addition, I wish to thank the following individuals and institutions for their unwavering assistance throughout this endeavor: Andrew and Holly Federle, Harrison, Nebraska; Charles E. Rankin, Helena, Montana; Paul L. Hedren, Omaha, Nebraska; Randy Kane, Crawford, Nebraska; the late L. Clifford Soubier, Charles Town, West Virginia; the late Thomas R. Buecker, Lincoln, Nebraska; the late John D. McDermott, Rapid City, South Dakota; David A. Wolff, Spearfish, South Dakota; John Warner, Billings, Montana; Ted Kooser, Garland, Nebraska; Vonnie Zullo, Fairfax, Virginia; William Stolldorf, Crawford, Nebraska; Vance and Karen Nelson, Ogallala, Nebraska; Loren K. Pospisil Jr., Chimney Rock, Nebraska; Sharon Small, Hardin, Montana; Ramon S. Powers, Topeka, Kansas; Margot Liberty, Sheridan, Wyoming; Chris Petersen, Corvallis, Oregon; Brian Dippie, Victoria, British Columbia; John Monnett, Lafayette, Colorado; Mort Wegman-French, Boulder, Colorado; Martha Vestecke Miller, History Nebraska, Lincoln, Nebraska; Annie Donofrio, Buffalo, New York; Carol A. Breuer, Fort Collins, Colorado; Edwin C. Bearss, Arlington, Virginia; Steven Fullmer, Fort Laramie National Historical Site, Wyoming; Douglas D. Scott, Grand Junction, Colorado; Greg Michno, Frederick, Colorado; Mary Jane Warde, Stillwater, Oklahoma; John A. Doerner, Hardin, Montana; Larry Ness, Yankton, South Dakota; Marc Abrams, Brooklyn, New York; R. Eli Paul, Kansas City, Missouri; Lori Cox-Paul, Kansas City, Missouri; Jeffrey M. Greene, Erie, Colorado; Jane Stark, Maxwell, Nebraska; the late Douglas C. McChristian, Tucson, Arizona; Daniel Martinez, Honolulu, Hawaii; Don Stevens, National Park Service, Omaha, Nebraska; Casey Madrick, West Point Archives, U.S. Military Academy, West Point, New York; Leanne Walther, Boulder, Colorado; April M. Sullivan, Las Vegas, Nevada; Erik Bittner, Don Dutcher, and Carol L. Donache, Historical Society of Cecil County, Maryland; Laura Jasiewicz and Rick Martinez, National Archives, Broomfield, Colorado; Jill Balcon, Harrison, Nebraska; Jerry Taylor, Fort Robinson State Park, Crawford, Nebraska; Michael J. Koury, Johnstown, Colorado; Jerome A. Greene Jr., Greenville, South Carolina; Paul Harbaugh, Cherry Hills Village, Colorado; the late Michael Her Many Horses, Wounded Knee, South Dakota; Gale Henry, Harrison, Nebraska; Cindy Hagen, Little Bighorn Battlefield National Monument,

Crow Agency, Montana; Jane Stark, Maxwell, Nebraska; Emily J. Schuster, Norman, Oklahoma; Steven Baker, Norman, Oklahoma; and Kathy Lewis, Iowa City, Iowa.

I must also acknowledge the assistance received from the following institutions: the National Archives and Records Administration, Broomfield, Colorado; Fort Robinson Museum, Fort Robinson State Park, Nebraska; Denver Public Library, Denver, Colorado; Jefferson County Public Libraries, Lakewood and Arvada, Colorado; University of Colorado Libraries, Boulder; Sioux County Historical Museum, Harrison, Nebraska; Wyoming State Archives, Cheyenne; Special Collections and Archives Research Center, Oregon State University, Corvallis, Oregon; Dull Knife Memorial College Library, Lame Deer, Montana; National Archives and Records Service, Washington, D.C.; National Park Service Library, Intermountain Regional Office, Lakewood, Colorado; Leland D. Case Library, Black Hills State University, Spearfish, South Dakota; Nebraska State Historical Society, Lincoln; Lilly Library at Indiana University, Bloomington, Indiana; Fordham University Archives, Bronx, New York; University of Pittsburgh Press, Pittsburgh, Pennsylvania; Brigham Young University Library, Provo, Utah; Amon Carter Museum, Fort Worth, Texas; Little Bighorn Battlefield National Monument, Crow Agency, Montana; Gilcrease Museum, Tulsa, Oklahoma; Order of the Indian Wars, Johnstown, Colorado; and Fort McPherson National Cemetery, Maxwell, Nebraska.

To all of these people and institutions, I extend heartfelt appreciation.

Jerome A. Greene
Arvada, Colorado

JANUARY MOON

PROLOGUE

On Thursday night, January 9, 1879, a natural phenomenon took place at Fort Robinson, Nebraska, that spontaneously foretold dire consequences for Northern Cheyenne Chief Dull Knife and his followers, who were then imprisoned at the post. The crusted snow blanketing the fort and its environs that night varied from three to eight inches deep in broad areas, perhaps a foot or more deep in places where drifts had accumulated. The mercury hovered around 10 degrees Fahrenheit.

That night a lunar spectacle further impacted the scene at Fort Robinson. On that unfathomably cold, clear, and lethal night in northwestern Nebraska the moon was 98.38 percent full, illuminating the snowy ground in all directions around the post, rendering near-perfect silhouettes of humans against the enhanced backdrop and suffusing surrounding trees, bushes, and buildings with its glow. The moon rose at 6:17 P.M. on January 9, reached its zenith at around 1:30 A.M. on the 10th, and finally set at 8:48 A.M., creating an eerie, enveloping radiance through much of the cloudless and deadly night.

Thirteen days later, on Wednesday, January 22, 1879, a new moon emerged, marking the initial lunar phase when the moon is not visible. The onset of that manifestation would presage further peril for Dull Knife's people.

1

Provenance

A Northern Cheyenne woman named Iron Teeth witnessed and endured much of the following story. She was born in the late summer of 1834 in the Black Hills of present western South Dakota, which meant that she was forty-four to forty-five years old in 1878–79, when the following events played out. Her father was Northern Cheyenne and her mother Lakota, and she had grown up with her father's people. Like other Native American families of the time, Iron Teeth's family roamed seasonally with her people, covering the vast territory between the northern plains and Mexico to trade with other tribes and with those few white people who had come early to the southern plains. Having graduated from using dogs to using horses to transport their possessions, they hunted wild game, principally buffalo, for their food and used the hides for clothing and shelter. Iron Teeth remembered a time when her people had planted corn using sharpened sticks, but she had also seen them gradually turn away from that enterprise to follow the migrating herds of buffalo more exclusively.

Iron Teeth told her story in 1926, when she was perhaps ninety-two years old, physically bent, worn, and furrowed. Yet she recalled many historical events in her people's past, which spanned from the Northern Cheyennes' earlier free-roaming days to those harder times of the later nineteenth century, when the U.S. government restricted her people to reservations. In particular, Iron Teeth had strong memories of warfare and of the struggles against government soldiers, particularly the agonizing events of the 1870s. She was in her late thirties and early forties then, married and with a family of her own. Perhaps because of her station among the Cheyennes, much of her memoir dwelt on the manifold historical tragedies that had beset her people in those days. Her account is straightforward and matter of fact, but it evokes emotions in the reading. Her story, among many other sources, describes and substantiates the human calamity that befell her people at Fort Robinson, Nebraska, in the snow and bitter cold of January 1879.[1]

Iron Teeth's people had experienced a long and arduous history. Originally, her ancestors had been part of a larger population of Cheyennes or Tsistsistas in their own Algonkian stock language (meaning "The People" or "The Human Beings"). They were hunters and agriculturalists who lived in the area of the western Great Lakes, in the wooded country of present northern Wisconsin and Minnesota. As with other regional tribes, the Cheyennes migrated west from the lakes country in the eighteenth century. Driven by enemy tribes who themselves were pushed by ascendant white populations farther east, they were also drawn west by the presence of horses and the ubiquitous buffalo that frequented the prairies and plains.

As time passed, the Cheyennes incorporated with other Indian peoples, notably the Suhtais, and their culture gradually transformed. They largely discarded their horticultural pursuits, adopted tipis, and followed the buffalo herds. By the late eighteenth century they had reached the Black Hills and ranged over lands from the Missouri and Yellowstone drainages in the north to the river valleys of the Platte and Arkansas in the central plains. As Iron Teeth remembered, it was a transient population that moved often according to the seasonal shifting of the buffalo.

During their early years on the plains, the Cheyennes fought with adjacent tribes, including the Teton Lakotas and Arapahos. In the mid-nineteenth century many Cheyennes, drawn by prospects for trade, gravitated more permanently to the southern plains. While retaining familial and band relationships to some degree, they effectively divided into two tribes, becoming the Northern Cheyennes and the Southern Cheyennes. The Northern Cheyennes, numbering about 1,200 people by June 1876, occasionally allied with the Lakotas and Arapahos through the years. They sometimes jointly fought enemy tribes: Crows and Kiowas in the north, sometimes Kiowas and Comanches farther south. In time, Northern Cheyennes intermarried with Arapahos and Lakotas and notably with the Oglala band of the Lakotas. Intertribal relationships with the Oglalas proved strong and enduring and would be important and culturally influential in determining the futures of both tribes.

As a society, the evolving Cheyenne horse culture revolved spiritually around two entities: Esevone (the Sacred Buffalo Hat) and Maahotse (the four Sacred Arrows). These were the cardinal covenants that fused them with their Creator and centered them spiritually in every facet of being. Through these entities all aspects of life drew renewal and spiritual nourishment. Hereditary keepers maintained these treasured relics, which in all ways reflected the people's purpose in life and living. Traditionally, the Sacred Hat remained in the north country with an assigned keeper, while the Sacred Arrows stayed in the south, also with a keeper.

Organizationally, Cheyenne society in both the north and the south was governed politically by two entities. One was the council of forty-four peace chiefs (the Council of Chiefs), which made decisions regarding tribal routines such as moving a village or determining when an annual buffalo hunt might start. The other entity was composed of warrior societies with fighting chiefs who, with their followers, defended the people from enemies. Mainstays within the council structure were four "Old Man Chiefs," also known as "Peace Chiefs." One of them, designated the "Sweet Medicine Peace Chief," epitomized the people's spiritual actuality. Each of the eleven bands composing the Cheyenne population contributed four chiefs to the governing council, thereby forming a Council of Chiefs. After division of the Cheyennes into northern and southern components at some time after 1850 and the subsequent band dispersal, band chiefs came to make the decisions formerly made by the Council of Chiefs. Following separation into northern and southern branches, the Cheyenne bands often moved unilaterally. Although the cohesiveness of their society required continued interaction, family visitation between northerners and southerners grew less frequent.[2] Consequently, while the Northern Cheyennes maintained hereditary contact with their southern kin, they gradually further evolved into largely separate tribal entities.[3]

The presence of whites gradually increased west of the Mississippi River in the early decades of the nineteenth century, but their numbers swelled substantially after the Mexican-American War and gold discoveries in California, Colorado Territory, and elsewhere. Encounters between white would-be prospectors and settlers bound west on the overland trails and Indian tribes, including the Cheyennes, could be friendly and benign, but they could also provoke conflict. Eventually the federal government sought to restrict the Indian presence along the emigrant trails across the plains and negotiated treaties with affected tribes.

At Fort Laramie, established in 1849 in present-day southeastern Wyoming, such an accord was struck in 1851 to acknowledge tribal boundaries for the northern Indians, including the Lakotas, Arapahos, Crows, and Northern Cheyennes, though not all bands of the various peoples subscribed faithfully to the protocols affirmed there. Moreover, government promises were not always kept, and Indians forcibly resisted the inevitable intrusions by whites onto dedicated Indian lands. The result was conflict. The inevitable presence of U.S. troops sent to protect citizens escalated turmoil involving the Cheyennes and collateral tribes during the 1850s, 1860s, and early 1870s, creating an atmosphere of distrust that persisted for the remainder of the century.

Much of the fighting that followed involved both Lakotas and Cheyennes. When Second Lieutenant John L. Grattan provoked the Sioux near Fort Laramie in 1854, warriors practically wiped out his small detachment.[4] Brevet Brigadier General William S. Harney retaliated the next year against a camp of Lakotas on Blue Water Creek in western Nebraska, killing eighty-five people. The Northern Cheyennes were not involved in either encounter but were nearby, and events soon engulfed them. In 1857 an expedition led by Colonel Edwin Sumner routed and destroyed a camp of Cheyennes along the south fork of the Solomon River in north-central Kansas, although only a few of the people were killed.

Sumner's engagement sparked the beginning of sustained military action against the Cheyennes over ensuing decades. During the Civil War, a major conflict involving Minnesota's Santee Dakota Indians in 1862 set in motion operations against their western kin that inevitably involved the Northern Cheyennes. Two years later, a federal undertaking targeted Southern Cheyennes following purported attacks on whites in the mining regions around Denver. Late in 1864 Colonel John Chivington led some 700 federalized territorial troops against a village of 500 Southern Cheyennes and Arapahos at Sand Creek in southeastern Colorado Territory. The result was butchery largely of noncombatants, after which the soldiers further desecrated the dead. Sand Creek brought home to the Cheyennes as well as other tribes of the plains the catastrophic threat that white Americans posed to their societies. Conversely, Sand Creek set off a reaction against the Cheyennes throughout the plains that lasted for almost two decades before those people, at last subdued, were driven onto reservations.

During the months following Sand Creek, the Cheyennes and their Lakota and Arapaho allies opened a broad reprisal throughout the plains against white miners, cattle ranchers, and settlers who symbolized the existential calamity that they faced. Fighting on the southern plains over the next decade encompassed notable army drives against the Southern Cheyennes and their Arapaho, Kiowa, and Comanche allies. A signal engagement occurred in November 1868 when Lieutenant Colonel George A. Custer led the Seventh U.S. Cavalry in a devastating strike against Cheyennes under Black Kettle along the Washita River in present Oklahoma. Those people and their Southern Arapaho colleagues presently settled on a reconfigured reserve, even as the fighting continued. Campaigns by Colonels Nelson A. Miles and Ranald S. Mackenzie in 1874–75 against Kiowas and Comanches in Texas and the Indian Territory largely stemmed fighting in that region.

Conflict raged on the northern plains following Sand Creek as well, especially along Wyoming's Bozeman Trail, which led to the goldfields of western Montana. Engagements from 1865 to 1868 included the killing of an entire command of soldiers under Captain William J. Fetterman near Fort Philip Kearny in northeastern Wyoming by Indians in late 1866. Lesser but still bloody engagements with troops followed in 1867. In 1868, again at Fort Laramie, the government negotiated broad treaties affecting the major regional tribes, including the Lakota Sioux, Northern Cheyennes, and Northern Arapahos. The agreements reached restricted these tribes to a large reservation in western Dakota Territory that included the Black Hills and permitted Indian use of a designated "unceded" zone for hunting. Peace proved fleeting, however, largely due to economic enterprise. After an army expedition into the Black Hills in 1874 found gold deposits on the Great Sioux Reservation, the Indians spurned federal attempts to purchase that part of their domain, ultimately leading the government to mount a broad campaign to at last drive all the Sioux onto the reservation.[5]

The Great Sioux War of 1876–77, as it was called, proved a lengthy affair. Disparate fighting between troops and Indians ranged over huge expanses and spanned eighteen months from March 1876 into September

1877. The conflict involved the nonreservation Lakotas and their Northern Cheyenne allies, who refused to remain on their designated reservation tracts. Also involved were many so-called summer roamers: Indians who lived on the Sioux reservation during the winter but departed each spring to join colleagues in the unceded territory.

Significantly, the Northern Cheyennes played prominent roles in every major action of the Great Sioux War, so named because the government targeted the larger and more diverse Lakota population (including their Cheyenne allies), believing that the Indians would obstruct white expansion in the Yellowstone Valley. In fact, the Northern Cheyennes were the first people attacked by troops in the opening action on March 17, 1876. Soldiers of Brigadier George Crook's field command had mistaken their Powder River village for the village of Crazy Horse's Lakotas in the engagement. After that, the proportionately smaller Cheyenne contingent aligned fully with the Sioux, who yielded to them the honored position of leading the intertribal assemblage as it proceeded finally to the Little Bighorn Valley in southeastern Montana Territory.[6]

The Northern Cheyennes further fought skillfully at Rosebud Creek, joining the Sioux to thwart Crook's campaign and momentarily put his force out of action. And a week later, on June 25–26, the coalition destroyed Lieutenant Colonel George A. Custer's immediate command at the Little Bighorn River in a resounding victory that left 268 soldiers dead on the field. Cheyenne warriors skirmished with troops at Warbonnet Creek in northwestern Nebraska in July and again joined some of their Lakota allies in September when General Crook's cavalry successfully routed their camp at Slim Buttes, in present northwestern South Dakota. Northern Cheyennes under chiefs Little Wolf and Dull Knife suffered a dawn assault by Colonel Ranald S. Mackenzie's forces along the Red Fork of Powder River in north-central Wyoming in late November 1876. The Cheyennes sustained devastating losses in people and matériel. Iron Teeth's husband was killed during the fighting at the Red Fork.[7]

Colonel Nelson A. Miles's campaigning in the Yellowstone hinterland in late 1876 and 1877 finally ended the Great Sioux War. Miles won a major engagement with Sioux and Cheyennes in the Wolf Mountains in January when he brought his artillery to bear and followed up with actions mostly involving Lakotas. The Indians at last yielded. Most of the Sioux surrendered at their agencies in Dakota Territory and Nebraska, although a large number under Sitting Bull instead withdrew across the international line into Canada. They remained there until 1880–81, when starvation forced their return and surrender. Several hundred Northern Cheyennes under chiefs Black Moccasin, White Bull, and Two Moon had previously surrendered to Miles on the Yellowstone, where they agreed to serve as army scouts. Because of this, the Two Moon Band, as it became known, was permitted to settle along the Yellowstone River. Most of the other Northern Cheyennes—under Little Wolf, Morning Star (Dull Knife), Old Bear, and Coal Bear (Keeper of the Sacred Buffalo Hat)—accompanied their leaders to what was then Camp Robinson, in northwest Nebraska, where they submitted on April 21, 1877.[8]

Camp Robinson was established in 1874 to guard Red Cloud Agency, which had been erected the previous year to attend the Lakotas, Northern Cheyennes, and Northern Arapahos. Moved considerably northwest from a previous site thirty miles down the North Platte River from Fort Laramie, Wyoming Territory, the relocated agency consisted of an enclosed compound with a warehouse, offices, living quarters, mess hall, and kitchen, together with a livestock corral. A ten-foot-high plank wall, gated on the south side, enclosed the whole compound, while two separate bastions guarded approaches to the agency from the west and north. Camp Robinson, still under construction in 1876, sat on a broad plain a mile to the west, adjoining White River with commanding bluffs on the north and pine-topped hills on the west. The government had hoped to remove all Indians from Nebraska and at the time both Red Cloud Agency and Camp Robinson were believed to be located in southwestern Dakota Territory, because of a yet unsurveyed boundary. (In reality, they stood west of the present community of Crawford in northwestern Nebraska.)[9]

As warfare receded following Mackenzie's attack on the Cheyennes in November 1876, many of the outstanding Lakotas headed for the agencies in Dakota and Nebraska the next spring. Following suit, on April 21, 1877, more than 500 Northern Cheyennes under Chiefs Dull Knife and Little Wolf, entirely destitute and hoisting a white flag, approached Red Cloud Agency and Camp Robinson to surrender to General Crook and hand over their guns. One Cheyenne leader reportedly said to Crook, "We want to shake hands and bury the hatchet." Many more Indians arrived on the following days. On May 6 the Oglala chief Crazy Horse and nearly 900 men, women, and children turned themselves in at the post, largely concluding the Great Sioux War.[10]

The Cheyennes did not tarry at Camp Robinson. In accordance with the wishes of Commanding General William T. Sherman and Lieutenant General Philip H. Sheridan, who commanded the Military Division of the Missouri in Chicago, they were to be sent south. On May 28—just three weeks after their arrival at Red Cloud Agency—First Lieutenant Henry W. Lawton and an escort of fifteen Fourth Cavalry soldiers started south from Camp Robinson with 933 Northern Cheyennes and 4 Arapahos. They were bound to join their kin at the Cheyenne-Arapaho Agency at Darlington, near Fort Reno, in the Indian Territory (near modern Oklahoma City). Overall, the move was in accord with the new Rutherford B. Hayes administration, which promoted allotment in severalty among the tribes, justice, fair treatment, and ultimate assimilation. Secretary of the interior Carl Schurz succeeded in blocking an effort by the War Department to take back control of Indian affairs. Despite such an encouraging policy, Hayes's years in office would occasion considerable strife with the Indians in the West.[11]

General Sheridan considered the decision to move the Northern Cheyennes south to live with their kin logical and final. But it was not without controversy. Whereas the Cheyennes who stayed on in Montana were subsequently allowed to remain there at the behest of Colonel Miles, those who yielded at Camp Robinson were sent south under the pretext that they had always belonged in the south and had previously agreed to go there. As early as November 12, 1874, Northern Cheyenne leaders, including Little Wolf, Big Wolf, and Standing Elk, had agreed "to go to the Southern Reservation [*sic*] whenever the President of the United States may so direct, provided we are allowed to remain at Red Cloud Agency and receive Rations and Annuity goods until that time arrives."[12]

Both Sherman and Sheridan advised the transfer, despite the Indians' objection, and on May 18 the Indian Department (as the Bureau of Indian Affairs was often called) concurred. Most of the Indians viewed the move as a temporary expedient whose permanence would be contingent on their adjustment and acceptance of new circumstances. If they did not like the new area, they thought that they would be free to return north. "None of us wanted to go there," remembered Iron Teeth. "We liked best the northern country." Furthermore, Standing Elk, who was in apparent disfavor with the majority, acceded to the move, giving the enterprise an air of legitimacy—to the dismay of most Northern Cheyennes.[13]

According to a traveler who encountered them en route, the reluctant people were mournful and quiet. "Events had forced them to this choice," he recalled, "and they had left their home with the regret of the emigrant." The men, he said, "were mostly mounted," while the women "carried their papooses on their backs, and led ponies that hauled the travois." Throughout their trek south the people retained their guns and ponies in accordance with their earlier surrender terms.[14]

Several of the Northern Cheyenne leaders who journeyed to Indian Territory with their people in 1878 played highly significant roles in the troubled months to come. The first, in the sense of tribal government hierarchy, was Morning Star, principal Old Man Chief of his people, who was known to whites of the time as Dull Knife. He belonged to the Omissis band, the largest among the Cheyennes, which had traditionally ranged the high plains country between the Black Hills and the Big Horn ranges. As a young warrior he had fought Pawnees and subsequently married a Pawnee girl whom he had captured years earlier. In 1878 he was about sixty-eight years old. During the past two years of fighting (1876–77), he had endured the loss of several of his ten children. Late in 1878, as Dull Knife rose to prominence in the newspapers, a *New York Herald* correspondent who visited with him portrayed him thus: "He seemed buried in deep reverie, his face smooth and classic as any ever put in marble, and much resembling that of the late Secretary [of state William H.] Seward in his most thoughtful moments."[15]

Dull Knife's able co-leader was Little Wolf, who was also an Old Man Chief, although considerably younger. A member of the Suhtaio band of Cheyennes, Little Wolf, along with Dull Knife, had first drawn notice from officers at Fort Laramie during the 1850s, when their encampments were variously located in the area of the North Platte River. Although Dull Knife had signed a document permitting the troops to build posts in the Powder River country of northern Wyoming in 1866, both leaders subsequently participated in the fighting near Fort Phil Kearny during Red Cloud's War. Later they both signed the Fort Laramie Treaty of May 10, 1868, which included the stipulations for them to accept homes in the Indian Territory or on lands of the Sioux Indians. By further arrangements with the federal government, the Northern Cheyennes received authority to collect supplies at Fort Fetterman until the Red Cloud Agency was erected farther east. An officer at Fort Fetterman, Lieutenant Colonel George A. Woodward, described Dull Knife as "tall and lithe in form [with] . . . the face of a statesman or church dignitary. . . . His manner of speech was earnest and dignified, and his whole bearing was that of a leader weighted with the cares of state." Little Wolf "had a less imposing presence, but looked more the soldier than the statesman."[16]

After Red Cloud Agency was relocated, Little Wolf earned the distinction of bearing the chief's bundle, with its sacred sweet root given the people by Sweet Medicine decades earlier and thereby incarnating Little Wolf as Sweet Medicine Chief. In 1873 both Dull Knife and Little Wolf journeyed to Washington, D.C., where they met President Ulysses S. Grant and other officials. There they remonstrated against any plan to remove the people to the Indian Territory and refused to recognize the Fort Laramie Treaty provision to that effect.[17]

It was Dull Knife and Little Wolf who exercised the primary tribal guidance for their people just before they moved south and during their tenancy in the Indian Territory. In addressing the individual capabilities of these two men, historian and ethnographer George Bird Grinnell said:

> Both were brave and good fighters, but they were very different. Dull Knife . . . fought merely as an individual leader of men. He was not an organizer, and did not plan his battles. Little Wolf . . . made a plan for each battle. During the progress of a fight Little Wolf constantly called out words of instruction and encouragement to his warriors, telling them to fight hard and advising them how to fight efficiently. He thought not merely of his individual deeds, but of the battle as a whole. In other words, he was what few Indians have been—an organizer. . . . Little Wolf always considered a situation in advance and planned what should be done. He possessed great foresight, tried to think of and to provide for every contingency, and to leave nothing to chance.[18]

Besides Morning Star and Little Wolf, several other Northern Cheyennes played prominent roles in succeeding events. One was Wild Hog. Born about 1840, Wild Hog became a chief of the Elkhorn Scraper Society in 1864 when he was still in his twenties. Following his people's surrender to General Crook in April 1877, Wild Hog served briefly as a scout. He had counseled with army officers as well as with Dull Knife, Little Wolf, and other Cheyenne leaders as they prepared to leave for the Indian Territory. The *New York Herald* correspondent cited above termed Wild Hog "the Achilles of the Cheyennes, with an immense head, and the devilishness attributed to Richard III by Shakespeare apparent in every feature."[19] Wild Hog's presence during the critical months ahead would prove especially consequential.

Another important Northern Cheyenne was Old Crow, also known as Crow. The eldest of the chiefs, he had served Colonel Mackenzie's attacking force as a scout during the strike against the Northern Cheyenne camp along the Red Fork of Powder River the previous November but had redeemed himself with his Cheyenne peers by leaving ammunition for them while the fighting raged. His people had forgiven him for his offense over the months since the attack. Among those Northern Cheyennes arriving in Indian Territory, others with leadership status included Tangle Hair, chief of the Dog Soldiers, a prominent military society. Tangle Hair was mixed-blood Lakota and could speak both languages fluently. With him also were Blacksmith, Noisy Walker (Old Man), and Left Hand, said to be an adept negotiator.[20]

It took Lieutenant Lawton seventy days to deliver the people to the south. Of the 972 Northern Cheyennes who left Red Cloud Agency, about 35 managed to break away and ostensibly headed north to join relatives in the Yellowstone country. Almost as soon as the Indians reached Fort Reno at noon on August 5, 1877, they were escorted to the adjacent Darlington Agency by Major John K. Mizner, the post commander. As they settled in, they quickly realized that the place was not for them. Some of them did not fit well among their southern kin, who referred to them as "Sioux." Nor did they exhibit much interest in farming. Coming from the high, dry northern plains, they soon found the humid climate discomforting. Several grew ill with assorted sicknesses and fevers. Indeed, many Northern Cheyennes died from the feverish malarial climate over the ensuing weeks and months. Medical help proved wanting, and within a year 28 adults and many more of the children had perished. As one observer noted, what followed for the Indians was "like telling a well man to sleep with a leper; as public policy, like courting war; as justice, like robbing a man of his home, and then compelling him to dwell roofless in an atmosphere of contagion." As a young Northern Cheyenne named Wooden Leg recalled, "Chills and fever and aching of the bones dragged down most of us to thin and weak bodies. Our people died, died, died."[21]

Having been introduced into a more humid climate at a significantly lower elevation, many of the Northern Cheyennes were unable to adapt to the conditions of their southern kin. In the following months they not only grew ill but became increasingly indisposed and desperate. As Iron Teeth related, "We all got sick with chills and fever. When we were not sick we were hungry. We had been promised food until we could plant corn and wait for it to grow, but much of the time we had not any food. . . . Guns were kept from them. Sometimes a few of them would take their bows and arrows and slip away to get buffalo or other meat, but soldiers would go after them and make them come back."[22] Whenever the people killed white ranchers' cattle, "the whole tribe was punished. The punishment would be the giving of less food to us."[23]

Food shortages made everything worse. As Wooden Leg recounted, "Some of our young men . . . would slip away from the reservation to get a buffalo or some other animal good to eat. . . . If any Indians did kill the white men['s] cattle they did so because they were very hungry and could not find any wild game. We ate the beef because it was the best we could get." The people grew homesick and missed Lakota friends at Red Cloud Agency.[24] Listlessness took hold of many. Old Crow recalled: "I did not feel like doing anything . . . because I had no heart. I did not want to be in this country. I was all the time wanting to get back to the better country where I was born, and where my children are buried, and where my mother and sister yet live. . . . As it is now, I feel as though I would just as soon be asleep with the rest."[25] Later Old Crow told how families were so split up: "[We] who have been removed down here have relatives at Tongue River, and on the Yellowstone and the White River, and all through that region. The old people up there have children down here; the young people up there have parents down here; the women up there have brothers down here; and our families are all split up in that way by this removal."[26]

Ben Clark, the interpreter at Fort Reno, knew well the despair of the people. Wild Hog spoke to him about conditions as Clark readied to head north to conduct even more Northern Cheyennes to the Indian

Territory. As Clark recalled late in 1878, "'Hog' . . . said to me, why are you going to bring the rest of the Cheyennes down here. Don't you see our people are starving and dying of sickness[?] Let them stay north. We want to go back ourselves." Just weeks after the people's arrival in the south Colonel Mackenzie opined that "the best-informed white men . . . are of the opinion that unless the Indians have justice in the matter of food from the government, there will be an outbreak within two years."[27]

As stated, another motivation for wanting to return north was the peoples' strong kinship with friends and relatives in the north, grounded in intertribal affiliations and especially long-term intermarriage among neighboring tribes, largely between Northern Cheyennes and Lakotas and Northern Arapahos on the Great Sioux Reservation. Through the years, despite linguistic differences, strong bonds had been forged through matrimony and resulting offspring. Intercultural alliances had solidified and grown as the people shared relatives—indeed, whole families—with related descent, thereby normalizing and extending their interrelationships. Cheyenne roots had grown and intertwined with Lakota roots and vice versa: the prospect of such cross-family cultural linkages and networks had grown profound. Such deep nostalgia for their northern homelands were not universal among all those who went south with Lawton, however. A majority of the Northern Cheyennes integrated well with their southern kin and would decide to remain, seemingly contentedly at Darlington. Unfortunately, those who chose to return north failed to realize that conditions in their home country were changing: their idealized landscapes were disappearing with the influx of railroads and ranching and mining economies throughout the West.[28]

In sum, by the early fall of 1879, beyond their estrangement from their southern kin, the Northern Cheyennes in the Indian Territory represented a seriously fractionated component of an already ruptured tribe whose societal disarray reflected a generation of upheaval. The proximate discord of Dull Knife and Little Wolf's people was further intensified by intraband dissension generated by those who, despite their discontent and majority, vowed to remain in the south with extended kinfolk and bear the consequences. Under these circumstances, and following a harrowing year in the region, many of the northerners became unequivocally dissatisfied with their extant conditions and circumstances. Some even assumed a threatening demeanor and boldly voiced their intention to leave and head north to agency officials. As the Indians at Darlington became increasingly disruptive, even Brigadier General John Pope, who commanded the Department of the Missouri from Fort Leavenworth, Kansas, advised his superiors that the people should be allowed to go home. As the Indians grew more outspoken, however, he directed troops at Fort Reno to halt any perceived attempt by the northern Indians to flee. The Bureau of Indian Affairs resisted any move north. Finally, Little Wolf told agent John D. Miles, "Since we have been in this country, we are dying every day. . . . We wish to return to our home in the mountains." Pleading with Miles for permission to move north, he added: "Before another year has passed, we may all be dead." With such unsettling commentary, the meeting ended. Little Wolf returned to his fortified camp along the North Canadian River, a dozen miles west of Darlington Agency. The dialogue was done, but not the Northern Cheyennes' resolve to do something about their plight.[29]

2

Coming Home

At about 10 o'clock on the night of Sunday, September 9, 1878, long before the first streaks of dawn lightened the eastern skies, Dull Knife and Little Wolf led a procession of diversely aged men, women, and children, with their ponies and dogs, setting out for their home in the north. As indicated, not all of the Northern Cheyennes who had arrived in August 1877 undertook the journey. Some had perished from starvation and disease during their detention, while others had melded—easily or uneasily—with kin among the communities at Darlington. Only 353 of the people who had arrived the previous year from Camp Robinson (a little more than a third of the original body—a fragment of the whole) slipped away in the shadows that night, optimistic about going home but heartsick at having to leave relatives behind. Cheyennes captured en route north said that they hoped to reach Montana, where they would surrender if they were allowed to remain; if not, some at least would endeavor to reach Sitting Bull's followers in Canada. Despite the need for spiritual protection on the journey, Esevone, the Sacred Buffalo Hat, did not accompany the people. The danger of taking it was too great to risk.[1]

The fragmented people left their tipis standing and campfires burning as they faded into the night, the better to dupe army pickets sent from Fort Reno to monitor them remotely. Many of the Cheyennes lacked horses, although some had stolen animals from neighboring Indians and a herd accompanied them. They carried only minimal trappings and supplies, some pilfered from the agency, as they followed a northwesterly course through the gloom that night. Not until about 3 A.M., some five hours later, did the troops discover their absence. Despite their recent differences with the Northern Cheyennes, authorities at the fort and agency were incredulous over the Indians' departure. Early the next morning, as couriers dashed off to deliver word of the Cheyennes' flight to other posts in the region, Captains Joseph H. Rendlebrock and Samuel Gunther with Troops G and H of the Fourth Cavalry left Fort Reno on Major Mizner's direction to pursue the fleeing people.[2]

That same morning agent Miles notified his superiors of the departure and provided names of most of the males, including leaders Dull Knife, Little Wolf, Wild Hog, Old Crow, Old Bear, and Black Horse. Miles said that the tribesmen carried more than 100 Springfield carbines that had been taken from Custer's dead at the Little Bighorn and somehow secreted during their passage south. Had they been properly disarmed and dismounted earlier, he maintained, "there would not have been the least possible show [reason] for them to have taken such desperate chances."[3]

No one expected the Indians to get far. Existing railroads could hurry troops forward, and the numerous white settlers who would no doubt see the Cheyennes would report their passage.[4] "Even if they did succeed in crossing the Arkansas river and the Santa Fe railroad without interception," declared General John Pope, "they would certainly be turned back before they could cross the Kansas Pacific."[5] In addition, troops to be collected at Sidney Barracks, Nebraska, along the Union Pacific Railroad across the Kansas line, could "throw all that could then be assembled (about one hundred and forty infantry and cavalry . . .) upon any point on the road where the fugitives from the south might attempt to cross."[6]

Northern Cheyenne history ascribes much of their anticipated success in their endeavor to their firm cultural instincts and sacred beliefs. They credit an elderly holy woman named North Woman, known also as Moving Against the Wind, with intuiting their course over the weeks ahead. They also credited her with using sanctified powers in hiding them from the soldiers as they proceeded north, disguising them as "small herds of buffalo" in particularly alarming circumstances. Indeed, much of the Northern Cheyennes' apparent success during the coming weeks was grounded in their inherent intuition about survival amid often desperate settings and threatening contexts.[7]

Initial encounters showed how adept the Cheyennes were in holding off their adversaries to allow their noncombatants to forge ahead in orderly fashion. As they moved, their outriders doubtless canvassed the countryside for troops. At mid-morning on September 13 Rendlebrock's soldiers found them at Turkey Springs, among the Red Hills along a tributary of the Cimarron River, 140 miles from Fort Reno. When the Cheyennes refused to parley, Rendlebrock elected to move in. Things did not go well for his soldiers, however: in the resulting skirmish the Indians, positioned in surrounding ravines and rocky gorges perhaps 400 feet away, killed three cavalrymen and wounded three more, besides an Arapaho scout. A number of army horses were also killed or wounded. Ultimately, Rendlebrock's position on a rising knoll was nearly surrounded. The troops passed the night where they remained with neither food nor water while the Indians burned the surrounding prairie.

The shooting resumed the next morning. After another day-long exchange of fire, Rendlebrock, desperate for water, ultimately withdrew, leading his troops and wounded to Camp Supply, thirty-five miles away. As he did, the Cheyennes resumed their journey northwest. Sherman feared that a successful escape might inspire other reservation internees to do the same, so when he was made aware of the events he directed General John Pope at Fort Leavenworth to take every measure in capturing or killing the Cheyennes.[8]

In the following days the resolute warriors again skirmished with Rendlebrock's cavalrymen, who were now resupplied. The first encounters occurred at Bluff Creek, Kansas, on September 18, with minimal casualties on either side, and at Sand Creek two days later. There Rendlebrock's command, now joined by civilian cattle ranchers from the Fort Dodge vicinity, exchanged long-distance gunfire with the Indians but inflicted no casualties. The shooting resumed on September 21 and 22 after more ranchers joined the troops in attacking fortified Cheyenne positions. In what proved a contest of maneuverability, the Indians withdrew with negligible losses for either side except for one army mount killed.[9] In each engagement the warriors took successful measures to protect their noncombatants, while effectively stymieing the troops as they continued in their course.[10]

The fleeing Indians forded the Arkansas River on September 23 without incident. But four days later, as troops alerted across the region converged on western Kansas, a significant engagement took place. By then, 250 cavalry had joined Rendlebrock as well as a company of Nineteenth Infantry soldiers borne in wagons from Fort Dodge under Lieutenant

Colonel William L. Lewis, who assumed command. At midday on September 27, as the troops rested along a tributary of the Smoky Hill River known as Punished Woman's Fork, the Cheyennes gathered their noncombatants in a large cave beyond range of the soldiers' rifles then initiated a sudden attack from the surrounding heights. Lewis placed his men as skirmishers and quickly advanced against fortified positions held by as many as sixty warriors. As firing quickened, Lewis, standing on the rim of a canyon, took a bullet to his right leg. Captain Clarence Mauck, Fourth Cavalry, assumed command. After a distant exchange Mauck pulled his men back to his wagons, where they spent the night. By dawn the Indians had departed, leaving one warrior dead and abandoning many of their ponies to effect their escape. The troops shot most of the animals. A detachment hurriedly bore the stricken Lewis toward Fort Wallace, forty-five miles away; despite application of a tourniquet, he died from loss of blood before gaining the post. Besides Colonel Lewis, three enlisted men were wounded in the fighting.[11]

The pace of army pursuit abruptly slowed following the clash at Punished Woman's Fork. Following Lewis's death no one properly assumed charge of affairs. The Indians were allowed to move away after dark on September 27, effectively gaining a march on the soldiers. More troops, positioned ahead along the east-west railroads, were expected to check the flight of the dissident Cheyennes and to halt their drive north. Yet notification was not received in a timely fashion: trains bearing troops never arrived. The Indians, incensed over the encounter at Punished Woman's Fork, now quickened their pace.[12] Moving hurriedly north without halting, they crossed the Kansas Pacific Railroad near Carlisle Station and began meting out vengeance among settlers whose farms they encountered along the Sappa and Beaver Creek watersheds in Decatur and Rawlins counties in the northwest corner of the state.[13]

Over a period of several days in late September and early October, apparently despite the protests of their chiefs, the young Cheyenne men devastated the countryside, burning farms and destroying equipment while stealing horses and slaughtering livestock, mostly in the country adjoining the Sappa. "It would seem that the very prince of devils possessed them," recorded one witness.[14] Families fled their homes to hide in cornfields as the Indians approached. Ten settlers were killed in southwestern Kansas. About thirty more died in the wide-ranging assaults in the area around the settlement of Oberlin, while women were reportedly raped. Only two Cheyenne warriors were killed.

As one woman asserted, "The havoc the Indians made . . . is beyond description. The savages took every horse they came across; and killed every pig, chicken, cat and dog they could come up with. They took little children two and three miles from their homes and left them." Another wrote: "Every house they entered was pillaged, furniture broken up and destroyed, and clothing and bedding carried off. Hogs in pens were killed and left untouched." The scare extended into Nebraska, although the tribesmen mostly took horses in that sector. "Mr. Connor, on the Republican in Dundy County, loses 45 horses, 2 mules and about 85 head of cattle were killed. Mr. Wilson loses 27 horses. Mr. Webster, on Stinking Water, in Chase County, loses about 25 horses and had seven or ten head of cattle killed." The rage of the Northern Cheyennes in striking out at virtually every aspect of white culture that they encountered in northwest Kansas reflects the frustration of being chased and attacked and the mounting cultural trauma that they were experiencing. They did need horses and supplies, but their anger may also have had origins in all that had befallen them at the hands of whites in recent decades, perhaps even including an attack on a Southern Cheyenne village in the area by troops in 1875.[15]

Modern examination of this significant episode suggests that much of the Cheyennes' violence directed against settlers was grounded in their mounting psychological despair following the battering of disease, starvation, and overall angst during their fretful year in the south, now aggravated by the blunt reality of permanent white occupancy manifested by railroads, farms, cultivated fields, livestock, and nascent communities. According to this explanation, episodes of aggravated rape of white women perceived as trespassers by young warriors during these raids demonstrated aspects of transitory Cheyenne dominance, manifested earlier during incidents of intertribal warfare, and were reportedly outside the knowledge of most of their leaders.[16]

In her account Iron Teeth told of aspects of the journey from Darlington, although she was ill from fever much of the time. Her oldest son believed it important to go north and that "it was better to be killed than to go back and die slowly." Apparently the Indians succeeded in killing only a single buffalo (a calf at that), during the entire march. Iron Teeth said that they purposely avoided white settlements as they proceeded. As for the attacks occurring in northwest Kansas, Iron Teeth said that the people were desperately hungry and that the settlers must have instigated the trouble if whites were killed. She explained that the people fashioned wickiups from willow branches for shelter. As for casualties from the soldiers en route, she recalled that "some of our people were killed, women and children the same as men. . . . More than sixty of our children were gone when we got to the Dakota country." In fact, twenty-seven Northern Cheyenne men, women, and children died during the fighting in northwestern Kansas.[17]

Whether justified or not, the Northern Cheyennes' raiding in Kansas cost them dearly in public opinion. While they had drawn considerable sympathy in escaping ill-treatment in the Indian Territory, the pillaging in Kansas largely negated it. As one editor commented: "A simple flight of the Cheyennes from the reservation might, under the circumstances, have been excusable, and they would have had a sort of sympathy from a great portion of the community. . . . But they chose to commence a savage war upon all the settlements in the line of their march, and they have thus deprived themselves of all the kindly feeling which existed for them."[18]

Whatever the opinions they evoked, the Cheyennes pressed on, moving quickly now. Bearing north, they left Kansas and crossed the Republican River on October 2. Two days later they forded the South Platte and crossed the Union Pacific Railroad tracks at Alkali Station, Nebraska, a few miles east of Ogallala. Farther west, at Sidney, the detached engine of a "special train" sat waiting "with a full head of steam on" to carry soldiers east. Unknown to Dull Knife and Little Wolf's people, 186 more Northern Cheyennes, who had been moving south to the Cheyenne and Arapaho Reservation, waited with their leader, Little Chief, under guard at Sidney Barracks as their relatives passed by to the east.[19]

Seeking to capture Dull Knife's people as much as to protect Nebraska citizens, 150 soldiers and horses under Major Thomas T. Thornburgh waited. Alerted to the Indians' crossing of the Union Pacific tracks, Thornburgh entrained with his cavalry and infantry from Sidney Barracks for Ogallala, sixty-two miles east. When they reached that community late that afternoon, the trailing Captain Mauck soon arrived from the south with his command. Although Thornburg pushed ahead with his cavalry, his foot troops followed in wagons, which were abandoned after a difficult fording of the North Platte River. Despite their hurried pursuit, they all remained far behind the Indians in desolate country without grass or water. Adding to their sense of futility, their scouts told them that the Cheyennes had dispersed and were now traveling in several bodies. On October 3 the plodding infantry and the wagons returned to the railroad. The cavalry resumed the search, passing "to all points of the compass" as the Indian trail began to scatter, though still bearing north.[20]

As they entered Nebraska and gained the North Platte basin, the Indians ran off stock from several area ranches. While some of the Cheyennes may have recognized their old hunting grounds as specified in the Treaty of 1868, few if any realized that they had crossed into jurisdictions of a different sort. Having left General Pope's administrative province, they had entered the Department of the Platte, headquartered in Omaha under their old adversary, General George Crook. Crook knew of the Indians' elusive tendencies. Catching them, he said, "would be as hard a task as to catch a flock of frightened crows."[21]

Anticipating the Indians' arrival and hoping to prevent them from joining the Lakota Sioux, in early October Crook directed Major Caleb H. Carlton (operating from Camp Robinson) to move south. In response, Carlton headed along the Sidney Road with five troops of the Third Cavalry, scouting the Sand Hills around the Niobrara River. His goal was to head off the Northern Cheyennes before they reached the new Lakota agency. Carlton was to coordinate his movement with Thornburg's famished soldiers from Sidney Barracks, who had thus far encountered constant difficulty in closing on the Cheyennes in the trackless expanse above the North Platte. At one point they encountered "a fog so dense that it obscured objects 20 yards away." By the time they had traveled eight miles, "20 miles had been traversed in objectless detours": the Cheyennes had eluded them altogether. On October 7 they hit the Sand Hills, where "ceaseless currents of wind piled it up . . . into drifts like snow." Mauck's worn command meantime abandoned the chase and returned to Sidney Barracks, eventually conducting Little Chief's followers to the Indian Territory.[22]

Carlton's and Thornburg's commands united on October 10 along the Niobrara. Then they moved west toward Camp Sheridan, located at the site of the former Spotted Tail (Brulé) Agency, forty-three miles northeast of Camp Robinson, where they hoped to consolidate information and determine their future course.[23] Troops of the Seventh Cavalry, operating from near Bear Butte in Dakota Territory, canvassed the country to the north and closed on Camp Sheridan. Concurrently, Major Alexander J. Dallas arrived from the south with several companies of mounted Twenty-Third Infantry soldiers.

Rumors that the Sioux were leaving their new Red Cloud Agency to support the Cheyennes coming north made these military movements of Carlton and Thornburg all the more urgent. Upon arriving at Red Cloud Agency, those officers met with Chief Red Cloud and his headmen, who quelled such stories and agreed to deliver to the troops any Cheyennes that might appear among them. A scarcity of rations caused Thornburgh and Carlton to move their troops southwest to Camp Robinson. At that point Thornburgh and Dallas took their commands back to Sidney Barracks.[24]

In the meantime, somewhere in the area of the upper Niobrara River at a point not precisely known today, Dull Knife and Little Wolf disagreed over their future course. Aged seventy and still mourning the loss of one of his wives killed accidentally in northwest Kansas, Dull Knife wished to move forward to the Red Cloud Agency, believed to be along the White River near Camp Robinson. Many Oglala Lakota friends and intermarried relatives were living there. Little Wolf apparently disagreed, evidently determined to keep the people together and stay on course to reach their homeland along the Yellowstone. Little Wolf could not change Dull Knife's mind, so the two parted. Perhaps half of the people went with Little Wolf, who moved more northerly toward the trackless Sand Hills of west-central Nebraska. There, he and his followers hoped to find refuge from the soldiers, hunt buffalo, and gain safe harbor from the coming winter weather.

Dull Knife, with the balance of the now riven people, including most of the women and children, took his column more northwesterly, in the general direction of Camp Robinson, adjacent to the site of the old Red Cloud Agency. Among the chiefs accompanying Dull Knife's group were Old Crow, Wild Hog, and Tangle Hair. Some said that Wild Hog thereafter assumed leadership among those accompanying Dull Knife. Iron Teeth and three of her children also went with Dull Knife, although a daughter and son may have gone with Little Wolf's followers. Unknown to either group at the time of their separation, the government had moved Red Cloud's agency into Dakota Territory during their incarceration in

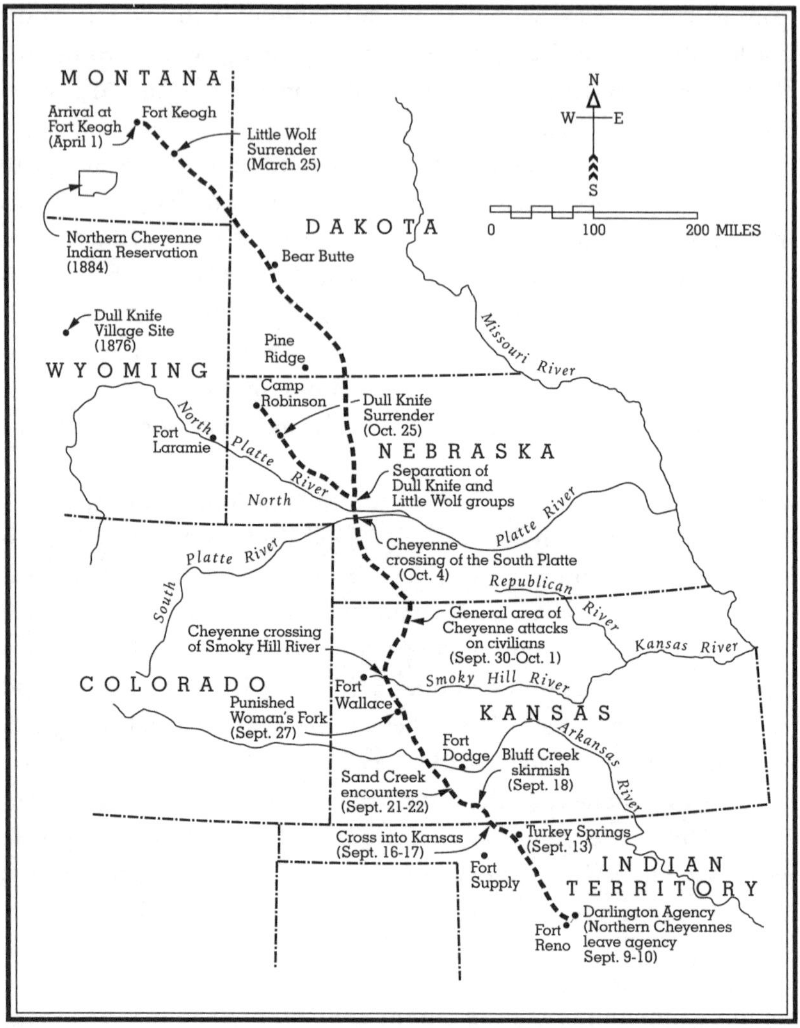

Northern Cheyenne Homecoming Trail, 1878–1879

the south. Construction of the new agency was underway at a site in the Pine Ridge country adjoining White Clay Creek (ultimately to be renamed Pine Ridge Agency), some fifty miles north of Camp Robinson.[25]

The Cheyennes' division into two groups and movement in largely different directions may explain at least in part why the soldiers had such difficulty finding them above the North Platte. "No Indians had been seen," recollected one area rancher of those times, "and the trails indicated that they were scattered in all directions, singly and in pairs, scattered like a flock of quail."[26]

But the soldiers were never all that far away. Seventh Cavalrymen scouted an area of the Sand Hills south-southeast of Wounded Knee Creek in Dakota Territory,[27] while Major Carlton's Third Cavalrymen from Camp Robinson ranged south and west to the source of White River. The Northern Cheyennes had run off stock from nearby ranches, while others had told the Sioux of their two parties, one moving into the ever-drifting Sand Hills. Within five days of the Indians' crossing of the North Platte, sightings by local ranchers indicated that the Cheyennes had arrived. Parties of them had been observed in the area of Crow Butte, a prominent landscape feature rising above lower outcroppings seven miles east of the post and just six miles from the recently vacated Red Cloud Agency. A party of Cheyenne men had reportedly managed to appropriate a number of horses kept near a store there, arousing ranchers in the area, who feared losing livestock. Army pickets reportedly had surrounded Crow Butte, but the Indians eluded them in the night.[28] Over the next several days the patrols from Camp Robinson traced the White River from its head all the way to Chadron Creek in the north, but they spotted only a few of the Cheyennes.[29]

With so many army units in the field searching for Dull Knife's people, who were moving ever closer to the old Red Cloud Agency site, and thus toward Camp Robinson, it was only a matter of time before they were found. On October 22 Carlton directed Captain John B. Johnson and First Lieutenant John C. Thompson with Companies B and D, Third Cavalry, and an interpreter and two Oglala scouts to search to the south along Chadron Creek and "see if they could see any trace of the Cheyennes."[30] The next day, while reconnoitering in mixed rain and snow toward the Niobrara and roughly eighteen miles east of Camp Robinson, they found Dull Knife and his people, including chiefs Wild Hog and Old Crow. "They were brandishing arms," wrote Johnson, "some wearing War-bonnets," so the captain readied his troops. Then he saw hands waving at them and making signs. He sent Lone Bear, one of his scouts, forward. Lone Bear returned shortly to announce that "the Indians were Cheyennes who did not want to fight, but wanted to talk." Johnson advanced and met Dull Knife, Wild Hog, and Old Crow, who told him that they wished to go to their old Red Cloud Agency. The captain told them that they must go with him and allowed them to discuss the matter with their people. As he reported, "They soon returned and said they would come with me."[31]

A correspondent accompanying the troops reported the confusion even among the Cheyennes:

> The Indians were on the march, a good deal strung out, but emerging from a pass where they could have made a stand with decided advantage. Many were disposed to do so, hastily donned war bonnets, and began dancing and singing in preparation for the fight, the women and children at the same time closing up the ponies and baggage in a spot so difficult of access that they afterwards had considerable trouble in getting the herd out to surrender. Others attempted to deceive the soldiers by waving cloths and shouting that they were "Sioux! Sioux!"[32]

Bad weather was brewing, but Captain Johnson's troops were ready. The people had little time to react. Swaddled in torn blankets and canvas pieces, they were cold, desperately hungry, and likely short of ammunition. "They were more dirty and ragged than usual," Captain Johnson noted, with "poor moccasins and . . . thin cloth that looked like sheets, using them for blankets."[33]

And so it was here—somewhere in an area between the head of Chadron Creek and the Niobrara River, after trudging north approximately 600 tortuous miles for more than forty-two days since leaving Fort Reno in the south—that Chief Dull Knife and his followers despairingly turned themselves over to the troops. The 149 Indians—46 men, 61 women, and 42 children, according to a count by the officers—apparently presumed that they would be well treated and would be permitted to stay in the north. With them were 131 horses and 9 mules.

Major Carlton was not present, having gone to Camp Sheridan and not yet returned. In his absence, Captain Johnson fed the Cheyennes bacon and crackers and dispatched word of his success to Carlton. The command then ushered the captured people eighteen miles northwest in the driving sleet, arriving along Chadron Creek just before dark. They were directed to camp in a thicket right at a bend near the edge of the stream and some 300 yards from the soldiers' own bivouac. Johnson ordered guards posted around the Indian camp. Dull Knife, Johnson said, had told him that "Little Wolf's band, said to be with them, would follow, but they did not. That . . . night it snowed, and we supposed they had halted somewhere on account of the storm, but we did not see them."[34] Mounted guards were enjoined not to permit any of the Indians to escape, and the troopers distributed pieces of canvas to help protect the children. It had been decided to withhold food pending the Northern Cheyennes' dismounting next day, but Captain Johnson seized a steer from a nearby ranch and delivered it to the Indians. Johnson's actions won praise from his superior. In forwarding the news afterward, Major Carlton noted, "Captain Johnson displayed great skill, firmness, and good judgment. Not an Indian was lost or a soldier injured."[35]

The next morning, October 24, Captain Johnson worked to dismount and disarm the Cheyennes. They eventually yielded only thirteen assorted long arms (including some that were obsolete), four handguns, and perhaps twenty sets of bows and arrows.[36] The Indians surrendered these arms only after frequent delays, as they repeatedly explained their treatment in the south. Some of the warriors exhibited their anger by dropping their guns or throwing them onto the pile.[37] At least one officer at the time thought that they possessed more guns that were not delivered: indeed, eight more long arms would be turned in to Second Lieutenant George F. Chase after the Indians reached Camp Robinson.[38]

Significantly, none of the people's bundles were searched before leaving. In view of later events, it is also noteworthy that the Cheyennes produced none of their ammunition, which for the moment likely remained hidden in the women's garments, and evidently were not pressed on the matter.[39] "It was vain to look for more," wrote a witness. "It was necessary either to accept as true their solemn assurance that they had no more, or else shoot in cold blood men, women and children already in our power." As would be discovered later, other guns had been disassembled and also secreted in women's clothing; parts of guns were hidden in plain sight, worn as ornaments. Some rifle parts were hung on the women's backs beneath their dresses. Although the Indians evinced great antagonism during the delivery of their arms, Johnson inexplicably ordered no individual searches for weapons at this juncture, and Dull Knife kept his young men from becoming violent. The soldiers' searches, however, did reveal clothing, toys, and other articles that indicated that at least some of the warriors had participated in the raiding in northwest Kansas.[40]

Hoping to forestall more resistance, Captain Johnson directed Lieutenant Thompson and Company D to occupy a high point north of the stream, directly overseeing the Indian camp. The soldiers discovered that the people were hiding ponies among tall weeds near their camp. At one point a warrior raised a bow and arrow aimed at an enlisted man in the process of leading a pony away from the camp, but nothing came of the incident. After further delay, Lieutenant Chase and Company A headed southeast with 138 ponies over the snowy twenty-two miles to Camp Robinson. Some of the horses were in such poor condition that they had to be shot en route. It took three hours to claim the guns and horses, after which Chase moved on and camped with his men and horses that night near Ash Creek. They reached the post early in the afternoon of October 25.[41]

Back at Chadron Creek, Johnson's soldiers distributed rations to the desperately hungry people. Major Carlton, freshly returned from Camp Sheridan, proposed that the warriors have their hands tied behind them in preparation for the move, but Captain Johnson talked him out of it. Late that day Carlton met with the leaders and explained the plan to them. The Cheyennes bristled upon learning that their Oglala friends had been moved to the New Red Cloud Agency. Now, they declared, they would rather die than go to Camp Robinson. Moving to the soldier post would negate their going to the Sioux and figuratively point them instead in the direction of the Indian Territory. They also refused to go to Camp Sheridan and returned to their camp amid growing tensions. In the closing darkness they vowed to die there and began excavating rifle pits and raising log barriers. They also notched breastworks to contest the troops, thereby indicating that they still had guns.

That night confusion marked the Northern Cheyenne camp. Some danced a "war dance," as Carlton construed it. An interpreter reported that they had grown suspicious and feared that the major "would get them out of the thicket and shoot them down."[42]

The next day, October 25, the standoff intensified even as Carlton bolstered his force. The major had called for a six-pounder gun to be sent from Camp Sheridan, along with two companies of the Seventh Cavalry. Meanwhile, one company of the Third Cavalry arrived with a howitzer from Camp Robinson. Still, the impasse proceeded for the balance of the day with the Cheyennes refusing to move. "I knew that the troops were in a delicate position," Carlton noted later. "If a fight had occurred we should have been compelled to kill nearly all of them, and would [have] been accused of first dismounting and disarming them and then murdering them." Overnight the troops raised their own entrenchments and began clearing a lane of fire for the guns. By dawn on October 26 the army encirclement of the Cheyennes was complete. Finally, after what Carlton termed "another interminable talk," the major at last told the leaders that they must yield and go to Camp Robinson. Additional delay ensued while the Oglala scouts helped convince them not to resist further. Without a shot being fired, the disconsolate chiefs relented.[43]

At around noon the people began the 25-mile journey to Camp Robinson. The women and children rode in wagons. The men, still protesting any return to Darlington, walked as Carlton's soldiers rode along on either side of the procession. As Captain Johnson related, "The principal thing that induced the Cheyennes to consent to come to Camp Robinson was the information derived from a Sioux." They were told that "there were no rations at [New] Red Cloud agency except beef, and that they had better go to Camp Robinson where they could be fed until the Great Father should decide what to do with them." At one point Wild Hog exhorted the people, and the young men began singing war songs. But the march never halted, and the troops and Indians reached the post between 10 and 11 P.M. Carlton directed that the Indians immediately be held all together in an unoccupied barrack building located at the southeast corner of the parade ground. "I promised to treat them as prisoners of war until they should arrive at Camp Robinson," Carlton notified headquarters in Omaha, "but persistently urged upon them that I would make no promises, as to their future disposition or punishment, and think they understand it."[44]

Almost immediately after the Cheyennes entered the vacant barrack, evidently with no guards around, some apparently managed to pry up a loose board on the floor and deposited beneath it the firearms that they had managed to hide from the soldiers. If the soldiers indeed believed that the Northern Cheyennes had no more guns, the Oglala scouts knew better. Sergeant Carter P. Johnson of the Third Cavalry later recalled: "When we got to Robinson the Sioux scouts wanted to know if they could have their pick of guns that would be taken from the Cheyennes & the officers said that they could not find any more than had already been given up, but that if they could find any with the Cheyennes to take them." Sergeant

Johnson further recollected that "[b]y this time most of the Chey[ennes] had gone into the barracks at the fort, but one of the Sioux went up to a tall buck as he was going into the door, reached up under his blanket, gave a quick jerk downward and brought forth a gun that the Ind[ian] had taken apart and slung under his blanket by a string tied around his neck. Another Sioux got another gun that a Cheyenne was trying to conceal."[45]

Sergeant Johnson said Major Carlton had ordered another search of the Indians about an hour after they had entered the barrack. "We did this thoroughly," he remembered, "going through their bundles and compelling the women to stand up, and found none." In light of later events, he suspected, "there can be no doubt but that the Ind[ian]s had taken a plank out of the floor and hidden their guns thereunder as soon as they got into the place. It is my opinion that no guns were ever smuggled in to them."[46]

During the early days of the Indians' incarceration, Seventh Cavalry First Lieutenant Hugh L. Scott, using the sign language that he would one day become famous for, spoke with Dull Knife, Wild Hog, and Old Crow about their circumstances in front of a group of the regiment's officers. "They told us with great earnestness," Scott recounted, "that they had run away from Fort Reno [Darlington Agency] on account of the many deaths from fever, determined to die quickly in battle rather than at a slower rate by fever, and they said they would die in the North rather than be sent back." Reporting on the meeting to Carlton, Scott told the major flatly that those Indians "would never go back alive." Old Crow soon afterward accompanied Scott and a column of Seventh Cavalrymen in seeking Little Wolf's followers in the snow-covered country east of Camp Sheridan, but they returned without success.[47]

3

Time, Place, and the River

Much had changed at Camp Robinson since the Cheyennes had left for Darlington Agency in May 1877. By that time, the warfare with the Sioux and Northern Cheyennes that had begun in March 1876 was largely over. In the wake of the Great Sioux War, the post had begun a significant downsizing but also had become well established and linked by roads and telegraph to the outside world.

By early 1878 the companies of the Ninth and Fourteenth Infantry had been dispatched to frontier service elsewhere. Only a single company of two officers and sixty-nine men of the Third Cavalry occupied the post. The camp and its ground area incorporated a tract along the north side of White River (also known as White Earth River), as an official document specified, "20 miles east of [the] western line of the State of Nebraska."[1] The land encompassing the post was at the time considered part of Sioux County, only recently designated in February 1877 and as yet neither organized nor surveyed. The estimated countywide nonmilitary white population at the time stood at 550.[2] There was a certain irony in the fact that units of the Third Cavalry had garrisoned nearby Camp Sheridan in 1877–78. Thereafter, elements of that regiment were omnipresent, with a force varying between one and four companies assigned from Fort Laramie between that date and early 1880, during which other units moved to different stations. The Third Cavalry's posting was also ironic in that its companies had already played primary roles in the recent campaigning against the Sioux and Northern Cheyennes and during the Great Sioux War had been variously instrumental against the Indians at Powder River, Rosebud Creek, Slim Buttes, and the Red Fork of the Powder: all core engagements of the conflict. Many of the Third's officers and troopers had served with distinction in those combats and were experienced, weathered, and primed for duty.[3]

While the Northern Cheyennes had been away important events had occurred at the post, perhaps none more significant than the killing of the venerated Oglala Sioux leader Crazy Horse on September 5, 1877. Crazy Horse's death especially affected the Lakota people who had previously surrendered with him. The young chieftain was bayoneted in front of the post guardhouse and died in the adjacent adjutant's office (post headquarters). The subsequent removal of the remaining Lakotas to a new agency along the Missouri River (prior to their removal back to Pine Ridge), in addition to the departure of the Arapaho residents of Red Cloud Agency for the Shoshoni Reservation in Wyoming Territory, had effectively cleared the Camp Robinson area of its Indian tenants.[4]

First Lieutenant Charles A. Johnson, Fourteenth Infantry, was the post's nominal commanding officer when Dull Knife and his followers were brought to the fort. A native of Pennsylvania and a Civil War veteran, Johnson had enlisted from civil life as a private in the Wisconsin infantry early in 1861 and been commissioned in the Second Wisconsin Infantry Regiment in 1865. After the war Johnson gained appointment as second lieutenant in the Fourteenth Infantry in 1867 and promotion to first lieutenant in 1876. He would serve in a detached capacity with the Bureau of Indian Affairs at Camp Robinson as agent at the Red Cloud Agency and later as post commander when its assigned command consisted of Company C, Third Cavalry. Johnson was in command in early December, when matters began to escalate with the Cheyenne prisoners and a second company of that regiment (H) reinforced the post. Normally Major Carlton would have been expected to assume command occasionally during his Third Cavalry operations in late October 1878 due to his superior rank, but he never did.[5]

The physical presence of Camp Robinson had evolved following the relocation of Red Cloud Agency from Wyoming Territory to the White River in Nebraska in 1873–74 over Red Cloud's initial objection. As established, the agency stood near the junction of White River and Soldier Creek and served Oglalas, Northern Cheyennes, and Northern Arapahos. Disruptions caused by the discordant presence of nonagency Indians seeking food and supplies often threatened conflict and created management issues. Following months of seemingly interminable annoyance over repeated physical threats at the new site, as well as ongoing interdepartmental jurisdictional clashes, a nonpermanent army camp had been established a short distance west of the agency in March 1874. Troops from Fort Laramie that had intermittently bivouacked in the area were at last permanently located there beginning in April.

In July 1874 Captain William H. Jordan, commanding a detachment of Ninth Infantrymen from Omaha Barracks, arrived at Camp Robinson to lay out the post and begin building the components to shelter the troops. As a "camp" or "cantonment" (a temporary or transient facility of comparatively short duration as opposed to a presumably permanent "fort"), Camp Robinson would be built in accordance with plans prepared in Omaha. It was to accommodate four companies, requiring six double sets of officer quarters and a single set for the post commander, two long infantry barracks (each divided by a center partition to hold two companies) and appropriate mess halls, a commissary and quartermaster storehouse, a hospital, a commanding officer's/adjutant's office, a guardhouse, a bakery, a blacksmith shop, and other appurtenances. The major buildings, all laid out along a 165-yard rectangular perimeter, would be completed with wood-shingled roofs.

After formal approval from Washington, D.C., construction began utilizing heavy pine logs harvested and hauled from conifer-forested hills to the west and north as well as in the vicinity of Soldier Creek, which flowed into the White River a short distance south of the proposed site. Fashioned adobe bricks would be used for the officer quarters and burned bricks for chimneys, while a location south of the site yielded stone for constructing building foundations. A steam-powered sawmill at Red Cloud Agency was acquired to cut lumber for all the structures. Work commenced in August 1874, based on projected costs of $15,000 in appropriated funds. Besides building the new post, the soldiers conducted patrols and escorted supply trains and treaty commissioners and army paymasters as needed.[6]

In late summer 1874, as an afterthought, a single one-story cavalry barrack (the barrack that would figure so prominently in the Northern Cheyenne breakout) was added to the plan. Its construction got underway in August, based on knowledge of a smaller number of projected occupants for a cavalry company (perhaps 60 to 68) than for infantry (between 70 and 100). Sited at the southeast corner of the post, the barrack measured 30 feet wide by 100 feet long (longer and wider than the standard infantry barrack). Its projected cost was $712.25. The cavalry barrack stood along the line 66 feet east of the adjutant's office. Its pine log walls were laid horizontally in 15-foot panels as with the other barracks. Accompanying horse stables and corrals were erected south of the cavalry barrack.

The squad room inside the barrack measured 30 by 90 feet. A first sergeant's room was built at the northwest corner of the main building to jut slightly toward the parade ground's south edge, while a storeroom occupied the northeast corner of the building in the same manner. A shed extension constructed along the rear of the structure, as in all the barracks, housed a partitioned kitchen, a mess area, and a washroom. The building had a pitched roof that extended over the room and shed areas in front and rear. A building housing the laundresses' quarters was erected a short distance east of the cavalry barrack. In the meantime, construction of the second long infantry barrack proceeded along the western perimeter of the post, as did one along the eastern perimeter, not far from where the cavalry barrack stood. Construction of most of the principal buildings of the post was complete by October 1874, when officers and troops occupied the place and prepared for winter, which tended to be harsh in far northwestern Nebraska.[7]

Significant structures were added to the post in subsequent fiscal years, including a post hospital, which had previously amounted to an assemblage of several tents used for the purpose. The formal hospital building raised between July and November 1875 stood some 100 yards west on a line with the officer quarters and included surgeons' office facilities and a twelve-bed recovery ward for patients. As was typical, the building was purposely isolated from the core of post activity. At Camp Robinson it was situated west of the parade ground, northwest of the westernmost infantry barrack and the commissary storehouse. Like the other post structures, it offered a simple appearance yet sported a gambrel-style roof. Besides its patient ward, it housed a dispensary, office, storeroom, and kitchen. Enlisted men known as stewards, as well as soldiers from the ranks, assisted the doctors in performing their work there.[8] The hospital together with its physicians and attendants would prove especially important as events played out at the post.

Camp Robinson occupied a generally level plateau providing available forage at an elevation of about 3,800 feet throughout its building expanse. The post's surrounding landscape for a distance to the north, east, and west was sharply rising terrain, however. As one inspector later put it, "The country right there at the post is quite level, a sort of small plateau; but on all sides there are ravines and hills and cañons."[9] These hills, vales, and high ranges constitute parts of the broad Pine Ridge Escarpment, which extends across the immediate region in a southwest-to-northeast swath from eastern Wyoming through northwest Nebraska and into South Dakota for a distance of perhaps 175 miles. In South Dakota, they embrace the Great White River Badlands (including today's Badlands National Park).

Equally important was the White River, which had carved fissures and pinnacles in gravel and sandstone terraces across eons west of the post. The rough White River country (a product of the Oligocene epoch) was barely hinted at in the immediate vicinity of Camp Robinson, yet the river, which marked the northern margin of the high plains, would profoundly affect coming events.[10] Rising scarcely fifteen miles southwest of the constructing camp (east of modern Harrison, Nebraska), the White was named for the color of its water, which washed volcanic ash, clay, and sand in its bed. The White River was pivotal to selecting a site for Camp Robinson. Water was a mandated prerequisite for locating a military post, and Soldier Creek and its host of springs and tributaries nearby assured that water would almost always be accessible. Adjacent resources from a forested domain with a diversity of animal life for hunting further enhanced the post's location.[11]

The intermittent forested terrain of the Pine Ridge plateau would also affect coming events. In draining the slopes of the Pine Ridge, the meandering White and nearby Niobrara farther south, along with branches of Soldier Creek and their subordinate streams and rivulets, fostered both variegated and high elevation tracts of pine as well as ash, box elder, and hackberry and irrigated assorted cottonwood, willow, and plum growth at lower levels. The region about the post supported bountiful wildlife, including deer, elk, buffalo, bighorn sheep, rabbits, foxes, wolves, coyotes, mountain lions, bobcats, raccoons, and other small mammals as well as wild turkeys, eagles, owls, and lesser birds. Together with the rich grama, buffalo, and other grasses, besides diminutive cacti, the river had sustained an ecosystem used by Indians for generations. These qualities aptly persuaded the army to establish its temporary station there. It was—and is—also cold in the winter. Waterways such as the White River and its tributaries were subject to winter water evaporation as well as water withdrawal and diversion. Coupled with minimal precipitation based largely on snowfall, the streams were generally shallow in winter.[12] The landscape surrounding Camp Robinson was impressive to view but forbidding to travel through. Two miles north of what would become Camp Robinson stood a towering aggregation of massive tan sandstone buttes that in 1878 were known as Soldier's Grove Buttes or the Giant's Coffin. Today they are commonly called Red Cloud Buttes. Part of the Pine Ridge Escarpment, some of them attain heights of 4,300 feet, about 500 feet above the elevation of the barracks and buildings of Camp Robinson.

Immediately east of Camp Robinson stood Crow Butte and its entanglement of pine-topped scarps and weathered ridges. Crow Butte, which period maps referenced as Crow Hill or Dancers Hill, stands almost as high as Red Cloud Buttes. East of the post it reaches 4,227 feet in height. Adjoining it is Little Crow Butte at 4,200 feet. Today Crow Butte and Little Crow Butte dominate roughly nine square miles of surrounding broken ground that is part of Nebraska National Forest, including the Ponderosa State Wildlife Area.

The Crow peaks and their adjacent highlands lie mainly between West Ash Creek on the east and Squaw Creek on the west. Together they rise about seven miles from where Camp Robinson was laid out in 1874 and eventually flow into the White River.[13] The course of the White River gradually angles northeast, approaching Camp Robinson's expanse about one-half mile from where the cavalry barrack was erected, not far from where Soldier Creek, narrowly hugging the post's southern perimeter, empties into it. Thick groves of cottonwood and willow trees, as well as assorted brush, crowd the banks of the White and lower Soldier Creek confluence and beyond. Across the river to the southeast the bottomland fans out in a broad open range cut by rivulets and eroded declivities.

Two miles west of Camp Robinson the ground arises abruptly, with some peaks attaining 4,300 to 4,500 feet in elevation. From there the incline evolves into a broad rolling grassland plateau continuing west into Wyoming. The surrounding hills are rough terrain, marked by numerous deep ravines, holes, pockets, and even caves. The high ground is covered in underbrush and laced with stands of Ponderosa pine. A natural defile running east-to-west through the forested range is today called Smiley Canyon, now threaded with a modern scenic byway. The White River passes through a floodplain area two miles south of Smiley Canyon then levels northeast in its course toward South Dakota and ultimately the Missouri River. Today's U.S. 20 runs between the modern community of Crawford west to Harrison and beyond and transects these national forest lands overlooking the White River valley. The rugged Pine Ridge terrain bordering Smiley Canyon to the north and west (geologically known as the Arikaree Group) contains sediments of sand and volcanic ash. The region harbors deep gorges and twisted ridges that adjoin Soldier Creek two miles north, while that stream's thicketed tributaries mesh with timbered expanses even farther northwest.[14]

Only two roads connected Camp Robinson to the world beyond when Dull Knife's Northern Cheyennes arrived there in October 1878. One route, the Fort Laramie road, extended 73 miles southwest to Fort Laramie, Wyoming Territory. The route followed an earlier trail that had continued northeast some 275 miles to the old trading post of Fort Pierre on the Missouri River in Dakota Territory. The second road, which became the primary route linking Camp Robinson with the railroad, connected the post with Sidney Barracks, Nebraska, and its adjoining civilian community, about 120 miles south. The principal freighted supplies and Indian annuity goods came from Sidney. Troops aided by Oglala Sioux from Red Cloud Agency had blazed the route north from Sidney in August 1874. Beyond Camp Robinson the Sidney Road continued north to Buffalo Gap, the southeastern entry into the Black Hills. A divergence of the road angled eastward to Camp Sheridan. Other subordinate trails led to the New Red Cloud Agency at Pine Ridge, 50 miles northeast, and beyond. Officers at Camp Robinson bound for business at department headquarters in Omaha journeyed south over the Sidney Road to Sidney then by train east over the Union Pacific track, for a one-way total of 534 miles.[15]

The telegraph, which came to Camp Robinson in March 1877, revolutionized communication for the post. Officers could now convey military communications with command centers, principally Fort Laramie to the southwest and army department headquarters in Omaha to the east (but elsewhere too) as well as by mail to the post by horseback twice a week from Fort Laramie, the nearest key station.

One other link to the telegraph would play an important role in the ensuing events that engulfed Dull Knife's Cheyennes. When a commercial line was at last installed from Fort Laramie to Deadwood in the Black Hills in 1876, it coincidentally passed through a Fort Laramie subpost and stage station on the route between Cheyenne and Deadwood in the Black Hills. Located along Sage Creek, Wyoming, and misnamed Hat Creek Station by the stage company, it stood on the northern edge of the windswept, eroded, often alkali-encrusted Hat Creek Breaks region. Fifty miles southwest of the Black Hills and fifty-three miles west-northwest of Camp Robinson, the station was a boon to army officers, who seized the opportunity to access the telegraph line there. Things further improved when in spring 1877 the Cheyenne and Black Hills Telegraph Company, which had previously opened a route to the Black Hills, now laid a line through from Hat Creek to Camp Robinson and the Red Cloud Agency.

The corridor that had to be cleared for installing the telegraph poles to carry the wire along the 53-mile route to Camp Robinson came to be called the Hat Creek Trail or Hat Creek Road and served also as a mail route from the post office established at Hat Creek Station in 1877. Soldiers from Camp Robinson became familiar with this new route west from the post because they had to monitor the line for breaks, which were frequent, maintain it in working order through sometimes heavily forested terrain, and see to improvements along its course. As the route approached extreme western Nebraska and passed into Wyoming Territory, the broken landscape alternated between deeply forested areas and largely wide open hilly tracts with little vegetation beyond underbrush and prairie grass. It was across this fragmented terrain, cut with steep gullies and ravines and marked by high cliffs, that many of Dull Knife's followers would struggle in the dead of winter in trying to escape Camp Robinson. The existence of the trail by October 1877 is attested in the report of a survey party that passed over the route in that month "from Hat Creek Station along the direct road to Camp Robinson."[16]

4

Prison House

The ordeal of the Northern Cheyennes that started on the morning of September 9 when they left Darlington Agency only intensified after they entered the vacant cavalry barrack at Camp Robinson almost seven weeks later. Certainly by then they had grown increasingly wary over their circumstances. The fall weather had turned "arctic in severity," General Crook reported.[1] Although the empty facility afforded them immediate shelter, they would never feel altogether secure in this new domicile. Their situation there might only become worse.

Over the months since the close of the Sioux War and the resulting surrenders at Camp Robinson, troop strength there had dropped from more than 1,100 officers and men in eleven cavalry and infantry companies (most of them not quartered directly at the post but bivouacked in the wider vicinity). This status continued through the fall and early winter of 1878–79, despite sundry arriving companies of the Third Cavalry, formally assigned to Fort Laramie but quartered in the direct environs of Camp Robinson as the search for the Northern Cheyennes proceeded. Thus, although many soldiers camped nearby, only the 69 men of Company C of the Third Cavalry were formally posted there as of October 1878. That situation remained unchanged when the Northern Cheyenne prisoners reached the post on Saturday night, October 26.[2]

To summarize, Camp Robinson's preliminary layout spanned 400 feet per side on a true plane running northwest to southeast. On a modified plane, the single-company barrack now interning the Indians stood along the southerly side of the parade ground, a few yards east of the post adjutant's office, which itself stood a short distance east of the post guardhouse. Farther east, beyond the Indians' barrack, were quarters assigned for laundresses. Centered along the east end of the parade ground stood the barrack of Troop C, Third Cavalry, the company quarters nearest to the barrack where the Indians were located. Across the parade ground stood the seven officer quarters, including those of the commanding officer. Completing the perimeter, at the west end stood another presently vacant barrack (soon to be occupied by Troop H, Third Cavalry), while a short distance behind that structure was the post hospital. At the southwest corner of the parade ground were the commissary and quartermaster storehouses, each measuring 80 feet long by 30 feet wide, fronted by the commissary, while behind them stood the small post bakery and yet another storeroom.

About 160 feet behind the adjutant's office were the stables for Company C (measuring 30 by 150 feet). At the same approximate distance behind the barrack occupied by the Cheyennes stood another long building harboring carpenter, saddler, and blacksmith shops, while immediately to its east was the empty stable (30 by 150 feet), soon to be occupied by the mounts of Troop H, Third Cavalry. Adjoining to the east were cavalry and quartermaster corrals as well as a nearby wagon master's office. To the rear of these facilities, roughly a quarter-mile to a half-mile behind the Northern Cheyennes' detention barrack, Soldier Creek flowed west-to-east toward White River, which itself angled northeasterly half a mile to three-quarters of a mile behind the Indians' residence. On the east side of White River, a short distance north of its junction with Soldier Creek, stood the post sawmill, sheltered in another long building approximately 75 feet south of a wooden bridge across the river.[3]

For the most part, with various degrees of tolerance, the Indians would remain confined to the formerly empty cavalry barrack over the succeeding seventy-five days. Inside the two-year-old building they occupied the long, largely empty dormitory room, now devoid of all furnishings normally contained therein (iron wood-slatted bunks, bedsacks [rude straw-filled mattresses], blankets, and footlockers). One exception was stoves. Both Sergeant Johnson and Lieutenant Chase recalled seeing a single large permanent cast-iron heating stove in the center of the room. According to accounts describing the dormitory, it was otherwise vacant except for the clothing and blankets that the people were wearing and personal belongings contained in the bundles that they had been

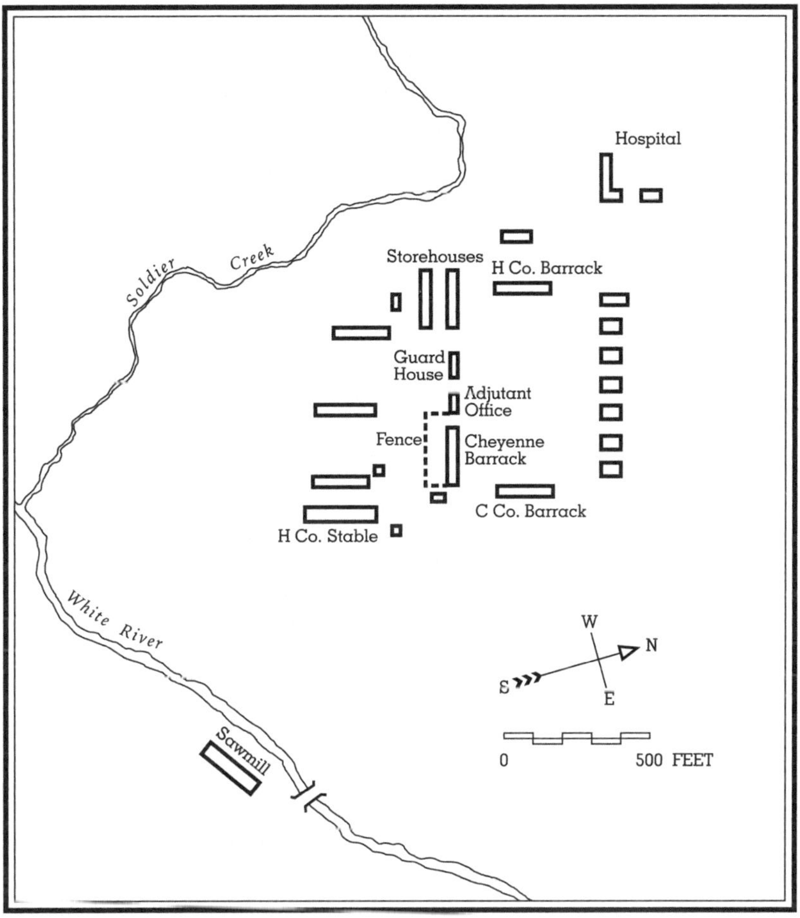

Fort Robinson in 1879

permitted to bring in with them. Whereas the building's exterior measured 30 feet wide by 90 feet long, the interior of the dormitory was surely slightly smaller. As stated, a small extension on the south side near the west end of the dormitory housed a kitchen containing a cooking range. The kitchen room had a single interior doorway accessing the dormitory proper as well as an exit door in its west wall. Similarly, on the south side of the west end of the building was a small projecting guardroom with a door on its west side exiting the building and an interior door accessing the dormitory. The glass-paned windows throughout were unbarred. The rear of the barrack was further bounded by a slab-plank fence enclosure approximately 6–7 feet tall extending some 40 feet from the east end of the building, running west for about 120 feet and then approximately 45 feet north to connect with the east end of the adjutant's office. The Cheyenne men were not permitted to go beyond this enclosed exterior area.[4]

Major Carlton initially had planned to separate the Northern Cheyenne men from the women and children, "placing the former in the most secure locality." He quickly changed his mind, however, and decided to keep everybody together. He explained that no building at the post was large and strong enough to enclose the men alone. Besides, maintaining two containment areas would require "too strong a guard" for the troops at hand. Carlton believed the Indians probably would not attempt to flee if they were kept together for a long period. "By separating the bucks [pejorative term for Indian men] from the women and children," he reported, "suspicion would be aroused that something was going to be done with them, and they would give us a great deal of trouble to guard them." Keeping them together would make them "comfortable [and] less suspicious." Furthermore, "we could hardly put the women and children in [a] camp" by themselves, "as although they had canvas, they had no lodge poles."[5]

As stated, the discovery of another firearm disrupted the entry of the people into the barrack and resulted in a further hunt for weapons.[6] The Sioux scouts with Carlton's troops had been assured that they could keep any Cheyenne arms subsequently discovered. A Lakota scout confiscated another gun when the 149 people crowded into the barrack. Carlton directed that a further search for weapons be made, now obliging the women to stand during the inspection process. The announcement created considerable excitement among the Cheyennes, but no further guns were found at the time. As Sergeant Johnson remembered, "This search was made but the women and children were crowded into this small quarters [in] such a dense mass that it was impossible to tell whether they had anything or not. It was afterwards learned that they had weapons, that some were carried by the women in their bundles and others were about the persons of the Indians."[7] It was later suggested that some Sioux (likely relatives by marriage) who were permitted to visit the Northern Cheyennes during their detention smuggled guns into them, but that scenario was never verified. Sergeant Johnson, among others, believed that the people had hidden firearms under the boards in the floor. He maintained that "no guns were ever smuggled in to them" but acknowledged that it would have been "easy for the women to carry in anything they pleased when they first went in." A man who had overheard that orphans and widows of deceased Cheyennes would be sent to Pine Ridge was alleged to have tried to kill himself with a pair of scissors.[8]

Lieutenant Chase oversaw security arrangements in the barrack building during the arrival of the Northern Cheyennes and for the weeks immediately following. His Company A took charge of guarding and feeding the captives. On the day after their arrival, Chase personally searched them yet again and discovered "lead, powder, caps and bows and arrows," which were taken from the building. He ordered his sentinels to observe the tribesmen closely for more armaments. At least one pistol surfaced, which was surrendered when Dull Knife intervened. Chase provided further details of the search: "I inspected the persons of many of the Indians. They willingly threw off their blankets and came up to me for inspection." Some asked to depart, promising to leave all their baggage "and go naked to [New] Red Cloud Agency."[9]

The guard regimen regarding the barrack was strictly enforced, Chase maintained. "I posted two sentinels inside the building, keeping them there night and day." Sufficient light was maintained always so that the guards might watch for arms. Another sentinel ranged outside, and all of them were told to permit only the interpreter and officers to enter the building without the lieutenant's approval. Chase directed his guards not to allow anyone to enter the barrack with arms. Within days, members of the Third Cavalry band from Fort Laramie augmented the Cheyenne barrack guard detail for the next three weeks. After November 20 Company B, Third Cavalry, took over direct charge of the Indian prisoners. Years later Chase elaborated on the entry of the Indians into the vacant barrack. "They were an ugly lot of Indians," he recalled. That first night "we gave them rations of bacon and bread & coffee, but they complained and said the children could not eat it," wanting flour and beef broth instead. Chase's cooks broke up the "beef heads and bones . . . and threw them into a big cauldron [in the kitchen area. We] kept soup constantly on hand for them, with a little rice stirred in . . . & they soon became jolly and well behaved & ki-yied & danced & seemed to be having a good time."[10]

On Crook's authorization the Indians were attached to Chase's Company A to receive rations. The lieutenant explained that he also acted as the Indians' direct commissary. Chase remained with them, sleeping in the barrack storeroom over the following three weeks. Because no one with the troops could speak the Cheyenne language, he explained, "we had an interpreter who could talk Sioux [Lakota] & when we wanted to talk to them had him converse with some of the Cheyennes who could talk that language. When we wanted to talk to any of the Inds [Indians] we had them come out into the office, so as to get them away from the rest." One interpreter was James Rowland, from New Red Cloud Agency. Grinnell identified another as Tangle Hair, who spoke both Lakota and Cheyenne.[11]

Soon after the placement in the barrack dormitory, First Lieutenant Edward B. Moseley, assistant surgeon, examined the people and found them in "pretty good condition." One bore a recent gunshot injury to his leg but recovered. Moseley reported that the Indians needed medication for chills and fevers derived from the trek north as well as from constipation, headaches, and other infirmities caused by overeating and lack of sufficient exercise. Each morning and as often as needed, Dr. Moseley visited the Cheyennes' barrack and cared for those who requested his attention. He stated that he believed that the enlisted men "have treated the Indian women & children in a kind and considerate manner." In early December Dr. Charles V. Petteys, acting assistant surgeon, succeeded Dr. Moseley in treating the people.[12]

One of the earliest guard details assigned to the Northern Cheyennes in their barrack environment was described by Second Lieutenant John W. Baxter Jr., Ninth Infantry, attached to Company F, Third Cavalry, as consisting of two noncommissioned officers and nine men of Company K, Third Cavalry, and the band. "Sergt. [James] Taggart and a detail from 'A' Co was in charge of cooking their rations. The Indians seemed to be perfectly satisfied with their rations, conveniences, and everything else." In his 1913 interview with the historian Walter M. Camp, Sergeant Johnson, who served with the guard details, recalled further specifics about the Cheyennes' guard unit as well as about the liberties granted to the people during the weeks immediately following their incarceration. "A guard was put outside the building," said Johnson, "one company being on guard all the time at the [nearby post] guardhouse, and inside the barracks there were three sergeants in a little room at one end, with a sentry pacing up and down [the dormitory] armed with a six-shooter among the Indians." Two sergeants, Johnson related, had to be continuously awake through each day, and at mealtime a "soldier cook" and two soldiers distributed the food among the people.[13]

"The women and children," Johnson said, "were allowed to go out and in the barracks and to walk around out of doors freely, but the men were not permitted to go out except singly and under guard." He found the Indians "pleasant and agreeable" toward their guards, freely talking with them, even smoking with them in the small guard room. In a liberal concession, their dogs were allowed to accompany them in the barrack. The large barrack heating stove made conditions satisfactory. Often, Johnson recounted, the Indians would "stick their heads out of the windows and talk with the guards outside. They had a club with the end driven with nails, which they had pulled out of the barracks. They would sometimes stick this out and wave it in fun."[14]

A Northern Cheyenne lady named Mrs. Black Bear further affirmed the good care accorded the captives during the weeks after their placement in the barrack. All were well treated, given sufficient food, and treated with friendliness. "They had good times and used to dance in the barracks," she said. The soldiers purchased food from the trader's store for the dances and would give money to the girls who danced with them to buy ornaments. For two months, said Mrs. Black Bear, "they had a fine time. No people could have been better treated than they were."[15]

Captain John B. Johnson elaborated on the Indians' diet and explained the procedures for feeding them, recalling that "they were fed 3 times a day, and as nearly as possible their tastes were consulted. . . . Potatoes and corn meal were purchased, [and] much more than the full ration of beef was issued them. . . . They got sugar, coffee, and salt . . . except that all rice was drawn instead of half beans and half rice." As Johnson explained, "Five minutes before a meal was to be served a cook entered the main prison room and beat on the top of a tin boiler, at which signal the Indians took their places along the wall, when the cooks passed around the entire building issuing to each his [or her] portion. They had coffee twice a day." Grinnell's informants told him that the people "had a good time, plenty to eat and nothing to fear."[16]

During their internment, the old people were allowed to go down to the stream and gather red-willow bark to make kinnikinnic for smoking and sage for purifying themselves and holy articles that they still possessed, and young people could go up on the nearby mountains, but all were back by suppertime. The women could visit the post slaughterhouse and obtain entrails and other leftovers for their families. Tangle Hair stated that he was occasionally called upon to take a horse and seek out trails nearby, while others told of working elsewhere on the post, including washing dishes, and going hunting for meat with some soldier scouts. In the barrack, the people spent time sitting, sleeping, and playing card games and hand games. The men often smoked, while the women completed beadwork projects, including moccasins. A reporter for the *Sidney Telegraph* stated that "about the only amusement they [the Cheyennes] are granted is an occasional dance with the officers [soldiers] stationed there. Both the squaws and white gallants get quite enthusiastic." So far as work was concerned, the officers generally preferred that only the women perform labor outside the barrack, such as unloading wagons and policing the grounds.[17]

Years later, George Bird Grinnell learned from his informants that Carlton had told them, "You will have the freedom of the post . . . but each night at supper time you must be here. If one man of you deserts or runs away, you will not be treated like this any longer." Dull Knife told the people to obey. "We are back on our own ground and have stopped fighting," he said. "We have found the place we started to come to."[18] The barrack internees with Dull Knife and the other chiefs and their families included Iron Teeth and her youngest children, a son and two daughters, as well as a youthful Northern Cheyenne man named Little Finger Nail, who along with some others created a strong visual record of the people's sojourn from the Indian Territory in a canvas-covered ledger that he kept belted to his body. (Second Lieutenant Francis H. Hardie, of Company D, Third Cavalry, tried to purchase the ledger while serving as post adjutant, but Little Finger Nail refused to sell it.)[19]

Despite the army cadre's indulgent treatment during the Cheyennes' early days at Camp Robinson, some of the people remained sick from malarial disorders that they had acquired during their stay at Darlington, which were accentuated by the increasingly cold temperatures. As indicated, a medical officer visited the dormitory each day to monitor their condition and care for anyone who required help. When permitted (mostly after mid-December), Northern Cheyenne women, guarded by sentries, would police the ground around their barrack and elsewhere on the post, picking up debris and using shovels to scoop up horse manure.

They also worked in the granary unloading corn and grain from wagons arriving at the post. Some of the parched corn that "rattled through the [storehouse] floor" apparently made it into small sacks kept hidden in the barrack for use in an emergency. For the same reason, they also saved small amounts of beef tallow from their meals.[20]

Throughout the Indians' detention, the officers and enlisted men thus seem to have generally treated them with tolerance and care. The resident doctors reported no callous treatment, and one medical officer pronounced the prisoners "leniently dealt with . . . more like distinguished guests than prisoners. As far as I have seen[,] the enlisted men . . . have treated the Indian women & children in a kind and considerable manner." Over the following weeks, the army's attitude toward the Northern Cheyennes seems to have vacillated between loose acceptance and rigid oversight, the former most evident during the early part of their detention. Yet, despite the army's seeming leniency at the outset of their internment at Camp Robinson, the Indian leaders repeatedly and strongly maintained their rigid opposition to being returned to Darlington Agency, being firmly convinced that they would die there. On October 31 Major Carlton notified General Crook that, "if these prisoners were to be taken south, it would be necessary to tie and haul them" and urged that "they not be informed at present [of that conclusion] or they will give trouble." General Sheridan, in response, recommended that more soldiers be sent to guard them, stating that at present Camp Robinson "is more important than Fort Laramie and other posts in the department."[21]

Since the time of his submission on Chadron Creek, Dull Knife and the other leaders had emphatically and repeatedly told the officers of the abject conditions that they had experienced at Darlington and of their steadfast refusal to return there. On one occasion during their initial detainment the old chief ardently told several of the officers of his concerns. According to Lieutenant Chase, the chief said: "Before we went south they told us it was a beautiful country with fine water, where we could kill game to feed our families and where our children could play upon the grass. When we got there we found it not so. The water made us sick . . . and that grass was burned up. There was no game & our children cried for meat. Our people died of fevers and we could not live there."[22]

Reflecting the people's feelings about returning south, a daughter of Chief Wild Hog coveted some calico that she saw in the post trader's store during the Indians' early weeks at Camp Robinson. When a clerk suggested that she might wait and purchase it at Sidney Barracks while en route back to the Indian Territory, the girl echoed the Cheyennes' doughty stance, responding that she was not going there. When the clerk asked where she would go if not to Sidney, she allegedly replied, "To Heaven."[23]

In this vein, on November 1 Major Carlton forwarded to Crook word from Red Cloud, who urged that "even knives" be confiscated from the prisoners because he feared they "would kill themselves to keep from going south."[24] In fact, the Indians had been allowed to keep their knives for cutting their food to eat. As Carlton put it, if the knives were taken from them they "would immediately have suspected something. . . . I thought that . . . it would at once excite their suspicion that something was to be done with them."[25]

Further communication with Red Cloud suggested that the followers of Little Wolf had been responsible for the Kansas atrocities, implying that was the reason they did not follow Dull Knife's model for surrender and that "those captured [with Dull Knife] had avoided committing [such] outrages." Whether this was true or not, soon after Dull Knife's people were imprisoned at Camp Robinson, Major Carlton's battalion renewed the active search for Little Wolf and his followers, still believed to be somewhere in the broad and inexact expanse of central and western Nebraska. Some held that those absentee Northern Cheyennes still hovered in the vicinity of the post and had in fact occasionally communicated with the prisoners. In one instance, Lakota scouts confronted two of Little Wolf's people not far from the post. One was the chief's son, who managed to escape. The other was brought to Major Carlton, who interrogated him. He led soldiers to bluffs not far from the post, where they found evidence of those people, who had fled.[26]

On November 1 the men of the Third Cavalry headquarters and staff, loosely bivouacked along White River a few miles from Camp Robinson, departed and marched to Fort Laramie, while the bandsmen returned to the post to guard the Cheyennes. On the previous day, soon after Dull Knife and his people had surrendered, elements of Carlton's battalion of Companies A, C, F, and K retook the field in their effort to locate Little Wolf and his followers. Chief Old Crow accompanied the column as a guide and interpreter. Lieutenant Chase with Company A scouted the country around Crow Butte early in November, while Company C patrolled the land south all the way to Fort Laramie and back and Company D kept vigil in the immediate area of Camp Robinson. Carlton and his battalion later ranged over the country around the Niobrara River to the mouth of Antelope Creek, as units under Lieutenant James Simpson patrolled along the Niobrara and White Rivers and Chase's company traced the Sand Hills to and from Snake River. But Little Wolf's people had by then apparently dispersed, aided by recent snows that blanketed much of the ground. All told, the units exceeded 200 miles in their fruitless search.

The hunt through the Sand Hills carried into December, with Carlton's men revisiting the Niobrara in the direction of Sidney before returning to Camp Robinson late that month. In mid-December the regimental band, which had been guarding the Indians, returned to Fort Laramie, while other companies again reconnoitered in the Niobrara country. Companies B and D marched to Fort Laramie, while Companies K and M (the latter lately at New Red Cloud Agency) were reassigned to Sidney Barracks, Nebraska; Company L, posted at New Red Cloud Agency, marched back to Camp Robinson. Companies G, H, and I accomplished "the usual garrison and escort duty" during the month. Companies A, C, F, G, H, I, and L were present at Camp Robinson or bivouacked in its vicinity by the end of December. A and F started for Fort Laramie on Christmas Day but instead returned to Camp Robinson on December 26 and occupied a bivouac area known as "Mackenzie's old camp" on a flat half a mile northeast of the sawmill near White River. (Sergeant Johnson later maintained that the recall of Companies A and F occurred after the discovery of a plot by the Indians to break out of their barrack late in December, a plan that, if true, was apparently abandoned.)[27]

During the troops' fruitless quest to find Little Wolf, Major Carlton proposed a grand ruse to entice the chief and his followers into Camp Robinson. He forwarded the scheme to General Crook on November 17. In his dispatch the major divulged that five parties of Sioux were helping the troops but to date had "found no fresh trails." He concluded that "some of the Little Wolf's band have scattered and gone north about the [time of the] last snow storm . . . , and they have either gone to the Arapahoes [in Wyoming Territory] or as Red Cloud says, are waiting to come in here [Camp Robinson] . . . after the troops leave and everything is quiet." Frustrated, Carlton was certain that Little Wolf's people had headed north, so that by "taking advantage of a [recent] snow storm they could cross almost anywhere between Ft. Randall on the east and Ft. Laramie on the west" and therefore might only be caught "by accident."[28]

Carlton's scenario grew more complicated. Those Northern Cheyennes related by marriage who were living with Red Cloud's Oglalas had, he believed, communicated with Little Wolf with regard to recent troop movements. Those people "claim many of the Cheyenne prisoners here as relatives." Thus Red Cloud might know the location of the wayward chief but was delaying "to see what we do with the prisoners before informing us." Carlton's convoluted scheme called for deceiving both the Northern Cheyennes and the Lakotas, and he detailed it at length to Crook:

> I would respectfully recommend that the scouts and interpreters be discharged with the impression that nothing further is to be done until spring; that the troops in camp [near Camp Robinson] march towards Ft. Laramie, return here in the night and go into quarters and stables; that two companies go quietly to Camp Sheridan and into quarters and stables there. It could be arranged so that the increase of garrisons need not be known by the Indians if the troops are in quarters and the tents disappear. . . . The Cheyennes or Sioux would probably at once inform Little Wolf that the troops had gone and everything was quiet, and as his people are not prepared for cold weather we would probably hear of his whereabouts. . . . The prisoners should [meantime] remain here. . . . [As for renewing the search,] it seems useless under the circumstances to continue scouting longer. If you approve of the plan proposed, please inform me by telegraph.[29]

Carlton's proposal was devoid of specifics, however, and was never attempted despite his earnest promotion. Instead, for the balance of November the major's troops recanvassed areas southwest to the Blue Water along the Platte River, as well as to the southeast and east, searching the country thoroughly but finding no sign of Little Wolf. On November 19, 1878, Carlton notified Omaha that the scout Little Big Man believed that Little Wolf's people might have captured forty-five Lakota ponies and headed north via Rawhide Buttes en route to join Sitting Bull in Canada. Word from Crook stressed that Carlton should use discretion if he found those Northern Cheyennes and that he should keep his command together and for the moment not consign any companies to Fort Laramie. Companies D (beyond its brief scouting activity), E, G, and I performed garrison duty and escort service at the post throughout November, including guarding the Cheyennes, as appropriate.[30]

The search for Little Wolf continued well into December as Third Cavalry troops reconnoitered the upper Niobrara and its tributaries, but the impression grew that Little Wolf's people had scattered. Although arrangements had been made by early in the month for the Fifth Cavalry to join the hunt if required, Major Carlton was convinced that nobody, including the Sioux, knew where those people had gone. On December 12 Crook notified Sheridan that "if not otherwise instructed by the Lieut. General . . . , I shall order the companies of Major Carlton's command to their stations." Crook still believed that the withdrawal of troops from the field might induce those elusive Northern Cheyennes to reveal themselves at last.[31]

While the army hunt for Little Wolf proceeded, on Thursday, November 7, a significant assembly was held at Camp Robinson inside the Northern Cheyenne barrack dormitory to address their situation. Important Oglala Lakota chiefs Red Cloud, American Horse, No Flesh, Red Dog, and Little Wound arrived from New Red Cloud Agency, while Third Cavalry officers Captain Peter D. Vroom, Company L, and Lieutenant George Chase, Company A, as well as other junior officers attended and monitored the proceeding. Partial evidence for the meeting comes from rancher Edgar Beecher Bronson, a former reporter for the *New York Tribune* who now owned a spread (Deadman's Ranch) five miles south of Camp Robinson and doubtless joined the session as a concerned property holder, as well as from period newspaper accounts. As Bronson recalled the moment in later years, the officers and attending Sioux chiefs occupied the center of a circle in the barrack, while the other Cheyenne men stood in the rear with the women and children behind them. Red Cloud apparently sat on a bench and addressed the gathering, conveying his people's empathy for the Northern Cheyennes and alluding to the tribes' close affinity with each other, which included intermarriage. "Our hearts are sore for you," he stated, "but what can we do? The Great Father is all-powerful. . . . We must do as he says. We have begged him to allow you to come to live among us. We hope he may let you come." According to

Bronson, Red Cloud offered to share with the people if they could come but warned that "what . . . [the Great Father] directs, that you must do."[32]

Red Dog told them: "The whites gave us good advice; we took it. You young men, look to your fathers, mothers, and little ones. . . . Have pity on them and do right." The words were moving and brought tears to the eyes of many warriors in the room.[33]

Dull Knife spoke next, as Bronson recalled, "with a face of a classical Roman . . . [and the] commanding bearing of a great leader of men," standing "in his worn canvas moccasins and ragged, threadbare blanket, the very personification of the greatness of heart and soul that cannot be subdued by poverty and defeat." He thanked the Lakotas for their offer "to share your lands." He averred that his fighting days were behind him and reflected on the tumult that his people had known in the south, where "those not worn by disease were wasted by hunger." He turned to Lieutenant Chase: "Tell the Great Father [that] Dull Knife and his people ask only to end their days here in the north where they were born. . . . Tell him if he tries to send us back we will butcher each other with our own knives."[34]

Dull Knife continued: "We meant to live with the Sioux and be at peace with the whites. Some of our young warriors ran away from us, murdered whites and escaped north. None of us have done wrong, and all we want is peace." He urged: "Let us go. . . . We will walk to Red Cloud's agency and live in peace with him, but we can't go south."[35] When Dull Knife told Chase to "tell the Great Father and General Crook about us," the lieutenant reportedly responded, "The Great Father and General Crook know about you. You are subject to their orders."[36] During the council, the Northern Cheyennes sat quietly, except for the chief's son, Bull Hump, who was said to have paced the dormitory back and forth with an incensed expression. After Chase further replied that the chief's concerns would be forwarded to the president, the council ended.

In the meantime, General Sheridan urged that a determination be made regarding a disposition of the prisoners held at Camp Robinson. He notified the adjutant general that "the whole reservation system will be endangered" unless the Indians were returned south, "except the ring-leaders," whom he felt should be imprisoned in Florida, and again called for increasing the garrison at Camp Robinson. "To encourage them to oppose the policy of the government is doubtful propriety," he said.

"Unless these Indians are sent back, the reservation system will receive a shock which will endanger its stability. If Indians can leave without punishment, they will not stay on the reservations." Furthermore, he stated, a decision was needed regarding the prisoners, who were "a source of great inconvenience and expense." On November 16 Commissioner of Indian Affairs Ezra A. Hayt forwarded Sheridan's recommendation through Secretary of the Interior Carl Schurz to Secretary of War George W. McCrary that the Cheyennes who committed the Kansas brutalities be removed to Fort Wallace or another Kansas post "with a view of the identification of such as committed outrages in that state, and their delivery to the proper civil authorities for trial." Hayt further advised that "the remainder of said Indians be returned to their agency in the Indian Territory."[37]

Throughout November the government evolved a strategy for prosecuting certain of the Northern Cheyennes for their wayward activities during their passage through northwestern Kansas in late September. General Sheridan counseled that the Indians should not be informed of any government decisions on their status until such preparations had been concluded and should remain under arrest at Camp Robinson until then. On November 11 Kansas governor George T. Anthony specified to Sheridan that the Cheyenne leaders must account for the murders of "more than forty men" and the rapes of numerous women. He called on the secretary of war "to surrender to the civil authorities of Kansas, for trial, the principal chiefs, Dull-Knife, Old Crow, [Wild] Hog, Little Wolf, and others . . . in the crimes of murder and woman ravishing." Fearful that other Cheyennes might flee Darlington, Sheridan rued the dearth of troops now in the Department of the Missouri and called for supplemental infantry and cavalry from the southeast and Texas to fill the need. "We have not half enough soldiers, and it is embarrassing to give orders to an inadequate force to engage an enemy where annihilation is the result of defeat, to say nothing of the responsibility to which the military is held for the murder of defenseless settlers."[38]

At Camp Robinson fears regarding the security of the barrack where the Northern Cheyennes were interned increased late in the month. On Saturday, November 23, officers discovered that Dull Knife's son, Bull Hump, had somehow fled the dormitory and made his way to New Red Cloud Agency at Pine Ridge and joined the Oglalas. In fact, the young man had gone there seeking his wife, who had earlier accompanied some

Oglala scouts to Pine Ridge. Captain Deane Monahan, Third Cavalry, temporarily commanding the post, insisted that agent James Irwin seize Bull Hump and return him. Bull Hump reappeared a few days later. Some of the Northern Cheyennes believed that this incident marked a turning point in the tolerance of army oversight, especially after new strictures on their leaving the barrack were imposed. Thereafter, ostensibly, the Indians were locked in the building day after day as sentries patrolled outside. The people henceforth lost all semblance of privacy. Men and boys now had to use the sole indoor facilities, consisting of a water closet and an earth sink, while guards ushered women and small children in groups of ten or fifteen to and from a tract beyond the stable "to respond to calls of nature." Although the women had been permitted free access to Soldier Creek to obtain water, after the Bull Hump incident this was only allowed when they were accompanied by a secure guard.[39]

5

Long Nose

While these events were happening at Camp Robinson, a significant change occurred on December 4, when Captain Henry W. Wessells Jr. and Company H, Third Cavalry, arrived from Wolf Creek, Dakota, close to New Red Cloud Agency at Pine Ridge. The next day Wessells assumed command of the post, as ordered. Company H moved into the vacant barrack east of the parade ground, thus bolstering Company C, which had served there permanently since October 1876.[1]

The mustachioed Wessells, thirty-two years old, had been born in Sackett's Harbor, along the eastern shore of Lake Ontario in northern New York. He was the son of an accomplished officer, retired Brigadier General Henry Walton Wessells (West Point class of 1833), who had served with distinction in the Mexican-American War and the Civil War as well as on the Sioux Expedition of 1855–56 and other frontier assignments. The younger Wessells was educated at the Deer Hill Institute, Danbury, Connecticut, and at the U.S. Naval Academy at Newport, Rhode Island. In 1864 he resigned from the academy to join the U.S. Army at New York City during the closing months of the Civil War. Wessells enlisted as a private in the Seventh Infantry, advanced to sergeant between March and August 1865, and served with the regiment in Florida, Nebraska, and Montana. Commissioned in the Third Cavalry in 1871 and promoted to captain the following year, Wessells remained with that regiment during the Great Sioux War, participating in Mackenzie's assault on Dull Knife and the Northern Cheyennes at the Red Fork of Powder River in November 1876. By late autumn 1878 Captain Wessells was well aware of the survival instincts and abilities of the Northern Cheyennes when under duress.[2]

During his initial weeks as post commander, Wessells took care to meet with the Indians repeatedly and learn of their concerns. He especially sought to get to know Dull Knife and his family. Years later Wessells reported that he particularly liked the chief's daughter, known as "the Princess," as well as a Sioux woman who had married a Northern Cheyenne and thus been away from her people during the stay at Darlington. Wessells claimed that he could converse in the Lakota language with her and that he engaged this woman whenever he wanted to speak with the Cheyennes. According to Wessells, the woman's brother came down from Pine Ridge to visit her on one occasion and the captain found the scene "very touching, the brother weeping like a baby." Wessells said that the Indians referred to him as "Long Nose." Although Major Carlton was technically the responsible officer and could have assumed command of the post, he remained at Fort Laramie or in the field. As designated commander Wessells (and sometimes others) took direct charge. Thus he appropriated much of Lieutenant Chase's former administration of the Cheyennes, kept the Third Cavalry band members on that duty, and occasionally substituted a "special Guard detail" composed of men from all the companies present. They operated under orders of the post officer of the day, who was charged to visit the Cheyennes often. Wessells himself "was in and around the [prisoners'] building at least 10 or 15 times a day."[3]

Wessells claimed that he inquired daily of the people regarding the quantity of their food and was assured by them that it was sufficient except that they did not receive enough meat. Wessells reported that "the sergeant in charge of [the] cookhouse told me they got full ration. They must have gotten more than soldiers, as full ration was issued to suckling children [too]." Overall, he said, "they were very contented and good natured." Regarding visits, Wessells directed his officers to permit only post military personnel to call on the Northern Cheyennes without written orders from himself or the designated officer of the day and always with the sergeant of the guard present. Oglala relatives from Pine Ridge occasionally visited, but visitation as a whole largely fell off after early December.[4]

As the weeks passed, debate resumed regarding the return of the prisoners to the south. The Bureau of Indian Affairs had urged such a course well before temperatures plummeted, but the army had seemingly vacillated. Soon after Wessells's arrival came word that General Sherman, in accordance with Commissioner Hayt's decision, had recommended that the Northern Cheyennes be sent by rail to Fort Leavenworth. Generals Sheridan, Crook, and Pope soon after assented to this. On their arrival at Fort Leavenworth, the suspected leaders of the Kansas raids were to be held for identification, while the rest of the people would continue on to Fort Reno and Darlington. Kansas authorities were also informed of this plan so that they might prepare for the Indians' arrival and make arrangements with witnesses from the northwest counties who might identify the perpetrators. General Pope, meanwhile, pressed for information about when the Indians should arrive: he wished to notify the governor as well as the identifying parties "to avoid delay as much as possible."[5]

As December proceeded, conditions among the imprisoned Cheyennes gradually worsened. The recent incident involving Bull Hump had changed the army's previous lenient attitude toward the people respecting their daily comings and goings. Thereafter, the Cheyennes largely stayed inside the barrack under rigorous guard. With security tightened, the freedoms and niceties earlier accorded to the prisoners disappeared. Already crowded conditions in the dormitory worsened, and the people became more fractious under the new restrictions. Furthermore, responsible officers at Camp Robinson realized that oncoming winter weather could pose serious health risks for the people harbored in the building. Most of them still wore the same frayed clothing that they had arrived in from the Indian Territory, which often had deteriorated into rags over the ensuing weeks. Some still wore the pieces of torn canvas acquired from the soldiers soon after their surrender. Wessells, however, stated that "they always had plenty[,] *for Indians.*" He noted that the Oglalas had contributed 104 pairs of moccasins for their welfare.[6]

Meanwhile, Crook asked Sheridan's office in Chicago whether clothing allotted in annuity goods for the Sioux agencies might be disbursed to the imprisoned Cheyennes and charged against such appropriations for people still harbored at Darlington. "Mercury in [the] vicinity of Camp Robinson has not been so high as zero for a number of days," he wired, "and it will be inhuman to move these Indians as ordered." Crook also notified divisional headquarters that adequate transportation was presently unavailable, so it would take time for it to arrive, while Major

Carlton now warned Crook that "in order to move them it will be necessary to handcuff the men."[7]

It has been suggested that by this time something of a schism had arisen between the chiefs present (Dull Knife, Old Crow, Wild Hog) and the younger men, perhaps including some headmen, who looked upon Little Wolf as their legitimate leader. These young men were said to have consulted with each other on their situation and kept their conversations from their seniors as well as from the women and children. It was primarily these younger men, some subsequently maintained, who had hidden the guns beneath the dormitory floor when they first entered the building. They reportedly had rejected entreaties by their elders to retrieve those weapons and turn them over to the soldiers. It was later stated that these young men kept to themselves, perhaps meeting together occasionally in the small room at the northeast corner of the building.[8] It is noteworthy that during his own tenure as post commander Captain Wessells conducted no further search for firearms in the Cheyenne dormitory. "Having heard much of their disarmament," he stated, "[I] took it for granted they had been properly disarmed. I never saw any arms myself in inspecting them. No sentinel could have been more vigilant nor exercised a more careful supervision over them than myself."[9]

General Crook again registered his concern about clothing for the people and on Christmas Day directed Captain Wessells to issue them military attire on hand at Camp Robinson. As Crook explained, however, this "last resort" action "could be productive of but little benefit, as [besides the men] there were 60 women and 40 children to be provided for, and the Quartermaster's Department is not supplied with clothing suitable for them." Again the army argued that it had requested proper clothing in November, but Indian commissioner Hayt claimed that no request had arrived until December 30. In the meantime, as the usual systemic inertia prevailed, the Indians stayed warm in their barrack environment only because of the heating stove within, not because of their apparel. It was impossible for them to proceed anywhere wearing tattered summer clothes in temperatures well below zero. Nonetheless, by early January plans proceeded to move the people in wagons down the Sidney road to the Union Pacific Railroad, where they would board the cars for Fort Leavenworth and whatever questionable future awaited them. Yet they remained without the needed clothing as several inches of snow now blanketed the region.[10]

On January 3, 1879, because Camp Robinson was anticipated to remain occupied for the long haul, the post was officially redesignated a fort on the direction of General Sheridan.[11] The formality produced no change affecting the Northern Cheyennes, however, who remained unsettled in their confinement, despite occasional rumors that they were now planning to escape from the barrack. More importantly, however, that Friday morning brought official word to move the people south. Wessells called Dull Knife, Wild Hog, Old Crow, Tangle Hair, Left Hand, and a few other Cheyenne men into his office, adjacent to the barrack. It was a critical meeting. With his officers present, and with James Rowland interpreting, Wessells told them of the decision. He said that they would be safe and that Captain Peter D. Vroom's soldiers would guard them en route to Sidney.

When several of the headmen readily acceded and were dismissed to gather their property, the others intervened and physically held them back. Dull Knife spoke uneasily, stressing to Wessells and his officers once again that the northern country was the people's home, where their children had been born and raised, where their fathers lay buried, and consequently where they wished to remain. He restated all of the problems that the Cheyennes had encountered in the south, specifically their dearth of food, that "fifty-eight of their people" had died there, and that the children did not want to go back.[12]

Wild Hog also spoke to the same concerns, adding that "we were very much surprised at being told that we would have to go at that time [of the year]." "Look at us," he told the officers. "See how we are clothed!" He asked that the people be allowed to stay until the temperature warmed in the spring, because "there was nothing on us hardly [little clothing]." By then Little Wolf's people might be found, as Wild Hog explained, and they could return all together. "If the order has come for us to go back [south], why not take us all back?" Dull Knife concurred, staunchly and definitively arguing, "We will not go. You may kill me here, but you cannot make me go back."[13]

In another account, Dull Knife allegedly concluded: "Great Grandfather [the president] sends death in that letter. You will have to kill us and take our bodies back down that trail. We will not go." Some believed that they were to be killed anyway before they reached Darlington "and might as well die here."[14] Wessells replied that the president had ordered this so "it had to be done," that he was merely obeying orders, and that "I hoped they would give us no trouble."[15] The leaders then withdrew to confer in the barrack with their people.

Wessells telegraphed Crook that he was prepared to move on the arrival of clothing for the Indians. He stated that he afterward "went through the [prisoners'] building during that day and the next, but avoided conversing with them. I increased the guard and took the sentinel that was inside and put him on the outside." On the afternoon of January 4, perhaps hoping to mitigate Dull Knife's influence, Wessells met alone with Wild Hog in his office and asked him what decision had been made. As the captain reported to Crook, "Hog said they would do anything that I wanted but go south, and that they would not do." According to Wessells, he responded to the chief that "I would have no more to say but would act. That night they had supper[,] but [I] ordered that it should be their last meal, and [they] should receive no more fuel. They understood that as soon as they would give up they could have fuel and food." Wessells maintained "at no time did they suffer for either," a nebulous conclusion. The captain then withdrew the cooks from the barrack and told the posted sentinels to be vigilant. Indians were not to be killed, he later wrote, "till it was absolutely necessary either to save their own lives or prevent escape."[16]

Regarding their food and fuel, Lieutenant Johnson later told Bishop William H. Hare that the withdrawal of food and fuel "was not done in any spirit of cruelty, but to avoid the great loss of life that would inevitably have followed any attempt to remove them from the building by force" and that they "had fires nearly all the time by breaking up and burning every thing [*sic*] in their room which they could convert into fuel."[17]

Wild Hog contended thereafter that Wessells withheld food from the Indians "because the President told him [to do so]." As he recalled, "The officer [Wessells] told me that the President had ordered that we should not receive any food, or any fuel for fire, because we had said we did not want to go south. He said, 'If you will go south now, right away, we will issue food and fuel to you again.' We said again we did not want to go, because we had not the clothing to keep us from freezing to death in such cold weather." Wild Hog further stated that he soon after conversed with

Lieutenant Johnson, the former post commander, who told him, "I am very sorry that you are being starved and used in this way; it makes me feel bad to see you suffering in the way you are. I would not have you suffer so if I could help it. I thought I had charge of you myself, but the government has decided otherwise, and it seems that this other officer [Wessells] has charge of you. It is not my fault that you are suffering in this way."[18] Wild Hog added that when Agent James Irwin of New Red Cloud Agency at Pine Ridge came to the post during this period the chief asked him to take his children and "send them to school, so as to keep them from suffering . . . but he said he could not do it."[19] About this time the Indians began singing and dancing "almost constantly," as Sergeant Johnson remembered.[20] Old Crow recalled that later in the dormitory "everything was quiet; they did not do anything but sleep, and try to pass away the time as well as they could, for they had nothing to eat."[21]

Following the meeting with Wild Hog, Captain Wessells notified Crook of the Indians' obdurate stance yet stated that he expected to "get them away" if not interfered with. The next morning he wired Crook and Sheridan of his action:

> The eleven [headmen?] have not come [to consult]. They say they will die before returning to the Indian Territory, and I have no recourse but taking their food and fuel away. They [the Cheyennes] have had no food for twenty[-]four hours. Dull Knife is inclined to give up, but the young men won't allow it. I offered to feed the young children but the Indians won't allow it.[22]

The decision to withhold food until the Indians consented to go south had a strong impact. Wild Hog, for one, feared that they would starve unless they complied with Wessells's demand. On Sunday, January 6, the captain announced that the Cheyenne men would proceed to Fort Leavenworth while the women and children would continue on to Darlington, a notice that brought even further trepidation because of the implication of direct prosecution of the men for the Kansas raids.[23] On January 7 Crook again pressed Sheridan about moving the prisoners. Sheridan could not "see how they can be moved without warm clothing" and told his brigadier to "exercise your own judgment." On January 8, when they still refused to yield despite the mounting duress, Wessells cut off their water supply. According to Sergeant Johnson, the Indians soon demanded that a certain sentinel be removed, threatening otherwise to kill him. But when an elderly Cheyenne man indeed tried to assault the guard with his knife, the warriors intervened to prevent it. In another instance, a woman reached out to swipe a knife at a guard as he walked by a window. As before, Johnson recalled, "the guards were now afraid to stay inside the building, and were withdrawn." They believed that the Indians were going to break from the barrack. Likely at this juncture Wessells directed Troops C and H to surround the barrack as further precaution. That lasted only a short time.[24]

Amid the rising tension, the troop components at the post consisted of the following Third Cavalry units: Companies C and H under Wessells's immediate command occupied the two available barracks; Companies A, E, F, and L, under Captain Peter Vroom, camped to the east along White River in the broad expanse near the now-defunct Red Cloud Agency, an area known to the troops as "Mudville," a mile and a half east of the Northern Cheyennes' barrack. Captain Vroom's troops, from Fort Laramie, had arrived to conduct the Indians south to the Union Pacific Railroad at Fort Sidney. As mentioned, the plan specified that the Indian men would then take the rail cars east to Fort Leavenworth, where their specific roles during the Kansas raiding would be determined, while the women and children would be escorted south to Darlington Agency.[25]

Evincing concern, Wessells telegraphed Crook's office yet again, remarking on the "destitute condition" of the prisoners and "their want of food and clothing," now stating that he feared that the animals of the escort troops were "rapidly consuming the little hay in the country" and that they should therefore proceed quickly. Crook meanwhile had forwarded Wessells's proposal that the Indian bureau "send an agent to superintend the move."[26] But in reality it was already too late. That afternoon a civilian named Henry Clifford, an occasional interpreter at the fort, heard an imprisoned Cheyenne acquaintance call out to him in Lakota, "I want to tell you something. We are all going to die tomorrow. You will not see me again." In the evening as darkness fell, Second Lieutenant Francis H. Hardie of Company D, who was Officer of the Day, approached the barrack and looked into the small guardroom, where an Indian was sitting. As Hardie related, "I put my head in the door and said to him in Sioux 'pretty cold.' He beckoned me with his hand and going into the prison room called out Big Head, who put his hand through a broken pane in the window and shook hands with me. He told me he was a Sioux and wanted to go away from these people and go to Red Cloud Agency. He told me he would rather die right here than go south again. Then he asked me for tobacco." Hours later, as temperatures plummeted in the murky dormitory, famished adults and youngsters garbed in rags agonized and chanted shrilly as they braced and waited in their "prison house."[27]

6

Commencement

Northern Cheyenne society called January Moon of Frost in the Lodge (tipi). January at Fort Robinson was true to form this year: the steady cold compounded the crisis for Dull Knife's people. Facing mounting anxiety under military confinement, they agonized over their predicament as temperatures plunged below zero on the night of January 8. Captain Wessells's disquiet about his prisoners was substantial too.[1] At his quarters across the parade ground at the west end of officers' row and diagonally northwest from the Cheyennes' barrack, Wessells contemplated over what to do. He believed that Wild Hog had emerged as the most forceful leader of the people during their incarceration, so the captain conceived a plan to remove him physically and thus eliminate his abiding influence. As Wessells later recounted, "I made up my mind to get Hog in irons, as I knew he was the leading spirit and the one by whom they were in great measure guided. By getting him separated from the rest, they would be without his counsel."[2]

As January 9 dawned clear, Wessells detailed his notion to Lieutenant George W. Baxter.[3] The plan was provocative: if it did not go as planned, things could get a lot worse. Wessells therefore directed Baxter to go over to the Company H barrack at the west end of the parade ground and remain ready there with the soldiers in case of an emergency. Shortly after noon Wessells crossed the parade ground to the Adjutant's Office, just seventy-five feet west of the barrack holding the Northern Cheyennes. There he charged "four trusty men" to post themselves in the adjacent clerk's room, directing them to appear only after Wild Hog had entered the building. Wessells sent for two more soldiers from the guardhouse:

the sergeant major, Lieutenant James F. Simpson (who was officer of the day), and Lieutenant Joseph F. Cummings of Company C were also present. When he solicited Wild Hog's presence, however, the suspicious chief balked and refused to leave the barrack. Instead he sent word for Wessells to come there so that all the people might hear what he had to say. Only after Old Crow was permitted to accompany Wild Hog did the two chiefs proceed over to the commander's office. Dull Knife, who had been reported sick and had an abscess on his leg, was not invited.[4]

As the office steadily filled with soldiers, Wessells again asked the two Indians if their people would go south. Standing up, by his own account, he demanded to know: "Will you go or will you not?" Before Wild Hog and Old Crow could respond, at a signal from the captain the soldiers abruptly jumped the chiefs. Old Crow submitted readily and was handcuffed, but the robust Wild Hog fought back vigorously. "I thought they were going to kill me," the chief recalled. In the ensuing melee, Wessells, Cummings, Sergeant Edward Dunne of Company H, and Private Thomas Ferguson of Company E wrestled the chief to the floor. During the ruckus, Wild Hog managed to pull a knife, seriously slashing Private Ferguson in the sternum and cutting Cummings's hand. The chief said later that he had been attempting to stab himself and commit suicide. Whatever the case, Wild Hog, at last subdued and handcuffed, told Wessells that he would now go south and further, if uncuffed, would obtain the other Cheyennes' assent to go. Fearing more alarm, however, Wessells refused to release him. Instead, he directed that the two chiefs be removed to Captain Vroom's lower camp, a mile and a half east of the post near the old Red Cloud Agency. Sergeant Johnson recollected that three companies of the Third Cavalry (E, F, and L) "were camping here partly in some small log huts erected there [two years earlier] . . . and partly in tents."[5]

With Wild Hog and Old Crow conducted to the lower camp, Wessells approached the front door of the prison dormitory and asked that those agreeable to going south come out, promising that they would get food and not be harmed. He got no response. He then sought out the relatives of Wild Hog and Old Crow in the barrack to take them to stay with the chiefs in the remote camp, but the Indians inside would not permit it. That afternoon near 4 P.M., however, Wessells allowed Wild Hog and Old Crow to return under guard to the east end exterior of the dormitory to speak with the people and to convince their relatives to go back to the lower camp with them. Johnson claimed that Wild Hog took his small daughter, "but none of his children who could take care of themselves." Additionally, he brought out nineteen infirm and elderly men and women, including Tangle Hair's relatives.[6]

Chief Left Hand emerged from the building, was handcuffed, and went with the others, leaving perhaps 130 men, women, and children in the barrack, although an exact count was never finally determined. When Wessells asked Dull Knife to come out, the old chief said that he wanted to oblige but the others would not permit it.[7] Notably, Wild Hog and Old Crow later told mixed-blood interpreter Rowland that the Indians planned to break out that very night.[8] The departure of the relatives of Wild Hog, Tangle Hair, and Old Crow, along with the infirm and elderly people, afforded a certain relief for those still in the overcrowded barrack but otherwise did little to curb the prevailing anxiety.[9]

After the Indians' initial alarm at hearing Wild Hog's cries during the scuffle in Wessells's office, his daughter "began chanting a war song which was taken up and participated in by the whole imprisoned band, . . . and for two hours the echoes of that prison-room produced a babel of sounds better imagined than described," according to a scribe. The sounds carried across the parade to officers' row. Angie Johnson wrote: "The rest of the day we could hear them tearing up the floor and smashing things generally and occasionally singing their death song, knowing that some of them would probably be killed when they made their attempt to escape." Some of the Cheyennes made two attempts to break down the barrack doors and during one such momentary effort spilled into the fenced compound area on the south side of the building. A son of Wild Hog was heard to call out, "Get out of the way, here we come!" But the guards drove them back.[10]

After this the Indians resumed singing, chanting, and dancing. They also began strategizing, for it was approximately during this period after Wild Hog's arrest that most of the imprisoned Cheyennes, especially the men, united in their resolve to break out. Tangle Hair later said that following the affray with Wild Hog "we who were inside thought they were getting ready to commence shooting us down. . . . We all consulted together and decided that, rather than be shot down in there, we would break out." One of the guards recalled: "I heard Indians tearing [the] floor up in [the] afternoon. We looked in the windows and saw them tearing up [the] floor and making war clubs [from pieces of the floor joists]. One of the Indians came and showed us a club made of a piece of board with six or eight spikes driven in the end of it."[11]

Soon afterward the Cheyennes used assorted fabrics, including blankets, to shield the windows and thus conceal their activities. At the same time, they fortified the doors and tore up more flooring to help barricade them. Using their knives, they excavated at least three rifle pits as well as a trench in the earth beneath the floorboards. From there they would command the barrack windows and doorways to the west if the soldiers directed gunfire inside.[12] Others meanwhile apparently salvaged or reassembled and then loaded the guns that had remained hidden during the intervening weeks. Altogether, they had perhaps a dozen long arms and three revolvers and a relatively small supply of ammunition (though the exact amount is unknown). For his part, Wessells had thought that the people had been fully disarmed, although he suspected that they might have "4 or 5 pistols."[13] As mentioned, the Indians had been permitted to keep their knives, which they could now use as weapons. The men also broke the stove apart to fashion various rude clubs from its pieces. "They now became very ugly," remembered Sergeant Johnson. As one officer observed, it "was like a den of rattlesnakes, and any white man who had shown his head in the room would have met certain death." Some of the Indians yelled threats to the troopers, and, as Johnson remembered, challenged them "through the windows to come and take them to the Indian Territory." Years later Sergeant Johnson recalled that at one point during the standoff Wessells trained a battery of six-pounder guns against the barrack to no avail; the Indians still refused to yield.[14]

The prisoners had clear reason for such a response. Over their long days of mounting desperation at Fort Robinson, the Northern Cheyenne leaders had prudently weighed their alternatives and in their growing hopelessness had prepared for this exigency. They indeed were willing to die rather than return to Darlington Agency. With neither food nor water, thirsty children were now reduced to scraping frost from the window panes. Leftover saved food was entirely gone. The reek of human waste assuredly mounted in their restricted confinement as all previous sanitary privileges for women and children were stopped. By January 9 the women were collaborating with the men to break out, realizing full well that they and their sons and daughters might die trying to escape.[15]

As Bull Hump later explained, "When it became evident that the soldiers intended to starve us to death, we thought we might as well die fighting as to return [south] & it was decided to break out." In her own gloom, Iron Teeth supported the plan. "The women were willing," she recalled. "Some of us, perhaps many of us, would be killed. But it was hoped that many would escape and get away to join other Indians somewhere."[16]

If there was any organized plan beyond forcibly breaking out and running from the barrack, it focused only on reaching the rugged fastness of the bluffs nearly three miles west of the post. The teenage son of a man named Pumpkinseed recalled overhearing the young men say that they would head for those bluffs, where their bodies would lie if all else failed, but apparently no further strategy was discussed. Over the preceding weeks Iron Teeth had made extra moccasins for herself and her children. In the frigid darkness, she and others now heaped their packs and other items beneath the windows so they might climb on them to aid their escape at the proper time. "The plan," she said, "was to break out just after the soldiers had gone to bed for the night. I gave to my son the six-shooter I had. He was my oldest child, then twenty-two years of age." The Indians now refused to allow anyone to come into the building or leave it. Earlier, when Wessells came to speak with Dull Knife to encourage him to come out, the chief had refused to leave his people: some young warriors had physically held him back to assure that he remained inside.[17]

Word of an imminent breakout spread quickly among the soldiers. Reacting to the overall tumult in the adjutant's office and subsequent uproar in the barrack, the soldiers worked to take measures during the late afternoon and evening to prevent escape. They hammered heavy planks sideways across the doorway leading between the kitchen and the dormitory and then stapled heavy chains over the planks. They fortified the doors on the north side of the barrack as well, at least one with a heavy bar screwed into place. An increased number of sentinels outside, seven in all (three at the east end of the building, one in front, one directly in the rear, and two at the west end next to the Adjutant's Office), closed around the building and the plank fence in back. Because Wessells and his officers felt certain that the Indians could not escape, most of the windows were left alone. Wessells also thought that the unarmed Cheyennes could be recaptured easily if they bolted through the windows. For their part, the Indians believed that the place was secure from the troops after they finished their own work.[18]

Besides the sentinels, other soldiers came and went, intermittently occupying the small room at the northwest corner (formerly designated as the company first sergeant's room) with an exterior door facing the porch and accessed from under the veranda. Extra men repaired to the guardhouse, distantly adjacent to the west wall of the adjutant's office. The small extension room in the northeast corner of the barrack (mirroring the one at the west end) was empty; until that morning it had served as interpreter James Rowland's bedroom, but he moved out in the evening because, as he said, "I thought they would break out." Finally, as Wild Hog and Old Crow were removed to the lower camp, supposedly to thwart such a breakout, Companies C and H formed under arms in ranks, the former on the parade ground between the unit's own barrack and the Indian quarters and the latter similarly positioned to the west.[19]

After an hour, as the initial excitement waned, Companies C and H were withdrawn and divided into reliefs. Company H took position near its stables for the time being, but late that afternoon, as a further precaution, Lieutenant Simpson gained permission from Wessells to increase the guard around the Indians' barrack. Three sentries were now posted at the east end: two at the west end adjoining the adjutant's office, one in the front, and one at the rear. Despite the tensions over a possible breakout, standard army routine proceeded at Fort Robinson. Garbed in their fur caps and caped overcoats, the garrison's troops paraded and formed in ranks before dusk as company sergeants and officers took roll.

The manner of these movements, especially the assignment of the reinforced guard, only intensified the Cheyennes' distress. One soldier, Private Arthur G. Ross of Company A of the Third, recalled hearing the Indians "continually working at the windows, as I thought loosening them so they could easily be pushed in [*sic*: out]. When I came off post [at 7 P.M.] I told the sentinel who relieved me to keep a good lookout on the windows and [I] told the corporal of the guard what I had observed." Most of this troop's own preparations were completed by around 7 P.M., when Captain Wessells again approached the building and described the sentinels as vigilant and "everything quiet inside." With the prisoners disarmed, as he believed, despite the unbarred windows, Wessells was convinced that no breakout would likely occur. Consequently, he stationed no supplemental body of troops nearby in the darkness beyond his reinforced guard detail. Others thought differently, however. Lieutenant Baxter of Company H, along with several other officers, kept their clothes on, expecting the worst. At 9:30 P.M. Lieutenant Simpson entered the Adjutant's Office adjacent to the barrack, expecting to remain an hour. When taps sounded that night, the vigilant officer alerted his first sergeant to "to have the men [of Company C] ready to turn out at a moment[']s notice."[20]

Temperatures had apparently now dipped below freezing inside the barrack, intimating the intense cold that would come that night, while outside the moonlight illumined a landscape of crusted snow at least three to eight inches deep and much deeper in places.[21] Most of the Indians, reconciled to what was about to happen, had dressed well in what little clothing they still possessed and tied about them whatever blankets they had to keep their hands free. Some painted their faces red and others applied different colors, as they effectually prepared to die. The warriors also planned to augment what few guns they possessed with weapons taken from the soldiers that they would shoot to initiate their escape. Several men, possibly preselected by lot to be the first out of the building, were designated as a rear guard to protect noncombatants, who would also be among the first to leave once the exit began. Most women and children apparently gathered themselves near windows and doors toward the east end of the barrack, while most of the armed men occupied the west end and its windows, to cover the area of the guard house. They expected the most immediate threat to come from that direction. They had also conceived certain routes to follow. Although their plans were perhaps indefinite, they included obtaining horses at area ranches at their first opportunity as they fled the immediate vicinity of the fort. Some women, and men as well, carried lariats, bridles, and saddles to enable this effort. Darkness was not in their favor, however: the moon in a cloudless sky would expose their flight despite their many prayers for success.

Through mindful discussion, the Cheyennes had almost certainly planned for a getaway once they were free: a route that might enable their escape, with the aid of their songs and hope. They must have made such preparations, though we have little direct evidence. The people knew the area well, having lived in the vicinity from the time of their agency relocation there from Fort Fetterman in 1873–74, and where they were assigned until their removal to Darlington in 1877. They further possessed intuitive skill about landscapes and had gained increased familiarity with the post and its locality over the previous two months. The soldiers had also treated them quite moderately at times, so they had collectively gleaned knowledge of the most practical routes that they might follow to escape the troops once free of the barrack. They were familiar with the immediate area surrounding the building and with the natural wooded cover afforded by nearby Soldier Creek and White River. Once they reached the closely rising rugged timbered bluffs to the west (part of the Pine Ridge Plateau), they might logically conceal themselves from pursuers. The streams could also provide relief for their thirst, but those icy waters also represented a physical hindrance. The Pine Ridge Agency, where their Lakota friends and relatives might harbor those who escaped, was a likely goal, but their pressing immediate objective in their desperate circumstances was to get away—to scatter and to hide. As they had repeatedly declared, they would escape and survive or they would die.

Inside the dormitory, some of the people now retrieved from their packs special objects to carry with them, sacred pieces with designs or colors that signified protection, such as shields and eagle feathers—hallowed items that they had kept with them for years, decades, lifetimes, even generations. Older men, including Dull Knife, planned to accompany the women and aid them, while several bold younger warriors, including the artist Little Finger Nail (who kept his treasured ledger book tucked in his belt), would oversee the immediate escape from the barrack to ensure that all got away quickly.

As stated, their plan called for breaking the glass and climbing through the windows at the northeast corner of the building—farthest from the guardhouse and closest to Soldier Creek and White River. From there, they would seek concealment amid the adjoining sheltering trees and foliage. All of their hefty property—parfleche bundles, saddles, assorted gear, some to be abandoned—was now stacked as climbing steps directly beneath the windows to accelerate the people's escape. A man named Little Shield, a soldier chief, took station at the window facing the parade ground inside the northeast angle of the building. Additional warriors posted themselves at the remaining appointed windows, while others aimed their guns between chinks in the log walls. At the proper moment, they would open fire on the posted sentries. Waiting anxiously amid their mounting trauma, the people hugged and kissed each other then paused in the bleak darkness. For a short while all grew quiet. At 9 P.M. the strains of "Taps" wafted over the post. The night was still and clear and crystal cold. The full moon was gliding toward the western horizon, with varying levels of crusted snow covering the ground.[22]

Northern Cheyenne leaders Little Wolf (*left*) and Dull Knife (*right*), photographed by Alexander Gardner in Washington, D.C., 1873. The chiefs initially left the Indian Territory with their respective followers but parted after reaching Nebraska, where Dull Knife remained with his people until the breakout from Fort Robinson. He and several family members finally reached New Red Cloud Agency at Pine Ridge, Dakota Territory, whereas Little Wolf and his followers eventually succeeded in gaining their Montana home. (Wikimedia Commons)

President Rutherford B. Hayes, whose administration embraced such tenets as concentration, farming, and education to assimilate the Indians. His tenure, however, coincided with several disquieting Indian wars, including the flight of the Northern Cheyennes from Oklahoma Territory and the subsequent imprisonment and breakout of Dull Knife's people from Fort Robinson. (Brady-Handy photograph collection, Library of Congress, Prints and Photographs Division, LC-BH826-400 [P&P])

Secretary of the interior Carl Schurz, German immigrant and a former prominent Civil War officer, espoused fair treatment of the Indians and desired to see them assimilated humanely. Such efforts, however, often resulted in disaster on the frontier, as exemplified by the Northern Cheyennes, while assuring the continuation of untenable reservation policies into the twentieth century. (Frontispiece of *Ehrenbankett für Carl Schurtz* [1899], courtesy Wikimedia Commons)

Secretary of war George W. McCrary, an Iowa lawyer and politician, whose tenure coincided with operations involving the Northern Cheyennes in 1878-79. McCrary implemented and oversaw policy considerations, while leaving military activities in the hands of Generals Sherman, Sheridan, and Crook and their subordinates. (Brady-Handy photograph collection, Library of Congress, Prints and Photographs Division, LC-BH832-633 [P&P])

Lieutenant General Philip H. Sheridan, commander of the Military Division of the Missouri headquartered in Chicago. He called for returning the Northern Cheyenne prisoners south to Indian Territory in order to secure the reservation system and ordered that they be held at Camp Robinson pending such transfer. Following the breakout, Sheridan directed the removal of the survivors to New Red Cloud Agency at Pine Ridge. He ultimately blamed Crook for the breakout. (Author's collection)

Brigadier General George Crook commanded the Department of the Platte from Omaha in 1878-79. Although Crook believed in treating Indians with honesty and authority, after the Fort Robinson breakout Generals Sherman and Sheridan directed him to convene a thorough investigation of the entire affair, at least partly to quell public furor over what had happened. (Author's collection)

Red Cloud Agency, Nebraska, on distribution day. View northeast toward the massive sandstone buttes later named for Chief Red Cloud as depicted in *Harper's Weekly*, May 13, 1876. Many of the agency buildings had been dismantled and moved to Pine Ridge, Dakota Territory, by the time of the Northern Cheyennes' arrival as prisoners at adjacent Camp Robinson in late October 1878.

Major Caleb H. Carlton (shown here as a Civil War officer) oversaw the troops who apprehended Dull Knife's followers along Chadron Creek in late October 1878. Carlton largely monitored Camp/Fort Robinson from his home station, Fort Laramie, while vainly leading operations in search of Chief Little Wolf's people during the weeks preceding the breakout. (Library of Congress, Prints & Photographs Division, LC-USZ62-105785)

Captain John B. Johnson, Company B, Third Cavalry, commanded the units credited with locating and capturing Dull Knife's followers during a snowstorm along Chadron Creek, Nebraska, on October 23, 1878. Three days later, the Indians were escorted to Camp Robinson to begin their imprisonment. Johnson later performed significantly in the breakout and its contiguous actions. (Courtesy of the Missouri Historical Society, St. Louis, http://collections.mohistory.org/resources/158628)

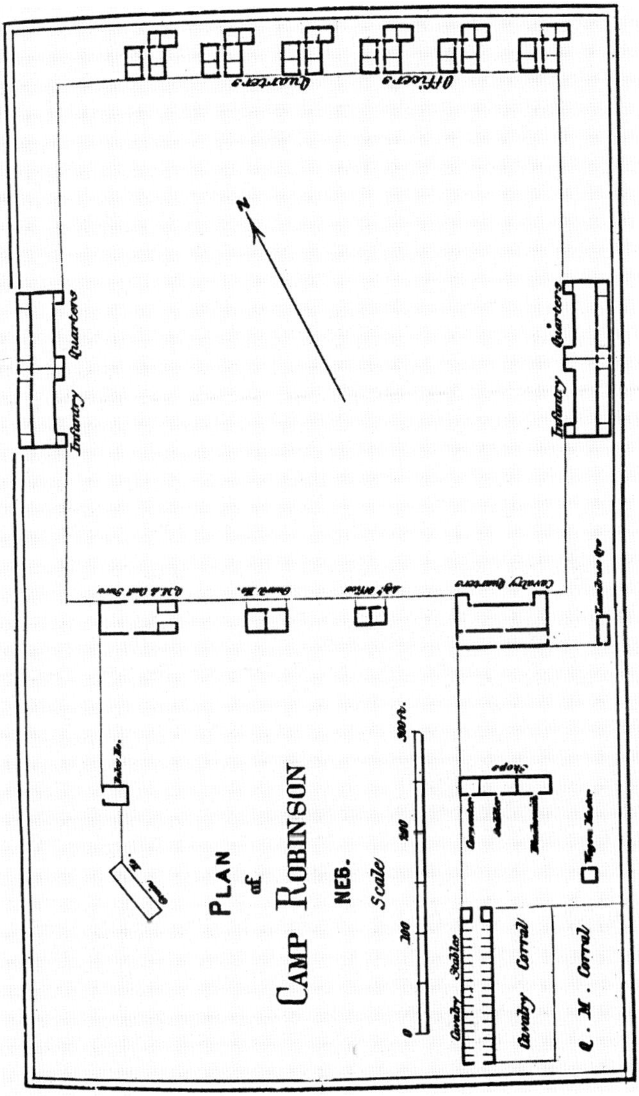

Plat of Camp Robinson, Nebraska, 1876. The cavalry barrack holding the Northern Cheyennes appears at the lower southeast corner of the parade ground. Officer quarters are at the north. The adjutant's office and the guardhouse appear immediately and consecutively to the west of the cavalry barrack. (From *Outline Descriptions of the Posts in the Military Division of the Missouri* [Chicago: Headquarters Military Division of the Missouri, 1876]).

View to the west of Camp Robinson, Nebraska, in 1876, showing tents of troops as well as elements of the neighboring Red Cloud Agency in the foreground, while trees and brush mark the relative course of White River. The east end of the new cavalry barrack appears at high left center, its broad roof apparent in the sunlight, while the adjutant's office and guard house stand immediately beyond. (U.S. Military Academy Library)

Camp Robinson, Nebraska, as completed in 1877, viewed from the southeast. Officers' row is at right in the upper distance, while one of the long infantry barracks appears on the east perimeter of the parade. Directly below the flagpole on the parade ground at right center appears a major part of the cavalry barrack (light-colored here) that would contain the Northern Cheyenne prisoners. The other structures were a guard house, along with various shops, storehouses, stables, and administrative offices. (Larry Ness and History Nebraska)

Detail of the photograph above showing (a) the cavalry barrack (directly beneath the flagpole) from which the Northern Cheyennes escaped; and the top of the roofs of (b) the adjutant's office, and, to its left, (c) the guardhouse. The lower part of the image includes the principal area that the Indians fled across in their break for White River as well as the bridge over the stream and the sawmill, which appears in the direct foreground.

Captain Henry W. Wessells commanded Fort Robinson during much of the Northern Cheyennes' confinement. He then prosecuted the two-week-long pursuit of the people following their breakout from the post and was wounded during the final engagement at Antelope Creek. Years later, Wessells evinced deep regret and personal guilt over what had happened, even calling the events akin to murder. He wears the medal of the Loyal Legion, a Civil War officer society to which Wessells belonged. (Author's collection)

Oglala Lakota Chief Red Cloud, who repeatedly interceded on behalf of the Northern Cheyenne prisoners at Fort Robinson in 1878-79. Following the breakout, Red Cloud welcomed the Cheyenne survivors to Pine Ridge Agency, thereby creating a special bond between the tribes that continues today. Photo taken in 1880. (South Dakota State Historical Society, courtesy Wikimedia Commons)

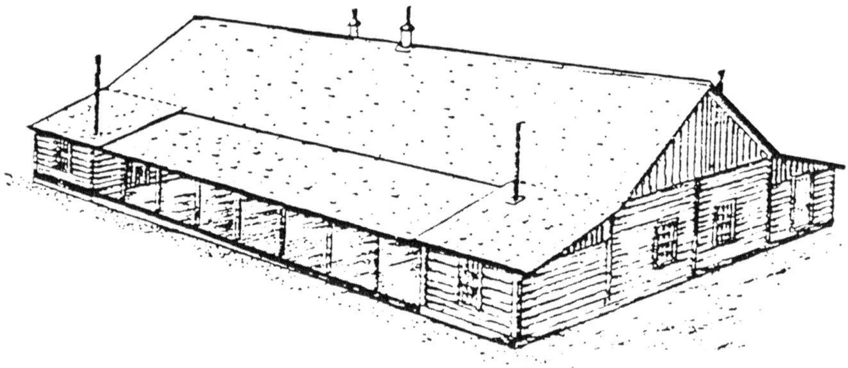

Modern drawing of the 1874 cavalry barrack at Fort Robinson, view to the southeast, showing the north side and west end. On the night of January 9, 1879, most of the Northern Cheyennes exited the building through doors and windows located beneath the porch roof on this nearest north-facing side as well as through egresses on the far (east) end. (Fort Robinson Museum)

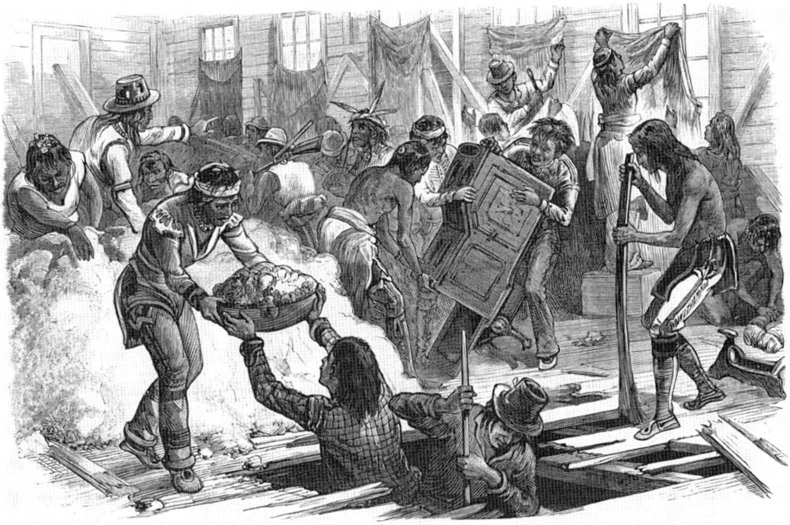

Artistic rendering of the Northern Cheyennes readying their escape from the barrack prison at Fort Robinson on January 8, 1877. Here some are shown excavating defenses beneath the floor, while retrieving and readying previously hidden firearms. Others are seen covering windows, bolstering doors, and obtaining stove parts for weaponry. (*Frank Leslie's Illustrated Weekly*, February 15, 1879)

Newspaper drawing showing the initial escape of the Northern Cheyennes from the prison barrack with troops in close pursuit. In this view, warriors endeavor to protect women and children as they run toward Soldier Creek and White River. (*Frank Leslie's Illustrated Newspaper,* February 15, 1879)

James R. O'Beirne, field correspondent for the *New York Herald,* whose immediate and thorough chronicling of the Northern Cheyenne breakout from Fort Robinson proved significant in enhancing the known history of the event. As depicted here, O'Beirne, who had coincidentally led the army's pursuit of John Wilkes Booth directly following President Abraham Lincoln's assassination, years later received a Medal of Honor for his service at Charlottesville, Virginia, during the Civil War. (Courtesy of Fordham University Library, Bronx, NY)

Captain Emmet Crawford, Company G, Third Cavalry. A Pennsylvania enlisted man and officer during the Civil War, Crawford later served with black infantry troops before transferring to the Third Cavalry in 1870. During the breakout in 1879, he actively pursued the Northern Cheyennes from Fort Robinson. Crawford died in 1886 at the hands of Mexican irregular troops during General Crook's pursuit of Apache renegades below the border. The town of Crawford, Nebraska, is named in his honor. (Wikimedia Commons and Carol A. Breuer)

Major Andrew W. Evans, Third Cavalry, whose Fort Laramie soldiers skirmished with the Northern Cheyennes near Castle Rock, west of Fort Robinson, an action that directly pressed the Indians in their course toward Antelope Creek, where Captain Wessells's scouts located them. (*Cecil Whig* newspaper and Creative Commons)

Newspaper drawing of the fight at Antelope Creek, January 22, 1879, which ended the Northern Cheyennes' breakout from Fort Robinson. The Indians' entrenchment differed significantly from that represented here by incorporating a single elongated pit. The troops closed on the position on foot rather than on horseback as depicted here. (*Frank Leslie's Illustrated Weekly*, February 15, 1879)

Second Lieutenant George W. Baxter, Company F, Third Cavalry, who provided details of the Northern Cheyenne breakout and pursuit from Fort Robinson. Baxter's men performed a major containment role at Antelope Creek before assisting in the final attack on the Indian position. Baxter later served briefly as governor of Wyoming Territory in 1886. (Wyoming State Archives)

Northern Cheyenne breakout survivors from Fort Robinson held prisoner as defendants for trial in Dodge City, Kansas, in 1879. *Top row, left to right*: Tangle Hair, Wild Hog, interpreter George Reynolds, Old Crow, Porcupine; *bottom row, left to right*: Left Hand, Noisy Walker, and Blacksmith. (New York Public Library Digital Collections, G90F195_035ZF)

(Susan) Iron Teeth, Northern Cheyenne survivor of the trek from Oklahoma and the Fort Robinson breakout, whose reminiscence helped chronicle this study, as she appeared in 1926 at age ninety-two. (National Park Service, Little Bighorn Battlefield National Monument, LIBI_00012_01920, Thomas B. Marquis, photographer)

The fight at Antelope Creek, Nebraska, January 22, 1878. Frederic Remington's *Through the Smoke Sprang the Daring Soldier* (1897) was used as an illustration in Remington's piece "A Sergeant of the Orphan Troop" in his book *Crooked Trails* (1898). Original in the Amon Carter Museum of American Art, Fort Worth, Texas. (Wikimedia Commons)

Aftermath of the fight at Antelope Creek, Nebraska, January 22, 1879, as depicted by Frederic Remington. This picture, entitled *This Time the Air Grew Clear*, was published in Remington's story in *Crooked Trails* in 1898 and is also known as *The Battle of Warbonnet Creek*. (Gilcrease Museum, Tulsa, OK)

Dedication of the Northern Cheyenne Memorial near the bluff below Fort Robinson, July 15, 2016. (Photo by John Warner)

7

Violent Night

Almost an hour later, near 10 P.M., soon after a sentinel shouted the time, four shots rang out from inside the Indians' barrack.[1] Northern Cheyenne warriors, taking advantage of the vivid moonlight, leveled their guns and quickly fired through the window glass, targeting sentries pacing within several feet of the east and west ends of the barrack. At the east end, Private Frank Schmidt of Company A took a carbine bullet in his lower stomach. He screamed and fell mortally wounded.[2] Another sentry near the west end of the barrack, Private Peter Hulse of Company A, was hit in his right thigh, a wound that would also prove fatal.[3] Several warriors rushed out to retrieve the sentries' weapons and cartridge belts then dashed back inside to resume the attack. Private Daniel Timmany of Company E, patrolling on the south side of the barrack, was hit in the right arm. Another sentry, Private James E. McHale, was struck in the leg by a shot from a carbine leveled between the gaps of the log wall as he sat in the guard room attached to the front northwest corner of the barrack.[4] Private James Emory was hit in a thigh by an incoming bullet through the closed door of the guard room. During the initial gunfire and accompanying racket, Edward F. Pulver, corporal of the guard, was struck in his right arm by a revolver bullet fired through a shattered porch window of the building.[5]

The remaining guards exited by breaking through the window fronting the parade and started shooting at the Indians who had begun fleeing the barrack. "The fire became heavy," one soldier recalled. The Indians, he said, "were firing both from inside and outside of [the] building."[6] Ultimately, seven soldiers were killed or wounded in the first seconds of the Northern Cheyennes' opening barrage.

During the shooting, warriors abruptly forced open the door on the north side while others broke windows from their sashes on the north and east sides of the building. Through these openings poured men, women, children, and the remaining elderly people, several of whom had apparently known little or nothing of the anticipated breakout and reacted in dazed confusion. Some men carried babies and toddlers as others dashed forward weighted down with their scant possessions. Most ran haltingly around the east end of the barrack as they fled southeastwardly, some passing between the south end of C Company barrack and the unit's nearby stable. Children became separated from their parents in the tumult. Some brothers and sisters carried their siblings. In all, the hurried evacuation lasted less than five minutes. The people—screaming, crying, and yelling in the uproar—labored past the adjacent laundress quarters and across the fields, in crusted snow up to a foot deep in places. Their immediate goal was the distant cottonwood, willow, and plum thickets clustered along Soldier Creek and White River. There they might find shelter and get water, which they had not had for two days. Rancher Bronson, who apparently arrived soon after the breakout, said that many Cheyennes had already discarded the gear with which they hoped to secure his animals, as their casualties and evident desperation mounted.[7]

Captain Wessells was just going to bed at his quarters when he heard the first shots. At the sound of the gunfire, he hurriedly rose, pulled on his trousers, overshoes, hat, and overcoat, and tore across the parade ground toward the south end of the C Company barrack and the east end of the Cheyennes' barrack. By then "the Indians were all out running away," he said later. Several Cheyenne warriors hurriedly assembled near the east end of the barrack to check the onrushing guard and cover the men, women, and children still emerging from the barrack (many of whom had been asleep when the first shots rang out).[8]

Half-dressed members of Company C, sprinting from their own barrack, loosely assembled east of the parade. At Wessells's direction, they pressed the Cheyennes in their advance through the tramped-down snow. One of those troopers, Sergeant Michael F. Lanigan of Company C, recalled: "I was awake when the first shots were fired. I got out of bed as quick as possible, put on my pants and boots and ran for the gun rack, took my carbine and ran outside putting on my belt as I went out. The Indians were scattering over the prairie [toward the river] and the company was scattered out to the left of the company quarters firing at them." The men of Company C were in disorder, but they quickly joined the guard and poured unremitting fire on the Indians. Over the next several minutes they killed twenty Cheyennes, only eight of whom were warriors, as they later learned. According to Sergeant Lanigan, Wessells ordered the troops "to follow them up and kill them or not let them get away." Some members of Company H joined the chase as well, making perhaps fifty soldiers in pursuit. "The Indians fired at us repeatedly with carbines," Wessells reported, "and we killed five bucks in a few moments." Soon after the initial firing on the guards, Surgeon Petteys was at hand treating the sentinels and directing their conveyance to the hospital for Surgeon Moseley's attention.[9]

Northern Cheyenne survivor accounts describe the escape from the barrack in particularly rich detail. Either Little Shield or Curly Hair fired the first shot through the window that killed the sentry patrolling at the west end. Whoever this was then rushed out and retrieved the sentry's arms and cartridge belt to augment the Indians' arsenal. Three more Cheyennes—Tangle Hair, Little Finger Nail, and Gathering His Medicine—also fired, wounding the sentry at the east end and garnering yet another gun and more ammunition. The warriors otherwise reportedly carried only five long arms and eleven revolvers among them, so the captured sentries' arms and cartridges would be useful in warding off the close pursuit.

Iron Teeth recalled that her son broke a window with the gun she had given him, while others did likewise. "We all jumped out. My son took the younger of the two daughters upon his back. The older daughter and I each carried a little pack. It was expected the soldiers would be asleep, except the few guards. But bands of them came hurrying to shoot at us. One of them fired a gun almost at my face, but I was not harmed. . . . All of the Indians followed one broken trail toward the river, but soon we had to scatter."[10]

An aged Cheyenne named Old Sitting Man, already enduring a protracted leg injury sustained on the march from the south, leaped from the barrack window just as a shot hit his good leg. As he fell, he reinjured his other leg and could not proceed. A passing soldier shot him dead. Not all of the action started in the front of the building. Bull Hump, son of Dull Knife, later told the historian Walter Camp that "I bursted the boards from the [rear?] window and was first out, and knocked a hole through the [back] fence with an ax. . . . I was nearly choked from long thirst and made up my mind that I must have a drink at all hazards. I . . . ran to the creek for a drink the first thing and the pursuing soldiers ran past me." A man named Three Fingers took a bullet in his heel as he bolted. Captured later, he would walk with a limp ever after.[11]

Mrs. Black Bear was one of the first to flee the barrack. She said that "the soldiers . . . followed them [afoot] in a half circle shooting into them all the time." The handful of warriors, known to be Dog Soldiers within the Northern Cheyenne military community, assumed a rearguard position behind the fleeing women and children and sought to protect the noncombatants from the brunt of the closing troopers. As one officer explained, "The Indians moved south towards the creek, the squaws being driven in a mass ahead of the men, at least five of the latter keeping up an incessant fire. It was in returning the fire that several women and children were killed. No woman or child was intentionally harmed, and in fact many officers and soldiers showed great daring in trying to save them." When the Cheyennes crossed a bend in Soldier Creek, then probably only a trickle, Mrs. Black Bear said that they paused momentarily to quench their thirst and broke "through the ice so that most of them were soon wet" amid the freezing temperatures.[12]

A military diagram prepared within weeks of the breakout revealed that many of the escaping Cheyennes forded the White River on the existing bridge one-third of a mile from the garrison and just below the post sawmill. They then turned southwest, passing the sawmill and moving upstream along the river's east bank amid the trees and brush. They were in a more dispersed body now, and many others remained on the west side of the White in ascending the stream. "By this time," Mrs. Black Bear recalled, "they were getting separated, some getting tired and falling behind and others longer winded and with no babies to carry getting ahead." As she later related to Grinnell, "It was hard to run in frozen clothing and besides they had not much strength from having starved so long."[13]

While passing the sawmill, a woman and a man suddenly turned and confronted their pursuers, the man armed with only his knife, the woman with a piece of broken stove. Both fell in a flurry of soldier bullets. In a particularly tragic scene near White River, a man named White Antelope (also known as Big Antelope) exited the barrack with his wife and baby and ran until the wife was wounded. Still they kept on, with White Antelope carrying the baby. When confronted by soldiers, he drew his knife and fought but was shot and wounded along with several other people. As his wife sought to reach him, she too was wounded. When he finally gained her side, White Antelope found the baby dead. Distraught with grief, White Antelope said that they should all die together and stabbed his wife before turning the blade on himself. They were eventually carted off to Fort Robinson with the other wounded, where both soon died.[14]

As the soldiers hurried their pursuit, they killed or wounded a large number of Cheyennes, many rushing toward and past the river. Tangle Hair was wounded but ultimately survived. Elderly noncombatants often could not be distinguished from the men. Lieutenant Johnson wrote: "During the [opening] firing, it was impossible to avoid hitting some women and children as they were all fleeing together." As the chase quickened, at least nine Indian men died and perhaps eighteen more of the people were wounded as they ran across the terrain toward the bridge or along the west bank itself. According to one report, "Their bleeding bodies, mangled and torn, bucks, squaws, and papooses all together literally strewed the road they had selected for their much hoped deliverance." The man who at the onset had shot the guards and secured their weapons and ammunition was hit in the thigh as the Indians pulled away. Unable to advance, he lay prone but unleashed further rounds against the advancing soldiers until he was killed.[15]

As they withdrew from the barrack, some of the warriors' initial shots tore across the parade in the direction of the officers' homes. "The balls flew pretty thick around our quarters," wrote Angie Johnson. She and others "were not very far from the Indian building. . . . I was afraid Charlie would get hit as he went down from our house to the office across the parade, when the balls were flying all around, but he didn't get hurt."[16]

More Indian noncombatants fell dead or wounded during this initial action, including an eighty-year-old woman. Wessells said that his troops thought she was a man. "The poor old soul no doubt became exhausted & could not go any further," he said. Soldiers were now arriving from the Company H barrack: some bareheaded and sparsely attired in undergarments and without shoes, yet armed. Wessells advanced directly on the trail of the escaping Indians, their route across the snow fully exposed in the brilliant moonglow. As he gained the bridge, Wessells crossed it. He saw no Indians ahead, so he returned to the post, gathered and mounted members of H Company, and then moved quickly southwest along the river. Following the Indian and soldier trail in the general direction of the bluffs, he joined Captain Vroom and Lieutenant Chase, who had preceded him. There he dispatched First Lieutenant Emmet Crawford back to the post to assemble army stragglers and rejoin the pursuit. Other cavalry under Lieutenants Simpson and Hardie shortly joined Crawford's effort.[17]

When the men, women, children, and elderly pulled away after the breakout, the five or six armed warriors remained as rearguard skirmishers to cover the Cheyennes' withdrawal to the river. They stayed well behind the noncombatants and seem to have anchored themselves just past the H Company stable building. Sergeant John J. Mitchell of Company C recalled that "they were the first [Indians] out [of the barrack,] and after the others had passed them they commenced jumping, yelling and firing and remained there until killed." The Dog Soldiers sought to draw the troopers' attention to themselves, but in the confusion of the moment many shots that the soldiers fired at them instead hit noncombatants running in front of them. While the bright moonlight helped show the way for Dull Knife's people, it simultaneously enabled the soldiers to shoot accurately.[18]

Indeed, the brightened tract between the prison barrack and the sawmill and beyond proved the critical zone where most of the Northern Cheyennes casualties occurred and many of them died. Company C's Private John Corbett offered one of the clearest accounts of this action:

> When the Cheyennes broke out they formed a skirmish line across by the "H" Company stable [southeast of the barrack], and fired a great many shots. We killed five of them and after we had passed the saw mill, the others fired a volley at us. I could not say whether any shots were fired by them after this time. I followed about two miles. We caught up to 15 or 16 between our [C Company] quarters and the point where I turned back. We captured women and children and killed the men. The volley was fired at us while we pursued these Indians. Some of those [men] killed had firearms. We could not have taken those men prisoners.[19]

By the time the Cheyennes gained the river, only about half a mile south of their barrack, they had lost almost thirty of their people: nine men dead, including the Dog Soldiers, and at least eighteen wounded, including women and children. (The wounded Tangle Hair slowly dragged himself to a barrack where soldiers found him and got medical help.)[20]

Private James W. Payne of Company C recalled:

> There were shots fired at us just after we crossed the bridge. . . . [The Indians] seemed to throw out a skirmish line like the one they formed when firing at us at the quarters. Then some men came up behind and they broke and ran in all directions. After that I did not notice them fire back. We could hardly see who was firing as we were all split up. I think there were three Indians killed about 500 yards beyond the saw mill. They could not be taken as they were desperate and seemed to want to die rather than surrender. Those who had arms and were wounded continued to fire as long as they could raise up.[21]

Indian gunfire from either side of the river slackened considerably once the escapees made a brief stand near the sawmill and passed it. The troops had closed quickly, and in their weakened condition the Cheyennes could not move swiftly through the snow after having gulped considerable water to quench their thirst. After the urgent shooting during the breakout, it is probable that their supply of ammunition was waning as well. Those warriors who had harbored notions of gaining horses nearby now began discarding the heavy saddles and impedimenta. Some took the occasion to hide in the underbrush or to find refuge in a hollow tree trunk, as did Miles Seminole and his mother, who were never discovered by the troops. Others escaped discovery in a similar manner. From their hiding places, they heard distant gunfire and the occasional sounds of soldiers dragging captured women past them. In a washout near the sawmill opposite the mouth of Soldier Creek, Lieutenant Joseph F. Cummings encountered two Indians who suddenly rushed him with their knives. He shot them both dead before discovering that they were women. Others died in similar face-offs along the route.[22]

Meanwhile, at the lower camp a mile and a half from the post, Captain Vroom had heard the distant shooting and quickly dispatched Company A under Lieutenant Chase to hasten afoot to the sound of the guns. He sent Company E, also on foot, east under Second Lieutenant George A. Dodd to guard against escape along the road leading northeast to Camp

Sheridan. Company A soon joined Company C and some members of H, who were doggedly following the Cheyennes as they moved toward and ultimately up the left (west) bank of White River. Company F, under Lieutenant Baxter, was directed to remain at the lower camp to guard the Cheyenne prisoners there. Vroom then ordered Company L to saddle up and personally led them toward the fort. On learning that Wessells was in pursuit with C and H troops, however, Vroom instead veered along the White River, skirting the trees in the bottom and moving toward the sounds of shooting farther upstream.[23]

Anticipating combat that night, Lieutenant Chase had told his men to go to bed fully clothed. On hearing the first gunfire at the barrack, and on word from Vroom, Chase's Company A men sprang into action. By the time they arrived near the post, however, the Indians were approaching the river, their main group already diverging southwest toward the distant bluffs.[24] By then, as Sergeant Michael Lanigan remembered, his own Company C "was [initially] so scattered that I could not tell where the fire was coming from, [and] there was cross fire in every direction. There was great confusion. The Company was not formed in any regular order, it was simply following the Indians." Significantly, Sergeant Mitchell, also of C Company, recalled that "after these few Indians who were armed and were firing were killed, there was very little firing by Indians, not above half a dozen shots." While some of the Indians crossed over the bridge, more seem to have angled right upon reaching the river and trudged forward under the shadowy foliage along the water's edge. Pressing the Cheyennes, the soldiers proceeded up the White toward a local pond known as Cramblett's Lake. The Indians' trail, now marked by casualties, was easy to follow in the moonlit snow.[25]

Exasperated by their nighttime pursuit, the soldiers, some still without shoes in the snow, began taking matters into their own hands. At least that is how *New York Herald* field correspondent James R. O'Beirne saw it. His report confirmed and elaborated on the account of Private John Corbett in regard to the targeting of men. "Where the first shot did not dispose of the victim," O'Beirne wrote, "a *coup de grace* was readily given by final pistol charge. Almost every one is shot through the head and the attitudes [positions] of the dead are of almost every variety." Implying that virtually *all* of the adult male Cheyenne fatalities were of this nature, O'Beirne added: "One of the Indians fought so tenaciously at close quarters that

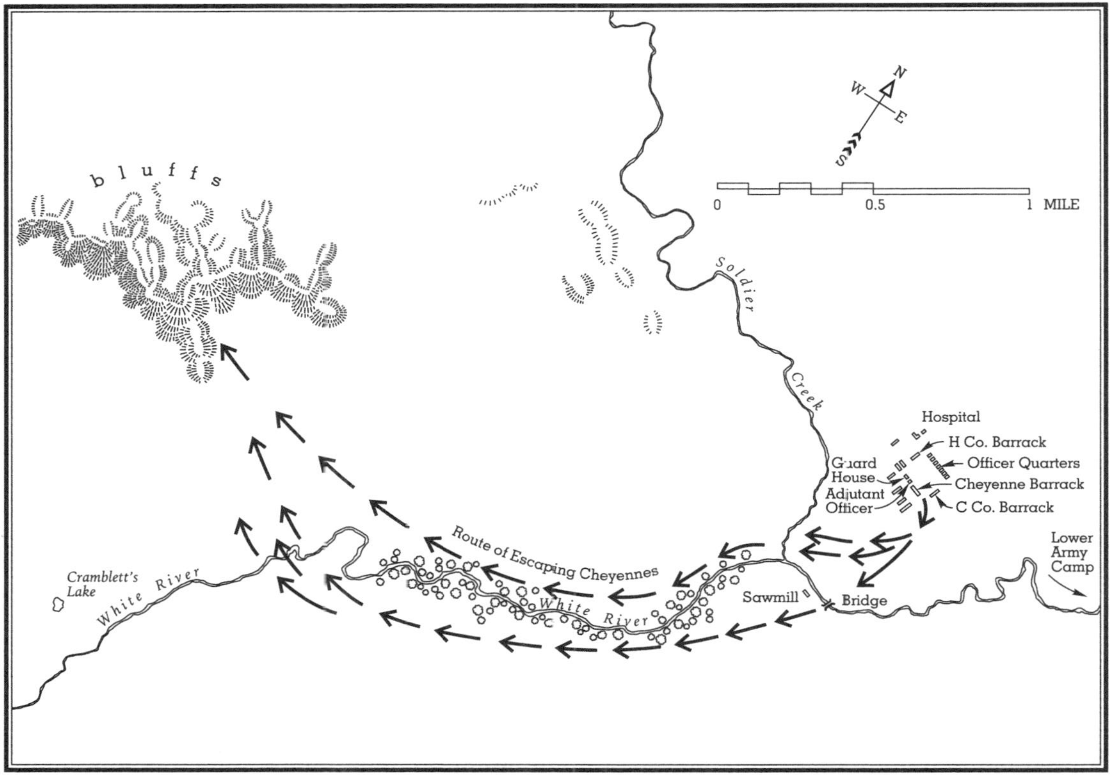

Northern Cheyenne Breakout, January 9, 1879

his garments were set on fire by the pistol which killed him." In contrast, O'Beirne claimed, the soldiers "were as tender in caring for the squaws as if they had done no harm. Captain Wessells himself [at one point] carried a child less than two years old for a hundred yards to a place of safety. Lieutenant Simpson brought a wagon and team to pick up the women and children, and Captain Wessells says that while it is to be regretted that any woman or child was killed it could not be helped."[26]

Among those joining in the pursuit was Captain Joseph Lawson, whose Company E had been in the lower camp. When the shooting erupted, Lawson was in his quarters along the north side of the parade ground. He rushed across to the adjutant's office and directed the men there to act as skirmishers and move with the others after the fleeing Cheyennes. "The Indians," he later stated, "at first kept up a pretty brisk fire. I could not see the Indians as I was late and many soldiers were ahead of me, but I heard the balls whistle over my head." In the course of the pursuit "I had the men pick up some children lying on the ground and carry them back to the post." Lawson also noted how disordered the responding companies were in the excitement, as they joined the opening chase toward Soldier Creek and the river. After Companies C and A afoot had trailed the Indians closely for nearly two miles along the west side of White River, the mounted Companies E and L under Captain Vroom arrived from downstream and the troops, now some 160 strong, succeeded in capturing many of the surviving people, mostly noncombatants, whom they returned to the post.[27]

Vroom's men then took up the pursuit along the White, which permitted the fatigued and freezing members of the dismounted companies to return to the fort with more wounded Indians. With temperatures hovering at 10 degrees, some soldiers had gone back even earlier. Sergeant Lanigan recalled, "the men were scattered all through the brush coming back in the bottom." Most of the firing by now having subsided, Vroom's troops proceeded on the trail leading up the bluffs. They killed several more Cheyennes before Wessells arrived with Companies C and H, now mounted and searching for stragglers. Rancher Bronson recalled seeing the Indians that night as "gaunt as wolves from starvation, awful with their wounds, infinitely pathetic on this bitter night in their ragged half-clothed nakedness." By the time of Bronson's arrival, most surviving Cheyennes had managed to wade the shallow waters of the icy White by foot or had crossed over the bridge. Most of them, however, had moved along the left or west side of the river, seeking relief in the surrounding wooded tracts before attempting the sharply rising bluffs and ridges north of Cramblett's Lake.[28]

Frightened and now grieving for lost family and friends, some of the people waded the icy stream in their shredded clothes then scattered individually or in clusters across three-quarters of a mile of snow-encrusted plain to reach the bluffs. There, with the troops in hot pursuit, they began their ascent. Some eventually gained cover in gullies and washes among the abrupt cliffs and ridges, hoping that these defiles would prove their salvation. But more of the people fell wounded or killed during the climb, shot by Vroom's men, who were now rapidly overtaking them on horseback. Other small groups became detached in the mounting darkness and uncertainty. It was likely here that Iron Teeth, her son, and her two daughters started up the slope but soon became separated. The young man, still bearing his small sister on his back, moved in one direction, while their mother and her older daughter went in another. Other exhausted but surviving women began to fail and to fall around them, among them Walking Woman, another of Dull Knife's daughters. Soldier bullets found her as she ascended the heights. She lay in the snow beneath some pines, with a lifeless child on her back, amid other dead women and children.[29]

As the first Cheyennes reached the bluffs and began climbing, more joined them, chased by the horse troops. After reaching the area near Cramblett's Lake, where the White River channel abruptly angled southwest, these people left the relative safety of the trees and undergrowth to cross over the open terrain lying between the stream and the bluffs. These were the survivors—mostly men—who escaped the running slaughter from the fort. Somewhere in this vicinity, conceivably in the sloping ground between the river and the bluffs, the mounted troops got ahead of these exhausted people. Vroom's men rode past them, circled, dismounted, and confronted them, shooting some of them there, although a few warriors managed to flee the trooper cordon. The soldiers dismounted and followed as skirmishers, soon gaining the heights. Vroom's men captured a number of wounded women and children who could not keep up with the men in their ascent. Most of those killed climbing the bluffs were women and children, while those who attained the sandstone summits and lived found refuge among holes and crevices in the walls. In their hiding places, the survivors could hear the cries of women and children and later the sounds of wagons arriving to carry them away.[30]

In the hours following the breakout, soldiers canvassing the terrain with wagons retrieved perhaps twenty wounded men, women, and children and took them to the post hospital. Other wagons ranged the same ground, especially the tract between the prison barrack and the bridge, picking up bodies where most of the fleeing Cheyennes had been killed.[31] Lieutenant Chase meanwhile returned to the lower camp with his exhausted soldiers then patrolled north along White River for several more miles.

Wessells soon directed Vroom to march with Company L through the valley below the bluffs in the direction of Hat Creek Road and the telegraph line, to keep any uncaptured Indians from stealing away north in the general direction of New Red Cloud Agency. Finding nothing, Vroom turned his troops back toward his camp near White River at about 3 A.M. Wessells also sent most of Company H under its first sergeant to scout east of White River. Company F, momentarily under Lieutenant Chase, proceeded to search the area between the post and the bluffs to the north of the fort. During that reconnaissance, Wessells's own party killed two more Indians before returning to Fort Robinson.[32]

In its entirety, the army pursuit from the prison barrack to White River and into the hills and peaks "rising like giant icebergs" west of the fort extended roughly four miles. In leaving the trees and undergrowth near White River, the Cheyennes passed diagonally across a gradually rising snow-covered grassland for three-quarters of a mile to reach the heights before them: a medley of nearly impregnable wooded sandstone bluffs approaching 700 feet in height. The bluffs there, part of the prairie plateau of the Pine Ridge Escarpment, harbor countless deep-walled gullies, rivulets, and washes, some cave-like. It was a remarkable feat to reach them, and it was supposed that the Northern Cheyennes knew the surrounding country well. Rancher Bronson, who himself was familiar with it, believed that "hidden away in an angle of the cliff lay a slope accessible to footmen, and this the Indians knew and sought."[33]

In their escape and flight from their barrack prison, the Northern Cheyennes lost approximately forty persons killed or wounded. Perhaps another fifty-five women, men, and children were recaptured, leaving some forty or so still alive and fleeing in the darkness or hiding and shivering tenuously amid bitter gully recesses somewhere in the frosty elevations. Besides the captured but uninjured, who were promptly returned to the barrack under guard, those with wounds were sent to the post hospital or returned to their barrack and the post guardhouse, where doctors Petteys and Moseley treated them. Of the troops, in addition to the two guards killed at the inception of the breakout, one of the six other soldiers shot would die. Altogether, the soldiers pursued the Northern Cheyennes for more than two hours that night. On attaining the highlands, however, the command, some still half-naked after hurrying out in their haste, began to flag. At 12:15 A.M., as the moon began to set, Wessells called off the chase and directed most of his men back to the post. He intended to resume pursuit and reconnoitering in the morning after they had rested, eaten, dressed appropriately, and regained their strength.

Some troops, however, under Adjutant Cummings's direction, continued recovering the dead and wounded Cheyennes in three wagons and moving them back to the post. All of the adult males brought back were dead. Some women and children had injuries and frozen limbs that required attention, and a few of them quickly died. Cummings reported that, with the other fatalities, the Cheyenne dead numbered "14 men, 9 women, [and] 4 children" in all among the "dead Cheyennes who were accessible." He pronounced them ready for burial. "All the Indians thus far killed who have been brought in are buried in one grave near the sawmill," the *New York Herald* would report, adding: "Some of the bodies still remain on the hillsides where they fell." As the morning progressed, the riddled bodies thus far retrieved were unloaded hastily near the river and placed in rows for interment, the men separated from women and children as relatives identified them. One of the wounded women proved to be the sister of Red Bear, a member of Red Cloud's Oglalas who had married a Northern Cheyenne. Red Bear had only recently arrived to visit his sister, and seeing her wounded now brought tears to his eyes.[34]

Area civilians, confounding army authorities, ranged over the ground through the night of January 9 to strip the dead Cheyennes of blankets and artifacts, take scalps for their own purposes, and otherwise mistreat and expose the corpses, particularly those of the women, after the troops moved along in their chase. Several persons reported the names of those civilians recognized either during or shortly after the soldiers' pursuit. The army officers present were incensed and tried to identify the perpetrators after the breakout. As the formal board proceedings later explained:

> On the morning of the 10th when the bodies of the dead Indians were being collected by the post adjutant for burial it was found that more than a dozen of them had been scalped, and too that many of the dead squaws' persons had been indecently exposed. We had no evidence that soldiers took part in this although due inquiry has been made. There is evidence that civilians were seen examining the dead and taking therefrom blankets that had been placed over them by the officers and soldiers, and the inference is that these men had not only robbed but committed these barbarities on the dead, and the evidence shows that one at least had boasted of having arrived in time to have killed a squaw.[35]

When the burials finally took place on Sunday, January 12, twenty-six bodies were consigned to eternity in a pit by the sawmill, "scarcely any one of them having been pierced with less than three bullets," reported the *New York Herald.* A small number of Cheyenne women and children watched the proceeding. The remaining few corpses, it was said, were buried in the field where they died.[36]

Early Friday morning, January 10, Wessells telegraphed an initial report to General Crook, which was duly forwarded to Sheridan and to the adjutant general's office in Washington, D.C.:

> The Cheyennes at 10 P.M. [last night] made a break from their building. Thirty-five (35) men were recaptured, about thirty (30) killed; eighteen (18) had previously surrendered, making a total of fifty-three (53) in our hands now, including [Wild] Hog, [Old] Crow, and Left Hand, three head men. It is reported to me that Dull Knife is dead, but I am not sure. We will have many [more] before dark, as the trailing is good and five (5) companies are out.[37]

In fact, the precise number of Northern Cheyenne fatalities resulting from the breakout stood at fourteen men, nine women, and three children at daylight on January 10: twenty-six in all. But others had been wounded and remained in the care of surgeons Petteys and Moseley, including four more women and children who would die from their injuries before noon, making a total of thirty dead to that point. "I never saw so many dead Indians than I did during this affair," Lieutenant Crawford wrote, "I had no idea that our men were such good marksmen." More of the wounded would perish subsequently. Besides those recaptured without injury and returned to the wrecked barrack, it was estimated that "thirty-four are still out, including about fifteen warriors, among whom is Chief Dull Knife, erroneously reported dead last night."[38]

In fact, Dull Knife with his wife, daughters, son Bull Hump, and extended family fled the barrack with the others. Somewhere in the growing dark as the moon began to set, and likely as they sought to elude troops on the north side of White River, they became separated. One daughter was shot along the White River, and Bull Hump and other warriors stayed to protect her. Others in the party, including the daughter known as the "Princess," broke away and headed to the bluffs after some of their protectors fell before the soldiers' guns. Dull Knife and Pawnee Woman, Bull Hump, and their party pressed on but diverged on an alternate route leading toward the bluffs. One of them, Great Eyes, elderly father-in-law of Dull Knife, attempted to cover the withdrawal but was shot dead in the snow. His thirteen-year-old nephew, Red Bird, shot in the knee during the flight from the barrack, managed somehow to proceed. Forging ahead, the dwindling party gained relief in a large grotto in the rocks and took refuge there. Perhaps a mile or more back on the trail, near the point where many of the people had turned from the river toward the bluffs, several women and children lay dead. Interpreter James Rowland, who had trailed the advancing soldiers, came upon the prone form of Walking Woman, another of Dull Knife's daughters, as she was dying. On her back she carried a lifeless child, retrieved in the course of her trek. Their bodies, too, ultimately joined those in the pit by the sawmill.[39]

For Dull Knife's followers, the forced escape from the barrack prison embodied an existential dynamic not only for them but for Northern Cheyenne society as a whole. By their spirited refusal to obey the army dictate at Fort Robinson—whatever their reason—in their anguished flight the people made their stand. Their defiance had been conditioned by decades of struggle. They would confront what seemed to them a troubled destiny that forsook instinctive societal freedom, acting for a purpose that they believed wholly just. In their recent past they had confronted the appallingly corrosive influences of U.S. colonialism on their tribal psyche, yet the breakout proved a moment of defiance in the face of their seemingly ever-evolving cultural trauma. Not to have countered the mounting duress that they faced in the manner that they did would have been wholly uncharacteristic. And for Dull Knife's people, at the least, it might have been culturally faithless.

Early on Friday morning, January 10, doubtless after he had wired his initial report of events to General Crook in Omaha, Captain Wessells briefly visited the recaptured Indians following their return to the trashed and guarded barrack prison. Perhaps intemperately, he inquired of the surviving people, including some of those wounded, now treated and bandaged after their frightful experience, whether they would now go south. One young woman, who had been struck in the foot by a bullet but managed to stand and face Wessells directly, said: "No. We will not go back. We will die instead. . . . Why do you not go ahead now and finish the job?"[40] There is no record of Wessells's reply, if indeed he had one.

8

Hat Creek Road

Officers at department headquarters in Omaha assessed the situation at Fort Robinson as best they could, based on information received over the wire. General Crook, who had been ailing from a cold augmented by malarial fever, had restricted himself to his quarters, several blocks from the command offices. Nonetheless, he addressed the telegraphic communications with his adjutant, Lieutenant Colonel Robert Williams, and other staff. Lacking direct information about affairs at the post, Crook dispatched his aide-de-camp, First Lieutenant Walter S. Schuyler, to Fort Robinson. Schuyler, whose reputation for "keenness and sagacity in unearthing facts" for intelligence purposes was renowned, was to monitor the situation and inform Crook of developments. He would arrive on January 15.[1]

While officers in Omaha tried to puzzle through the scant information, Captain Wessells's fatigued companies rekindled their search among the bluffs, ridges, gullies, and stream bottoms around Fort Robinson. In the early hours of Friday, January 10, they combed the area for the Indians who had eluded them. "On the morning of the 10th small parties of troops were coming in all day long bringing in two or three women and children," recalled Sergeant Johnson, "and this kept up almost daily."[2] Wessells also directed troops to reconnoiter northeast down the White River, seeking Indians who might have eluded the soldiers and gone in that direction. To that end, Lieutenant Chase returned to the post with captives, relieved his own troop, then advanced with Lieutenant Baxter's mounted Company F northeast from the post. Thwarted by rugged terrain and deep encrusted snow, however, Chase covered only five miles before turning back without sign of the Cheyennes.[3]

Chase's men were targeting the immediate breakout survivors. Notwithstanding a growing aura of mortality and physical loss, in addition to their emotional and mental trauma, some of the Indians would persist through coming days amid the stark realities of danger, fear, and depression. Knowledge of the ground and countryside was in their favor, however. It was an expansive geographical landscape that they understood intuitively after decades of living there. Furthermore, having succeeded thus far in their flight from Fort Robinson, the survivors among Dull Knife's people would take advantage of that familiarity time and again, despite the almost overwhelming odds against them.

The Northern Cheyenne survivors essentially fell into two groups. One was composed of young folks and older adults, including some seniors, and several children, mostly toddlers. A smaller group, moving separately, included only four women, one of whom was named Old Meat Woman. The troops' primarily focused on the first group, which numbered perhaps twenty people. The men of this body included the warrior-artist Little Finger Nail as well as the warriors Roached Hair, Roman Nose, Bullet Proof, and a few others. Little Finger Nail and the young men served as formal protectors of the women and children and as "wolves" (scouts), watching for soldiers operating in any vicinity even as they sought opportunities to secure food and water for all. (It is conceivable that the people were using their knives to kill and eat their dogs that might have followed them from the barrack.) Among the younger women were Singing Woman, Lame Girl, and Brave One as well as a daughter of Wild Hog who had not been moved to the lower camp with the chief's relatives.[4]

Five companies of soldiers from Fort Robinson, outfitted in wool overcoats and buffalo hide coats with fur caps and arctic overshoes against the snow and incessant cold, traversed miles of the varied terrain composing the Pine Ridge Escarpment. Operating together or in smaller separate bodies, these soldiers sought to ferret out the Indians who had thus far survived the breakout. Their efforts produced only marginal success. Persistently hiding among the recesses and declivities in that rugged country, the weary Cheyennes adroitly moved in several directions from the fort while trending progressively west and north. They circumvented the land southwest of the post to assume the general course of Hat Creek Road, the telegraph line access path laid down in 1877 to connect Fort Robinson by wire with Hat Creek Station, fifty-three miles east in Wyoming

Territory. From there, the line extended to Fort Laramie and the world beyond. The Indians mostly steered clear of primary roads and trails broadly leading to and from Forts Laramie and Sidney and avoided direct routes north to New Red Cloud Agency in Dakota and the southern Black Hills, although that station, with its prospect for ultimate relief, became their primary target.[5]

As the Northern Cheyennes forged through the country bordering Hat Creek Road, it seems never to have occurred to them to sever the telegraph line and disrupt direct communication between Wessells's headquarters at Fort Robinson and command centers at Fort Laramie, Omaha, Chicago, and Washington, D.C. Admittedly, the technology was recent and had not existed at Camp Robinson in 1876, when they might have observed it. Moreover, the shock and trauma of their escape and fearful prospects for their long-term existence must have shaken their sensibilities, for cutting the telegraph wires would have stalled or otherwise complicated government communication only temporarily. So the telegraph remained in service. The escaping Cheyennes in their desperation seem to have focused on immediate survival.

The Indians' desperation would continue for at least two more weeks as they became the primary object of the army pursuit. For those like Dull Knife and his family, who sought hiding places from which to monitor their circumstances and mount separate courses, the time spent in cold and uncertain settings proved grueling. One of those who endured was Iron Teeth, whose twenty-two-year-old son and small daughter had become separated from their mother and sister in the aftershock of the breakout. Distraught with worry over them, Iron Teeth forged ahead, seeking shelter away from the soldiers. Not knowing their fate, somewhere in the craggy pine-covered setting west of the post, "I and the daughter with me found a cave and crawled into it," she related decades afterward. A Cheyenne man named Crooked Nose also found shelter there. During the rest of the night, as she remembered, "we could hear lots of shooting. The next day we still heard shots, but not so many." The distant firing gradually diminished. "We stayed in the cave seven nights and almost seven days" until about January 16, as the soldiers refocused their efforts. "More snow kept falling. It was very cold, but we were afraid to build a fire." Her fingers and toes froze. She and Crooked Nose ate dried meat and snow. They occasionally heard horses and soldiers' chatter as they passed by. When an officer found them after a week or so, they yielded. "He and his soldiers then took us back to Fort Robinson," she said.[6] Others who had ascended the bluffs, with or without wounds that varied from trifling to severe, may have survived similarly.

George Bird Grinnell later acquired the account of a Northern Cheyenne youth, Big Beaver, who was about fourteen years old at the time of the breakout. He told Grinnell how he and others also sought shelter in the holes in the bluffs southwest of the post and recalled hearing the distant "guns and the yelling." He related his story:

> A troop of cavalry came to where we were hidden. There were five of us, and we had one [long] gun and one pistol. The troops began to shoot into the holes where we were and kept shooting, and presently all had been killed except me. When I looked about and saw that every one of my friends was dead, I did not know what to do. I waited, and at length the soldiers stopped firing. . . . I walked out of the hole . . . and went toward the soldiers. A white man called out something and no one fired at me. The officer rode toward me and drew his saber, but did not strike me with it. He . . . reached out his hand and I stretched out my hand, and we shook hands. I was . . . helped up behind a soldier on his horse and taken into the post.[7]

At the fort, the soldiers placed Big Beaver in the guardhouse with the wounded Tangle Hair as well as Blacksmith and his wife, Enemy Woman.[8]

In the early hours of January 10 a few cavalrymen remained in the highlands but called off their search as receding moonglow obscured the trail. Within a short time, however, when daylight revealed the trail, the troops resumed the chase. They had to speculate on the Northern Cheyennes' precise route—or routes—following their withdrawal to the bluffs. The broken terrain may have been unfamiliar to them, but they joined other bodies of soldiers as they gradually moved north and west in small groups.

During the first few days, many Cheyennes remained alone or clustered in washouts and other recesses among the forested growth in the vicinity of today's Smiley Canyon and modern U.S. 20. Some of the Cheyennes, such as Dull Knife's family, appear to have passed days undercover in this area then proceeded northwest when the immediate tumult passed. The troops occasionally targeted them as they sought water in tributaries and snow pools as well as small creatures for food in the sheltering timberlands. They followed the branches of Soldier Creek and intersected the course of Hat Creek Road, tracing the telegraph line along the north side of the stream's middle fork and only three miles beyond the bluffs that they had vacated overlooking White River. Cold, hunger, and danger accompanied every step, and their trail was almost always evident in the layered crusted snow.

Most of the army's pursuit over the coming days was focused along this area of the telegraph line and its attending road. Paralleling the middle fork, Hat Creek Road headed west northwest through spotty wooded growth. About nine miles northwest of modern Smiley Canyon it reached an elevation of 4,800 feet, passing through a stretch of ground today named Beans Canyon, Horse Creek, and Boggy Creek, some fourteen to sixteen miles west of Fort Robinson and just two miles shy of the road's crossing of Hat Creek proper.[9] Most of the isolated combat between soldiers and Northern Cheyennes in the vicinity of Hat Creek Road took place here, in a desolate expanse that was alternately wooded or open and craggy.

The army search that had slackened on the night of January 9–10 quickened as dawn gave way to a cold and clear but sunny day. Lieutenant Crawford initially joined with Lieutenants Simpson and Hardie and soldiers of Company C in locating three Cheyenne women, two of them wounded, and getting them to the fort.[10] One of the first postbreakout encounters occurred about six miles east of Fort Robinson as Lieutenant Baxter led a detachment of fifteen Company H soldiers in searching for Indian trails. Near Crow Butte they encountered a boy who surrendered. About 2 P.M., as Baxter's group examined the area, Private William W. Everett was shot in the stomach while calling upon an Indian to yield. As Baxter reported, "my party . . . fired and killed the Indian." Everett reached the post hospital in an army ambulance but died the following morning.[11]

Late on the afternoon of January 10 Lieutenant Cummings ascended the bluffs southwest of Fort Robinson with a detail of guardhouse prisoners. They followed along the previous night's trail of the Northern Cheyennes, "repeatedly passing [discarded] blankets, lariats, moccasins and pools of blood." As they gained the summit, they heard shots. Cummings quickly advanced, calling on his men to refrain from killing Indians "unless you have got to." He later described the encounter that followed:

> Just outside the mouth of a cave sitting on a rock I saw a squaw of about 40, a young man of about 18 and a girl of about 15 and a little child, with this private standing guard over them. The Corporal was standing at the mouth of the cave examining the bodies of two young bucks. Both were shot through the head. I asked the Corporal if it had been absolutely necessary for him to kill those two bucks. He then showed me a Springfield carbine with a loaded cartridge, and a Colt's revolver with one chamber just emptied, and said that these two Indians had these arms and refused to surrender. The Corporal and his companion suspected the presence of Indians, and were on their guard. As soon as they discovered the Indians he called out to them, "How How and Washte, Washte." The eldest squaw commenced crying and started to get out of the cave. She was rudely pulled back by one of the bucks who immediately loaded his carbine. The other buck raised his pistol and the Corporal called out to his companion to shoot. Both soldiers then raised their pieces and fired. At the same time the Indian with the pistol fired. The one with the pistol was killed instantly. The Indian who had the carbine had 38 rounds of copper cartridges in a belt, and the one with the pistol had five shots left in his pistol, also a pouch of bullets and a bag of powder, about half a pound with a few caps. It was an old pattern pistol using paper cartridges. I had to leave the bodies there as I could not get them down. . . . The boy who was captured had a knife but threw it into the snow in token of surrender.[12]

Nearby that day, Captains Wessells and Vroom and their companies (H and L) jointly ventured south and then west from the post, along the divide overlooking White River and into the upper drainage of Soldier Creek. Eventually they trended northwest and along Hat Creek Road, while Company E under Captain Lawson advanced southwest up the White River bottom for a dozen miles, encountering, as he said, "several bodies of Indians on my way." Wessells and Vroom located the primary Indian trail, which they followed until reaching a "knoll upon which the Indians had taken position."[13]

From their own camp east of the fort near White River, Lieutenant Chase and Company A had resumed their earlier search north along the Camp Sheridan road. In accordance with Wessells's directions, after a short distance they turned west, along and through the imposing Red Cloud Buttes. Their primary purpose was to head off Indians fleeing to Pine Ridge Agency to seek relief among the Oglalas. Chase recalled surmounting the bluffs and continuing through them and beyond for twelve miles. Encountering an Indian trail, he sent Corporal Henry P. Ore and five troopers in pursuit. Ore soon captured four Cheyenne women, including Old Meat Woman, who had become separated from the larger group of breakout survivors. Ore would turn them in at the post the following morning. Hearing shooting in a distant canyon, Chase and his men probed into the valley of Soldier Creek, where they shortly encountered Lieutenants Crawford and Simpson, who explained that Vroom's Company L was under fire from the Indians. With Crawford's approval, Chase and his troopers advanced but soon came under long-distance gunfire themselves from warriors entrenched behind fallen timbers atop an outlying hill a dozen miles from the fort. Wessells's troops had effectually surrounded these Indians.[14]

Chase sheltered his men behind an embankment and approached Captain Wessells, who explained that "Vroom's company had been ambushed[,] that one of his men had been seriously wounded and several of his horses shot."[15] The injured soldier was Private William H. Good, of Company L, who said he had "got an Indian yesterday, but that they had got him today." He had been "shot from a high bluff not fifty yards distant," and his comrades had carried him beyond range of the Indians to a small streambed to protect him. The men fashioned an Indian travois on which to carry him, but Good, wounded in the abdomen, died before reaching the hospital.[16]

Lacking provisions, Wessells returned with most of his fatigued command to Fort Robinson after dark on January 10, while troops under Lieutenants Crawford and Hardie encircled the Indians' position at a distance. As Wessells maintained, "I was perfectly satisfied for the Indians to get away here because I knew they could travel but very slowly through the deep snow, but was determined to watch them."[17] By then it was calculated that fifty-two of the Northern Cheyennes were in custody, with many of them wounded, while thirty-seven others were dead. Approximately sixty still remained unaccounted for and presumably were alive.[18]

The iron cold persisted, and at dawn on January 11 Crawford's soldiers learned that the Cheyennes had strengthened their breastworks. Returning to the location with Companies E, F, and H, Captain Wessells reconnoitered and found it impossible to advance his command within 200 yards of their defenses. After nightfall he withdrew F and H back to Fort Robinson, calling for artillery with which to assail the stronghold. Soon two twelve-pounder Napoleon guns rolled out of the post under Second Lieutenant George A. Dodd. Captain Lawson's Company E monitored the Indians through the night and guarded against their escape west. When warriors succeeded in killing a cavalry mount, Lawson directed that the carcass be incinerated to prevent the famished people from devouring it.[19]

The next day Wessells sent a wire to General Crook:

> Those Indians were as well armed and supplied with as much ammunition as any Indians that ever went on the warpath. I had a fight with some of them who are entrenched twelve miles from here all day yesterday, and left them in position after dark last night. I crawled with the interpreter to within five hundred yards of them about noon yesterday and told them if they would surrender the women and children we would not hurt them. Their reply was a bullet sent close to our heads.[20]

When Lieutenants Simpson and Chase with Companies C and A reached the Cheyenne defenses on upper Soldier Creek on Sunday morning, January 12, they learned that the people had abandoned their breastworks for another site seven miles farther west. The Northern Cheyennes could not move quickly, however, and their lack of horses hindered their prospect of gaining Pine Ridge. Scattered and ever-wary ranchers in the broad vicinity guarded their herds accordingly. Captain Vroom's Company L bolstered the units that day, bringing news that Captain Wessells would arrive on the morrow with Companies F and H and the artillery.[21]

A newspaper correspondent chronicled particulars of the soldiers' frustrating efforts along Hat Creek Road on January 12: "Troops [A and C] were unceasingly watchful. At the first gray light of morning those . . . nearest and to the west of the stronghold discovered a large trail apparently coming therefrom and leading in a northwesterly direction. This news was immediately made known to the commanding officer [Vroom], who suspected that the savages had flown under cover of the darkness." To determine whether the Indians had indeed departed,

> three soldiers of Company C, 3d Cavalry, volunteered their services to ascertain if such was the case. Creeping down [from atop] the bluff to within twenty yards of the stronghold, and failing to discover the[m] . . . , the trail was again followed, which led through a succession of bluffs, ravines, and heavy timber. The advance guard, consisting of Corporal Henry Ore and six men of company A, 3d cavalry, were in the act of ascending a steep bluff, when Ore, who was a little in advance, was instantly killed by a volley from . . . a rifle-pit near the summit, the ball entering his heart. His men, seeing their comrade fall, charged on the savages, numbering only three, who were doubtless covering the retreat of the main band. The soldiers succeeded in killing one . . . , the others escaping unhurt.[22]

Two miles farther, as the command mounted a hill rising over a valley, Northern Cheyennes concealed in distant timber again unleashed gunfire, wounding farrier Peter W. Painter of Company C. The troops continued targeting the Indian position until darkness fell.[23]

In describing this perilous skirmishing along Hat Creek Road, First Lieutenant George F. Chase, a participant throughout, provided supplementary details on the killing of Corporal Ore and its immediate aftermath:

> Before arriving . . . [near the Cheyennes' position], our advance guard under Sergt. [James] Taggart, Company A, discovered a large trail leading in the direction of the Hat Creek road. . . . Sergt. Taggart's party reconnoitered the position occupied by this small party of Indians and definitely located it. I [then] sent for Corporal Ore and four men of my own Company, giving him orders to go around the head of the ravine and advance cautiously down to the hole where the Indians were. I was going to advance with Sergt. Taggart and four other men from the other side of the ravine.[24]

According to Chase,

> Corporal Ore had not left me more than two minutes when he was killed instantly by a shot from the Indians. Lieutenant Simpson then ordered a portion of the command to surround the position

> and decided not to charge it, but left a sergeant and twelve men to . . . get Corporal Ore's body and his arms. . . . I gave him orders not to leave the place until relieved by other troops, and under no circumstances to allow the Indians to get Corporal Ore's body or his arms. Sergeant [Gottlieb] Bigalsky that night obtained Corporal Ore's body and brought it in to Camp [*sic*] Robinson. His carbine was subsequently obtained from the place where he was killed.[25]

Chase's narrative described further aspects of the troop movements along Hat Creek Road. As he related, he and Lieutenant Simpson with Companies A and C (about thirty-five men) followed an easily discerned trail. Some five miles from Hat Creek Road "we found where large numbers of cattle had been roaming in all directions and it was impossible to follow the trail."[26] Yet they proceeded "down a very rough canyon" and for a time detected moccasin tracks but then lost the trail as they approached Hat Creek. "We found one moccasin track evidently made by a lame Indian, for we could see the prints of a stick he had used for a cane." The troops crossed two rugged ravines until a number of Indians, rising suddenly from behind a crest in front, opened fire on them. Chase yelled for his men to take cover, but in the ensuing melee "my horse [mis]behaved, and I couldn't get back to the companies." Sergeant Taggart and several men managed to dismount and deliver a covering fire as Chase withdrew to his troops. Only one soldier and three horses were wounded in the fray.[27]

Chase primed his troops and continued to occupy the position. At 1 A.M. on January 13 Captain Vroom and Company L arrived, and at 10 o'clock that morning Wessells appeared with Companies F and H. At noon the two Napoleon guns trundled into the command from Fort Robinson. (Chase's brief narrative offers further critical aspects of the only and largely innocuous artillery barrage of the entire pursuit, directed that afternoon against the Northern Cheyennes, who still responded with tenacity and resolve. Besides furnishing essential details about activities bearing on the army pursuit along Hat Creek, it notably affords knowledge of one of the very few known instances in the course of the western Indian campaigns wherein artillery was brought to bear against Indians.)

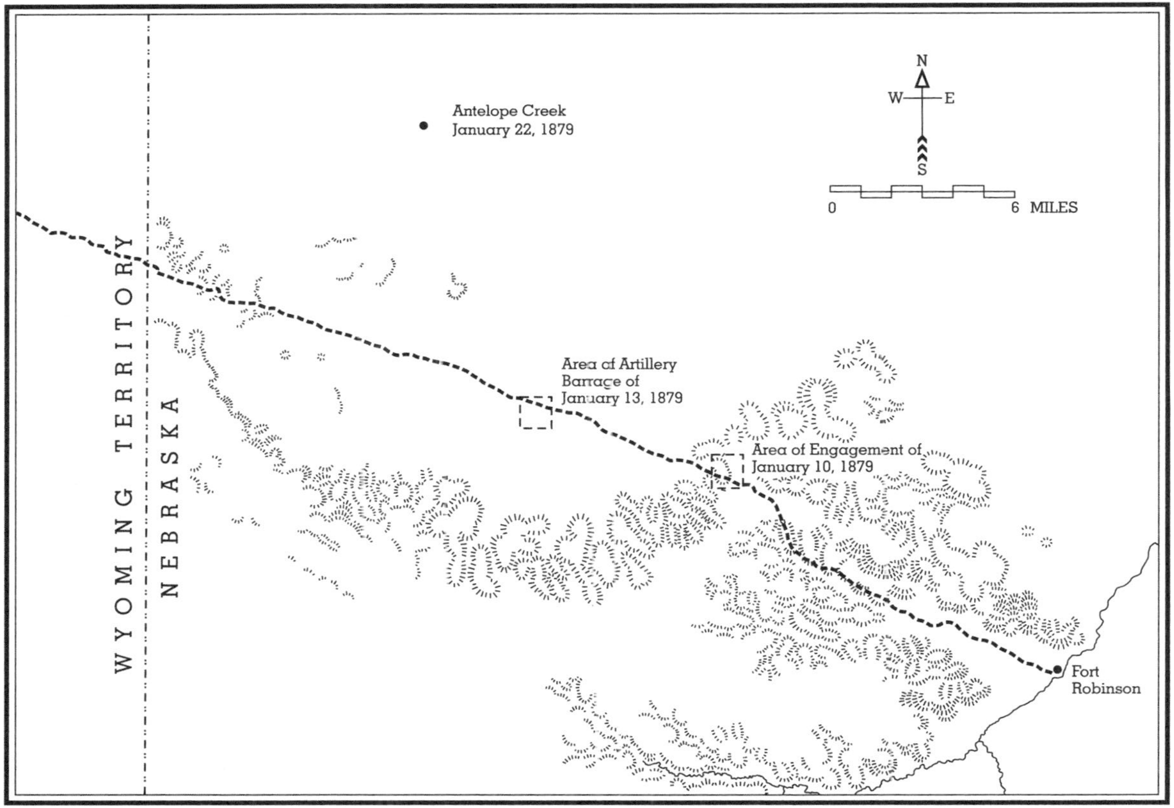

Army Pursuit along Hat Creek Road and Environs, January 10–22, 1879

> Captain Wessells directed me with my entire company to proceed to a point between 900 and 1000 yards from the Indians up this ravine. I then found 12 men of Captain Vroom's company, of whom I assumed command. This position threw me into the foothills on a point overlooking the position of the Indians. Captain Vroom was ordered with a portion of his company [L], and his entire Company F . . . to a point down the ravine about 1000 yds. from the position of the Indians.[28] The artillery under Lieutenant Baxter [Company F], 3rd Cavalry, was to play upon the Indians from a point on the hill just above Capt. Vroom's position. Several shots were fired from this position. I could see the effect. I sent a courier to Capt. Wessells stating that I thought the shots from the artillery were doing little or no damage to the Indians, also suggesting that the piece be brought to the position which I occupied.
>
> Captain Wessells sent me word that he was going to change the position of the piece to a point on the right of [the] ravine about 100 yds from it. This was done. I could see the effects of the shot from the new position, and sent again to Capt. Wessells asking that the artillery be sent to the position assigned me. The piece soon afterwards came to me and by request of Lieut. Baxter I took personal charge of it. I fired 12 or 15 shots from the piece, the effect of which could be plainly seen. Several of the shells burst immediately over the rifle pits supposed to be occupied by a portion of the Indians. Iron and pieces of shell were subsequently found in these rifle pits. It seems, however, that the main portion of the Indians were in a rifle pit on the crest of the ravine and in my opinion there were no Indians in the rifle pit in the bottom of the ravine while the artillery was playing from my position.[29]

In sum, the artillery bombardment ended when the ammunition played out. Wessells directed the troops to camp in the general vicinity. As Lieutenant Simpson explained, "[That night] we had no transportation, no rations [and] but one saddle blanket to the man." The next morning, moreover, they learned that the Northern Cheyennes had vacated their position. Lacking sufficient resources to continue, Wessells headed his weary troops back to Fort Robinson to resupply.[30]

During the January 13 salvo, only one of the two pieces brought from Fort Robinson discharged on the Indians because of difficulty in depressing the carriage trail of the other gun to elevate the barrel sufficiently to reach the target. As Lieutenant Baxter recalled, Companies F and L "proceeded to the north and below the Indian fortifications 600 yards [distant from them], Capt. Vroom with a small detachment of his company [L] remaining in the ravine where the Indians had fortified themselves. I proceeded with my company [H] up on the plateau to [the] west of [the] Indians under orders to charge and capture them should the shelling drive them out." (The Cheyenne warrior named Bullet Proof [also known as Wolf Man], who had fought soldiers under Colonel Nelson Cole along the Powder River in present Wyoming fourteen years earlier, perished in the bombardment that day.)[31]

In all, some forty rounds of both exploding shell and spherical case shot were discharged in the artillery assault, according to Baxter.[32] "They burst right around them [but] none were injured." In evaluating the encounter, Wessells asserted that he had considered charging the Indians' position

> but I felt certain I could get a good chance at some later time. . . . They were bound to go to Red Cloud Agency, so I thought it would be risking too many [lives] and did not do it. I thought that night [that] it would be just as well to let them go again if they wanted to[,] as they might get further out of the hills, and I felt quite confident I could overtake them no matter where they went. That night they left again. Instead of going out they went back towards the hills. I was going to pursue them with F and H Companies but we were poorly prepared for winter weather, so I went back to the post and got a refit for a week.[33]

Correspondent James O'Beirne (who was conceivably present) reported the group deliberations over Wessells's idea of rushing the Indians' position. He stated that Wessells had called his officers together to direct a charge against the Indians. "It was judged to be unwise," wrote O'Beirne, "as it would result in the loss of several men before the Indians could be dislodged. They were at that time thought to be completely surrounded and it seemed only a question of a short time, in their famished condition, before the entire band would be compelled to surrender." But the Indians "had slipped away" by morning.[34] Furthermore, a report in the *Chicago Times* opined that the Indians would have been "capable of inflicting severe loss upon the number selected for what may be almost termed a forlorn hope."[35] Years later, Wessells commented that he was advised to assault the Indian position but "did not wish to lose men [un]necessarily & he allowed [the] Ind[ian]s to escape from there."[36]

As indicated, on the morning of January 14 Lieutenant Crawford and another soldier reconnoitered the Cheyennes' lofty position and learned that they had vacated their rifle pits in the night as before, slipping southwestwardly, possibly (and inexplicably) in the direction of Fort Laramie. This was thought perhaps to be a misleading ploy before striking northwest.[37] In their famished condition, the Indians had managed to find, kill, and consume yet another beef, leaving nothing but its hide behind. Bereft of provisions and learning that part of his anticipated supply train had overturned en route from the post, Wessells determined to withdraw his weary command (Companies A, C, H, and L) and return about twenty-three miles to Fort Robinson to refurbish.[38] While referencing the "stoical character of both the [Northern Cheyenne] men and women," correspondent O'Beirne noted: "The companies and detachments of troops that were sent out in pursuit of the ragged and supposed unarmed Cheyennes returned to camp late last night [January 14] for the purpose of resting after their brief and exhausting campaign, which for suddenness and effectiveness has not been equaled in the records of Indian warfare."[39]

O'Beirne recalled Wessells saying that "the Cheyennes cannot go away successfully or make much progress, as it has already taken them five days to cover twenty-odd miles to the position where they were for the last time held temporarily in check." The correspondent stated that judgment was divided as to the course that the Indians would now take. Some believed that once they obtained horses they would "speed into the mountains and strike for the Big Horn [River country]," whereas others thought they would circumvent this "last stronghold" and head northeast seeking refuge (and potential auxiliaries) among Red Cloud's Oglalas.[40] After the encounter in the hills on January 13, the people certainly forsook that oft-sheltering high terrain for the open plains, where their chances of survival grew even more ominous as they became vulnerable to further exposure in their quest to gain the newly renamed Pine Ridge Agency, still sixty miles away, where few, if any, had ever been. On his return to Fort Robinson, Wessells alerted Crook to the recent engagement "twenty miles from here on the Hat Creek Road" and praised his men's zeal throughout.[41]

In the meantime, as news of the breakout reached the nation, the army hierarchy began to deflect blame for what had occurred at Fort Robinson. General Sheridan in Chicago kept a measured silence after hearing of the event, evidently pondering the facts as they reached his desk. On January 11, in his earliest-known reaction, the division commander telegraphed General Pope that "the devil has been to play at Camp [*sic*] Robinson" and began assigning fault for what had happened there. He complained that his attempts to have the Cheyenne matter transferred to the Bureau of Indian Affairs had been ignored until "it was too cold to move them, especially as they had no clothing—in fact, were nearly naked." And he directly criticized Schurz, who, he claimed, had "played the adroit in the correspondence," stating that "the evidence [to be] furnished will have its effect."[42]

On January 14 Crook, impatient at the seeming delay in the field, notified Sheridan that Wessells and his men "are making strenuous exertions" to recapture the Northern Cheyennes. The next day he wired Wessells and Major Andrew W. Evans at Fort Laramie, ordering them to press the pursuit, "to take up the Cheyenne trail and follow it until the Indians are recaptured." Soon after this directive, two companies of the Third Cavalry departed from Fort Laramie hoping to head off the Indians from the west. Telegraphic dispatches now flowed readily between Forts Robinson and Laramie as to the respective troop movements, just as horseback couriers operated between the field commands and the posts. Crook, lacking full details of the outbreak, and concerned over news stories citing increasing public indignation over the troops' killing of fleeing Cheyennes, sought details from Lieutenant Schuyler, who was to investigate and report on the situation. In response to Crook's demand for information, Wessells wired the general a six-page account of the breakout and the events preceding it, while Schuyler notified Crook that "of the escaped Cheyennes there are fully forty-five [*sic*] not yet accounted for [by] death or capture." Of these, only nineteen or so warriors were said to remain alive. "It is probable," Schuyler maintained, "that the troops will overtake nearly all of them."[43]

Prompted by the edict from Crook, Wessells reoutfitted detachments from Company E and his own Company H, now complete with pack mules provisioned for six days and supply wagons with tents to protect against freezing winds, and sent them out at noon on Wednesday, January 15, under Captain Lawson to pursue a course well beyond the drainage of upper Soldier Creek. Before dawn on Thursday Wessells and the remainder of Company H followed, along with acting assistant surgeon Petteys. Also joining the column as a scout was Woman's Dress (a prominent Oglala and grandson of the venerated Lakota chief Smoke), whose sister with her daughter and baby remained quartered with the wounded prisoners in the barrack prison pending approval for their release. Yet another recruited scout was John Shangrau, a mixed-blood from Pine Ridge Agency, who was Woman's Dress's nephew.[44]

A newsman noted that in the barrack prison that day were fifty-two men, women, and children. "Of this number fourteen are wounded. One aged squaw has just died from the effects of six different wounds." The correspondent wrote: "The sight presented by the [wounded] captives was sickening in the extreme. Crowded together in a long, narrow apartment, . . . from the infant to the decrepit old hag, all ages are represented in the most hideous aspects of the human form, and most grotesque and horrible contrasts are seen." Some officers feared that in addition to trying to reach Pine Ridge Agency, the escaping Indians might also seek to reconnect somewhere with Little Wolf and his followers. On the evening of January 17 Red Cloud and agent Irwin from Pine Ridge arrived at Fort Robinson to visit wounded Lakota kin among the Northern Cheyennes held in the barrack and "to see what is to be done about them." Irwin reported that the Sioux in his charge were considerably agitated over the Cheyenne breakout. The next morning he and Red Cloud met with Lieutenant Schuyler, requesting that the women and children, as relatives of the Oglalas, be given into the chief's care.[45]

Near midnight on January 16 Wessells's command, including Lawson's force and now totaling about 100 men, bivouacked with their wagons some twenty miles from the post and within a few miles of the Indians, who remained sheltered in the profoundly harsh terrain. On Friday morning, January 17, Wessells sent Woman's Dress with Shangrau and the Sioux trailers to reconnoiter the Cheyennes' position. As the column proceeded beneath a looming bluff, warriors suddenly let loose a "rattling volley" from an entrenchment less than 100 yards away. Riding some distance ahead was Private Amos J. Barber of Company H, recently enlisted at Buffalo, New York, who was struck in the chest and instantly killed. Woman's Dress, whose horse was also shot in the encounter, pronounced it "a perfect hornet's nest." As the troops fell back, the warriors swept in, stripped Barber's body, seized his weapons and ammunition, then boldly scalped him before racing off, while notably failing to capture his horse.[46]

According to a witness, on the morning of January 18, after ascertaining that the field was clear, Wessells and eight soldiers sought to recover Barber's body. Alarmed at "seeing their comrade lying nude and scalped on the frozen snow," they at last advanced mounted with drawn sabers and pistols and "were much surprised on reaching the summit of the hill to find two rifle-pits but no Indians." They finally retrieved the fallen man's remains, which were returned to Fort Robinson. The Northern Cheyennes lost at least two of their own that day, a warrior named Pug Nose, shot by John Shangrau, and a female named Small Woman. Both were apparently buried by their people among the rocks.[47] Wessells soon after dispatched Lieutenant Dodd back to the post to enlist additional Lakota scouts from Pine Ridge Agency.[48]

The engagement of January 17 stimulated controversy. It was suggested in O'Beirne's commentary that "strictures" had been imposed on Wessells (presumably from higher authority) before leaving Fort Robinson, in regard to close and dangerous advances on the Indians, including storming them, evidently because of inherent perils of the inhospitable landscape. O'Beirne said that Wessells had been "galled" by the levied constraints and thereafter "intends to keep the Cheyennes in full sight, if such a thing is possible, though he is debarred from charging them, owing to the steepness of the bluff on which they are, rendering the place completely impassible for men on foot or horseback."[49]

On the night of January 18 the Indians again left their position, "one of the strongest they had held," Wessells reported, and appeared now to be headed toward distant bluffs overlooking Prairie Dog and Warbonnet Creeks. Asked why the Cheyennes had remained so long in the area of

Fort Robinson after effecting their escape, Woman's Dress guessed that they might have anticipated aid from unknown sources. In addition, the relatively short distance that the Indians had covered since their last encounter perhaps evoked a desperate resolve to die rather than to yield. Both Woman's Dress and Shangrau that day scouted ahead with a detachment from the command; they found evidence that the warriors had killed and consumed a beef along their route and notified Wessells that they were "but two or three miles ahead." The scouts and their soldier accessories soon after briefly exchanged fire with Cheyennes ensconced in yet another distant rifle pit. The captain, however, determined not to keep an intense watch that night "as it was deemed desirable that the Indians should move into less (to them) advantageous ground." He instead dispatched Captain Lawson and Company E to Bluff Station, some ten miles west near the intersection of Hat Creek Road with the Fort Laramie–Black Hills Road, now fearing that warriors might attempt to run off and capture horses corralled there. The detachment composed of Companies B and D of the Third Cavalry, which had departed Fort Laramie on January 15 under Captain John B. Johnson, also reached Bluff Station that night.[50]

On Sunday, January 19, Captain Wessells led Company H to Bluff Station. Major Evans arrived by stagecoach that afternoon and assumed command of the campaign.[51] Twelve wagons bearing supplies and forage came in during the day from Fort Robinson to support operations. In addition, two companies of the Third Cavalry left the post to join Evans's command: Company A on January 19 and Company F the next day.[52] Evans suggested that the Indian trail had not yet crossed the north-south stage road leading to and from the Black Hills. At his direction, Company E reconnoitered along the bluffs in the area for several miles without success, leading Captain Lawson to conclude that the Indians were "pursuing the plan of descending in the night to ground where they could travel and get beef and holding by day strong points in the bluffs. Evidences were found of their killing a beef which they had encountered." Shangrau told him that the Northern Cheyennes were only days away, but no more than "20 miles in advance as they have a lot of cripples with them." At Evans's direction, Wessells patrolled northeast of the station, returning at nightfall.[53]

On Monday, January 20, the major again dispatched Wessells with Companies E, G, and H and his packs and wagons northeast of Bluff

Station toward Hat Creek, directing him to probe the base of the bluffs for trails leading to or from the eastern hills.[54] Evans with Companies B and D meantime moved southwest of the station, searching the ridgelines for signs until Shangrau located them above the steep, broken terrain. That afternoon, "on a high point of rocks" among the cliffs, Evans's men "exchanged shots" with distant Indians, who managed to shoot the major's horse from beneath him. As Evans would later notify Crook: "Companies B and D[,] Third Cavalry[,] Captain Johnson and Lieut. Thompson with myself found Cheyennes in strong position in cliffs north of [the] stage road . . . and cut off their progress on [the] heights. Indians escaped down cliffs in [the] night and moved east towards Red Cloud Agency." Evans camped in the vicinity on the prairie that night, below and away from the rocks. Wessells, meantime, met with little success as his troops crossed Hat Creek Road and advanced northeast to camp eleven miles above Bluff Station, somewhere below the ascending topography bordering Warbonnet and Squaw Creeks.[55]

Early on January 21, with Companies E and H and Woman's Dress accompanying, Wessells pressed his search northeast toward Hat Creek, combing the edge of the bluffs for about ten miles. That morning Shangrau appeared with news of Evans's skirmish and a vaguely worded dispatch stating that the Indians were believed to be in the area of a "Butte between where I [Wessells] was [yesterday] and Bluff Station." Then Shangrau pointed to a height three miles away and declared, "They [the Cheyennes] are right over on that point." The scout further informed Wessells that during the night as he camped alone on the prairie floor en route from Evans he heard voices in the dark and allowed that the Indians "may have come down [from their previous heights]." Shangrau went out and soon brought news that he had found the trail. Word was dispatched to Evans. Shangrau then departed for Bluff Station. Soon thereafter Lieutenant Chase rode in with Company A and joined the search, and Wessells grew more anxious to learn if the Indians yet remained in the area.[56] He continued to examine the lowlands for signs of their proximity. Then, as he later recalled, while "going [a]round the base of the bluff, a corporal [and] a private of my company and myself saw plenty of moccasin tracks. Soon after more were discovered by Woman's Dress. I then started on the trail[.] We followed out about 3 miles from the bluff and found a dead beef killed by Indians and soon after lost the trail."[57]

Wessells said that as night fell he moved closer to the foot of the bluffs edging the eastern prairie and "almost immediately saw a camp-fire. I went to it and saw . . . some men of my Co. [H] who had been sent ahead during the afternoon to look for the Indian trail. They told me that they had discovered the whole thing. . . . At [the] same time I saw the reflection of a campfire in exactly the place where the Indians ought to be. So I did not remain at the bluffs."[58]

9

Mortal End

The remaining Northern Cheyennes had sustained no significant losses in their brush with Major Evans's soldiers near Castle Rock on Monday, January 20. That night they managed an orderly descent and withdrawal from the rocky pinnacle. Gaining the prairie floor, they dauntingly set out east-northeast toward the Sioux at Pine Ridge Agency, sixty miles away. They hoped that Lakota friends and relatives there would provide them food and shelter and that they might blend with the Indian population there. Wessells and his officers feared that if they reached the agency "the task of identifying . . . and getting them . . . will prove more troublesome and dangerous than the present so far fruitless pursuit."[1] But most of the Northern Cheyennes had not yet been to the new agency and did not know precisely where it was. Still, they planned to navigate the fingered courses of Antelope Creek—and any other routes trending that way—to the stage road area, even as they tried to maintain a muted profile and a sufficient lead and distance from patrolling troops. It was during that night when they set on their course that John Shangrau thought he heard their voices nearby.[2]

Passing through the darkness and hoping to avoid further confrontation, the people looked increasingly to Little Finger Nail, whose stature had grown measurably since the breakout, for leadership. They needed such a leader with so many others having been killed, captured, or incarcerated or with their present status altogether unknown (such as Dull Knife). Beyond the meat taken from the few random beeves killed en route, their food resources were scant. With prospects for obtaining horses to augment their journey now fading, the Northern Cheyennes faced constant uncertainty and ever-mounting anguish. During the night of January 20–21, they covered about eight or nine miles before stopping to rest and build fires for warmth and perhaps for roasting whatever meat they still retained. Then they moved on. Always they sought to screen themselves from the soldiers. With their ammunition running extremely low, they wanted no further soldier encounters. The group accompanying (and including) Little Finger Nail now numbered thirty-two people: seventeen warriors and fifteen women and children.[3]

Continually fearful that the troops would find them as they crossed the open prairie, the Cheyennes found secluded places by day where they could remain together yet evade discovery. When darkness settled, they moved on. Still, they left footprints in the melting snow, evidence of their passing that Wessells's soldiers had discerned during the night.[4] Ascending to the brim of a low, gently rising escarpment amid grassy rolling ridges before dawn, they found what they thought would be a safe hiding place. Located some thirteen miles northeast of the site of the skirmish with Evans and about eight or nine miles northeast of Bluff Station, the surviving clutch of Dull Knife's people settled into what would seem a natural entrenchment: a large blowout perhaps thirty-five feet long and a dozen feet wide, varying between three and six feet deep.

New York Herald correspondent O'Beirne later described the Indians' entrenchment of January 22 after consulting with officers and soldiers who had examined it: "The position of the Indians was in an oblong hole about thirty feet long, ten or twelve feet wide and five feet deep, with ridges in it here and there, where the invested Indians had dug out some holes, so as to get down low from the range of our fire, and to alternately step up on ridges to deliver theirs in return. This was within a few feet of the edge of a high bank which broke off abruptly from the dry bed of a branch of Indian [later Antelope] Creek, thirty feet below."[5]

The refuge offered only modest protection, but it occupied high ground. Situated some twenty-five feet above the trifling streambed, it enabled the Cheyennes to survey the adjacent plain and upland approaches to the south and west. They further improved the setting by digging with knives to improve rude natural breastworks and to forge other trappings. At the front of the pit, a gulch some two feet wide ran down fifty feet to the sparse tributary of Antelope Creek, which provided water. The stream's webbed complex of rivulets coursed a few miles east to Hat Creek, which in turn passed north, alternately converging with a spate of streams before joining the Cheyenne River below what is today's community of Hot Springs, South Dakota, about forty-five miles away.

Cognizant of their precarious circumstances, the people hunkered beneath the lip of their make-do redoubt. They planned to pass the day until darkness enabled them all (or perhaps only the women) to proceed on their course. Some of them—the older ones, at least—realized the site's vulnerabilities. If the troops found them there, they were trapped, yet if they moved on they were sure to be discovered. So they stayed there, once again prepared to die. In this manner, remaining members of Dull Knife's people reconciled themselves to their dilemma atop a gentle bluff overlooking Antelope Creek.[6]

The troops, in fact, were close at hand. On a morning that Wessells would recall as "clear and pleasant," the captain's command found the Indians' trail as it passed through a large prairie dog town then quickly lost it again. His men nonetheless proceeded ever closer to the rising ground on the northeast. Returning from Bluff Station with Lieutenant Hardie that morning, Shangrau brought word that the supply wagons were en route and also learned that Woman's Dress had located a spot where the Indians had butchered yet another beef.[7] As Wessells later reflected on the Indians' hideaway, "this was the position most favorable to us, that they had been in since I had been operating against them."[8] After advancing a mile or so, Wessells directed Lieutenant Chase to move ahead and to the left of the column with Shangrau, Woman's Dress, and two Company A soldiers as an advance guard, urging the officer to "keep the general direction of the stream."[9]

The troops proceeded in this manner for two miles, at last approaching a slightly timbered and sage-covered bottom fronting the area of the Indians' concealed position atop the bluff. There Little Finger Nail, Roached Hair, Roman Nose, and the other Northern Cheyenne men had carefully painted their faces, prepared for any exigency. The women with the children and elderly took shelter as best they could, bracing for discovery and the climax that now appeared inevitable.

Near one o'clock, as the army scouts came within several hundred yards of the rising ground, shots abruptly rang out from the Cheyennes' lofty berth, immediately felling Shangrau's mule and damaging the scout's revolver. Shangrau and Woman's Dress ran for cover in the bottom growth while the advance guard pulled back. Directly behind them, Companies A and E dismounted and returned fire. Wessells ordered a mounted charge but then quickly countered the command, directing Lieutenant Chase instead to dismount and hold his position. For several moments Chase's men returned fire toward the Cheyennes' entrenchment. Woman's Dress received a gunshot wound to his arm in the brief exchange. Private Henry A. Deblois of Company A also fell wounded from his saddle, his horse shot beneath him. To keep the Cheyennes in place, Wessells sent Lieutenant Chase with Company A to take position below and opposite the bluff top while the balance of the soldiers waited expectantly for Lieutenant Baxter to arrive with Company F.[10]

As they paused, however, Wessells, who maintained a 200-yard distance from the Indians, now determined to surround and finally attack them on foot from several directions. With Companies E and H, he moved left and then north of the entrenchment, directing Captain Lawson to advance with E on his left and secure a location to cover the Indians' position. Below and some 125 yards southwest of the Cheyennes, Chase's Company A completed the encirclement, effectively "hemming them in on all four sides." Appointed troopers thereupon removed most of the company mounts to secure ravines or sheltered areas beyond range of the Indians' guns. Lieutenant Chase in the meantime dispatched riders on the back trail to find Lieutenant Baxter and Company F and hasten them forward. As before, Wessells directed interpreter James Rowland to call out to the Indians that the women and children "would be protected" if they came forward. There was no response.[11]

From these several positions, the soldiers girded for battle, sporadically exchanging shots with the Northern Cheyennes over the next two hours or so, until Baxter and his unit at last arrived to increase Wessells's immediate force to four understrength companies totaling 100 men.[12] On Wessells's direction, the soldiers deployed several paces apart in skirmish formation. While Baxter's Company F took position below the Indians, Chase and Company A proceeded "to a point occupied by Capt. Lawson's [E] company and thence down the ravine [that led] in the direction of the Indians' position." Chase's men took cover behind a crest and "prepared to charge the rifle pits occupied by the Indians." Baxter's Company F covered Wessells's and Chase's units during the maneuver. After the companies had realigned to complete the investment, Chase

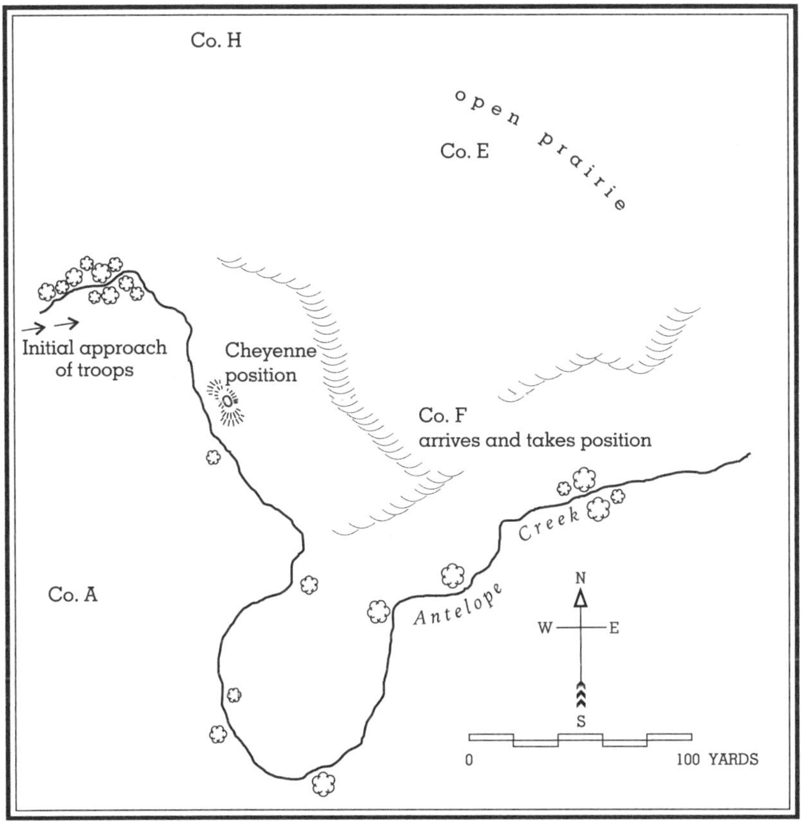

Antelope Creek, January 22, 1879, First Army Positions

reported to Captain Wessells, who laid out his plan. He explained that he "would advance up the ravine from the position his company [H] then occupied [north of the Cheyennes' entrenchment,] and at a given signal the two companies [H and A] would charge the ravine together."[13] In short, the combined force would form a semicircle "so as to bring the right and left of the line respectively toward the edge of the steep creek bank," where the Indians were sheltered. A detachment of Company F would also later move to advance from the east, while the remainder of that unit stayed in the bottom to monitor the west side of the Northern Cheyennes' position.[14]

Prior to opening the attack, Wessells told his command: "We have lost enough men now waiting for these Indians, and we must charge them."[15] Company A men pulled off their overcoats and arctic overshoes to enable them to move more freely. Before the assault could proceed, however, Lieutenant Chase sustained a grievous loss to his unit when reliable Sergeant James Taggart was abruptly killed by a carbine bullet to his neck as Company A took position fifty yards from the Cheyennes' pit.[16] Chase's men suddenly took the direct brunt of the ensuing opening melee. As Chase recalled, "I found my men subject to a flank[,] rear[,] and front fire." He continued: "I determined not to wait for the arrival of H Company, but ordered an immediate advance on the rifle pits of the Indians. We came under their fire at a point about 12 yds distant [east] from [the east side of] the pits. The Indians raised from the pits as my men . . . [reached] the crest and volleys were simultaneously exchanged. Farrier [George] Brown of my company was killed here."[17]

Lieutenant Chase described the continuing engagement:

> The Company then advanced to within about 5 yards of the pit and fired two or three volleys into it. Capt. Wessells seeing "A" Company in action moved at double time and within 5 or ten minutes had surrounded the pit with his company and a few men from the other companies.[18] In the meantime Private [George E.] Nelson of my company was [also] killed.[19] From this time [forward] I did not see an Indian take aim except the one who [subsequently] wounded Capt. Wessells with a revolver. The line fought in this position for nearly three-quarters of an hour during which time Captain Wessells twice ordered the firing to cease and called to the Indians to surrender and come out. The answer in both cases were shots from the Indians.[20] The firing eventually ceased. I formed my company in line [and] directed that the bodies of the Indians should be taken from the pit. Upon removal it was ascertained that 17 bucks were dead and one buck wounded. There were eight women and children alive and seven women and children dead.[21]

As mentioned, a detachment of F Company had been brought around so as to be out of range of fire during the assault from the north and east, but Sergeant Johnson, accompanying that unit, recalled that in the final storming of the pit, "When we charged into it [we] found only 3 of their pickets [warriors]. They now began firing at us from above. They were on the bank, and were firing lively, but we could not just see their exact position. Finally one of them jumped up and ran to another [part of] the pit. We finally charged right upon them, firing at each other not farther apart than 20 feet, and killed every fighting man."[22]

Chase remembered a certain hesitation among the troops in finally surmounting the crown of the Indians' defenses as well as specifics about the wounding of Captain Wessells:

> [During the assault] we found it difficult to force the men onto the crest of the pit occupied by the Indians. I called around me men [from Company A] whom I thought I could trust. Capt. Wessells did the same in his company [H]. Capt. Wessells and I walked side by side with cocked pistols[,] determined to lead the few men around us up to the very edge of the pit. As we advanced I saw an Indian's head and his hand with a pistol in it raised above the other Indians, but not above the level of the crest. Captain Wessells and I both fired. The Indian fired at the same time, the bullet taking effect in Capt. Wessells['s] head. Capt. Wessells staggered. I caught him to prevent his falling, ran back with him about 15 yards to where I found a place out of the range of fire.[23] I then went back to the skirmish line [and] told the men Capt. Wessells was wounded and called for a general advance on all sides.[24]

Shangrau recalled the scene similarly, noting that Chase's men clambered up the slope to a height equal to that of the Indians, while Wessells with Companies E and H advanced from upstream seeking level ground on the north. Finally, Lieutenant Baxter led the detachment of Company F in charging directly across the plain from the southeast. As Chase explained, Wessells's men initially met strong resistance. Fifteen yards from the Cheyennes' entrenchment a glancing bullet bloodied the captain's forehead, sidelining him while several of his men simultaneously collapsed before the Indians' shots. Another felled by a bullet in the assault was First Sergeant Edward F. Ambrose of Company E, who survived. Following the wounding of Wessells, Lieutenant Chase called for a general advance. "The men," he later reported, "now rushed right to the very edge of the pit and fired, I suppose 200 shots into it, and again fell back some six or eight yards. The line wavered backward and forward

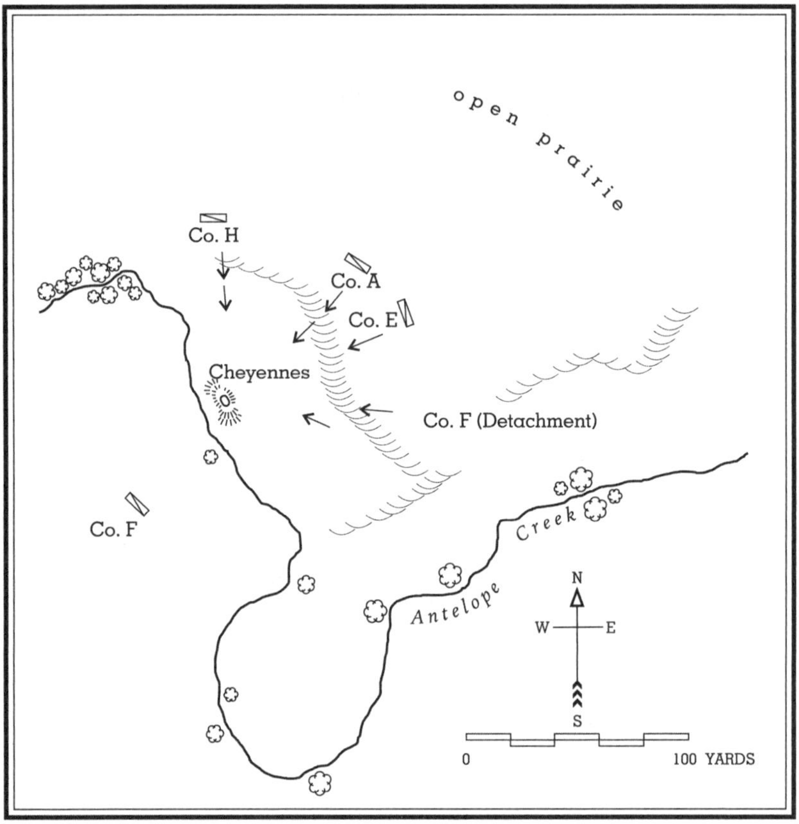

Antelope Creek, January 22, 1879, Final Army Assault

within 10 yards of this Indian rifle pit for some 10 or 15 minutes after Capt. Wessells was wounded."[25]

It was quickly apparent that the fighting was over. When the soldiers closed at last, most of the Indians were dead or immobile from wounds, their shots trailing off as their ammunition played out. At the very end, two warriors rose from the ditch in a forlorn final charge with only an empty revolver and two knives. They were quickly "riddled with bullets and fell dead."[26]

From start to finish, the bloody carnage of Antelope Creek lasted perhaps three hours. The initial shooting between the soldiers and the Northern Cheyennes began about 1 P.M., with the fighting intensifying after Company F arrived. The standoff ended about 4 o'clock.[27] "When the fight was over," remembered Shangrau, "the Cheyennes had fired their last cartridge."[28] For the Cheyennes, their defensive pit had become a cauldron of dashed hopes, frustration, and loss.

When the shooting subsided, Captain Lawson recalled, "I saw a little girl on the opposite side of the pit looking imploringly at us. I instantly gave the order [to] cease firing and[,] leaping in onto the dead bodies[,] took the child by the hand and helped her out. I also took hold of a squaw's hand and assisted her in getting up from amongst the dead, and called on the men to assist all those that were wounded and living out of the pit."[29]

10

Scrutiny

Captain Wessells's Third Cavalry companies, now under the command of Major Evans, returned to Fort Robinson late on Friday, January 25, bearing the army casualties and Northern Cheyenne wounded and survivors from Antelope Creek.[1] Post returns transmitted at the end of January indicated that the Northern Cheyennes had been good shots. Throughout the operations that month, the returns showed that altogether the regiment lost eleven soldiers who were killed outright or died of wounds and ten men (including Wessells) who were wounded and eventually returned to duty. The wounded scout, Woman's Dress, also survived and returned to Pine Ridge. Considering the number of troops engaged over the fourteen days between January 9 and 22, the twenty-one army casualties speak well of the Cheyennes' prowess and marksmanship under the extraordinary duress and trauma of a rigorous army pursuit in the dead of winter, especially given the limitations of their weapons and ammunition. Further evidence of the Cheyennes' shooting proficiency is the fact that ten of the eleven army fatalities (one being accidental) resulted from shots to the chest, neck, or stomach regions.[2]

After Antelope Creek, Companies B and D of the Third Cavalry returned to Fort Laramie, where they arrived on January 27. Three days later Companies A and F also departed for Fort Laramie, their permanently assigned post. Company H returned to its dormitory in the west barrack building, while Company E reoccupied its tented quarters in the lower camp. Company C, which had performed normal garrison duties while the other units were away and was permanently assigned at the post, also occupied its own barrack.[3]

The wounded and uninjured Indians brought back from Antelope Creek underwent examination and treatment at the post hospital and were then returned to the barrack prison. Other breakout survivors had been incarcerated there since or shortly following the night of January 9. Altogether, the number of Northern Cheyennes wounded and subsequently given medical treatment and still living at the end of January totaled at least twenty-four. Although there may have been more, no records for them have been found.[4] As the curator Roger Grange later determined of breakout casualties, "twenty-five percent of the soldiers wounded in the field died en route to the hospital. A similar death rate existed among wounded Indians dying before arrival at the hospital."[5] The Cheyenne dead were buried together with those previously interred in the single pit near the post sawmill. By contrast, soldier fatalities rested in individual plots in the post cemetery, on the west side of White River not far from the Indian burial site.[6] Sixty-four Indians had been killed during the breakout, seventy-eight had been captured and reconfined, and seven other women and children and one man—including Chief Dull Knife and his family—remained unaccounted for. The army believed that he had "died in the bluffs." Certainly, as George Bird Grinnell later intimated, others "were never again heard of, and no doubt were killed or starved to death in the hills."[7]

Responding to Major Evans's telegram of late January 22, General Crook extolled the command's "gallantry and energy," adding that "the charge made by Capt. Wessells upon the Indians in trenches is worthy of the highest praise." Crook thanked the command for "trying to save women and children" and for performing with fortitude despite the "cold, hunger, and privations . . . under circumstances more disagreeable than any which have yet presented themselves to our Army." Later Crook would praise some of the Cheyennes as well. "Among these Cheyenne Indians," he said, "were some of the bravest and most efficient of the auxiliaries who had acted under General Mackenzie and myself in the campaign against the hostile Sioux in 1876 and 1877, and . . . I still preserve a grateful remembrance of their distinguished services which the government seems to have forgotten."[8] Even General Sheridan, although holding to a hard line, acknowledged that the Northern Cheyennes "were treated in a bungling and impolitic manner."[9]

In the wake of Antelope Creek, pressure mounted as to what to do with the Cheyenne prisoners held at the post. Approximately sixty of the people, including those wounded on the night of the breakout, now occupied their appointed barrack, which had since been sufficiently repaired and guarded to prevent escape. For a while some of the recaptured prisoners were kept temporarily at an outdoor location secured partly by an earthen cut bank. Iron Teeth, among those held there, recalled her anxiety: "I was afraid to ask anybody about my son and the little daughter, as my asking might inform the soldiers of them. After a while the little girl [was found and] came to me. I asked her about her brother. It appeared to me she did not hear me, so I asked again. This time she burst out crying. Then I knew he had been killed."[10]

"We were hungry as wolves" in confinement, Iron Teeth said. The women and children were fed coffee and lots of crackers, but the soldiers also "hurried us, so that many of the people did not have time to eat much." She added that "some shoes and socks and blankets were given to us, [but] we had no place for shelter," so "my daughters and I got some cottonwood branches and built for ourselves a kind of lodge." Ultimately, "all of us were put again into the prison house a day or two later. The number now was only about half what it had been."[11]

Chief Red Cloud had favored moving the Northern Cheyennes to Pine Ridge Agency, Dakota Territory, since at least the November 7 council inside the barrack prison with the Oglala leaders in attendance. Wessells's attempt to recruit Lakota scouts during the days preceding events at Antelope Creek seemed to fuel the idea further. Agent Irwin, moreover, likely endorsed such a course too, based on the tribes' cultural, historical, and familial affinities. Early in January Irwin, referring to the Oglala leader's commentary in council, wrote to Crook again, urging their transfer. Irwin told him that Red Cloud

> listens to the Great Father and will make them [the Northern Cheyennes] do the same and will make new rules for them and hold them secure; that the prisoners are old men, women and children and related to his people; that the [Kansas] murders were committed by young men who have all gone north, and he does not want the innocent to suffer for the crimes of others. That, if they are given to him, he will turn them all over to the Great Father, if desired, and that if the guilty ones come to him, he will deliver them up. That his people will do right and want the Cheyennes to do right.[12]

To that end, Irwin and Red Cloud had visited the post again on January 17–18 for the purpose of consulting to obtain "some of the captive widows and orphans."[13] The War Department's concurrence came within a week, directing that "all widows and orphans with Oglallalla [*sic*] blood be turned over to Red Cloud," although the order had to be approved by General Sheridan and conveyed to Fort Robinson.[14] The directive provided major resolution for at least most of the remnant of Dull Knife's followers, "thus ending," according to the *New York Herald*, "the question concerning the removal southward."[15]

After approval by the secretary of the interior, the War Department endorsed the release of the people on January 31.[16] That morning, as some thirty-three Northern Cheyenne women and twenty-two children boarded wagons and departed the post with rations en route to Red Cloud's people at Pine Ridge, yet another misfortune befell them. As the wagons halted at the lower camp to load women and children of Lakota extraction, they encountered grieving wives, including Wild Hog's wife, who was a sister to the Oglala chief American Horse. She was wailing and gesticulating wildly "with lean and shriveled arms, her rags flaunting in the wind." When the soldiers searched her they found self-inflicted wounds and a sharp scissor blade as well as a fork fashioned into a "miniature stiletto." Apparently, as the wagons rolled out, Wild Hog, while confined in the lower camp where Old Crow, Left Hand, and fifteen other men also remained imprisoned, had attempted to take his own life. Wild Hog's twelve-year-old daughter, Blanche, had survived Antelope Creek, and he himself had been incarcerated since hours before the breakout on January 9. Not until noon on January 31 did a sentinel discover the manacled leader sprawled unresponsive in his enclosed space on the ground. Stressed over his family's imminent departure and his own prospect of going south to face charges in connections with the Kansas raids, Wild Hog was found bleeding from four apparently self-inflicted stab wounds near his sternum and below his heart. Acting assistant surgeon Petteys administered morphine and proclaimed the wounds potentially fatal. Some believed that Wild Hog's wife had caused the injuries to prevent his being sent south to Fort Leavenworth. Others thought that by taking his life he believed that he would ensure his family's safe transport to Red Cloud.[17]

That night *New York Herald* reporter James O'Beirne accompanied Lieutenant Dodd to Wild Hog's lodge at the lower camp, where the tragic events had played out:

> The oldest daughter of Wild Hog laid asleep. She is one of the three survivors from the pit where the fighting Cheyennes made their last stand,[18] and where she was shot through the neck. Lying head to head with her was the wounded chief. . . . Wild Hog, wounded unto death, breathed heavily and moaned with pain, though under the influence of morphine administered to him by Dr. Petteys. Corporal Lewis gave him another pill, with some words kindly spoken in Indian dialect. The mother, wild and terrified, sat at the portal of the lodge, one old gash under the right eye being the most prominent sign on her averted face, which looked at the lodge fire. Suddenly the wounded girl . . . awoke with a shrill cry of pain, and seeing the soldiers through the smoke of the lodge fire she shrieked hysterically and acted as though she thought she was again under the murderous rain of bullets. . . . She was finally quieted and your correspondent withdrew from the heartrending scene.[19]

Meanwhile, the five wagons bearing the former prisoners "with canvas enough to cover them" and bound for Pine Ridge, sixty-five miles away, lurched northeast along the road to Camp Sheridan. William T. Corbusier, the young son of the post surgeon, witnessed their arrival. "The most pitiable sight I ever saw was . . . fifty women and children, many of them suffering from wounds," he remembered. "They stopped several days at Camp Sheridan where father [assistant surgeon William H. Corbusier] was stationed. He dressed their wounds and we took them cakes and sweets and such other foods that the soldiers did not have to give them. The oldest boy [among them] could not have been over fourteen years old and he was badly wounded."[20]

On their arrival at the Red Cloud Agency at Pine Ridge, the Northern Cheyennes gathered in a commodious space. Trader Charles P. Jordan detailed at length their joyous and tearful welcome among the Sioux:

> The [Northern Cheyenne] survivors were brought into the large council room. The [Lakota] Indians were collecting in great numbers

> and were loudly bewailing the fate of their allies & kinsmen. A pandemonium prevailed. . . . They presented a horrible sight. The weather was bitterly cold and there was no fire in the council room. They stood there shivering with fear and cold. It was thought that when they appeared, the Sioux would become so angered at [the] sight of them and with the knowledge of the slaughter at [Fort] Robinson that they would lose all control of themselves and turn loose, as many of them were intermarried with the Cheyennes. The daughter of the noted Cheyenne chief Dull Knife was one of the party, and . . . she advanced from the line of trembling and frightened sufferers and extended her hand to me. . . . The faces of those who apparently were bereft of all hope [now] brightened up, and they seemed to feel they had a friend there in position to help them. This beautiful Indian girl had been called the princess by the military officers when at old Red Cloud [near Fort Robinson], and her character was unimpeachable. . . . The Indians had already learned who the survivors were. . . . As they entered the room and saw the pitiful sight and recognized those they sought, the wailing was heartrending, and they had to be directed to pass out and make room for another [to enter]. . . . I was indeed glad to get away from the harrowing sight and horrible wailing.[21]

As Jordan noted, many Oglalas were on hand to welcome these bereft and melancholy survivors. As a Sioux witness of the scene, Susan Bordeaux Bettelyoun, recalled years later, "It made many of the Indians cry to see them so sick and starved."[22] Other Northern Cheyennes who had eluded the troops in the days and weeks following the breakout and managed to survive the elements likely joined the Lakotas and their Cheyenne relatives at the Sioux agency over time. Some fought lingering illnesses and wounds related to the Fort Robinson flight for weeks, months, and even years. Others seemingly made their way back to Montana, while some were doubtless never seen again.

Four days later, on February 4, the remaining twenty-one Northern Cheyennes—seven men with their accompanying wives and children escorted by Captain Vroom and Companies E and L of the Third Cavalry—departed from Fort Robinson in two "canvas-topped wagons" and a train bearing rations and supplies. In January Lieutenant Schuyler had learned from Wild Hog, Old Crow, and Left Hand that *all* the young men had been "actively engaged in the Kansas outrages, though the old men [had] tried hard to restrain them," and that "at least fifteen" of those recently imprisoned at the post had been involved.[23] Now the seven Cheyenne men—all who were available at that time but not all who had been involved—were bound for Fort Leavenworth, Missouri, ultimately to face civil prosecution for their participation in the Kansas raids of the previous September.

It was a bitterly cold trip, and several soldiers suffered frozen feet and ears. When they reached Fort Sidney four days later, the Indians were placed in the post guardhouse—the men in a large single cell and the women and children together in another. The exceedingly tall Wild Hog, "bent double by wounds," was still shackled, but "he smiled, as did all the other Indians, and shook hands all around," according to an *Omaha Herald* reporter who was present. Wild Hog, said another, "acted as if it was the pleasantest moment of his life." During the layover, wherein the post surgeon redressed the wounds of the injured, Vroom granted the reporter an unprecedented wide-ranging interview with Wild Hog and the other leaders in which the gentle Old Crow averred that "the braves who killed the [Kansas] settlers are still out."[24]

On Sunday evening, February 9, as the Indians, none of whom had previously been on a train, waited to board a special passenger car for transit east, "the locomotive came down with its hissing steam, clanging bell and brilliant headlight [and] several of the Indians started nervously and the children screamed." First Lieutenant Morris C. Foote and a detachment of armed Ninth Infantrymen took charge of them as Vroom and his detachment prepared to return to Fort Robinson. When the train stopped in Omaha on Monday evening, Foote and the Indians faced a throng of several hundred interested residents. A few distinguished citizens entered the car, where Wild Hog, still in irons, proudly flaunted "a large metal star . . . bearing Wild Hog's name [and] . . . 'Newark [New Jersey] Industrial Exhibition, 1873.'"[25]

The Indians reached Union Depot in Leavenworth, Kansas, and went from there to Fort Leavenworth to be jailed until bound over to state authorities to face prosecution for the previous year's offenses. Warrants for the arrest of 150 Cheyennes had been filed in Ford County, where the incidents had occurred, and the U.S. attorney had urged that the Northern

Cheyennes be fully prosecuted. General Pope, commanding the Department of the Missouri, notified Governor George T. Anthony that the prisoners would be turned over to the civil authorities. Ford County authorities forwarded appropriate demands to new Kansas governor John P. St. John in January to arrest the Cheyennes. A delegation of witnesses together with the county sheriff arrived to conduct the designated tribesmen and their family members by train via Topeka to Dodge City.[26] There the defendants remained jailed for nearly five months, during which time agent John D. Miles, from Darlington Agency, managed to achieve the release of the wizened Old Crow, who returned to Darlington.[27]

The succeeding trial, *The State of Kansas vs. Wild Hog et al.*, which convened on June 24, began with an abrupt change of venue, based on alleged predisposition on the part of Judge Samuel M. Peters, 9th Kansas Judicial District. The shackled defendants (who had been indicted for the murder of Kansas rancher Washington O'Connor) were all removed three hundred miles east to Lawrence, in the 4th Judicial District.[28] Ultimately, however, the prosecution was doomed. The maneuver to move the accused to a more moderate political venue, the state's subsequent failure to produce lead witnesses, and a major dearth of evidence were all factors, along with sentiment evoked by the Indians' defense, which focused on the conditions that had inspired their initial departure from Darlington. In essence, the prosecution was unprepared. On October 13, 1879, presiding Judge Nelson T. Stephens denied a continuance and dismissed all charges by virtue of a motion of *nolle prosequi*, by which the case was dropped. As rationalized in fitting legal parlance of the time, it "appears that each Judicial District, through the county attorney of each county in said Judicial District[,] . . . takes cognizance at law for the crimes committed in the several counties of each said Judicial District. This mode of judicial procedure in the case of the Cheyenne Indian murderers is equivalent to a positive acquittal of the prisoners."[29]

Following the ruling, the Northern Cheyennes were turned over to Indian agent Miles, who was present to accompany them back to Darlington Agency, where the men were to be retained as scouts for the government. Miles and the Cheyennes reached Wichita the next night. A number of Cheyenne men and women, coincidentally in town from the agency to receive supplies, greeted them there. As one newspaper noted, "Great was the rejoicing among the sons and daughters of the plains, after the long separation." Also present were Cheyenne and Arapaho youths bound for the new off-reservation Indian boarding school in Carlisle, Pennsylvania.[30] Still, the irony and disappointment that Wild Hog, his associates, and their family members were returning to the dreaded southern agency must have been further devastating.[31]

Months before the trial of the Northern Cheyennes in Kansas, and within days of the army command's arrival back at Fort Robinson after its engagement at Antelope Creek in late January, an official inquiry got underway at the post to look into the Northern Cheyenne breakout of January 9 and its aftermath. On January 21—even before the closing engagement had occurred—General Crook transmitted Special Orders No. 8 from his headquarters in Omaha, directing the convening of a board of officers. Crook had been urged to do so by Sherman and Sheridan and was no doubt influenced by public antipathy over the killing of virtually helpless men, women, and children during and after the January 9 breakout.[32] Crook ordered that the board should "consist of Major Andrew W. Evans, Third Cavalry, Capt. John M. Hamilton, Fifth Cavalry, and First Lieut. Walter S. Schuyler, Fifth Cavalry [as recorder]."[33] As soon as possible, it should "examine into and report the facts attending the arrest, confinement, disarmament, escape, and recapture of a number of Cheyenne Indians, recently at and in the vicinity of Fort Robinson, Nebr." Crook added: "The board will make a thorough investigation and full report of all the facts, as well as of the causes which led to them, so that the whole case may be thoroughly and correctly understood. The board will also express an opinion as to who, if any person in the military service, is to blame in the matter, and will recommend what further action, if any, is in its judgment necessary."[34]

The board convened at the Fort Robinson adjutant's office on Saturday, January 25, just three days after the events at Antelope Creek, and undertook proceedings that would continue until February 7. The transcript of the proceedings indicates that the board presented its testimonial record consecutively from the beginning to the end and did not particularize the dates or times of individual testimonies during that period.[35] Major Evans, the senior officer present, as well as the other appointees, examined a variety of participants and witnesses. The board asked about the troubles that the Cheyennes endured while in the Indian Territory, their departure from Darlington, and their journey north, including the raiding in Kansas, the schism between Little Wolf and Dull Knife, and the surrender of Dull Knife and his followers along Chadron Creek in late October 1878. The members heard testimony about the dismounting and disarmament of the Indians, their subsequent movement to Camp Robinson, and virtually all considerations involving the Cheyennes' quartering and treatment on the night of January 9, 1879. They also heard testimony about the subsequent pursuit and engagements with the breakout survivors, including the closing events at Antelope Creek.[36]

The evidence presented was based on the recollections of individual participants drawn from memory, viewpoints, personal insights, and motivations as they supported and/or diverged from other renderings of the topics examined. As in all formal evidentiary proceedings, subtle shades and disparities appeared among the presenters, rendering much of the Fort Robinson 1879 board testimony not altogether clear or precise. While it is altogether possible that personal agendas played into the responses of witnesses, as a whole the testimony yielded sound information to benefit historical knowledge. When the testimony is considered along with the other sources bearing on these events (and in the hope of learning more from the Northern Cheyenne perspective), it is clear that the story thus far presented is likely the closest we can get to understanding the totality of what happened between the troops and Northern Cheyennes at Fort Robinson and environs in 1878–79.

On January 25, as its first order of business, the board examined several Northern Cheyenne men and women, including those under guard at the lower camp (among them Old Crow, Wild Hog, and Blacksmith, who had not yet departed for Kansas); Pumpkinseed's son, Big Head; and women named Red Feather and The Enemy. The two women were examined together, "the board hoping that they would talk more freely than if examined separately." One of the two, still in despair over the events at Antelope Creek, which obviously remained fresh in her mind, described the stabbing of a child by her own mother, who had then stabbed herself.[37]

The men spoke of their time in the south and their later difficulties in restraining the young warriors from raiding on the way north. After two days of questioning the Indians,[38] and likely because of the Cheyennes' expected departure for Pine Ridge Agency, the board took up the much anticipated matter of how the Northern Cheyennes came to have significant firearms to use during their breakout. The Indians supposedly had surrendered their weapons during their earlier disarmament and removal to the barrack. Besides those known weapons seized on October 24, 1878, as well as those yielded to Lieutenant Chase within days of the Indians' arrival at Camp Robinson, others had been "captured from Indians after the outbreak," as the board noted, indicating "long possession by the Indians." The latter weapons made a noteworthy list:

Seven Springfield breech-loading rifles, caliber .50
One Springfield carbine, caliber .45
Three Sharp's carbines, caliber .50
One Sharp's rifle (old reliable)
One Colt's revolver, caliber .36
One Colt's revolver, Navy, old pattern
One Remington revolver, Army, old pattern.[39]

Beyond the discussion of Indian weaponry, several junior officers and enlisted men testified on aspects of the Indians' initial surrender, the condition of the barrack, and the Indians' overall situation there. They also described the Cheyennes' imprisonment as well as aspects of the breakout that they either had witnessed or were involved in. Captain Wessells, who was directly engaged in almost all events surrounding the breakout and who had made the key decision to seize and isolate Wild Hog and other Northern Cheyenne leaders on January 9, provided essential information regarding those activities and subsequent events, including details of the soldiers' advance against the Cheyennes during the horrendous closing action at Antelope Creek.

Captain John B. Johnson, Company B, and First Lieutenant John C. Thompson, Company D, told of the search and capture of Dull Knife and his followers and their disarmament and movement to Camp Robinson as well as the discovery of significant evidence of the Indians' raiding activities in Kansas. First Lieutenant Charles A. Johnson of the Fourteenth Infantry, on duty with the Third Cavalry, provided additional statements verifying Northern Cheyenne involvement in those forays.[40]

First Lieutenant James F. Simpson addressed the Indians' stay in the barrack, the manacling of Wild Hog and Old Crow, and the matter of civilian atrocities against the Indian dead. Captain Peter D. Vroom,

Company L, detailed the efforts of troops in the lower camp in racing forward to help during the opening emergency of the breakout and later pursuit of the people into the bluffs west of the post as well as the events of the succeeding search and encounters beyond the post along Hat Creek Road and at Antelope Creek.[41]

Other junior officers offered significant testimony about essential troop movements and scouts and combat details following the breakout. Second Lieutenant George F. Chase of Company A described his role in searching and guarding the Indians following their arrival at the army bivouac on Chadron Creek as well as his unit's involvement in the guarding and monitoring of the people in the barrack before the breakout. Chase's testimony about his company's part at Antelope Creek added significantly to an understanding of the landscape and troop deployment preceding and throughout that tragic engagement. Captain Joseph Lawson of Company E offered specifics about the breakout as well as the purported civilian atrocities to Cheyenne bodies, the Indian burials, the details of incidents and actions along Hat Creek Road, and the climax at Antelope Creek. Second Lieutenant George W. Baxter of Company F also testified about the barrack confinement, the breakout, the movements around Crow Butte on January 10, and the artillery barrage near Hat Creek Road on January 13.[42] Together, the information gathered would contribute to and enhance the historical chronicle.

In other testimony, Second Lieutenant Francis H. Hardie, Company D, Third Cavalry, explained details of the killing of women and children during the initial flight from the barrack as well as Cheyenne deaths ascribed to civilians in the bluffs. Assistant surgeon Edward B. Moseley provided descriptions of several scalped Cheyenne remains that he had viewed, verifying Hardie's statement. Both Moseley and acting assistant surgeon Charles V. Petteys testified to the overall medical treatment accorded to the wounded soldiers and Indians. Petteys specifically addressed the self-inflicted stabbing of Wild Hog on January 31, along with aspects of the treatment given to soldiers and Northern Cheyennes wounded at Antelope Creek. First Lieutenant Emmet Crawford of Company G, Third Cavalry, addressed the initial breakout, the reputed killings by civilians in the bluffs, and the succeeding army chase along Hat Creek Road. Second Lieutenant Joseph F. Cummings of Company C, who was post adjutant at the time of the breakout, testified about finding survivors in the western bluffs as well as the killing of Indians there and collecting their bodies for burial.[43]

Several enlisted men gave testimony about the events, notably the Third Cavalry guards who were on duty before, during, and after the critical moment when the Northern Cheyennes' barrack erupted.[44] Civilian Henry Clifford expressed his belief that the women had sneaked guns into the dormitory and told of gathering bodies of Indians in the bluffs, including several that were scalped.[45]

A noteworthy informant was mixed-blood interpreter James Rowland, who told the court of the reaction among Indians in the barrack when they learned of the government's decision to return them to the Indian Territory. Rowland also spoke of the breakout, the Indian burials, and the later return of the captured and wounded people to confinement. He had frequently conversed with the Northern Cheyennes during their incarceration in the barrack as well as later during the Hat Creek Road encounters and the closing action at Antelope Creek.

Both James and his father, William Rowland, had accompanied the Indians south in the summer of 1877. William described the people's experiences there and especially what the people had told him about their time at Darlington, focusing on their scant food ration there: "corn meal and a little beef, [so] we were starving." James Rowland said that at one point Wild Hog told the soldiers that "they could not go back [to the agency] because they were starving." He added, "I think it would have been easier to take them south when first captured on Chadron Creek, than subsequently, but it would have been pretty hard to take them any way without killing them." Finally, he said, "They thought that after the rations [at Fort Robinson] were cut down if they did not conclude to go south they would be starved to death. When they broke out [of the barrack] there is no doubt they expected that most of them would be killed." Significantly, he stated that after the breakout "a squaw told me that the young men had their guns under the floor."[46]

Following the formal statements, the board called upon Major Caleb H. Carlton of the Third Cavalry, under whose command the Northern Cheyennes with Dull Knife were initially halted along Chadron Creek and escorted to Camp Robinson in late October, to "relate the circumstances of the capture, disarmaments and confinement of the Cheyenne Indians lately at this post." In a lengthy recital, Carlton described his command's movements from its departure from Camp Robinson on October 21 through the capture, disarmament, and confinement of Dull Knife's people in the barrack on October 26 (when another search for weapons occurred); how he allowed the people to keep their knives for eating purposes; and his departure from the post to continue the search for Little Wolf and his followers. Carlton testified that he had directed that 3 of the 149 individuals brought in by Captain Johnson—an Oglala woman who had married a Northern Cheyenne, along with her two children—be turned over to Two Lance, the woman's father, to take to Red Cloud Agency, thereby reducing the number of prisoners to 146. Soon afterward three stragglers—one badly frozen—turned up, bringing the number of those incarcerated back to 149.[47]

The board members deliberated the evidence and walked through and around the breakout barrack. The members then summarized their understanding of the imprisonment and the breakout from Fort Robinson. Their final document contextually related the recent history of the Northern Cheyennes following the Great Sioux War (1876–77), particularly their dispatch to Fort Reno, Indian Territory, and the agency of their Southern Cheyenne kin at Darlington. The board members concluded that

> they remained until, about the 1st of September 1878, rendered desperate by hunger and the Ague contracted in a climate to which they were unaccustomed, imbued with a superstition that they were all to die if they remained in that country, and tired . . . of a territory which they could not regard as their home, a large number of them, almost all who still had horses to carry them . . . took their families, and started for Red Cloud Agency in the North.[48]

When troops caught up with them, the people parleyed, with Wild Hog speaking for them, explaining the quandary of living at Darlington and that they would continue north.

The report recounted the Cheyennes' sequential engagements with troops after leaving Darlington, "the most horrible atrocities" that they committed in northwestern Kansas, and how they bore "each night to their women and children the spoils of the Whites." It told of the crossing of the Union Pacific Railroad, the split with Little Wolf, and the flight of Dull Knife and Wild Hog through the Nebraska Sand Hills until their capture and subsequent imprisonment at Camp Robinson, where they were again searched for weapons on October 27 as well as several days later. The board stated that "it was deemed impracticable to seperate [*sic*] the men from the women and children as there was not at the post any building except the weak barrack in which they were all put, and furthermore . . . it would have made them suspicious of an intended movement south, to have seperated them." Major Carlton, the report affirmed, "desired to use all available troops to try and recapture the other Cheyennes still at large, and could not spare enough men to guard the Indians unless that duty be made easy by keeping them in good disposition."[49]

The report described the mounting fears among the people about going south again for the health reasons noted, stating also that the young men now feared punishment for the Kansas raids and were well aware of the government's practice of exiling Indians to Florida. The views of the imprisoned young men gradually came to dominate in the barrack, and some came to learn of the hidden guns "deposited under the floor." "The cool headed old men endeavored in vain to have all the arms surrendered, but were far more terrorized by the young bloods to give to the whites the knowledge they must certainly have had of the possession of these arms." When Wessells informed the people on January 3 of their imminent transport back to the Indian Territory, and their spokesman proclaimed their "unalterable decision to die rather than return," the captain determined to cut off their food and notified Crook of his decision. Over the next several days Wessells repeatedly asked that the children be allowed to eat, but the Indians rejected the request, further hardening their position.[50]

On January 9 the removal from the barrack and arrest of Wild Hog, who, Wessells believed, had inspired the Indians' defiance, intensified the unrest and directly precipitated the calamitous breakout that night along with the engagements that followed over the next thirteen days. The board report described details of the Cheyennes' rush from the barrack, noting the urgent need for noncombatants to gain the bridge and the rough country near the White River, and highlighted the protective rear-guard action of the warriors en route; the pursuit of the people by Captain Vroom's men to and beyond the bluffs; the collecting of bodies of the dead and the evidence of civilian atrocities on them; the subsequent days spent searching and ferreting out men, women, and children from recesses and declivities across the snowy landscape north, east, southwest, and west of Fort Robinson; the attempt to roust the people with artillery fire along Hat Creek Road on January 13; the repeated need for the troops to pull back and resupply at the fort; and the conclusive fighting, in which the warriors succeeded in killing several soldiers.[51]

As for army strength and efficiency at the outset of the breakout, the board asked Captain Vroom whether in his opinion having a company saddled and ready at the post could have affected the outcome. Vroom responded: "I think it would. I think that most of the Indians would have been captured, and I think that if I had brought 3 companies up that night instead of one, we could have got most of the Indians that night [January 9]."[52]

The addition of two more companies of the Third Cavalry under Major Evans arriving from Fort Laramie bolstered the field command. The major's brush with the Indians on January 20 at Castle Rock drove them into their final defensive position, where Wessells confronted them two days later at Antelope Creek. According to the board's report: "Of the 32 Indians in the pit[,] 17 men and 4 women and 2 children were killed[,] 1 man, 1 woman and 1 child mortally wounded, died next day. That women and children should be killed, however much to be regretted, was simply unavoidable in the assault of this small hole. During the fight one squaw stabbed her own child and then herself." The board's final breakout casualty tally among the 149 Indians stood at 64 killed, while 78 had been captured and were in confinement. Another 7 remained unaccounted for.[53]

Nowhere in the proceedings is there the hint of any consideration for Wessells's command to starve out the Northern Cheyennes at Antelope Creek and avoid a final confrontation. Clearly, he felt an immediate sense of urgency, not only because of the troops' own losses but because of the nagging need to bring a conclusive end to the operation after two aggravating weeks in accord with the wishes of the army hierarchy as manifested by Crook and Sheridan. In the heat of the moment, however, the troops may have been affected—even angered—by the Indians' success in killing and wounding their fellows. The possible injustice of the climactic conclusion at Antelope Creek, however immoral this approach might have seemed, did not hinder Wessells's resolve or prosecution, even though he knew of the presence of women and children among that forlorn bunch. Other options did not seem plausible at that time. This was the core nature of warfare as it existed then and as it remains in essence today.

The board adjourned on February 7. Its conclusion, suitably bureaucratic for all intents and purposes, was surprisingly moderate in observation and inference given its contextual parameters:

> It is difficult to arrive at a correct estimate of all the motives which influenced the Cheyennes to their desperate course, without going beyond the strict limits of this investigation, or considering facts not developed by it. The village of these Indians, numbering over a thousand souls, was destroyed by General Mackenzie in the Big Horn range, in the fall of 1876. Left at an inclement season, without a tepee, they applied to their allies—the Sioux—for shelter, and were refused, or were at least received very coldly. Having no other recourse, they surrendered at Camp Robinson and were persuaded to go to the Indian Territory, largely influenced thereto by Chief Standing Elk, supposed to be a Southern Cheyenne. It is not known to the Board what assurances were given them by the Government, or what promises, if any, were broken. They were probably received very coolly by the Southern Indians, and they are unanimous in their complaints of hardship and ill treatment. It is easy to imagine that they were quite justified in their flight, at least in their own minds. After their surrender and incarceration at Fort Robinson in October last, it is understood that certain State authorities intended to make a demand upon the General Government for the surrender to their tribunals of the perpetrators of certain outrages charged upon these Indians. That demand would be eminently proper and right—but it could only refer to the guilty individuals, upon due identification. The punishment for their acts, of the entire band, tribe, or nation, as a body was the province of the General Government, and not properly to be delegated to any inferior authority. It is quite probable that identification of the guilty might have proved impossible; but might it not as well have been attempted at Fort Robinson as elsewhere? Could not the State officers have gone to that place for the purpose? Apart from these outrages, did the dignity of the Government require the forcible removal of these people

back to the Indian Territory at any rate prior to a full investigation into the merit of their complaints? It is neither the province—nor the intent of the Board to criticize its superiors; but it is convinced that the return of these Indians to the south could only have been accomplished by bloodshed; and it desires to point out the only course which, it seems to them, could have avoided that issue. In view of the orders received, the only question left to the military authorities at Fort Robinson was, what steps, to be taken by them, would involve the least shedding of blood. The recourse to measures of starvation bears too strong an analogy to the ancient, but now exploded, practice of torture applied to a prisoner to compel confession, not to startle the supporters of modern leniency. But what milder course could have been devised? It was evident to the Indians that they had no alternative but to consent to return.

That a violent outbreak of some sort must occur should have been apparent to every one [*sic*] who considered the temper of the Indians. Had it been practicable by secure barricades, to prevent their actual exit from prison, it is altogether probable that they would have immolated themselves rather than surrender. That they would attempt escape on the night of January 9th seems to have been clearly indicated that day—and was even predicted.

In view of these circumstances, it would seem that sufficient precautions were not taken. It was manifestly an error of judgment to relinquish the guard, or at least the watch over the Indians when discovered in their intrenchments [at Chadron Creek].

But it is so much easier to point out *after the event* what might or ought to have been done *before it*, that the Board finds it difficult to condemn an officer [Wessells] who was zealous in the discharge of his duties, who seems to have acted upon the best of his judgment, and who finally crowned his work by deeds of personal gallantry. It must be borne in mind that he supposed the prisoners to be without fire-arms, and that such was not the fact is a state of things which the Board finds itself—unable to clear up.

The responsibility for the continued possession of fire-arms by the prisoners seems, of course, to rest upon the officer who was in command when they were captured. To disarm them was the first and most natural idea. Yet the Board is satisfied that its accomplishment was impracticable on Chadron Creek. After their imprisonment at Fort Robinson, while they were apparently contented and satisfied and before the determination of the Government was announced to them, it is possible that disarmament might have been effectually and thoroughly done. The officer who undertook it [Major Carlton] certainly supposed that he was being successful in his attempt. The Board is of the opinion that the arms and ammunition used by the Cheyennes at their outbreak [breakout from the barrack] (except those captured by them from the troops) were previously in their possession; and had been introduced into and concealed by them in the prison.

It is possible that a very few may have been conveyed to them by visitors, but certainly not all, nor nearly all. With regard to his arms the Indian is so adroit and cunning, that it is not surprising he should have eluded the vigilance of his jaolers [*sic*]. The arms were most probably taken apart and concealed upon the persons of the squaws, until a favorable opportunity of hiding them—perhaps under the floor of the room—presented itself.

Colonel Carlton, in his evidence, has given his reasons why he deemed it impracticable or unwise to confine the men separately from the women and children. It has occurred to the Board that the latter class might have been simply placed in camp near by—without guard and without probability of escape. This suggestion is founded on similar cases that have occurred in Arizona and Texas, and at first view commends itself to the judgment. But this marked difference seems to exist, that in those cases the Indians had first been thoroughly whipped, while here this was not only not so, but the ultimate escape of the *bucks* would have been greatly facilitated by the absence of an incumbrance to flight; and it is doubtful if this seperation [*sic*] could have been made without exciting the suspicions of the Indians and precipitating the final result. While the Board has felt it its duty to call attention to what it deems errors of judgment committed by Captain Wessells, it cannot overlook the fact that that officer was so unfortunate as to succeed to a policy inaugurated by his predecessor and superior in rank[,] Major Carlton, and almost necessarily committed in advance to the pursuance of his system. Captain Wessells found these Indians imprisoned in

> a certain fashion, and seems if anything to have added precautions to their security. It was natural and reasonable that he should have supposed they had been really disarmed.
>
> The Board has pointed out certain errors, it believes to have been committed; but beyond that, attaches no blame to anyone in the Military Service, and in view of all the circumstances of this unfortunate business, of the manifest fact that collision with these Indians and consequent loss of life was unavoidable; of the evident desire of everyone concerned to carry out the orders of the Government in the most effective and yet most humane manner; and of the probability that no one else—of equal experience or judgment—could have done any better, recommends that no further action be taken.[54]

Clearly, despite its attempted neutrality, the board expressed a conclusion wholly compatible with military hierarchical needs and assumptions. Effectively, the authority of Crook and Sheridan—and even Sherman—overshadowed the proceedings. In its particulars, the board gently chastised Major Carlton for not sufficiently determining that the Indians were fully disarmed, either at the time of their surrender and encampment at Chadron Creek or before they entered the empty barrack at Camp Robinson. Although the members agreed that the enforced starvation initiated by Captain Wessells had been ill-applied, the devastating loss of human life was blamed on the Indians themselves and their fundamental refusal to obey federal administrative mandates that they return south. Beyond assorted details that contributed to or otherwise compounded the tragedy, the board members agreed that they could not hold any officers responsible for what had happened. Despite the oblique censure of Major Carlton, no direct charges resulted. To a large extent, during the Northern Cheyennes' desperate flight from their barrack prison—many of them anticipating or perhaps even seeking death—the people had shown their last measure of resolve. The troops responded in full measure, making what occurred throughout essentially nothing short of extended mass execution.

Following the disastrous days of the breakout, Sheridan unveiled a plan to abandon Forts Robinson and Hartsuff (in central Nebraska), along with Camp Sheridan, in favor of stationing troops nearer Pine Ridge and

Spotted Tail agencies. Although the general visited the post in March, he finally dropped the notion after the Bureau of Indian Affairs rejected the placement of soldiers so close to the Indian agencies. Instead, Secretary of War McCrary, with Sheridan's concurrence, urged the construction of a new post on the Niobrara River near the mouth of Snake River to protect cattle interests in the area.[55] But in the end the presence of Fort Robinson was sustained: the post would endure for decades to come.

11

Pine Ridge Interlude

At almost the same time that the board at Fort Robinson rendered and approved its findings and adjourned, an elderly man and his wife and son, the older two in wretchedly bad condition and suffering the effects of cold and long starvation, appeared in the doorway of a cabin near New Red Cloud Agency at Pine Ridge, Dakota Territory. The old man was Dull Knife: Morning Star to his people. Miraculously, they had endured ten days with little or no food as they hid in the freezing grotto among the bluffs west of Fort Robinson before finally breaking away as the soldiers focused along Hat Creek Road, northwest of the post. Around January 19, apparently while most of the soldiers remained to the west, Dull Knife and his wife, Pawnee Woman, and their son, Bull Hump, set out under the veil of darkness, circumventing Fort Robinson as they traced the forested gullies and breaks adjoining Crow Butte and trekked north-northeast toward Pine Ridge Agency, sixty-five miles away. They bypassed Camp Sheridan en route, moving at night and avoiding where possible snow-covered terrain that might expose their passage. Faced constantly with starvation, they consumed dried roots and berries, even gnawed their rawhide moccasin soles for meager sustenance in their dilemma.

After perhaps eighteen days (on February 6 or 7) Dull Knife and his little entourage appeared in the night at the dwelling of Gus Craven, a white man married to a Lakota woman. Dull Knife had known Craven years earlier. There the chief and his party found food and rest as well as assistance to the reservation home of William Rowland, interpreter at Pine Ridge and father of James Rowland, the interpreter at Fort Robinson.

From that domicile they at last reached the lodge of Little Big Man, the Oglala leader who had gained notoriety in the events attending the killing of Crazy Horse at the fort less than two years earlier. "They were very cold and had no clothes on and no blankets," Little Big Man said. "The old man shivered a great deal as he talked to me, and asked to come in to the fire and warm himself. I took pity on him, gave him something to eat, some clothes, two pair of moccasins and all my blankets." There at Pine Ridge, under the aegis of Little Big Man and other caring Oglalas, Dull Knife and his surviving family found seclusion and relief in a lodge along Wounded Knee Creek among other Northern Cheyenne arrivals only a short distance from the agency. Dull Knife's wounded daughter rejoined her family, and it was likely there that he learned of the deaths of his son and daughter in the nighttime furor of Fort Robinson and perhaps of the final trauma at Antelope Creek.[1]

Within weeks of his arrival at Pine Ridge, Dull Knife joined an interpreter for an extended interview with *New York Herald* correspondent James R. O'Beirne. The journey from Fort Robinson, the chief recalled, "was a hard time": "I have had a good many very hard times, but that was the hardest of them all." Still reconciling himself to the loss of his children, he grew melancholy. "I had nothing to eat for four days [before the breakout]." He told of the eruption that night:

> I jumped through the broken windows of the barracks among the first, followed immediately by my people. The firing was very fast and the bullets seemed to pass all around me and right by both sides of my head. I saw the Cheyennes falling all about me and thought every moment I would be killed, but that was what we expected when we broke out, and we didn't care, for we thought our time had come to die, and it did not make any difference to us how we were killed. . . . I ran until I got a short distance away from where the soldiers were shouting and firing, and I laid down in a little hollow in the snow. The soldiers kept going to and fro near us, and I thought they would trample upon us and we would be killed. When everything became quiet about us[,] my squaw and my little girl, who were with me, and myself crawled off to one of the ravines close by, and there we stayed. We had one blanket each among us, but nothing to eat. I had no arms. We worked out of one ravine

> into another after that, during the night time, to get further away, but sometimes, on account of the way they would [merge] into one another[,] after we had been traveling all night long we would find ourselves in the morning just where we started, or within a few feet of it. We were very sad, and commenced to think it was no use trying to get away. But at last we reached Crow Butte and hid there. Then we worked on, still keeping out of sight in the daytime, going around Camp Sheridan to the northward, until we got near the agency of the Sioux, our old friends and relatives. This took us 14 days, and we came then to a ranche [*sic*] on the prairie belonging to a white man named Craven.[2]

The old man said that he and his family survived by eating dried rosebuds. "I had a little tin can in which I gathered and carried them. . . . We could not keep warm. We would get under the three blankets we had among us, but we suffered awfully from the cold. I had my toes frozen." As O'Beirne related, "Here the chief pulled off a moccason [*sic*] and showed where two of the toes on his left foot had disappeared." Dull Knife continued: "Then when we arrived near here, during the four days following I staggered about and did not hardly know where I was going. My head got bad and I was dizzy, very weak and sick. I thought I would give up. I reached Little Big Man's tepee, and then got warm and something to eat. . . . I cannot believe that this is me, an old man, who went through all this. I shut my eyes and it seems to me like a great, frightful dream."[3]

As the dialogue concluded, O'Beirne inquired how Dull Knife was doing with regard to the other Northern Cheyennes who had at last been released to the Lakotas. "Very well now," he replied through the interpreter. Referencing his own family losses, he remarked, "If I only had those who are dear to me now, so I could take care of them, I would be content." This last remark, noted the reporter, "was said with a slight convulsion, and when I next looked at the fearless old warrior a tear was trickling down his weather beaten cheek. He brushed it away quickly and busied himself breaking twigs into pieces."[4]

12

Denouement

General Sheridan from his offices in Chicago assessed the events at Fort Robinson. Overall, he blamed mismanagement in the Bureau of Indian Affairs for the root problems. Yet he quietly notified General Sherman that Crook deserved criticism for failing to take appropriate safeguards in view of the Northern Cheyennes' oft-stated resolve not to return south. He told Sherman that he had directed "a full and accurate report" from Crook "which will reach you in due time." In his "strictly confidential" dispatch, Sheridan repeatedly lambasted his junior. "It is apparent," he told Sherman, "that trouble was apprehended in moving the prisoners south & proper precautions should have been taken in anticipation of an outbreak. This was not done. *Writing confidentially*[,] I am sorry to say that but very few things have been well done in that Department since Crook came in command of it."[1]

Sheridan continued his reflective harangue, condemning what he saw as Crook's long-standing leadership failures, including his ineptness in failing to disarm the Indians adequately following the Great Sioux War: "The troops complain that he has a want of confidence in them & they have a corresponding want of confidence in him, & from these existing conditions we must expect indifference and bad results." He complained that "Crook's decision to have the hostile Indians surrender compromised him to such an extent that he did not carry out the orders to disarm & dismount the Red Cloud & Spotted Tail hostiles after the termination of the Sioux War. Hence much of our trouble and much yet to come. If he had done this as [General] Terry did[,] Red Cloud & Spotted Tail agencies would have been as quiet as the agencies along the Missouri River."

Sheridan closed solemnly. "I am a warm personal friend of Crook & have stuck by him[,] but he has given me a great deal of disappointment."[2]

Later that day Sheridan self-servingly declared that he was convinced that no cruelty had taken place at Fort Robinson, that the officers had evinced the "highest sentiments of humanity," and that—seemingly more realistically—the failure to capture the elusive people had been "attributed to [the troops'] necessity" of repeatedly obtaining provisions during the pursuit over the Hat Creek Road. On balance, he asserted, "I blame the want of precaution to guard against this outbreak."[3]

Regardless of his misgivings about Crook's performance, Sheridan remained committed to wrapping up the Northern Cheyenne matter conclusively. Most immediately, questions prevailed over the whereabouts of Little Wolf, their Sweet Medicine Chief, and his followers. Many believed that Little Wolf and his people had remained securely harbored from winter's elements somewhere amid the vast and impervious Nebraska Sand Hills. Although not extremely far from Fort Robinson, the Sand Hills in their infinite emptiness were mostly beyond the capacities of the soldiers. They were, in fact, largely devoid of human habitation. Army efforts launched from Fort Robinson, Fort Laramie, and other points to seek out Little Wolf and his followers had come to naught and had virtually ceased weeks earlier with the onset of freezing weather well before the breakout by Dull Knife's people.

After separating from Dull Knife and his followers in October, Little Wolf and his people, including approximately 100 men, had headed northeast under the cover of an enveloping fog while bearing toward the tortuous Sand Hills in west-central Nebraska. Little Wolf's faction was protected by the attributes inherent in the Sacred Buffalo Hat and collateral relics that would guide them spiritually and nurture their advance as they sought their Montana homeland. As Little Wolf's people proceeded into the Sand Hills, other small groups of Northern Cheyennes from the south occasionally joined them. (These Cheyennes had left Darlington Agency before—and even days after—Dull Knife and Little Wolf had departed.) To avoid detection by soldiers, Little Wolf's people traveled by night, occasionally scattering into smaller bodies and converging again when the way seemed clear. They penetrated ever deeper among the dunes, with their scouts perpetually canvassing the country ahead for troops.

At a point below the forks of the Niobrara River,[4] Little Wolf's people halted in a small valley where they found temporary safe harbor against winter's cold and driving winds. The vale offered game, including deer, elk, and pronghorn, and even a lake where ducks and fish abounded. White ranchers' cattle grazing openly over the surrounding countryside might tempt them as well, especially after the snows arrived. Sheltering hills crowned with trees ringed the valley, and thriving grass for the ponies carpeted the bottomlands. Safeguarded in this secluded place, Little Wolf's people passed the following weeks in rude shelters of brushwood and reeds as they awaited warmer weather.[5]

All was not entirely peaceful, however. During their time in the valley, some of the Northern Cheyenne men, including one named Black Horse, set out to steal horses and possibly even kill a white man in apparent retaliation for the people's agonizing flight from the Indian Territory. Evidently well-armed, they journeyed north to the open range lands along the Niobrara River, where a consortium of ranchers grazed stock. When opportunity afforded, they approached ranchers at their homes, where they managed to count coup upon some and then killed them. Such was the case when the Cheyennes seized thirty or more horses to drive back to their valley refuge and distribute among the people. The raid took place on January 26, 1879, at the Lazy H Ranch south of modern Cody, Nebraska, some fifty miles northeast of the Indians' sojourn site. Period newspapers identified the casualties as twenty-six-year-old Franklin M. Moorehead, foreman James Ashbaugh (both scalped), and two men (named Alsop and Hopper) from neighboring outfits. The warriors reportedly burned the house, stable, and wagons and made off with eighty head of cattle, inciting ranchers throughout the Niobrara range, some of whom began searching for them. Five days later, along the Fort Randall Road near Little White River in Dakota Territory, the same body of Indians (about 100, according to one report, "armed with breech-loading guns and pistols" and with several hundred horses) attacked a Weatherell Ranch supply train bound for the Missouri River. The Indians made off with provisions but harmed no one physically. They indicated that they were bound for the Cheyenne River, and one was said to have handed a Weatherell man a silver watch stolen during the Moorehead raid.[6]

These Cheyenne sorties may have been preparation for Little Wolf's people to resume their trek home. During a thaw in late January when the winds moderated, and despite their wariness of soldiers and Lakota scouts operating in the region, the Sweet Medicine Chief led his people north toward the Niobrara River. Their raiding, although successful, was costly. Their leader, Black Horse, was severely wounded in the encounter at the Lazy H. Beyond such rare and desperate sorties, Little Wolf's followers for the most part remained isolated in their valley and perhaps yet knew little if anything of the fate that had befallen Dull Knife's people.[7]

About the time of the Niobrara and Weatherell train raids, G. T. Newman, a rancher who owned a spread on the Niobrara River, visited Fort Robinson accompanied by his foreman to report the discovery of a large Indian trail along Snake River, south of the Niobrara. That area, determined to be "about sixty miles from Pine Ridge Agency and perhaps about eighty from Rosebud Agency," was apparently not far from the secluded zone that Little Wolf's people had so recently inhabited. Based on this information and Crook's concern for Little Wolf's possible influence upon nearby Sioux, Captain Samuel P. Ferris departed Fort D. A. Russell, near Cheyenne, Wyoming Territory, on January 19 with about 300 of six companies (A, B, D, F, I, and M) of the Fifth Cavalry to reconnoiter the Sand Hills in search of Little Wolf's people. The troops passed through Fort Robinson on January 25, Camp Sheridan on the 27th, and Knowman's Ranch on the 29th then went east to the Snake River on the 30th, where they encamped until February 6. From there five of the companies pursued an Indian trail said to include women and children as well as a herd of stock, southeast toward Loup River and its tributaries, but the going was slow. Below-zero temperatures and deep snow hindered their progress, and the march proved fruitless. Upon returning to Camp Sheridan, the troops learned from newspapers that the Indians had indeed crossed the Niobrara en route north.[8]

By the end of February Ferris's troops had returned to Fort Russell with nothing to show for their efforts. Correspondent O'Beirne wrote that "both officers and men are very much disgusted with their mission." Reporting for the *New York Herald*, he observed that the cavalry's problem lay with the "intractable nature" of the country and "the superior animals of the Cheyennes." The soldiers were at a clear disadvantage, claimed O'Beirne. "It is a literal impossibility," he stated, "to make rapid progress through the country in which they are, owing to the sand, and, besides, there is no grazing of much account." He added that "the grain used by the [army] horses has to be carried on pack mules, and as much cannot be carried in this way the cavalry horses are reduced to short forage, and already the supply is nearly exhausted." O'Beirne described the Indians' eventual route as "a little east of north up to the point where they were encountered by Wetherell's train near White River [in Dakota Territory]." He predicted that "from there the course of the Cheyennes will be northwest and northerly."[9] Wisely, the troops did not proceed north onto the Great Sioux Reservation.[10]

While their precise route remains unknown, Little Wolf's people likely passed into Dakota Territory somewhere around and north of modern Merriman, Nebraska. From there they seem to have headed almost due north, possibly even northeast for some distance, decisively circumventing Red Cloud Agency, forty miles to the west. Throughout their trek they protected themselves against the elements with hides and robes and sought to avoid white communities and major trails as they pressed ahead. Still, they apparently took to raiding when opportunities existed. A report in February told of twenty-five raiders, presumably Cheyenne, striking a small camp of hunters thirty miles east of Rapid City, where they seized a gun and a horse, besides blankets and supplies.[11]

The Indians' main column moved through the Badlands, fording White River and gradually arcing northwest toward the northern Black Hills and distant southeastern Montana Territory. They were most certainly guided by the distantly towering outline of their Sacred Mountain, Nóvávóse, also known as Bear Butte. The uplift, looming near the eastern edge of the Black Hills, was (and remains) the quintessential focal point of their religion. Nóvávóse constitutes the Northern Cheyennes' transcendent foundation—indeed, the very cornerstone of their worldly and postworldly tribal being. The cultural prophet Sweet Medicine's spirit dwells there and imbues the very essence of being in all Cheyenne people.

Fittingly, Little Wolf's followers paused to rest in that hallowed sanctuary, assuredly aware of soldiers stationed at Fort Meade but a few miles to the west. While at Nóvávóse, Little Wolf—the Sweet Medicine Chief who personally bore the hallowed medicine bundle—ascended the summit to fast, smoke, and pray over the succeeding four days, seeking to safeguard peace and well-being among all his people and particularly this fragment of them during their long, precarious passage home.[12] Acquainted with these holy environs, and ever the planner, Little Wolf led his people northwesterly, moving furtively to avoid chance encounters with whites north of the Black Hills. He and his followers likely skirted tracts adjoining Owl, Indian, and Frozen Horse Creeks while moving deliberately diagonally into what was for many the increasingly familiar features of the Little Missouri River drainage of southeastern Montana Territory.[13]

As unobtrusive as Little Wolf and his people tried to be, O'Beirne reported for the *New York Herald* on several run-ins between the chief's followers and whites in the Belle Fourche country north of the Black Hills. Some of the encounters occurred on ranches along the Bismarck stage road, where Cheyennes seized necessities to sustain their passage into Montana. At the Belle Fourche stage station "the Indians rode up and . . . gave the friendly salutation of 'How'" and then "took all the provisions they could get," as well as a rifle, telling those present that "they did not care to kill anyone." Still, at least four killings reportedly happened along that road, although Seventh Cavalry troops from Fort Meade failed to find and pursue the perpetrators. Some persons believed that Little Wolf's followers were bound to join Sitting Bull and his people in Canada, where the Lakota leader had withdrawn after the warfare of 1876–77.[14]

Whatever the source of such rumors, O'Beirne reported that "Arkansas" John Seckler, a freighter and trader married to a Cheyenne woman and living at Fort Robinson, told of anticipated "retaliation against this place and vicinity for the punishment inflicted on them [the Northern Cheyennes] by the troops." O'Beirne correctly stated that many Northern Cheyennes were now integrated among the Sioux at Red Cloud, "with their old chief Dull Knife in their midst." If the Northern Cheyennes were successful in joining Red Cloud's people, "the agencies," he wrote, "may become grand recruiting depots for the hostiles."[15] Providentially or otherwise, O'Beirne's prediction never materialized.

Little Wolf's passage through the Little Missouri country was further stressful because of the earlier raid in which the warrior Black Horse had been wounded. Growing anxiety among his relatives eventually climaxed when Black Coyote, a younger man, shot and killed Black Crane, an elderly chief. The incident caused schism and familial disarray and, adding to the turmoil of recent months, strained tempers all around. Societal strictures governing the murder of one Cheyenne by another decreed that Black Coyote and his family had to leave the group. They evidently departed, but their exile was not without discord, even as Little Wolf's followers pressed on into eastern Montana, deeper into the country that they considered home.[16]

By this time army authorities had been alerted and were waiting. Indeed, scouting parties from Fort Custer, along the Big Horn River, and particularly from Fort Keogh, along the lower Yellowstone River, were raptly watching for them. In fact, Northern Cheyennes under Two Moon and other leaders and their families had remained by exemption in the employ of Colonel Nelson A. Miles and his command following the conclusion of the Great Sioux War. As recently as February 16, 1879, a company of Second Cavalry and a company of Fifth Infantry under Captain Simon Snyder had patrolled from Fort Keogh to Glendive looking for Little Wolf's people.

Anticipating Little Wolf's appearance in the region, Lieutenant Colonel Joseph N. G. Whistler, commanding in Miles's absence, on February 22 dispatched Companies E and L, Second Cavalry, to patrol east along the Yellowstone. Accompanying them were Cheyenne scouts, under the command of First Lieutenant William P. Clark, whom they knew as "White Hat" because of the white skimmer he always wore. Clark had been aide-de-camp to General Crook two years earlier and had headed a contingent of Indian scouts when Ranald S. Mackenzie attacked Dull Knife's village along the Red Fork of Powder River in Wyoming in November 1876. At Camp Robinson, Clark had monitored the Red Cloud and Spotted Tail agencies for Crook and had later worked with Little Wolf's Northern Cheyenne scouts. Clark's scouts now hoped to locate and intercept the Cheyennes before they reached the Yellowstone. Whistler further ordered a body of Sixth Infantrymen dispatched from Fort Buford on the Yellowstone, 191 miles downstream and northeast of Fort Keogh in Dakota Territory. They were to patrol west along the river, also hoping to intercept those elusive Cheyennes before returning to their base.[17]

Lieutenant Clark's command included Second Lieutenant Frederick W. Kingsbury and a doctor as well as an infantry detachment, a Hotchkiss gun and its squad, ten supply wagons, and forty pack animals bearing equipment and rations. Afield for several weeks, the unit scoured the backcountry despite dreadful weather conditions. En route, Clark established a picket post atop Sheridan Butte overlooking the mouth of Powder River on the Yellowstone. Fast-rising waters in the Yellowstone and its tributaries near O'Fallon's Creek caused him to seek higher ground along the banks of the stream, where he and his scouts remained several days.

On March 8 Clark dispatched two Lakota scouts and a mixed-blood interpreter up Powder River, directing them to divert east on the Black Hills road to the Little Missouri and beyond, searching for Little Wolf's Cheyennes. After three days, the scouts sent word of a hunting party spotted some fifty miles up that stream. Clark took pursuit, passing through mounting cold and snowstorms, but without success. He sent several Lakotas farther east to probe the Little Missouri country as he led his weary troops back to Powder River, where they remained until March 17. After Clark asked Whistler for Northern Cheyenne scouts to accompany him, five soon arrived, as well as an especially adept Cheyenne mixed-blood interpreter named Jules Semineau (commonly known as Seminole).[18]

Clark hoped to use the Cheyenne scouts to achieve the surrender of Little Wolf's people without bloodshed, but he understood that the scouts would be in a precarious position if they were to help him toward that end. In a revealing report Clark later set down his candid feelings about these scouts, explaining the necessity of hiring Semineau at his own expense to ensure that a "perfect understanding" with them existed. He related his orders "to capture or kill these hostiles" and his hope that the scouts might "save their kinfolk": by surprising them and capturing their horses "it might open their ears and they would surrender without fighting." Clark moreover explained to them:

> If I could not surprise them, then when I got very close, they [the Cheyenne scouts] could go into the camp, represent the danger of an engagement, the number of troops out after them, [and] the extreme difficulty of crossing the [dangerously flooded] streams to the north. . . . [I told them] that Little Wolf had [formerly] been an enlisted scout under my command, and I thought [he] would have confidence in any message he might get from me. . . . I could only say, give up ponies and guns, and I would not fight them. That, if after this understanding, they (the Cheyenne scouts) did not feel they could act earnestly in the matter with me, they could go back to the post.[19]

Four days later, on March 21, Clark learned that Little Wolf's followers had captured his interpreter and two Lakota scouts near Box Elder Creek on the Yellowstone, 100 miles northeast (downstream from modern Glendive, Montana). Although captured, the interpreter and Lakota scouts had convinced the Northern Cheyennes that they had been headed into Canada to join Sitting Bull.[20] One of them managed to slip away to inform Clark, who rationed his men, left his wagons, and set out on the stage road to Bismarck determined to find Little Wolf. That night the other scout rejoined the command, having also escaped the Cheyennes. Believing that those people would attempt crossing the Yellowstone to evade capture, Clark sent a scout to Whistler, who directed a company of Fifth Infantrymen downstream (northeast) to guard the logical ford opposite Cabin Creek on the Yellowstone. Whistler also sent a company from the cantonment at the mouth of Glendive Creek to move upstream (southwest) with the hope of intercepting the Indians should they attempt to cross the river at that point.[21]

As these maneuvers played out, Clark pressed forward, his Cheyenne scouts moving well in advance to seek Little Wolf's exact location. They carried a personal message from the lieutenant to present to the chief. Four days later, on March 25, in the vicinity of Charcoal Butte near Box Elder Creek (in present Dawson County, Montana),[22] two of Clark's Cheyenne scouts returned to camp with three of Little Wolf's warriors, bringing word that the Northern Cheyenne chief, whose people were tired, hungry, and outnumbered, would comply with the terms the scouts had delivered. As Clark later reported, "I . . . selected the two head-men, Brave Wolf and Two Moon, of my Cheyenne scouts, to ride on ahead and renew briefly, kindly, and firmly my terms, and bring Little Wolf out to meet me as I approached the village with my command."[23]

In delivering Clark's message, the scout Brave Wolf told Little Wolf: "I love the soldiers at [Fort] Keogh. . . . If you will not listen you will force me to fight my own people, for you are my kinfolk." Soon afterward Little Wolf rode forward to tell Clark that he would accept the terms presented. As Clark recounted, "he was glad to meet me again." The lieutenant then advanced his command within three hundred feet of the Northern Cheyenne camp, which he found harbored "in a natural fortress," which "they had strengthened . . . by breastworks of stone and dirt."[24]

Clark ordered his troops to surround the Northern Cheyenne camp, "both for their protection and to attack in case there should be any necessity for such a measure."[25] As he related,

> After about an hour, to allow the excitement to wear away and give my Cheyenne scouts time to talk the matter over with them, I went over to the camp, taking off my arms, to show them that I had confidence in them, and briefly told them in council what they must do, as far as I was concerned. That I had told my scouts to give them no lies, and I hoped they had done so, as I told them; that the guns and ponies must be given up. This was the price of peace, and they must pay it. I wanted the guns then, and would take the ponies when we reached Keogh; that I was truly and heartily glad we had arranged this matter without loss of life on either side; they had ears and sense; they must listen and use their reason; there were many troops and Indian scouts in the country, and I thought they were wise to surrender.[26]

In response, Little Wolf emphasized to Clark the strife that his people had endured over the past several years since they had seen each other at Red Cloud Agency. "We have been south [in Indian Territory], and have suffered a great deal down there," Little Wolf observed, explaining: "Many have died of diseases which we have no name for. Our hearts looked and longed for this country where we were born. There are only a few of us left, and we only wanted a little ground, where we could live." He explained how they left Indian Territory. "The troops followed us. I rode out and told the troops we did not want to fight; we only wanted to go north, and if they would let us alone we would kill no one. The only reply we got was a volley. After that we had to fight our way. . . . My brother, Dull Knife, took one-half of the band and surrendered near Camp Robinson. . . . They gave up their guns, and then the whites killed them all." Regarding his present status, Little Wolf explained: "I am out on the prairie, and need my guns here. When I get to Keogh I will give you the guns and ponies, but I cannot give up the guns now. You are the only one who has offered to talk before fighting, and it looks as though the wind, which has made our hearts flutter for so long, would now go down. I am very glad we did not fight, and that none of my people or yours are killed."[27]

Just when and where Little Wolf had learned of the disaster that befell Dull Knife's followers is unknown, but his people conceivably heard of it within days of the January breakout, probably from Lakotas that they encountered in the Nebraska Sand Hills or after crossing into Montana Territory and communicating with Lieutenant Clark's scouts and interpreters. Whatever the source, the Sweet Medicine Chief knew enough after submitting to Clark to reference the events in his subsequent discussions with government authorities. This tragic knowledge certainly clouded the result.

Understandably, Little Wolf's people remained fearful and suspicious and at first were not inclined to turn over their weapons. Clark held firm "as long as I deemed judicious," but agreed to let the Indians keep their weapons until they reached the place where he had left his wagons. With their concurrence, the assemblage moved out together, camping after only a short distance. Clark distributed them rations while an accompanying doctor treated their sick and wounded. By the time they reached the wagons at Powder River on March 31, "a great deal of confidence had been restored and good feeling nearly established," Clark observed. Altogether, the group with Little Wolf totaled thirty-three men and eighty-one women and children, together with three hundred ponies.[28] At Powder River, the lieutenant reported, the Northern Cheyennes turned over the following firearms:

> 4 Springfield carbines, caliber 45; 3 Springfield rifles, caliber 50; 4 Sharp's carbines, caliber 50 [1 Sharp's carbine, ca. 50]; 4 Sharp's rifles, caliber 45; 1 muzzle-loading rifle; 3 Winchester-Henry repeating carbines, caliber 45; 3 Colt's revolvers, caliber 45; 2 Smith & Wesson revolvers, caliber 45; 5 Colt's revolvers, caliber 44 and 31; and 1 Remington revolver.[29]

On Tuesday, April 1, as he approached Fort Keogh, Clark halted his command and gathered the Indians together, telling them he must search again for weapons. "I had no option in the matter," he told Little Wolf's people. "I must not only satisfy myself, but I must take such measures as would satisfy those who issued the orders in regard to the terms through which they secured peace." When the Cheyennes responded that they had given up all their guns, Clark said, "I asked them if they could all arise, throw back their blankets, and show me that none of them had arms on their persons; they said they could, and did." Clark's scouts searched and affirmed that the Cheyennes' bundles contained no additional arms. The column gained the post at 11 A.M., where Little Wolf yielded his people. As previously arranged, the Indians relinquished 250 ponies, and the men later agreed to serve as army scouts.[30]

Clark had succeeded under difficult circumstances and without major incident. During his effort to find Little Wolf and usher him into Fort Keogh, he said that temperatures had plunged to 33 degrees below zero. It snowed and rained, according to Clark, and "the ice has gone out of the streams, leaving them swollen, difficult and dangerous to ford." Despite such intemperate conditions, Clark lost none of his men; nor were any Cheyennes killed or wounded.[31] Major George Gibson, Fifth Infantry, duty stationed at Fort Keogh, in transmitting Clark's report concluded that "it is particularly gratifying . . . , in view of the difficulty which has attended in some cases the management of captive Cheyenne Indians, that this band was recaptured without firing a shot."[32]

Lieutenant Colonel Whistler at Fort Keogh received Lieutenant Clark's final report, which included his remarkably enlightened view of the Northern Cheyennes' recent plight and of their current status:

> I know . . . "Little Wolf," who . . . was an enlisted scout under my command at Red Cloud [Agency], particularly well. No fears need be entertained of treachery or an attempt to escape. . . . They want peace, rest and a home somewhere in this country, where they were born and reared. The longing and yearning, born of homesickness, killed many of them when [in the] south. Should they be ordered back there they may seek escape by throwing themselves against the bullets and bayonets of the soldier, or by [other] suicide; if allowed to remain they would be among our strongest and bravest allies. . . . Among the forces which caused them to surrender, the strongest was the hope in their hearts that they would have a home in this country.

Clark added that he hoped that Whistler "will allow me to distribute [the captured] ponies to my scouts and command. Without the hearty assistance of the former I would have been helpless, and though I have made no positive promises, yet they expect this extra reward, and good effect will be lost if they do not get it."[33]

Whistler approved the recommendation and General Terry concurred, urging that "a limited number" of ponies be retained for Clark's scouts. General Sheridan, however, annulled the matter altogether, responding, "I doubt the propriety of rewarding Indian scouts by distributing to them captured ponies. It leads to looseness, [and] besides, some of these animals may have been stolen."[34]

In the immediate aftermath of Little Wolf's surrender, a cannon boomed at Fort Keogh while the Fifth Infantry regimental band regaled troops and Indians with "Hail to the Chief." A host of citizens and their children thronged around Clark. It "was the true soldier's triumph," affirmed the *Minneapolis Pioneer Press*, "and yet he hadn't killed anybody."[35] General Terry commended the lieutenant for his "energy, skill, perseverance and excellent judgment while commanding troops in the country of the Yellowstone, Powder, and Little Missouri rivers," where he "performed despite adverse circumstances of arctic weather, broken and inhospitable ground and swollen streams."[36]

Peace was not entirely at hand on the high plains, however, at least not yet. Within days of Little Wolf's surrender and the celebrations attending it at Fort Keogh, the turmoil that yet festered among the chief's followers exploded anew with an attack on two soldiers forty-five miles from the fort. The five Indian culprits included Black Coyote, who had earlier been involved with the murder of two Northern Cheyennes and banished along with eight colluding tribesmen from Little Wolf's camp. Black Coyote and his cohorts surprised Dennis Kennedy, an Irish immigrant and signal sergeant, and Second Cavalry private Leo Baader, an enlistee from Germany, in an ambush along Mizpah Creek. The attackers killed Baader in an initial volley and wounded Kennedy as he mounted his horse. Kennedy fled to the brush to hide. Returning to the scene later, the Indians took the soldiers' mounts, scalped Baader's corpse, and took the private's revolver but never located Kennedy.[37] Next day, a party passing through from Deadwood found the wounded sergeant and took him to Fort Keogh.

On learning of the attack and murder, still within days following Little Wolf's surrender, Sergeant Thomas B. Glover, Company B, Second Cavalry, with a detachment of ten soldiers and three scouts went in pursuit of Black Coyote's party. Glover and his men apprehended the Indians on April 10 and took them to Fort Keogh, for which service Glover subsequently received a Medal of Honor.[38] Finally convicted in civilian court and awaiting death, Black Coyote and two others precipitately hanged themselves in the Custer County jail.[39] For his part, Little Wolf had no sympathy for Black Coyote and his companions. "Your laws punish such crimes," he told the whites. "Hang them or imprison them for life. I never want to see their faces again." The chief added: "They knew I had made peace with you, and they killed your soldiers." He thought it would be a good thing if they were sent to Dry Tortugas, Florida, or some other place of confinement.[40]

Those Northern Cheyennes who had opted against following Little Wolf and Dull Knife north in September 1878, in the meantime, toughed out their coexistence with the Southern Cheyennes in the Indian Territory. Some, including Wild Hog and others of Dull Knife's followers who had been forcibly returned in 1879, were eventually permitted to join their families and relatives at Pine Ridge in southwestern Dakota Territory. Despite fleeting notions to transfer Little Wolf's people to the Bannock and Shoshoni agency in Wyoming,[41] they were at last permitted to remain in Montana, a status denied Dull Knife's followers in the years after their breakout from Fort Robinson.

The fate of still other Northern Cheyennes also remained undetermined. As noted, troops had escorted the followers of Little Chief south to Fort Reno in September 1878.[42] They had departed from Fort Abraham Lincoln, Dakota Territory, and coincidentally reached Sidney Barracks on September 16, where Little Chief and his people were held as precaution as the northbound Dull Knife and Little Wolf warriors raided homesteads in northwestern Kansas. Little Chief had become a prominent peace advocate and was one of several Cheyenne leaders who, like Two Moon, had deliberated favorably with Colonel Nelson A. Miles at the Tongue River Cantonment early in 1877, as the Great Sioux War concluded. Whereas Two Moon and others had continued as scouts for Miles in operations against the Sioux and Nez Percés and were thereby permitted to remain along the Yellowstone with their families, Little Chief's people had been directed to Fort Lincoln, Dakota Territory, along the Missouri River. At General Sheridan's bidding, they had then proceeded to the Indian Territory.

Little Chief's 221 people reached Fort Reno in early December 1878, joining more than 640 Northern Cheyennes who had remained there despite the Dull Knife and Little Wolf exodus.[43] Within weeks of their own disarmament and rationing, however, most of them also wanted to return north, largely because of their aversion for the Southern Cheyennes. Little Chief at last appealed his request to leave directly to Secretary Schurz in 1879. Only in 1881 and 1883, however, did the government permit his people, as well as those followers of Dull Knife and Little Wolf still remaining in the Indian Territory who so desired, to join those Northern Cheyennes now living on the Pine Ridge Reservation in Dakota Territory. On November 20, 1881, some 235 passed through Fort Robinson en route north with Little Chief and escorted by a unit of Fifth Cavalrymen. "Fifty of them are men, the balance are women and children, not counting their dogs, which seem to be almost as numerous as their children," commented an observer. They remained there for nearly a decade. In 1891, following the Ghost Dance agitation and the resultant Wounded Knee slaughter of Chief Big Foot's Lakotas, those Northern Cheyennes remaining on the Pine Ridge Reservation who were still desirous of doing so were at last permitted to return to their beloved Montana homes. Seven years earlier, in late November 1884, the Northern Cheyenne Reservation had been established by executive order. Initially the reserve encompassed more than 317,000 acres—some 580 square miles in what was then southeastern Montana Territory.[44]

Many of the Northern Cheyennes who returned to Montana in 1891 had been Dull Knife's followers who had survived the breakout from Fort Robinson and the fighting that followed. Over time the memory of the heartrending tragedy in Nebraska, coupled with more liberal consideration of the Indians by politicians as well as the army hierarchy, yielded a more favorable climate to promote a common home for the Northern Cheyenne people. Motivated by a coming together of the breakout survivors with relatives newly arrived with Little Chief from Darlington, most of them chose to return to Montana after Wounded Knee, which had surely evoked memories among them of their own calamity at Fort Robinson. Going home at last, after so long, nonetheless offered welcome respite and promise. At the urging of the War Department, President Benjamin Harrison directed the resettlement of 281 Northern Cheyennes from Pine Ridge to the Tongue River Reservation. Those people who had cultivated marriages and families among the Sioux and chose to stay remained at Pine Ridge.[45]

During the closing years of the nineteenth century and the early decades of the twentieth, the Northern Cheyennes in Montana grappled with their recent circumstances while trying to adhere to the dictates of their agents and their own hearts. Even there, however, the people's lives, fraught with anxieties fostered by such new issues as encroachment by white settlers (including squatters), mounting apprehensions over property rights, reservation expansion, education, inept agents, and eventually allotment in severalty, remained difficult and tenuous. Uncertain husbandry and economic agendas, cultural change, issues of kinship, and rising social and economic insecurity continued to plague the people well into the twentieth century. But they were at last together in their northern home.[46]

13

Reflections

In the first days after the breakout, during an interview with the *Omaha Herald* (circulated among Associated Press members), General Crook was asked if the Northern Cheyennes could have been returned to the Indian Territory after Major Carlton's men had captured them the previous October. He answered: "I think they would have gone back two months ago without any trouble. They then *expected* to be taken back." By January, he said, "they had been allowed to remain at the camp so long that they had about made up their minds that they were to be allowed to stay and [then] were opposed to returning." By the time of the breakout, Crook stated adamantly if excessively, "there was not military force enough in this department to have taken them back alive."[1]

Elsewhere, however, and perhaps in retrospect, Crook admitted, "I am satisfied they never would have surrendered [in late October 1878] had they not thought that they would have been permitted to remain north. They adhered so firmly to their statements that it was impossible *not* to believe that there must have been some good grounds for their leaving the Indian Territory." Crook added that in his nearly three decades of experience with Indians, "I have never known a band of Indians to make peace with our government and then . . . leave their reservation, without some ground of complaint."[2]

In consequence, Crook told the reporter that all of the recent history between the troops and the Northern Cheyennes in January 1879 could have been mitigated, perhaps avoided altogether, had matters been dealt with promptly and more rationally. While he was stating his measured opinion, such a course would assuredly have compounded the Indians' dilemma in the south. Yet repeated delays, coupled with seeming bureaucratic indifference, neglect, and overall inaction—to say nothing of poor decision-making and stifled communication on several levels respecting the prisoners and their welfare—contributed to the festering reality of what had happened at Fort Robinson, as Crook and other federal officials must have comprehended. To a fair degree, General Sheridan had been correct in leveling blame at his brigadier in Omaha. Add to this a pervasive ingrained institutional prejudice of the U.S. Army in its relationships with the tribes, notably in its campaigns from the 1850s forward, which thirty years later were still impacting the long-maligned Cheyennes. That mind-set was present at Fort Robinson too.

Most eastern tabloids, accustomed to reporting recent Indian troubles, used pejorative terms in describing what had happened at Antelope Creek. The phrases "repetition of an oft-told tale" and "this disgraceful and cruel affair" are representative of the editorial tone of such publications as *Frank Leslie's Illustrated Weekly*.[3] For an opposing view, General Sherman, well known for his altogether uncompromising attitude toward Indians, called Dull Knife's followers "insubordinate," "cunning," and "treacherous" people who had "attempted to escape from the custody of our troops and used violence to carry on their rebellious act." Sherman's comments in the immediate aftermath of the breakout expressed his sentiment that "the measures enforced were . . . precisely what the exigencies of the occasion demanded."[4] It was a time-worn response that Sherman was expected to make in his nominal role but doubtless also reflected his true instinctive reaction.

Regarding the killing of women and children during the breakout and successive engagements, which had aroused public opinion in the Indians' favor, Crook thought that most had been killed accidentally and that the soldiers "displayed great gallantry in endeavoring to protect them. [At Fort Robinson] an effort was made to remove the children and care for them when it was decided to starve or freeze the Cheyennes into submission." He believed that those women who detached themselves from the main body "were well cared for. . . . [But] when they had determined to die together rather than be removed[,] they took the chances of war in a hand-to-hand fight."[5]

Crook personally laid blame on Wessells, according to the *New York Herald*, for having been "outwitted" by the Northern Cheyennes. The finding of a few guns during their initial incarceration had been only a ploy—"an Indian artifice to hide their magazine . . . under the floor of their barracks. Had they concealed them all[,] the floor might have been taken up and the magazine discovered, but the visible arms warded off suspicion and prevented further search." The guns, allegedly derived from visiting Lakota friends, made the situation worse. "Of course," said the *Herald*, "they had to be shot down after they broke forth, but the necessity resulted from an unpardonable want of shrewdness and vigilance." The root cause of the Fort Robinson breakout, the paper contended, lay with faulty rationing of the people as well as their overall condition while in the south. Proper care and feeding on their Indian Territory reservation could likely have assuaged their needs and avoided the circumstances that compelled their leaving altogether. Their cruel treatment by Wessells in cutting off their food and water only exacerbated their situation.[6]

The *New York Herald*, of all the national newspapers, provided the most direct coverage and liberal editorial views generally sympathetic to the Northern Cheyennes, ultimately labeling the totality of events "an unpardonable blunder."[7] The *Herald* had the benefit of the most contemporary and detailed accounts of what had happened thanks to the on-site presence of James R. O'Beirne. An Indian Department employee from New Red Cloud Agency and the *Herald*'s reporter on the scene, O'Beirne relayed his detailed reports by telegraph almost every day. Based upon his dispatches, the editorial staff in New York generally reflected an opinion sympathetic to the Cheyennes in most of its accounting, from the breakout itself on the night of January 9 to the final bloodletting at Antelope Creek. O'Beirne apparently transcribed most of his reports in the trader's quarters at the post, where he resided. The exception seems to have been a solitary venture with the troops up Hat Creek Road, where he assembled the information gleaned from participants and witnesses of the engagements in preparing his dispatches. He then telegraphed these from the fort to the paper's New York office.

Together with pertinent data collected from other sources by the *Herald* staff in New York, O'Beirne's reports formed the basis for the paper's news and editorial coverage. The *Herald*'s stance, likely echoing its man on the scene, was sharply manifested on January 17, when the newspaper asserted that the killing of Indian men, women, and children "may not have been blamable under the circumstances, but it was an unpardonable blunder which opened the way for the existence of such a state of circumstances." The tragedy was compelling in its touching sadness, such as the reports describing "the child who had formed a doll of a bloody blanket and was swaying her little body back and forth, as in an attempt to lull this doll to sleep" or the "death-defying courage" of "resolute braves in their desperate attempt to regain their liberty."[8]

The *New York Times* even gave editorial voice to the charge that the breakout was foreseen and allowed by the army. Conceivably based on O'Beirne's reports in the *Herald*, that paper theorized that the army may have preplanned the event. It is "a belief among some that not only was the attempt to escape foreseen, but was actually permitted," noted the *Times*. "It was asked last night in camp by critics reviewing the occurrence, whether it was not intended to allow the Cheyennes to escape. . . . Strange coincidences . . . point that way, and with the apparently deliberate opportunity afforded to the Indians, [it] could be easily distorted to give plausibility to the revolting theory." The *Times* report continued: "Beyond the implied culpability in not securely guarding against the escape of the Cheyennes[,] the most serious charge is that of their possession of serviceable arms after it had been taken for granted that they had been thoroughly disarmed after their surrender." The *Times* writer intimated that Captain Johnson had failed to search the Indians carefully immediately after their surrender on Chadron Creek and that their delivery of only a few arms had "thrown Johnson . . . off his guard, and he failed to [thoroughly] search them. When they [at last] surrendered to Capt. Johnson they had numerous bundles in which their spare 'traps' were tied up, and it is the belief of the soldiers who assisted in their capture, and who escorted them from Chadron [Creek] to [Camp] Robinson, that the arms and ammunition were concealed in these bundles."[9]

Whatever the truth in the *New York Times* critic's speculation, the Indians had been searched two more times after entering the barrack, as other sources maintained. Nonetheless, the *Times* writer argued that "it was not only a blunder on the part of Capt. Johnson not to make a thorough search for arms at the time of the capture, but it was as great a blunder on the part of Major Carlton, who was in command at Robinson when the Indians were received there, in not searching them before placing them under guard."[10]

What the *New York Times* correspondent appeared to overlook, however, was the widespread belief that the Cheyennes had hidden weapons in the barrack by disassembling them and hiding the pieces. As Lieutenant Schuyler suggestively maintained, based on an exchange with Wild Hog, despite all precautions and searches, arms could indeed have been disassembled and "secreted in unsuspected places. . . . It is thought that the squaws, who through delicacy were not searched, had them concealed. From their peculiar make [physical attributes?] it would be quite feasible. They may [thus] have taken them [the gun parts] into the barracks unnoticed, after which they were placed under the floor. From all these facts an idea can be formed as to where the responsibility rests."[11]

A compelling component of the arms-hidden-in-barrack question suggested that visiting Oglala relatives of the Northern Cheyennes had spirited guns to the prisoners. One wide-ranging rumor held that a Cheyenne wife of trader John W. Dear commiserated with the internees and conveyed supplies to them in her husband's absence, perhaps including arms. The suspicion was never verified, however. During the relatively halcyon period of their earlier captivity in November and December, Northern Cheyenne women prisoners were said to have been allowed to roam relatively freely and converse with Dear's wives, who gave them arms to sneak into the barrack. "To say the least," wrote O'Beirne, "there was great indulgence, if not laxity, of restraint, shown in the treatment of the Cheyennes from the time of their capture."[12]

The question of hidden guns persisted but was never fully resolved. The *Herald* charged editorially that officers at the post either failed to disarm the people properly at the outset or negligently allowed weapons to be smuggled in. Thus "the blame must be at the doors of the military officers at Fort Robinson."[13] It was alleged that years after his retirement from the army Wessells expressed a personal view that the Northern Cheyennes had indeed been armed at the time of the breakout. When he took command at Fort Robinson in December 1878, he was said to have later recalled, "I assumed that when the Indians were captured [in late October] they had been disarmed, but it was not so. They had hidden their weapons, or some of them."[14]

Others questioned how unprepared the army was to prevent a breakout. Why had bars not been added to the barrack windows and more sentinel guards not been put on duty to retard the Indians' ability to escape?

Still another question leveled at Fort Robinson's leadership centered on why the Northern Cheyennes were not separated (men in one group and women and children in another) during their detention at the post. Such alignment, it was argued, would have averted the breakout, because the men would not have considered abandoning their families by doing so. One critic ludicrously suggested that too many soldiers went afield in pursuit of the fleeing Indians, thus providing "too much surface for the marksmanship capacity of a dozen or so of 'dead shots,' such as the Cheyennes." The army was also criticized for a lack of artillery at the outset of the breakout, which presumably might have been directed against the Indians' flight path from the barrack. Its absence was thus "sadly paid for in the loss of good men."[15]

An even broader and potentially more consequential critique regarding the breakout had to do with the response and alacrity of the Fort Robinson soldiers. It included the notion that the soldiers in the adjacent barracks had not been properly advised to remain "in readiness." Many if not most were retired in their bunks and ill prepared to respond more quickly to the breakout, especially to support the few guards stationed around the Northern Cheyennes' barrack. Furthermore, no officers were immediately present: the men, initially at least, "acted for the time being on their own responsibility." The soldiers' "wild shooting" was criticized. Much was made, too, of Little Finger Nail's targeting and shooting of Private Schmidt then bounding out and capturing his rifle and ammunition belt as he fled into the night. Even when the officers finally appeared to take charge, "orders and counter orders" flew about. Successive troop commands pressed the pursuit until 4:30 A.M., when Wessells at last returned to the post. "The escaped Indians," observed the *New York Herald*, "were thus allowed to pursue their way."[16]

Even in that enterprise, the soldiers' efforts fell short, it was said. By their returning to the post, they failed to press the pursuit immediately. Instead, they should have endeavored to encircle an anticipated zone to head off the Indians. That would likely have been an impossible task in the emergency of the moment, and no one seemed to consider it then or subsequently. When the troops positioned themselves to thwart the escaped Indians on January 12, they had to await the arrival of their artillery. By the time the bombardment could be undertaken the next day, the Indians had once more fled to relative safety. Lieutenant Schuyler, as Crook's on-site representative, could draw no firm conclusions about blame, even as the pursuit proceeded. If the troops had indeed charged at once into the barrack prison (which probably could not have happened given the rapidly unfolding events) he suspected that many more lives would have been lost.[17]

As the pursuit of the escapees continued over ensuing days, the specter of the captured, wounded, anguished, and traumatized noncombatants, all bloodied and lying in the wrecked barrack room from which they had fled, played in the eastern press. As a conscientious Indian Department employee, O'Beirne described their plight in heartfelt terms:

> In spite of their dusky complexion squaws are none the less women, and the sad variety of woe exhibited in that comfortless room proves that in all races woman is true to her own nature and that the varnish of civilization is no necessary accompaniment of feminine sensibilities. The grey-haired old squaw who lay in the agonies of death pierced with half a dozen bullets would have been an affecting spectacle, even if she had lain there alone in the throes of dissolution. But she served as the dark background of more pathetic scenes. The younger and orphaned squaws, some of them mere children, who displayed the native gentleness of their sex in trying to soothe one another, will unlock the deepest fountains of sympathy in the hearts of such of their civilized sisters as may read this description. . . . The time has come for a thorough reconstruction of our Indian policy. . . . The Modoc war, the Nez Perces war, the horrible Custer massacre, and now this bloody work at Fort Robinson are startling reminders, and the time has come when they must not longer be neglected.[18]

Furthermore, as one reader protested to the *Herald*, the commissioner's earlier proposal to send Northern Cheyenne men to Florida and their women back to Darlington seemed to compound the government's heartlessness:

> The inhumanity of this . . . proposition can only be realized by those who know something of the treatment of those Indians taken south in 1873 [*sic*: 1875]. It means death—slow, but certain. Then

> the vindictive spirit that could urge this request—the sending of all male adults to a lingering torture because a few bad members of their tribe had committed murder while escaping from a climate which was killing their wives and children, and from an agency where they were suffering from hunger and privation—is a sad commentary upon the justice of the Indian Department and the nation which tolerates it.[19]

Beyond the direct concerns registered over the Fort Robinson breakout, the fate of the Northern Cheyennes had aroused other national sentiments. In addition to humanitarian concerns, the *Herald* noted the irony of post–Civil War American society striving to do much for the freed slaves and so little for Indian peoples. "While we are affecting so much interest in the welfare of the negro [*sic*] race[,] it is a pity that we cannot do something for the substantial good of the Indians instead of shooting them down like wild beasts for manifesting the instincts which lie at the foundation of human liberty," read one *Herald* report. The commentary may have been filtered through editors in New York, but the author was most likely O'Beirne, whose own involvement and background—Irish, immigrant, Republican, abolitionist, soldier, and Bureau of Indian Affairs employee—undoubtedly shaped the response. Whatever their ultimate source, the remarks made a valid and timely assertion:

> It may be that [the Cheyennes'] slaughter and extermination are marked out for them by destiny; but considering that they are the original possessors of the soil and that we are intruders on their long occupation, it would be just and humane to give this truly heroic race a chance for its life. . . . As yet the national conscience has not been awakened respecting the Indians as it has toward the negroes. It is time to put an end to these sickening tales of slaughter which form the staple of our Indian history, and to substitute wise, firm, comprehensive, forecasting and paternal policy for the race which we are driving out of their original possessions and are provoking to desperate resistance by our blundering management.[20]

However discerning these assertions were, they went unheeded. Over the next decade and beyond, including the horrific massacre of Lakota

Sioux at Wounded Knee Creek on the Pine Ridge Reservation in 1890, many Northern Cheyennes remained indirect victims, considering they had settled there contentedly with their Lakota or Northern Cheyenne spouses and offspring.[21] Regardless, in the wake of Fort Robinson some observers forecast presciently that "bloodshed and incendiarism will reign unrestrained as the country fills up with white settlement unless our government 'takes time by the forelock' and settles the Indian question effectually within the ensuing five or ten years."[22]

The repeated Northern Cheyenne complaints—from their abrupt removal to the Indian Territory in 1877 and their poor treatment there, to their consequential decision to leave with Dull Knife and Little Wolf after a year of strife, to the concluding butchery that they experienced at Fort Robinson—ultimately came under the purview of broad congressional inquiry in 1879 and 1880.[23] While some attention was given to what directly caused the Fort Robinson breakout, most testimony fixated on matters affecting the Cheyennes after their arrival on the Cheyenne and Arapaho Reservation at Fort Reno. The food shortages, particularly of beef and flour, as well as the resulting hunger and starvation and pervasive sicknesses and other chronic ailments driven by the regional climate that devastated and killed many drew special notice. Critics complained that congressional appropriations for maintaining Cheyennes in the Indian Territory were even less than those dedicated *before* the Northern Cheyennes arrived and that all the affected people suffered in consequence. "Thus, while the population was increased, the gross appropriation for its support was reduced." Further, a regular appropriation of several thousand dollars expressly for those people while living in the north was denied them altogether following their transfer south rather than being used to improve their rations.[24] When Commissioner of Indian Affairs Hayt argued in his 1879 annual report that the Northern Cheyennes were not forced by starvation to head north the previous year, he was found to be untruthful: "the Indians were actually, as they had claimed, 'starving.' 'We were *always* hungry; we *never* had enough,'" complained one chief. Nor did the people receive sufficient and proper clothing in accord with treaty stipulations.[25]

Conclusive proof emerged to buttress the Indians' grievances that during their stay in the Indian Territory they had not been allocated their correct proportions of food staples. According to one report, the confirmation "in connection with the fact that for some weeks their scant [individual] rations were still further decreased by a half pound per diem of flour, . . . [is] not only sufficient evidence that the Northern Cheyennes did not receive rations to the amount to which they were entitled under the [1868] treaty, but sustain[s] the charge that they were [indeed] being starved."[26]

Congress and the army both received editorial criticism and were censured for their perceived shortcomings regarding the tragedy. While blaming Congress, the *Herald*, whose coverage of the Fort Robinson events superseded that of all other newspapers, laid much blame on the army, an institution that it believed had suffered various professional deficiencies since the Civil War. "The Cheyenne business, so far as these beggarly few are concerned, is at an end," it opined, "and it is a startling reflection to consider how many men, how much money, it has cost the government, and all through improvident or weak military management." The editorial (probably inspired if not generated by O'Beirne) fairly pilloried the officer cadre, stating that "there is a class among them . . . who have foisted themselves into important places in the ranks, who failed at the close of the rebellion to follow the example of thousands who had soldierly ability, but went into the ranks of private life to sustain themselves. The exceptions clung to the army, because [they were] powerless to sustain themselves elsewhere. The army now suffers because of inefficiency, as we have seen in cases connected with the slaughtered Cheyennes."[27]

The *Herald* editorial concluded bitterly that the pervasive faults of the military rested in large measure with a "tinkering" Congress and suggested that formal inquiry into the Cheyenne breakout would show that "our army is not a fighting machine, but a resort for the shiftless and those who dodge the other stern demands of life. Let the conduct of the late military campaign be examined and our recent contemptible and puerile contribution to it be also included, and it will be shown what a monstrous fraud the government is now paying millions of dollars for, on which it cannot rely for defence in the hour of need."[28] Largely omitted in the postbreakout conversation that circulated in the press was the imbalance evident in the army's failure to hold Little Wolf's people to the same standards of accountability that it had imposed upon those of Dull Knife. The vicissitudes of fortune apparently enabled Little Wolf to succeed in eluding the troops before they reached their Montana homeland even as Dull Knife's followers, who surrendered, ultimately bore the brunt of the army's response.

What happened to the Northern Cheyennes in 1878 and 1879 appeared symbiotic with the reservation system affecting the tribes as a whole. Even as the "cleanup" proceeded at Fort Robinson, rumblings from eastern Nebraska signaled the return home of Poncas who—much like the Cheyennes—had been coerced to go to the Indian Territory and—like the Cheyennes—rejected their tenure there. Although the Poncas' arrival was eventually resolved peacefully, still later in 1879 the Ute tribe of Colorado offered further systemic disruption. It climaxed in more fighting and death for the Utes and government soldiers, some of whom had been involved earlier in the year with the Northern Cheyennes. Together, these events denoted the continued resistance of the tribes in response to intolerable government demands and the dysfunctional vagaries of reservation policy.[29] While broadly related to those immediate misfortunes, the Fort Robinson breakout and its collateral actions—given their place, players, and results—were linked to earlier actions at Powder River, Rosebud, and Little Bighorn and can also fittingly be deemed a lingering and sad vestige of the Great Sioux War.

Memories of the Northern Cheyenne breakout from Fort Robinson, while never forgotten, ebbed significantly in the tribe's daily consciousness as the years passed into decades, notably by the early twentieth century. Area newspaper articles sometimes called attention to the event, often referencing the soldiers killed in early 1879, "whose graves now form a long row in the little post cemetery" located on the north (west) side of White River and just south of Soldier Creek.[30]

Following the fort's deactivation in 1948, the bodies of those dead with all the other military burials were removed and consigned to orderly rows in Fort McPherson National Cemetery near Maxwell, Nebraska. The fate of the Northern Cheyenne burials in the large pit above the rude bridge and near the post sawmill southwest of the fort on the southeast side of White River in January 1879, however, remained unclear.[31] Quite properly, it would become a point of contention decades later.

As part of the army's formal postaction inquiry into the Fort Robinson breakout, the number of Northern Cheyenne people who were killed outright or died of wounds received in the various actions stood at 39 men and 22 women and children. These, however, were the "accessible" dead. Lieutenant Cummings testified that "on the 12th [of January] I had all the dead Cheyennes *who were accessible*, buried, 14 men, 9 women, 4 children."[32] Cummings was not including the Indian fatalities from Antelope Creek, who were buried separately at that site on January 23. The word "accessible" implies that the remains of some Northern Cheyennes killed on the night of January 9 and in subsequent actions along Hat Creek Road and preceding Antelope Creek were deemed beyond retrieval. Nor did the number include those who may have died of exposure and starvation or were otherwise killed while hiding from discovery in the rough country around Fort Robinson and were presumably never found.

The burial area adjoining Fort Robinson originally harboring the remains of the Northern Cheyennes killed in the breakout apparently experienced aberrant and unwarranted attention. Almost immediately, according to one report, a cowboy cook working in the area somehow desecrated at least two of the remains, reportedly sending the skulls to his family in New Jersey.[33] Scientific inquiry of the period added to the mystery of the Indian dead too. Three years after the breakout, the ethnologist Alice C. Fletcher, later president of the American Folklore Society, inquired of her mentor, Professor Frederic Ward Putnam, curator of the Peabody Museum of Archaeology and Ethnology at Harvard University, about collecting Native American research specimens. The methodology was endemic to emergent anthropology and archeology at the time. Fletcher, then living and studying on the Omaha reservation in northeastern Nebraska, asked about locating various specimens and the likelihood of obtaining skeletal examples of Native American tribes in the area. At one point she told Putnam of a man named Mr. Miles, who could obtain "several Cheyenne skulls & skeletons from [the] Fort Robinson vicinity." However ethically and morally reprehensible, such period inquiries signified common regional knowledge of the whereabouts of at least some of the Northern Cheyenne dead as well as specific professional interest in those interred there.[34]

In spite of such harrowing probes, the site of the Northern Cheyenne mass burial near the old sawmill seems to have escaped such scientific notice over the years. As late as April 1904 it appeared, at least outwardly, to have remained undisturbed, according to area newspaper references,[35] although the place of the mass Northern Cheyenne burial at Fort Robinson perhaps may never have been formally marked.[36]

However undisturbed by human intrusion the site remained, it also went unattended and thus did not escape the dynamism of mother nature. At some point during the intervening decades, natural erosion gradually obscured the saw pit near the sawmill, which had burned in 1883. The historically significant confluence of Soldier Creek with White River endured repeated flooding during the early decades of the twentieth century, while threatening the post cemetery and surrounding ground fronting the river on both sides, apparently including the burial site. Coupled with recurring floods and erosion, heavy equipment used to adjust the active channels of White River and Soldier Creek to impede such physical degradation may have helped destroy the area harboring the grave and its contents. If it is indeed at all intact in the area across White River from the old military cemetery, it plausibly lies beneath heavy layers of accumulated sediment that conceivably may have secured and preserved some of the remains.[37]

In the 1960s a coterie of Northern Cheyennes from Montana, including tribal elder John Stands In Timber, as well as a consortium of local avocational historians keenly absorbed in the search, endeavored to find the location of the former sawmill and, by inference, the resting place of those who were buried nearby. If the site could be discovered, they hoped that it could be permanently marked with an appropriate monument. As late as the 1990s the Mari Sandoz Heritage Society at nearby Chadron State College joined with the Nebraska State Historical Society in an apparently fruitless endeavor to locate the burial site.[38]

Still other efforts continued into the 1990s, but with minimal success. Using technological advances, archeologists employed remote-sensing devices in the presumed area of the sawmill where the Indian remains were known to have been interred, but identified just a few "buried anomalies." In 2002, based on conclusions of his cultural resources staff about the feasibility of locating the resource, Nebraska State Historical Society director Lawrence Sommer concluded: "The 1991 flood deposited some 6–8 feet of silt on the location. In combination with several possible similar floods in the past[,] the 1879 land surface has been buried under an unknown depth of overburden. The water table has also been raised and probing has proved impossible under the current conditions and with the available equipment."[39] The remains of those victims seem to rest only in eternity.

By contrast, those people interred by troops in the Indians' blowout defensive position the day after the engagement of January 22, 1879, at

Antelope Creek experienced a different fate. After the burial there of twenty-six Northern Cheyenne dead, including three wounded who had died on January 23, the grave remained largely undisturbed following the soldiers' retirement from the field. The peaceful interment lasted only about a year, however. During the spring of 1880, in compliance with a program wherein the U.S. Army sought human remains from the scenes of recent Indian combat with which to evaluate the proficiency of army service weapons, Fort Laramie's post surgeon responded to a request from the Army Medical Museum in Washington, D.C., to collect Indian skulls "at the site[s] of Indian hostilities between Fort Laramie and Red Cloud Agency." Dr. Carlos Carvallo requested that Private Charles Ruby, Company D, Fourth Infantry, be dispatched with two men and a wagon "to Ames Ranche [*sic*], about 113 miles distance [and] between Hat Creek and Red Cloud Agency to collect the Indian skulls." As Dr. Carvallo explained, "This is an opportunity which the Commanding Officer [Colonel Wesley Merritt] has of rendering a valuable contribution to the Army Medical Museum and of furnishing data for the development of anthropology, and thereby contributing to the promotion of science."[40]

Merritt denied Carvallo's request. Private Ruby "does not know exactly where the skulls are and it is not practicable to furnish the detail asked for." Undaunted, the surgeon then requested an ambulance and driver for himself to find and retrieve the skulls, along with notice that he would be gone five days in the effort. Merritt thereupon endorsed the request.[41] An excerpt in Fort Laramie's medical history provided the following data regarding Carvallo's grisly mission:

> Detached service. Asst Surgeon Carlos Carvallo, U.S. Army, pursuant to S.O. No. 169, c.s. [current series] Post Headqrs, went Sept. 23d to Antelope Creek, Wyo.[,] 80 miles north of Fort Laramie, to seek the Indian Skulls of the Cheyennes which escaped from Fort Robinson January 1879, and returned Sept. 27th with 4 complete skulls and fragments of ten more, also long bones representing 19 Indians—obtained for Army Medical Museum at the instigation of Col. Geo. A. Otis, Surgeon, U.S. Army.[42]
>
> Specimens: Forwarded Oct. 2nd and 23d, to the Surgeon General U.S. Army, quartermaster's receipts for box of Specimens comprising the bones collected at Antelope Creek, Sept. 26, 1880.[43]

For many years thereafter the remains occupied specimen containers in the Army Medical Museum, established in 1867 in the old Ford's Theatre building on 10th Street NW in Washington, D.C. Eventually they were transferred for safekeeping to the National Museum of Health and Medicine in Silver Spring, Maryland, where they reposed in storage, ostensibly for medical and scientific study and for research purposes. Over the ensuing decades, elements of the collected remains were seemingly exchanged, donated, or placed on loan with other government or learned institutions, and some were perhaps casually lost by the borrowing entities.[44] Those referenced above appear in the cited catalog notations of the Smithsonian Institution, where they apparently rested for decades following the Fort Robinson breakout as they awaited final physical and spiritual reunification with their people.

EPILOGUE

Homecoming

Over the years, essential recollections of the night of January 9, 1879, emerged from the Northern Cheyenne people, but only a single Cheyenne account of the Antelope Creek engagement of January 22 is known to exist. Indeed, nearly all of those men, women, and children who fled west from the post along the Hat Creek Telegraph Road succumbed either during the fighting along that route or at their final fatal stand in the blowout entrenchment. In their tribal memory, the totality of the Fort Robinson experience—the breakout, the pursuit, the time at Red Cloud Agency at Pine Ridge, family separations and disruptions—proved shattering and, sadly, enduring. As historians James Leiker and Ramon Powers suggest, "For many of the families . . . it was a very difficult time. . . . Between the fighting and the removal from one reservation to another, families were split up, broken and torn apart. . . . At this point in their history, [the] Northern Cheyennes may well have lacked the type of unified community necessary for collective memories of the exodus to develop, at least to the extent to which all . . . could have found in it a sense of shared ownership."[1]

This changed over time, however, especially following later reunions among the people and notably among breakout survivor descendants. Most of those people later returned to the Tongue River Reservation in Montana, where they have retained the name "White River Cheyennes" after the stream that factored in their lives during those desperate days at Fort Robinson. When Mari Sandoz's sympathetic book *Cheyenne Autumn* appeared in 1953 to present a more balanced if semifictional depiction of Northern Cheyenne strife in 1878–79, people who still knew little of the history at last took notice, especially after John Ford's historical cinematic version debuted in 1964.[2]

Many of those Northern Cheyenne survivors of the trauma of Fort Robinson lived for years, some even decades, beyond the events. Among them was Dull Knife, the Old Man Chief, who had valiantly led his people north and suffered the brunt of their subsequent capture, imprisonment, and desperate flight from the post. He stayed with the Lakotas on the reservation at Pine Ridge, Dakota Territory, until late 1879, when his family joined other Cheyennes in reuniting with Little Wolf's followers at Fort Keogh, Montana Territory. Within a short time the elderly chief and his family moved to Rosebud Valley within the area of the proposed Northern Cheyenne Reservation, in the country where he had been born. There he remained until his death in March 1883, at approximately seventy-three years old.[3]

Another enigmatic leader was Wild Hog. Along with others, he had been threatened with prosecution for the Kansas raids and had factored significantly in events preceding and following the breakout. In the immediate aftermath of Fort Robinson, he was returned to Darlington Agency with other Northern Cheyennes but later was allowed to relocate with relatives to Pine Ridge. In early August 1889 the warrior-chief, aged fifty-four, died from pneumonia and was buried near White River.[4]

Iron Teeth, the widow who left Darlington with her children, whose son died violently in the breakout from Fort Robinson, became noted for her clear recollections of the events and for providing important context for what had happened there. In the wake of the turmoil, she stayed at Pine Ridge with her two daughters for twelve years before returning with them to Tongue River, where she remained until her death in 1928.[5]

Among Fort Robinson's officers who played important roles in the breakout, Captain Joseph Lawson with his Company E had been a premier player throughout. He joined in the opening action through the chase along Hat Creek Road and at Antelope Creek, where he accompanied the closing charge on the pit and ultimately extricated a Northern Cheyenne woman and child who were still alive. Lawson fought prominently in the Third Cavalry's fight with the Utes in the mountains of northern Colorado eight months later, for which he garnered a citation from the Wyoming legislature. He died from paralysis in January 1881 at Fort Fred Steele, Wyoming Territory.[6]

Above all, however, Captain Henry Wessells had been pivotal in the events of the breakout. In the following years he remained with the Third Cavalry, earning promotion to major in 1892. During the Spanish-American War, Wessells helped lead the Third U.S. Volunteer Cavalry in the assault on San Juan Hill near Santiago de Cuba, where he was severely wounded—again in the head: as before, he remained in the battle. He was later breveted for gallantry in action and consequently garnered a Silver Star for his service. Promoted lieutenant colonel, Wessells accompanied the Third Cavalry to the Philippines in 1899 and two years later advanced to colonel, whereupon he retired on a disability incurred in the line of duty. Promoted in retirement to brigadier general in 1904, Wessells took up residence in Washington, D.C., where he died in 1929.[7]

During his retirement, Wessells often brooded over what had happened to the Northern Cheyennes under his charge in 1878–79 and perhaps felt guilt over their treatment. Echoing the anti-German sentiment during World War I, he wrote: "When I think of the murder of those Indians who had every right on their side—being compelled by a cruel govt [*sic*] to leave the land of their birth & go to a strange country & then [to be] shot down because they would not return . . . It was all quite German like on the part of the Americans & they allowed a German—[secretary of the interior] Carl Schurz to do the thing. It would have been easily settled by a fair man." Wessells reflected that his sympathies had been with the Northern Cheyennes throughout their ordeal. He blamed Schurz for the directive ordering them back to the Indian Territory.[8]

While Wessells believed that he had done his duty as commanding officer, he remained torn over the event. He told the historian Walter Camp that he had often joked with Dull Knife about the chief's giving him his beautiful daughter. When Wessells chanced to see Dull Knife some time later, he teased him, asking "if he were going to give him his daughter." Wessells related, however, that "Dull Knife replied, 'No—the one you wanted—you killed.'" The response brought tears to Wessells's eyes.[9]

Of the enlisted men who served during the breakout, Sergeant Carter P. Johnson had participated in virtually all aspects of the capture, imprisonment, and subsequent pursuit of the Indians between late October 1878 and the closing engagement at Antelope Creek in late January 1879. It was he, moreover, who treated Wild Hog's daughter charitably after she had been wounded at Antelope Creek. When Johnson happened to encounter Wild Hog in Sidney, Nebraska, a few years later as the chief was transferring from Darlington to the Pine Ridge Reservation, Johnson accepted the Northern Cheyenne's gratitude for his earlier care of the girl. Johnson's role during the breakout was only one of many events he experienced in his several tenures at Fort Robinson. In 1882 the army formally commissioned him. He transferred to the Tenth Cavalry the following year and in 1902, as a captain, completed a stint as commanding officer at the post. Johnson later served in Cuba and the Philippines and retired as a major in 1909. Reactivated in 1916, he again commanded Fort Robinson but died from heart failure within the year.[10]

Through the decades the Northern Cheyennes have remained an extraordinarily resilient people. Highly devoted to their past and to those who came before, they have continued to foster and preserve an accurate and enviable record of their compelling history. Through the years since their journey from the Indian Territory under Dull Knife and Little Wolf, and beyond their calamitous imprisonment, escape, and pursuit from Fort Robinson, the people have never forgotten. Their forbears and the distant memories will forever remain in their hearts. Since the 1970s nearly one hundred years after the events of 1878–79, in their reverence for their illustrious history, the Northern Cheyennes have sought to perpetuate the remembrance of those people and times among their young people, so that they will always retain understanding of what happened: an enduring legacy that continuing generations of Tsistsistas, as well as all others, can learn from, cherish, and respect.[11]

Beginning in the late 1970s, the people began nurturing aspects of the Fort Robinson breakout. Over time, occasional visits evolved into an annual pilgrimage, a memorable ritual as well as an essential learning experience for their young. At the forefront was Ted Rising Sun, whose grandmother and aunt—both daughters of Dull Knife—had experienced the trauma of January 9, 1879, and who himself had become reconciled to the event through an abiding Christian faith. Over succeeding years, the White River Powwow and its associated feast became an annual Christmas tradition for descendants and for the extended families of breakout participants. In 1994 the Fort Robinson Outbreak Spiritual Run was organized by Lynette Two Bulls and Philip Whiteman Jr. It initially encompassed the perimeter of the Northern Cheyenne Reservation. In 1996 the course extended to 400 miles—the approximate distance from Fort Robinson to Busby, Montana.

Each year at the anniversary of the Fort Robinson breakout, Northern Cheyenne youths are bused with elders from the reservation to the fort. In preparing for the Spiritual Run, they learn and cultivate those pertinent aspects of their history. Many have visited not only the spot where their ancestors were confined, as represented in a reconstruction of the 1874 cavalry barrack dedicated in 2003 (the original building burned in 1898) but also the very ground over which the people had fled the pursuing troops on that deadly night. Some have visited the hallowed ground at Antelope Creek, thirty miles northwest of the fort, where the few survivors made their final stand and where other dead remain buried. Current landowners protect the site and encourage the people's homage and visitation. Visits to these locations, augmented by the Spiritual Run, in addition to bonding youths and elders, further honor the strength and tenacity of the people's ancestors who endured the profound events of 1878–79.[12]

In 1994, in addition to the inauguration of the site visitation and Spiritual Run, the Northern Cheyennes also celebrated the homecoming of their ancestors' remains, which brought further solace and unity respecting the Fort Robinson dead. Under provisions of the Native American Graves Protection and Repatriation Act (NAGPRA) (Public Law 101–601) passed by Congress in 1990, American museums supported by federal funds were obligated to notify tribes of identifiable objects and remains held in their collections. Among remains identified in the holdings of the Smithsonian Institution in Washington, D.C.; the National Museum of Health and Medicine in Silver Spring, Maryland; and the Peabody Museum of Archaeology and Ethnology at Harvard University in Massachusetts (on loan from the Smithsonian) were those removed from the Northern Cheyenne defense and burial site at Antelope Creek, Nebraska, by Assistant Surgeon Carvallo in 1880. As early as February 1991 a Northern Cheyenne delegation had visited the Smithsonian to consult regarding the repatriation of previously collected tribal remains.

More than two years later, in October 1993, at the behest of tribal vice president William Walksalong, sixteen Northern Cheyenne tribal members traveled to the Smithsonian offices in Washington, D.C., to receive the unnamed, bullet-shattered remains of twenty-five of their people. As

Alfred Strange Owl, a member of the delegation and a descendant of Chief Dull Knife's followers, recalled, "They traveled a bloody trail [and] we were finally bringing them home to the place where they were trying to go. It made me feel whole again." Tribal chairman Llevando Fisher noted how "appropriate" the repatriation effort was, as the people had initially been seeking to return to their homeland. "When they are reburied there, they will rest in peace," he said. Chief James Black Wolf, Keeper of the Sacred Buffalo Hat, completed ceremonial ministrations. The remains were then solemnly wrapped, with each set consigned to its own cedar box.[13]

On Sunday morning a van bearing the precious cargo left Washington, D.C., escorted by members of the Northern Cheyenne Crazy Dog Society. En route home, the group paused at Fort Robinson for a brief observance before moving on to the Northern Cheyenne Reservation. There a formal procession greeted the Crazy Dog delegates and escorted the remains to Busby, Montana, where interment occurred on Saturday, October 16, 1993, nearly 115 years after the breakout. On the plain near a monument to Chief Two Moon stood twenty-five cedar boxes. One held the remains of a child, aged three to five. "They think it was a little girl," commented Steve Brady of the Northern Cheyenne Cultural Commission, which had facilitated the transfers. In her grave, attending families placed a teddy bear along with a tiny blanket to "comfort her spirit."[14]

In this manner the Northern Cheyennes' fidelity to their people, culture, and history endures. Their memorialization of the human tragedies embodied in their experience at Fort Robinson in 1878–79 at last came full circle in 2016, more than two decades after the homecoming in Busby and the inaugural run from Fort Robinson. During the interlude, two Northern Cheyenne women, Edna Seminole and Rose Eagle Feathers, who had visited Fort Robinson, determined that a commemorative monument should be raised there to educate the public and promote healing and renewal. In 2004 they selected a site west of the state park, in the precise area that the terrorized people crossed on January 9, 1879, as they struggled from White River to the bluffs that they climbed, fleeing the troops. Area ranchers T. R. and Kay Hughes generously donated 220 acres of land to Chief Dull Knife Memorial College in Lame Deer, while members of a Fort Robinson Northern Cheyenne Breakout Committee helped raise additional funding essential for completing a monument, road, and footpath as well as appropriate interpretive markers. The land was further protected by the Nebraska Land Trust under a designated conservation easement.[15]

It took a decade to complete the monument, which stands today on a site 100 yards north of U.S. Highway 20. The memorial, consisting of a sixteen-foot-tall concrete tower with four sloping sides facing in the cardinal directions, is capped by the Northern Cheyenne Morning Star tribal emblem. The sides of the tower are faced with red pipestone slabs brought from a sacred site in Minnesota. Each side bears a mounted bronze tablet containing the names of the Northern Cheyennes who died in the breakout as well as those who survived the subsequent pursuit. Four long wooden poles were planned to trace the sloping corners and intersect at the top, above the Morning Star, to complete a tipi configuration. Beyond commemorating the men, women, and children who died, the site further honors those who escaped and lived.

On July 15, 2016, about 100 Northern Cheyennes, including some descendants of those who fled Fort Robinson that night 137 years earlier, gathered to pray and dedicate the memorial. Many of them had walked more than two miles along U.S. 20 in approximating the route that their ancestors had taken in fleeing from the post.[16] On one of the tablets, the stark words of Chief Dull Knife now resonate as the wind whips through the tufted buffalo grass and ascends the nearby bluffs. They speak for the ages and assure that his people will always remember:

> We do not wish to go back there, and we will not go. I am here on my own ground, and I will never go back. You may kill me here, but you cannot make me go back. . . . We will not go.

APPENDIX A

List of Indians Wounded

List of Indians wounded that have arrived at Camp [*sic*] Robinson, Neb.[,] to January 24, 1879, from various engagements with the troops," included in "Proceedings of a Board of Officers," January 25–February 7, 1879, Records of the Military Division of the Missouri, Special File 905-M-1879, RG 98, NA (punctuation inconsistent in the original), as reproduced in Roger T. Grange Jr., "Treating the Wounded at Fort Robinson," *Nebraska History* 45 (September 1964): 291–92. (This list is not altogether complete: the Cheyenne leader Tangle Hair, who was wounded, does not appear, as Grange noted. Others probably were also treated but not listed.) The total number of Indians killed or who died of wounds is 39 men and 22 women and children.

1. Yellow Woman, G.S.W.R.A. [Gunshot wound right arm] upper third. Ball penetrating R L [right leg]. . . . [illegible]. Died.
2. Short Woman. G.S.W.R. Hand, Head and chest & back, thigh fractured.
3. Red Woman. G.S.W.L. Thigh (flesh) Little finger fractures, scalp wounded.
4. Buffalo Girl (child) 5 years. G.S.W. thigh flesh wound severe.
5. Little Boy 7 years[.] G.S.W. Head Humerous [*sic*]. Serious.
6. Stub Foot 16 years. G.S.W. Arm twice and lower third of thigh.
7. Big Head. G.S.W. Thigh, upper third[.] (Buck) flesh.
8. Medicine Robe (old woman)[.] G.S.W. Fore arm middle. Flesh.
9. Medicine Woman G.S.W. Head R Eye shot out dangerous.
10. Little Bear G.S.W. Scalp slight[.] 10 years.

11. Moccason [*sic*] Woman G.S.W. Thigh L. third, flesh. 50 years.
12. Lost Woman. G.S.W. R Shoulder, serious.
13. Medicine [illegible] Girl 6 years left shoulder. Head of humerous [*sic*].
14. Lame Girl 6 years. G.S.W. Left side [illegible] lung.
15. Little Girl 5 years. Penetrating wound of abdomen[,] died 12 hours after being brought in.
16. Baby Girl, 1 year, fracture both thighs upper third. Died one hour after being brought in.
17. White Antelope G.S.W. of thigh and knife stab done by buck after both were wounded[,] died one hour after being brought in.
18. Squaw. G.S.W. Thigh upper third comminuted fracture. Died 10 hours after being brought in.
19. Noisy Walker (buck) G.S.W. thigh and knee.
20. Baby (girl) 6 month**[,]** fracture L thigh[,] died Jan[.] 12. 79 morning.
21. Hogs Girl G.S.W. R. arm flesh.
22. Boy G.S.W. both legs fracture of tibia leg.
23. Girl G.S.W. ankle spent Ball**[,]** slight fracture of bone.

APPENDIX B

List of Army Casualties

"List of Army Casualties, Fort Robinson Breakout, January 9–22, 1879," as identified in "Proceedings of a Board of Officers," January 25-February 7, 1879, Records of the Military Division of the Missouri, Special File 905-M-1879, RG 98, NA, as reproduced in Roger T. Grange Jr., "Treating the Wounded at Fort Robinson, *Nebraska History* 45 (September 1964): 278–90, and corrected. For specific details and data regarding individual cases, see Grange's article.

1. Private Thomas Ferguson, Company E, Third Cavalry. Wounded January 9, 1879.
2. Private Frank Schmidt, Company A, Third Cavalry. Killed January 9, 1879.
3. Private Peter Hulse, Company A, Third Cavalry. Wounded January 9, 1879, died January 24, 1879.
4. Private James Emory, Company C, Third Cavalry. Wounded January 9, 1879.
5. Corporal Edward F. Pulver, Company L, Third Cavalry. Wounded January 9, 1879.
6. Private Daniel Timmany, Company E, Third Cavalry. Wounded January 9, 1879.
7. Private James E. McHale, Company F, Third Cavalry. Wounded January 9, 1879.
8. Private Edward Glavin, Company E, Third Cavalry. Wounded January 9, 1879.

9. Private William H. Good, Company L, Third Cavalry. Killed January 10, 1879.
10. Private William W. Everett, Company H, Third Cavalry. Wounded January 10, 1879, died January 11, 1879.
11. Private Bernard Kelley, Company E, Third Cavalry. Accidentally wounded January 11, 1879, died January 12, 1879.
12. Corporal Henry P. Ore, Company A, Third Cavalry. Killed January 12, 1879.
13. Farrier Peter W. Painter, Company C, Third Cavalry. Wounded January 12, 1879.
14. Private Amos J. Barber, Company H, Third Cavalry. Killed January 17, 1879.
15. Private Henry A. Deblois, Company H, Third Cavalry. Wounded January 22, 1879, died January 24, 1879.
16. Woman's Dress, scout. Wounded January 22, 1879.
17. Sergeant James Taggart, Company A, Third Cavalry. Killed January 22, 1879.
18. Farrier George Brown, Company A, Third Cavalry. Killed January 22, 1879.
19. Private George E. Nelson, Company A, Third Cavalry. Killed January 22, 1879.
20. First Sergeant Edward F. Ambrose, Company E, Third Cavalry. Wounded January 22, 1879.
21. Sergeant Willard D. Reed, Company H, Third Cavalry. Wounded January 22, 1879.
22. Captain Henry W. Wessells, Company H, Third Cavalry. Wounded January 22, 1879.

APPENDIX C

Captain Wessells's Account

Captain Wessells's Account of the Fort Robinson Breakout, January 9, 1879," in Wessells to the Assistant Adjutant General, Headquarters Department of the Platte, Omaha, Nebraska, January 12, 1879, National Archives, copy in the Fort Robinson Archive, Nebraska State Historical Society. Also published in the *Chicago Daily Times*, January 24, 1879.

To the Assistant Adjutant-General, Headquarters Department of the Platte, Fort Omaha, Neb.:

I have the honor to state that I arrived at this post Dec. 4, 1878. Lieut. Johnson, Fourteenth Infantry, was in command of the post, but Capt. Johnson, Third Cavalry, was the senior officer present. Col. Carlton was absent after Little Wolf. Capt. Johnson with his company, were guarding the Cheyenne prisoners, and I told him to continue doing so, and added the band to his command. With the other companies I guarded the post and performed the usual garrison duty. When Capt. Johnson left I put the Indians under a guard detailed daily from all the companies of the command, and put a corporal and two men of my company to cook for the Indians, and instructed them the officer of the day to visit them frequently, and did the same myself.

On taking charge I found these Cheyennes prisoners of war, and though of course that, as they had been in Col. Carlton's possession for over a month, they were thoroughly disarmed. In fact, I am informed that they had been searched twice, and all arms found taken away. Still I knew they had knives, for I saw them daily, and thought there might be two or three pistols among them. After Col. Carlton went away I discouraged the Sioux visiting this post, and none had been here for a long while previous to the outbreak. When Sioux visited the building when in charge of B Company, there were always two sentinels in the room, besides non-commissioned officers of the guard, and officers constantly passing through the rooms.

Everything went on nicely; the Indians were good-natured, and said they were well treated, but told myself and other officers, repeatedly, that they never would go south. I, however, never said much to them on that subject, for the reason that I did not know anything about it myself.

When I received orders to move them to Sidney, I well knew that I had a most difficult and responsible task before me, but felt perfect confidence in myself, and resolved to do the best I knew how. My principal object from the start was to avoid bloodshed and exciting the Indians, and in all my conversation I was calm but decided.

When everything was ready, on the morning of the 3d, I called Hog, Crow, Dull Knife, Tangle-Hair, and Left Hand into my office, and told them that the Great Father had decided that they should be sent back to the Indian Territory; that they would receive plenty of food and clothing. Dull Knife got up first and said that this was the home of the Northern Cheyennes, and their fathers were buried and their children raised here. They left their Agency to come to this place, and here they wanted to remain; that they did not get enough to eat at their Agency; and that since going south with Lieut. Lawton, Fourth Cavalry, fifty-eight of their people had died, and even the children did not wish to return. Hog repeated what Dull Knife had said. I answered that I had nothing to do in the premises; that I was simply obeying orders; their going could not be avoided; and that I hoped they would go quietly and without trouble. Capt. Vroom, who was present at the talk, told them he was going as far as Sidney with them, and would see they were well cared for. They then went back to their quarters to communicate the news. I went through the building during that day and the next, but avoided conversing with them. I increased the guard and took the sentinel that was on the inside and put him on the outside.

On the afternoon of the 4th I called Hog in the office, and asked him what they were going to do. Hog said they would do anything that I wanted them to do except go south, and that they would not do. I told Hog that I would have no more to say, but act. That night they had supper, but I ordered that it should be their last meal, and that they should receive no more fuel. They understood that as soon as they would give up they could have fuel and food. However, at no time did they suffer for either. I gave instructions to the officer of the day to keep a good lookout and have his sentinels vigilant, and not under any circumstances to kill Indians until it was absolutely necessary, either to save their own lives or prevent escape. On the night of the 8th I made up my mind to get Hog in irons, as I knew he was the leading spirit and the one by whom they were in a great measure guided. By getting him separated from the rest they would be without his counsel. I said nothing to any one until the next morning, when I told Lieut. Baxter, Third Cavalry, what I was going to do. I told him to go to "H" Company quarters, and be ready for any emergency. I then instructed four trusty men to be in the clerk's room and come into my office when Hog entered, and what to do when I gave the signal. Hog would not come, but wanted me to go in their quarters, where all might hear what I had to say. I told him he might bring Crow, and they came. In the meantime I sent for two more men to [come to?] the guard-house. When Hog and Crow entered I asked them if they would go south, and continued talking while the room was filling with soldiers, Lieut. Cummings being already present. I gave the signal, when we all jumped on the two Indians at the same time, Lieut. Cummings, Sergt. Dunne, Company H, Third Cavalry, a man of Company E, Third Cavalry, and myself took Hog. Crow gave up at once, but we had to struggle very hard to get Hog handcuffed. Before we did it he stabbed Private Ferguson, Company E, Third Cavalry, slightly with a knife; he had three on his person. After he was handcuffed, he called me to him and said they would go south, and that if I would take off the irons, and let him go back to the people, he would get their consent to the move. While we were waiting for an ambulance to convey them to Capt. Vroom's camp, I sent word to the Indians that the relatives of the two Indians could come out and go with them. Hog's wife came out, but when she went back to the building to get her effects they would not let her come out. Hog, before getting into the ambulance, said he wished I would stay with them to see they were not hurt on the road. The Indians made two attempts in the course of the afternoon to get out the doors, but were driven back by the sentries. At no time were any firearms shown by the Indians. During the afternoon the excitement died out, and toward night Hog was allowed to come up and talk with the Indians. He got his and Crow's relatives out, and they went back to the lower camp. At 7 that night I was around the building, and found the sentinels alert and everything quiet inside. Lieut. Simpson, the Officer of the Day, just about 9:30 o'clock P.M. went to the Adjutant's office, which is about twenty-five yards from the Indian quarters, intending to stay about an hour or so. At 10 o'clock the Indians commenced firing through windows and doors, killing one sentry and wounding two, and the Corporal of the Guard, and immediately followed the shots. I had just gotten into bed. I got up, put on my pants, a pair of arctics, and no stockings, my overcoat and hat, and ran down to the east end of the Indians' building. The Indians were all out running away. I got Company C, Third Cavalry, to follow. The Indians fired at us repeatedly with carbines, and we killed five bucks in a few moments. Capt. Vroom, when the firing commenced, saddled his company, sent A Company up to the post dismounted, and E Company dismounted to cover the Sheridan road. I followed with C Company and men of H Company, who joined a few at a time. I passed two wounded squaws, both of whom I had carefully carried back to the post. I carried a 2-year-old child back on the road till I met an H Company man, whom I told to take the baby to a comfortable place. I then returned and told H Company men to saddle, dress themselves warmly, and assemble at the stables. On mounting, I went on a gallop to where Capt. Vroom was fighting the Indians in the bluffs about four miles out on the Laramie Road, accompanied by Lieut. Crawford. On my arrival I found Lieut. Chase and part of A Company there also; they had killed about eight Indians at that spot. I sent Capt. Vroom around on the Hat-Creek road, and Lieut. Chase back with the wounded squaws, and told him to go afterwards on the Deadwood road to prevent the Indians crossing towards Pine Ridge Agency.

I sent orders to E Company to go down White River. Lieut. Crawford was to gather up stragglers and come back to the bluffs, and in the morning look for Indians. I sent most of my men under the First Sergeant across to the right bank of White River, and went on top of bluffs north of river myself with six men. We struck fresh moccasin tracks on top of them, and soon overtook and killed two Indians. A third one got away. One of the Indians had twenty-five Sharp's carbine cartridges with brass shells and a Remington pistol. The man who held our horses let them go, and we had to walk about six miles towards the post before we got them again. We then rode in and went to bed.

This report will be continued as soon as possible. I have to prepare for another scout.

Very respectfully, H. W. Wessells, Jr.

Captain Third Cavalry, Commanding Post.

APPENDIX D

Cheyenne Names and Relationships

Northern] Cheyenne Outbreak January 1879 [Fort Robinson], Cheyenne Names and Relationships [undated typed document]," John L. Sipes Jr., Collection 88.32, Box 10, Folder 158, "Northern Cheyenne Indians," Research Division, Oklahoma Historical Society, Oklahoma City, Oklahoma, copy also in the Fort Robinson Archive, Nebraska State Historical Society. (The following list does not contain the many genealogical annotations included in the cited original. References to "outbreak" herein denote the breakout from Fort Robinson.)

1.	Big Antelope	Man
2.	Unknown	Wife of Big Antelope
3.	Big Bear	Younger leader, killed in last fight Jan. 22
4.	Unknown	Wife of Big Bear[,] wounded in flight, brought back to hospital
	[Added in ink: Big Crow, wife and 2 children]	
5.	Black Horse	mentioned in Powell
6.	Blacksmith	mentioned in Powell—also questioned by the Board of Inquiry
7.	Brave One	woman, killed in last fight Jan. 22
8.	Bridge	medicine man, killed Jan. 9
9.	Broad-Faced One	wife of Limpy [added in ink: daughter of Big Foot]
10.	Bull Hump	older son of Dull Knife, young leader
11.	Red Leaf Woman	[Leaf] escaped with Dull Knife group to Pine Ridge

12.	Unknown	daughter of Bull Hump
13.	Bullet Proof	killed Jan. 12
14.	Calf	grandson of Dull Knife
15.	Charging Bear	young brother of Broad-Faced One[.] Also cousin of Big Beaver . . . killed Jan. 10 maybe later [added in ink: son of Big Foot]
16.	Clubfoot	mentioned in Powell
17.	Crooked Nose Man	mentioned in Iron Teeth narrative
18.	Dull Knife	(Morning Star) old leader, escaped to Pine Ridge
19.	Unknown	older daughter of Dull Knife, killed Jan. 9 in flight with Dull Knife group
20.	Unknown	daughter of Dull Knife, killed Jan[.] 9 in flight with Dull Knife Group (probably Walking Woman)
21.	The Enemy	(Enemy Woman) woman, captured Jan. 9.
22.	Gathering His Medicine	son of Iron Teeth killed around Jan. 10, mentioned in Powell
23.	Great Eyes	uncle of Red Bird, older man, father-in-law of Bull Hump killed Jan. 9 in flight with Dull Knife group
24.	Hog's daughter	oldest daughter of Wild Hog. Remained in barracks in afternoon of January 9. Survived last fight Jan. 22
25.	Iron Teeth	woman, mother of Gathering His Medicine. Captured in hills several days after outbreak[,] mentioned in Powell.
26.	Unknown	middle daughter of Iron Teeth. Captured with her mother
27.	Unknown	younger daughter of Iron Teeth. Captured with Gathering His Medicine when he was killed Jan. 10
28.	Lame Girl	6[-]year[-]old orphan, survived last fight Jan. 22. Wounded, treated at post. [added in ink: daughter of One Eye]
29.	Young Elk	mentioned in Sandoz'[s] "Cheyenne Autumn." At last fight Jan. 22

30. Left Hand	(Strong Left Hand) went out of barracks in afternoon of Jan. 9. Surrendered to go with Hog & Crow. Held in lower camp. Interviewed by Board of Inquiry.
31. Unknown	wife of Left Hand. Went out of barracks in afternoon of Jan. 9. Surrendered to go with Hog & Crow. Held in lower camp. Mentioned in Powell. [Added in ink: also 1 child]
32. Limpy	older warrior. Husband of Broad-Faced-One
33. Little Bear	13 year old son of Tangle Hair. Captured Jan. 10 (with mother, sister & orphan)[.] Slight wound, treated at Fort Robinson
34. Little Finger Nail	young leader, led outbreak through east side of barracks. Killed in last fight Jan. 22
35. Little Hump	younger son of Dull Knife. Killed Jan. 9 in flight with Dull Knife group (see Bronson)
36. Little Shield	younger leader, led outbreak with Little Finger nail *[sic]*. Spokesman for young men
37. Meat Woman	(Old Meat Woman) Captured with small group of women Jan. 10 in northwest flight.
38. Medicine Woman	woman, wounded and treated at post.
39. Miles Seminole	12[-]year[-]old boy survived. This boy and his mother mentioned in Powell.
40. Unknown	mother of Miles Seminole
41. Noisy Walker	(Noisy Walking) older man, captured in outbreak. Wounded as part of 5[-]man rear guard. Treated at post.
42. Old Crow	older leader, subdued with Hog at noon on Jan. 9. Held in lower camp.
43. (Unknown)	wife of Old Crow. Released from barracks 5 pm Jan. 9. Also held in lower camp.
44. Old Eagle	older man
45. Pawnee Woman	wife of Dull Knife, escaped to Pine Ridge
46. Porcupine	Captured at old agency after Cheyenne brought to post. Held in lower camp.

47.	Pug Nose	young man, Southern Cheyenne? Killed Jan. 17 during flight toward Hat Creek. Shot by Shangreau [*sic*].
48.	Pumpkin Seed's Son	(Big Beaver) 13[-]year[-]old, cousin of Charging Bear. Captured Jan. 10. Interviewed by Board of Inquiry.
49.	Red Bird #1	13[-]year[-]old nephew of Great Eyes, wounded in initial flight with Dull Knife. Later surrendered.
50.	Red Bird #2	7[-]year[-]old cousin of Red Bird #1
51.	Red Feather	[Red Feather Woman] woman [*sic*]
52.	Roached Hair	mentioned in Powell. Warrior killed in last fight Jan. 22
53.	Roman Nose	One of the young leaders. Wounded when Bullet Proof was killed. Killed in last fight Jan. 22
54.	She Bear	Warrior
55.	(Unknown)	wife of She Bear
56.	Singing Cloud	(Singing Woman mentioned in Powell.) Young woman killed in last fight Jan. 22
57.	Singing Wolf	warrior, with rear guard [at breakout]? Had the Sharps.
58.	The Sioux	old man, captured with baby on his back, Jan. 10
59.	(Unknown)	Baby girl carried by The Sioux
60.	Sitting Man	leg broke on flight north [Indian Territory], killed Jan. 9 just outside barracks
61.	(Unknown)	wife of Sitting Man?
62.	Small Woman	woman, killed Jan. 17 in flight mentioned in Powell.
63.	Squint Eye	mentioned in Powell.
64.	Tangle Hair	(Bighead) Sioux Dog Soldier Chief, captured Jan 9 as part of rear guard. Interviewed by Board of Inquiry. Wounded
65.	(Unknown)	Wife of Tangle Hair, captured Jan. 10
66.	(Unknown)	Daughter of Tangle Hair

67. (Unknown)	Mother of Tangle Hair. Left barracks afternoon of Jan. 9[,] mentioned in Powell.
68. (Unknown)	Aunt of Tangle Hair, left barracks afternoon of Jan. 9[,] mentioned by Powell.
69. White Antelope	(Big Antelope) warrior, died of wounds Jan. 9 in post hospital. [Same as No. 1 above?]
70. (Unknown)	Wife of White Antelope[,] died of wounds Jan. 9 in post hospital. [Same as No. 2 above?]
71. (Unknown)	Baby of White Antelope[,] died of wounds Jan. 9 in post hospital.
72. Wild Hog	leader. Captured noon Jan. 9[.] In confinement in lower camp during outbreak. Interviewed by Board of Inquiry
73. (Unknown)	Wife of Wild Hog. Taken out of barracks 5 pm Jan. 9[.] Held in lower camp during outbreak.
74. (Unknown)	Young child of Wild Hog. Left barracks with Mother[,] mentioned in Powell.
75. (Unknown)	Young child of Wild Hog. Left barracks with Mother[,] mentioned in Powell.
76. (Unknown)	Young child of Wild Hog[.] Left barracks with Mother[,] mentioned in Powell.
77. Young Hog	Son of Wild Hog. Stayed in barracks. Was in the outbreak.
78. (Unknown)	Brother of Young Hog. Stayed in barracks. Was in the outbreak.
79. Young Magpie	killed in last fight Jan. 22
80. Young Medicine Man	Mentioned in Sandoz. Probably at last fight Jan[.] 22
81. (Unknown)	Wife of Young Medicine Man
82. Bird	Scout from Little Wolf, captured Oct. 29. Held in barracks
83. Walking Bear	killed in outbreak
84. Red Woman	wife of Walking Bear. Daughter of Spotted Wolf. Attempted rescue from barracks

		Jan. 9 wounded—treated at post. Mentioned in Powell.
85.	(Unknown)	Son of Walking Bear
86.	(Unknown)	Daughter of Walking Bear
87.	(Unknown)	Daughter of Walking Bear
88.	(Unknown)	Daughter of Walking Bear
89.	(Unknown)	One of 4 older people allowed to leave barracks late with Crow & Hog family members
90.	(Unknown)	One of 4 older people allowed to leave barracks late with Crow & Hog family members
91.	(Unknown)	One of 4 older people allowed to leave barracks late with Crow & Hog family members
92.	(Unknown)	One of 4 older people allowed to leave barracks late with Crow & Hog family members
93.	Stubfoot	Captured Jan. 10
94.	(Unknown)	Wife of Stubfoot. Wounded running to bridge
95.	(Unknown)	Nephew of Stubfoot. Captured Jan. 10
96.	Yellow Woman	Mother of Young Magpie. Died of wounds at Fort Robinson. (Sandoz)
97.	Short Woman	Wounded, treated at post.
98.	Buffalo Girl	5 years old[,] wounded, treated at post.
99.	(Little boy)	7 years old[,] wounded, treated at post.
100.	Stub Foot	16 years old[,] wounded, treated at post. Possibly a different Stub Foot. Could be Club Foot
101.	Medicine Woman	Old woman, wounded, treated at post.
102.	Moccasin Woman	50[-]year[-]old wounded, treated at post.
103.	Lost Woman	wounded, treated at post.
104.	Medicine	girl 6 years old[,] wounded, treated at post.
105.	(Little girl)	5 years old[,] wounded, treated at post. Died of wounds 12 hours after being brought in

106. (Baby girl) — 6 months old. Died while treated Jan. 12
107. (Boy) — wounded, treated at post.
108. (Girl) — wounded, treated at post.
109. Bushy Head — Killed. Great, great, great grandfather of Rick Williams
110. (Unknown) — Grandfather of Ida White Eyes—survived

[No entry 111.]

112. [Added in ink] Fast Whirlwind
113. [Added in ink] Buffalo Calf

APPENDIX E

General Sheridan's Report to the Adjutant General, February 25, 1879

General:

I have the honor to transmit herewith a report of a Board of officers convened by the Commanding General, Department of the Platte, "To examine into and report the facts attending the arrest, confinement, disarmament, escape and recapture of a number of Cheyenne Indians recently at and in the vicinity of Fort Robinson, Neb.—and also a copy of all correspondence, regarding the same Indians, which came to or was sent from these headquarters [omitted]."

For a more complete understanding of this case, and to make it perhaps a little more intelligible to persons unacquainted with the history of the Cheyennes, it may be as well for me to state briefly; that the Cheyennes and Sioux Indians are of two separate and distinct nationalities. All the country lying north of the Union Pacific Railroad was originally the country of the Cheyennes, but the Sioux, a warlike and aggressive people who greatly outnumbered the Cheyennes (who are equally brave and warlike), came down from points east and northeast of the Missouri river; invaded this country and drove them south into Kansas and Eastern Colorado. The Cheyennes in turn made war upon the Arapahoes who occupied that land and drove them further south, and they drove their southern neighbors the Kiowas, down on the Comanches.

For the purpose of this letter, however it is not necessary to follow out this matter, but to simply state, that as late as the year

1868, the main camps of the Cheyennes were spread throughout the country embraced by the Beaver and Sappa Creeks in Kansas. This country was the summer range of the great southern band of buffalo, and after having made peace with the Cheyennes, it was the usual custom of the Sioux to come to this vicinity for a yearly hunt, and in the course of time many of the young men of the Cheyennes intermarried with the Sioux.

Our Indian war of 1868 resulted in the Cheyennes' country being taken from them, and in fact all the country between the Arkansas and Platte rivers fell into the hands of the whites. When peace obtained[,] the Cheyennes were finally located in 1861 at what is now known as the Cheyenne Agency, on the North Canadian river, Indian Territory, near where the post of Fort Reno now stands.

When this forcible settlement took place, nearly all of the Cheyenne, who had intermarried with the Sioux remained north with that tribe, and a more distinct division of the Cheyenne people took place.

After the war of 1876 was over and these Northern Cheyennes had surrendered at Red Cloud Agency, it was discovered, that they harbored a great deal of ill will against their Sioux relatives, the details of which cannot be fully entered into here; but some of the discontent grew out of their defeat by Colonel MacKenzie [*sic*] in the Big Horn mountains, after which the Sioux refused them aid and shelter when they were in a most destitute condition, and as the Cheyennes had done most of the hard fighting, they held that the Sioux had treated them very badly in giving them the cold shoulder when they were in sore need and distress. While in this state of mind, they concluded to abandon the Sioux and decided to go south and join their own people on the Canadian river. This was a purely voluntary act upon their part, and upon their own application, a small escort under command of Lieut. Lawton[,] Fourth Cavalry[,] was sent to accompany them and they were turned over to the care of the Indian Agent at the Southern Agency.

These poor wandring [*sic*] people, after reaching the Agency, became very much dissatisfied and reports heretofore sent to the War Department show that they were pinched for food and were wasting away by sickness.

After brooding over their troubles for two years, a small band, under Little Wolf, became desperate and started north. They had some skirmishing with an insufficient force sent to intercept them and when they reached Beaver and Sappa Creeks, the old homes of their people[,] and found this beautiful country in the possession of thrifty farmers, all the ferocity of their savage nature seemed to be suddenly developed and the most cruel and bloodthirsty acts were committed by them. Many peaceful farmers were killed and women were brutally outraged, and happy homes robbed and desolated. The memory of the joyous days, when they were the possessors of this country, with its herds of buffalo and other game and the thoughts of their wild war dances when returning to this very spot, from a successful foray upon their enemies, seemed to add additional cruelty to their nature and they bathed their hands in the blood of innocent beings and gratified their beastly lusts upon women and even children of extreme youth, then mounting themselves upon fresh horses stolen throughout the country, they fled further north. When nearing the northern boundary line of Nebraska, they found themselves hard pressed by the pursuing troops, [and] they divided, perhaps hoping thereby to facilitate their escape, but the party who were under the leadership of Dull Knife, numbering about fifty warriors and one hundred women and children, were overtaken and captured by the soldiers. The other band under Little Wolf succeeded in escaping.

From the moment of their capture, the men seemed to be conscious, that if they were sent back through Kansas to their Agency, they would be arrested and tried by the Civil authorities for the outrages committed in that State, and they were well convinced that if found guilty they would be hanged, and therefore with the desperate resolution of desperadoes, they deliberately made up their minds that they would die before being taken back. They only allowed themselves to be captured, in the first place, in the hope that they might be permitted to stay in the north. While in confinement at Fort Robinson they repeatedly reiterated it as their fined [*sic*: final] determination, to die sooner than return. These statements were duly forwarded to the War Department for the information of the proper authorities, but no reply was received, except the final order to remove them south, turning over all who were identified as having committed outrages in the State of Kansas, to the proper civil authorities there.

For a further and more detailed history of what happened subsequently, I respectfully call your attention to the report of the Board of officers first named in this communication.

I am Sir,
Your obedient servant
(Signed)
P.H. Sheridan
Lieut. General

APPENDIX F

Northern Cheyenne Guns Surrendered or Captured, 1878–1879

Extracted from "Report of the Chief of Ordnance, June 26, 1879," as published in *Report of the Secretary of War, 1879* (Washington, D.C.: Government Printing Office, 1879), vol. 3, pp. 326–28.

HEADQUARTERS MILITARY DIVISION OF MISSOURI,
OFFICE OF CHIEF ORDNANCE OFFICER,
Chicago, June 26, 1879.

CHIEF OF ORDNANCE, U.S.A.,
Washington, D.C.

SIR: Replying to your letter to me of October 10, 1878, which is inclosed, I have the honor to state that it was referred by me to the assistant adjutant-general of the division October 12, with request for action, as will be seen by the indorsement on its back. The Lieutenant General [Sheridan] forwarded copies of this letter to the department commanders, requesting compliance with its terms. Up to this date I have received the papers which are appended and four rifles. The latter are forwarded to you to-day by express.

The subject covers a broader field than any one officer can possibly investigate, and especially when department, post, and regimental officers are not heartily in accord with its purpose.

There are also as many opinions on the subject as there are officers in the service. It would be presumption on my part, therefore, to offer a solution of the general question of the proper armament for cavalry in Indian warfare.

Coming to the special case of the officer in the Department of Missouri, between certain companies of the Fourth Cavalry and the Northern Cheyennes, which was the immediate cause of your letter, I think the papers appended will show the general character of the armament of this band at the time. From these papers I abstract the following lists:

Surrendered by Cheyennes to Captain Johnson, Third Cavalry, at Chadron Creek, Nebr., October 24, 1878.

One Winchester rifle.
One Schofield-Smith & Wesson revolver.
One Sharp's carbine, caliber .50.
One Colt's revolver, old pattern.
One Spencer carbine.
One Remington revolver, old pattern.
One shot-gun, double-barreled.
One horse-pistol, and
Nine muzzle-loading rifles, various patterns.
Fifteen or twenty sets of bows and arrows.

Surrendered at Camp Robinson to Lieutenant Chase, Third Cavalry.

One Henry rifle.
One Springfield carbine, and
One Sharp's rifle.
Two unknown patterns.
Three muzzle-loading rifles.

Captured from Indians after the outbreak at Camp Robinson, giving indication of long possession by Indians.

Seven Springfield breech-loading rifles, caliber .50.

One Colt's revolver, caliber .36.
One Colt's revolver, Navy, old pattern.
One Springfield carbine .45.
One Remington revolver, Army, old pattern.
Three Sharp's carbines, caliber .50.
One Sharp's rifle (old reliable).

Surrendered to Lieutenant Clarke [*sic*], *Second Cavalry.*

Four Springfield carbines, caliber .45.
Two Colt's revolvers, caliber .45.
Three Springfield rifles, caliber .50.
Two Smith & Wesson revolvers, caliber .44.
Four Sharp's rifles, caliber .45.
One Sharp's rifle, caliber .50.
Five Colt's revolvers, calibers .44 and .31.
Four Sharp's carbines, caliber .50.
One muzzle-loading rifle (old).
One Remington revolver, caliber .44.
Three Winchester and Henry repeating rifles.

Or a total armament, as far as ascertained, of fifty-three rifles, carbines, and muskets or various patterns, seventeen revolvers of various patterns, and fifteen or twenty sets of bow and arrows.

In this number there are:

Ten Springfield rifles, caliber .50.
Four Sharp's rifles, caliber .45.
One Sharp's rifle.
One Sharp's rifle, caliber .50.
One Sharp's rifle (old reliable).

Which with proper charges of powder and lead give a greater range than the Springfield carbine with its own special cartridge. I hardly think it just to the command concerned in this affair to exclude United States service arms in possession of the Indians in determining whether there was proper ground for the prevailing opinion that the Indian arms were superior in range and accuracy to the carbine armament of the command.

The four rifles referred to as sent you to-day by express are—

One Sharp's rifle, long.
One Sharp's rifle, short.
One Henry repeating rifle (surrendered at Camp Robinson).
One Winchester repeating rifle (sent from Fort Keogh by order of General Terry).

And are, I believe, selected specimens of the best arms in the possession of the Indians. As is well known to all acquainted with arms, the Henry and Winchester are vastly inferior in range and accuracy to the Springfield carbine, though these seem to be preferred by the Indians on account of their rapidity of fire to the extent of the contents of the magazines, in this respect offering some advantages in a moment of emergency to a horseman.

While adhering to my resolution not to attempt a solution of the proper armament of our cavalry, I think it is patent, and that I should state it more explicitly here, that our Springfield carbine, caliber .45, has a greater effective range and greater accuracy than any carbine made, and much greater than the Winchester and Henry repeating rifles. But the Indians do possess a *rifle* here and there, possibly one in ten of their armament, that exceeds it in range and accuracy at long range. To overcome this advantage the method in use in the Fifth Cavalry, giving to each company five Springfield rifles for selected marksmen, and in the Seventh Cavalry, giving ten rifles per company for the same purpose, seems to answer.

As bearing on the question at issue, it might be stated here that aside from the companies of the Fourth Cavalry serving in the Department of Missouri, which were ordered to be armed with the Springfield rifle, and Companies K and M, Third Cavalry, which had been for some time so armed, none of the companies of cavalry serving in this division have availed themselves of the permission granted by the General of the Army to exchange their carbines for rifles. The only inference from this is that a large majority of cavalry still have faith in the carbine.

Some weeks since I ascertained that 406 surrendered Indian (Sioux and Cheyenne) arms of various patterns had been in the possession of the depot quartermaster at Cheyenne for a year or more. I believe these have been sent, as requested, to the commanding officer of the National Armory, and his special knowledge and the facilities at his disposal will enable him to report upon their merits as compared with the carbine more definitely than I have attempted.

I have delayed forwarding this report in the expectation of receiving the arms before mentioned as capture by Lieutenant Clark, but they have not yet reached me.

Very respectfully, your obedient servant,

J. W. Reilly
Captain of Ordnance, Chief Ordnance Officer.

Notes

Abbreviations

AAG	Assistant Adjutant General
AG	Adjutant General
AGO	Adjutant General's Office
DPL	Denver Public Library
LC	Library of Congress
NA	National Archives
NSHS	Nebraska State Historical Society
RG	Record Group
USGS	United States Geological Survey

Prologue

"Record of Medical History of Post," cited in Roger T. Grange Jr., "Fort Robinson: Outpost on the Plains," *Nebraska History* 39 (September 1958): 224; Robert B. Thomas, *The Old Farmer's Almanac 1879* (Boston: H. A. Young and Company, 1878), 6; Time and Date.com, "Harrison, Nebraska, USA—Moonrise, Moonset, and Moon Phases, March 1879," www.timeanddate.com/moon/usa/harrison-ne?month+1&year=1879.

Chapter 1. Provenance

1. Iron Teeth's story appears in several publications. The purest rendering, used here, is entitled "Iron Teeth, a Cheyenne Old Woman," in Thomas B. Marquis, *Cheyenne and Sioux: The Reminiscences of Four Indians and a White Soldier,* ed. Ronald H. Limbaugh (Stockton, Calif.: Pacific Center for Western Historical Studies, University of the Pacific, 1973), pp. 4–26. See also Thomas B. Marquis, "Red Ripe's Squaw: Recollections of a Long Life Interpreted by Thomas B. Marquis," *Century Magazine* 118 (June 1929): 201–209; and Thomas B. Marquis, *The Cheyennes of Montana*, ed.

Thomas D. Weist (Algonac, Mich.: Reference Publications, 1978), pp. 52–81. For broader perspectives, see John H. Monnett, "'My heart now has become changed to softer feelings': A Northern Cheyenne Woman and Her Family Remember the Long Journey Home," *Montana The Magazine of Western History* 59 (Summer 2009): 45–61; and that author's recounting in *Tell Them We Are Going Home: The Odyssey of the Northern Cheyennes* (Norman: University of Oklahoma Press, 2001).

2. Aspects of Cheyenne political and social organization as well as history are condensed here from John H. Moore, Margot P. Liberty, and A. Terry Straus, "Cheyenne," in *Plains*, ed. Raymond J. DeMallie, vol. 13, part 2, pp. 863–85, in William C. Sturtevant (gen. ed.), *Handbook of North American Indians* (Washington, D.C.: Smithsonian Institution, 2001); see also pertinent parts of the following texts: John H. Moore, *The Cheyenne Nation* (Lincoln: University of Nebraska Press, 1987); George Bird Grinnell, *The Cheyenne Indians: Their History and Ways of Life*, 2 vols. (New Haven, Conn.: Yale University Press, 1923); Peter M. Powell, *People of the Sacred Mountain: A History of the Northern Cheyenne Chiefs and Warrior Societies, 1830–1879, with an Epilogue, 1969–1974*, 2 vols. (San Francisco: Harper and Row, 1981); John Stands In Timber and Margot Liberty, *Cheyenne Memories* (New Haven, Conn.: Yale University Press, 1967); and Marquis, *The Cheyennes of Montana.* See also the innovative interpretation in Elliott West, "Called Out People: The Cheyennes and the Central Plains," *Montana The Magazine of Western History* 48 (Summer 1998): 2–15. Further important contemporary material is conveyed in William P. Clark, "Cheyenne," in William P. Clark, *The Indian Sign Language* (Philadelphia: L. R. Hamersly, 1885), pp. 98–107. Northern Cheyenne population estimates during the mid-1870s are based on Harry H. Anderson, "Cheyennes at the Little Big Horn: A Study of Statistics," *North Dakota History* 27 (Spring 1960): 3–15. For the larger story of time, place, and interpretive perspectives on what happened and where and their full meaning today, readers are encouraged to consult James N. Leiker and Ramon Powers, *The Northern Cheyenne Exodus in History and Memory* (Norman: University of Oklahoma Press, 2011), particularly chaps. 4 and 5; and Alan Boye, *Holding Stone Hands: On the Trail of the Cheyenne Exodus* (Lincoln: University of Nebraska Press, 1999).

3. In regard to this separation, Chief Whirlwind of the Southern Cheyennes told First Lieutenant William P. Clark: "We drifted apart. We used to come together at times, but not just like one people. We would go north and live with the Northern Cheyennes, and they would come and live with us; but this was only for a short time. We were like two different tribes, only we spoke the same language and had the same habits and customs." Clark, *Indian Sign Language*, p. 101.

4. The Grattan affair affected the course and trajectory of relations with the Lakotas and their allies for the next several decades. See especially John D. McDermott, R. Eli Paul, and Sandra J. Lowry, eds., *All Because of A Mormon Cow: Historical Accounts of the Grattan Massacre, 1854–1855* (Norman: University of Oklahoma Press, 2018).

5. Early confrontations between the Cheyennes and the U.S. government are detailed in Powell, *People of the Sacred Mountain*, 1:180–82, 212–13, 451–61; George Bird Grinnell, *The Fighting Cheyennes* (Norman: University of Oklahoma Press, 1956), pp. 105–23, 123–263; R. Eli Paul, *Blue Water Creek and the First Sioux War* (Norman: University of Oklahoma Press, 2004); Gary L. Roberts, *Massacre at Sand Creek: How*

Methodists Were Involved in an American Tragedy (Nashville, Tenn.: Abingdon Press, 2016); Jerome A. Greene, *Washita: The U.S. Army and the Southern Cheyennes, 1867–1869* (Norman: University of Oklahoma Press, 2004); Robert M. Utley, *Frontiersmen in Blue: The United States Army and the Indian, 1848–1865* (New York: Macmillan, 1967); and Robert M. Utley, *Frontier Regulars: The United States Army and the Indian, 1866–1890* (New York: Macmillan, 1973).

6. The protracted Great Sioux War was also contemporaneously known as the "Sioux War" and the "War with the Sioux" and continues to be designated by these terms today. The term "Great" referenced its expansive reach and length as well as the overall intensity and significance of the struggle's component engagements and today also includes its modern symbolism. Regarding the Cheyennes' involvement, see in particular Margot Liberty, "Cheyenne Primacy: New Perspectives on a Great Plains Tribe," *Plains Anthropologist* 56, no. 218 (2011): 155–74 (revised and republished in pamphlet format in 2016 to include co-author W. Raymond Wood). Cheyenne participation in the action at Powder River is thoroughly explicated in Paul L. Hedren, *Powder River: Disastrous Opening of the Great Sioux War* (Norman: University of Oklahoma Press, 2016). The Great Sioux War (1876–77) is variously chronicled in a plethora of books, but for an overview and personal perspectives on its varied encounters, see Jerome A. Greene, comp., *Battles and Skirmishes of the Great Sioux War, 1876–1877: The Military View* (Norman: University of Oklahoma Press, 1993); Jerome A. Greene, comp., *Lakota and Cheyenne: Indian Views of the Great Sioux War, 1876–1877* (Norman: University of Oklahoma Press, 1994); and Paul L. Hedren, *Traveler's Guide to the Great Sioux War* (Helena: Montana Historical Society Press, 1996). It is important to note that Arapaho involvement in the Great Sioux War was negligible, although five Arapaho men happened by the Little Bighorn encampment and were initially taken prisoner by the Sioux, who feared that they were scouts for the army. (Late in the Sioux War some Arapahos served Crook's command against the Northern Cheyennes.) The fleeting appearance of five Arapahos at the Little Bighorn in no way suggested a purposeful tribal commitment during the fighting of 1876–77. Indeed, on March 17, 1877, Colonel Ranald Mackenzie informed the secretary of the interior that "the Arapahoes . . . have been entirely loyal to the Government through all the troubles with the Sioux and Cheyennes." Thomas R. Buecker, *Fort Robinson and the American West, 1874–1899* (Lincoln: Nebraska State Historical Society, 1999), pp. 101, 227 (quotation). For further explication of the term "Great Sioux War," see Paul L. Hedren, *After Custer: Loss and Transformation in Sioux Country* (Norman: University of Oklahoma Press, 2011), pp. 6, 199n2.

7. The Battle of the Rosebud is insightfully recounted in Paul L. Hedren, *Rosebud, June 17, 1876: Prelude to the Little Big Horn* (Norman: University of Oklahoma Press, 2019), while the Battle of the Little Bighorn is covered in James Donovan, *A Terrible Glory: Custer and the Little Bighorn—The Last Great Battle of the American West* (Boston: Little, Brown, 2008). For the Red Fork action, see Jerome A. Greene, *Morning Star Dawn: The Powder River Expedition and the Northern Cheyennes, 1876* (Norman: University of Oklahoma Press, 2003), pp. 90–177, 189–91.

8. See Jerome A. Greene, *Yellowstone Command: Colonel Nelson A. Miles and the Great Sioux War, 1876–1877* (Norman: University of Oklahoma Press, 2006), pp. 147–218; Orlan J. Svingen, *The Northern Cheyenne Indian Reservation, 1877–1900* (Niwot: University Press of Colorado, 1993), pp. 16–17; and Peter J. Powell, *The Cheyennes,*

Måheoô's People: A Critical Bibliography (Bloomington: Indiana University Press, 1980), p. 44.

9. Buecker, *Fort Robinson and the American West, 1874–1899*, pp. 18–36; Thomas R. Buecker, *Last Days of Red Cloud Agency: Peter T. Buckley's Photograph Collection, 1876–1877* (Lincoln: Nebraska Historical Society, 2016), pp. 16, 18–19.

10. Buecker, *Last Days of Red Cloud Agency*, pp. 92–95; *New York Herald*, May 11, 1877; Powell, *People of the Sacred Mountain*, 2:1144–45; Greene, *Morning Star Dawn*, pp. 190–91 (quotation). As indicated, Sitting Bull and his followers, perhaps numbering as many as 5,000 people, crossed the border into Canada, where they remained until 1880–81. Jerome A. Greene, *Beyond Bear's Paw: The Nez Perce Indians in Canada* (Norman: University of Oklahoma Press, 2010), pp. 26–27; Buecker, *Fort Robinson and the American West*, p. 103. Some names of the heads of families of Northern Cheyennes who surrendered at Camp Robinson and then went south appear in Thomas R. Buecker and R. Eli Paul, eds., *The Crazy Horse Surrender Ledger* (Lincoln: Nebraska Historical Society, 1994).

11. Hans L. Trefousse, *Rutherford B. Hayes* (New York: Henry Holt, 2002), pp. 100, 106, 109, 117, 126.

12. U.S. Congress, Senate, *Letter from the Secretary of War, to the Chairman of the Committee on Indian Affairs, Communicating Information in Relation to the Escape of the Cheyenne Indians from Fort Robinson.* Misc. Doc. No. 64, 45th Cong., 3rd sess., 1879, p. 32 (hereinafter cited as Senate, *Escape of the Cheyenne Indians*). For the 933 Cheyennes and 4 Arapahos, see Major John K. Mizner to Agent John D. Miles, August 8, 1878, in *Report of the Secretary of War, 1878* (Washington, D.C.: Government Printing Office, 1878), p. 50. In 1880 General Crook wrote that "in 1875, at the time of my coming to this department, the Northern Cheyennes were constantly running between the Red Cloud Agency and the Indian Territory, and were regarded as the same people with the Southern Cheyennes." When the northern people opposed a plan to send them to the Missouri River, Crook told them that the Interior Department offered them an option of going south to join their relatives. He reported that "they were not a unit in this matter, and had many councils among themselves before coming to tell me that they had decided to go [south]." Crook to Senator Samuel J. Kirkwood of Iowa, Chairman of the Select Committee on the Removal of the Northern Cheyennes, February 22, 1880, in U.S. Congress, Senate, *Report of the Select Committee to Examine into the Circumstances Connected with the Removal of the Northern Cheyennes from the Sioux Reservation to the Indian Territory*, Senate Report 708, 46th Cong., 2nd sess., 1880 (hereinafter cited as Senate, *Select Committee Report*), p. 224. See also Mackenzie to Kirkwood, February 24, 1880, in ibid., pp. 224–25.

13. "Iron Teeth, a Cheyenne Old Woman," p. 19 (quotation); James Mooney, "The Cheyenne Indians," *Memoirs of the American Anthropological Association* 1 (September 1907): 397.

14. George W. Manypenny, *Our Indian Wards* (Cincinnati: Robert Clarke, 1880), pp. 334–35. Telegrams to Sheridan on May 14, 15, and 20, 1877, suggest that many of the Northern Cheyennes desired to go south at this time. Sioux War Papers, 4163 AGO 1876, RG 393, Records of the U.S. Army Continental Commands, Microfilm Publication M666, Reel 281, National Archives. According to the treaty of May 10, 1868, Northern Cheyennes (and Arapahos) agreed

> to accept for their permanent home some portion of the tract of country set apart and designated as a permanent reservation for the Southern Cheyenne and Arapahoe Indians . . . by virtue of an earlier accord at Medicine Lodge Creek, Kansas, on the [28th] day of October [1867], *or* some portion of the country and reservation set apart and designated as a permanent home for the Brulé and other bands of Sioux Indians, by a treaty entered into by and between said Indians and the United States, at Fort Laramie, D.T., on the twenty-ninth day of April [1868].

Charles J. Kappler, comp. and ed., *Indian Affairs: Laws and Treaties*, 2 vols. (Washington, D.C.: Government Printing Office, 1904), 2:1012. The following almost identical phrasing appears in article 2 of the October 1867 and April 1868 treaties: "The same [land] is set apart for the absolute and undisturbed use and occupation of the Indians herein named, *and for such other friendly tribes or individual Indians, as from time to time they may be willing, with the consent of the United States, to admit among them.*" Ibid., 2:985 (quotation; emphasis added), 998. This locution seemingly explained the government's anticipated extended use of land on either reservation to harbor the Northern Cheyennes and/or the Northern Arapahos. A subsequent agreement on September 26, 1876, ratified by Congress on February 28, 1877, authorizing the government to take the Black Hills, prevented the removal of the Lakota Indians to the Indian Territory but not the removal of the Northern Cheyennes and Arapahos (although the latter were subsequently sent to join the Shoshonis on their reservation in Wyoming). Ibid., 1:168–72. An earlier council that failed is covered in depth in James E. Potter, ed., *From Our Special Correspondent: Dispatches from the 1875 Black Hills Council at Red Cloud Agency, Nebraska* (Lincoln: Nebraska State Historical Society, 2016).

On the Indians' retention of their arms, see Major General Philip H. Sheridan to Brigadier General John Pope, June 6, 1877, Sioux War Papers, NA, wherein Sheridan stated: "I was under the impression that the Cheyennes had been disarmed and dismounted [last April] and am sorry it was not most thoroughly done [at that time]." In fact, the Indians had surrendered their guns (many taken from Custer's dead at the Little Bighorn) on their arrival at Camp Robinson in April 1877. "They were given a good many of them back again to hunt with—both horses and arms—and those guns were the guns they brought down here [to the Indian Territory]." Those guns subsequently had been turned in and were not given back to the Indians, who instead acquired guns from other Indians: "Pawnees, Sacs, and Indians of other neighboring tribes [in the Indian Territory]." Senate, *Select Committee Report*, p. 20; Mooney, "Cheyenne Indians," p. 397. The controversy regarding Standing Elk is discussed at length in Monnett, *Tell Them We Are Going Home*, pp. 22–24, as well as in Ramon Powers, "The Northern Cheyenne Trek through Western Kansas in 1878: Frontiersmen, Indians and Cultural Conflict," *Trail Guide* 17, nos. 3–4: 7.

15. *New York Herald*, January 15, 1879.

16. George A. Woodward, "Some Experiences with the Cheyennes," *United Service* 1 (April 1879): 188.

17. Leo Killsback, "Morning Star, Violence, and the Rights of Indigenous Peoples," in "Remembering the Battle of Punished Woman's Fork: The 2013 Scott City Symposium," *Kansas History: A Journal of the Central Plains* 38 (Winter 2015–16): 242; Rubie Sooktis, "Surviving the Odds: People of Dull Knife and Little Wolf,"

Kansas History: A Journal of the Central Plains 38 (Winter 2015–16): 236; Woodward, "Some Experiences with the Cheyennes," pp. 188–91. See also Charles A. Eastman, *Indian Heroes and Great Chieftains* (Boston: Little, Brown, 1929), pp. 179–88.

18. Grinnell, *Cheyenne Indians*, 1:51–52.

19. *New York Herald*, January 15, 1879.

20. Peter J. Powell, *The Killing of Morning Star's People* (Chadron, Nebr.: Mari Sandoz Heritage Society, 1994), pp. 1–2; Denise Low and Ramon Powers, "Northern Cheyenne Warrior Ledger Art: Captivity Narratives of Northern Cheyenne Prisoners in 1879 Dodge City," *Kansas History: A Journal of the Central Plains* 35 (Spring 2012): 19–22; Moore, *Cheyenne Nation*, pp. 196–97. The composition of the affected people, including the leadership, is discussed in depth in Powell, *Killing of Morning Star's People*, pp. 1–4.

21. Mizner to Agent J. D. Miles, August 8, 1878, in *Report of the Secretary of War, 1878*, p. 50; Christina Gish Hill, *Webs of Kinship: Family in Northern Cheyenne Nationhood* (Norman: University of Oklahoma Press, 2017), pp. 166–67; Manypenny, *Our Indian Wards*, p. 335; Mooney, "Cheyenne Indians," p. 397; Edgar Beecher Bronson, *Cowboy Life on the Western Plains: The Reminiscences of a Ranchman* (New York: Grosset and Dunlap, 1910), p. 137 (first quotation); Thomas B. Marquis, *A Warrior Who Fought Custer* (Minneapolis: Midwest Company, 1931), p. 320 (second quotation); Powell, *Killing of Morning Star's People*, p. 1; Stan Hoig, *The Peace Chiefs of the Cheyennes* (Norman: University of Oklahoma Press, 1980), pp. 131–32; *We, the Northern Cheyenne People: Our Land, Our History, Our Culture* (Lame Deer, Mont.: Chief Dull Knife College, 2008), pp. 25–26; Tom Weist, *A History of the Cheyenne People* (Billings: Montana Council for Indian Education, 1977), pp. 77–80. See especially Ramon Powers, "Why the Northern Cheyennes Left Indian Territory in 1878: A Cultural Analysis," *Kansas Quarterly* 3 (Fall 1971): 72–81. "Northerners Slandered as 'Sioux,'" cited in Svingen, *Northern Cheyenne Indian Reservation*, p. 19.

22. Marquis, *A Warrior Who Fought Custer*, p. 320; George Bird Grinnell, *The Fighting Cheyennes* (Norman: University of Oklahoma Press, 1956), p. 398; "Iron Teeth, a Cheyenne Old Woman," pp. 19–20 (quotation). The dearth of adequate agency-provided footstuffs proved a bane but reflected the attitude of Congress and the American people in the matter of appropriations for Indians in the aftermath of the Great Sioux War. See Henry E. Fritz, *The Movement for Indian Assimilation, 1860–1890* (Philadelphia: University of Pennsylvania Press, 1963), pp. 137–38.

23. "Iron Teeth, a Cheyenne Old Woman," p. 20 (quotation). For Darlington Agency and Fort Reno, see *Outline Descriptions of the Posts in the Military Division of the Missouri* (Chicago: Headquarters Military Division of the Missouri, 1876; reprint, Bellevue, Nebr.: Old Army Press, 1969), p. 178; Robert G. Ferris, ed., *Soldier and Brave: Historic Places Associated with Indian Affairs in the Trans-Mississippi West* (Washington, D.C.: National Park Service, 1971), pp. 266–68; W. Edwin Derrick, "Fort Reno, Indian Territory: Frontier Guardian, *Periodical, Journal of the Council on Abandoned Military Posts* 10 (Winter 1978–79): 14–17; and Robert W. Frazer, *Forts of the West: Military Forts and Presidios and Posts Commonly Called Forts West of the Mississippi River* (Norman: University of Oklahoma Press, 1965), p. 123.

24. Wooden Leg in Marquis, *A Warrior Who Fought Custer*, p. 320. Agent Miles reported that the "Dull-Knife band were displeased with the system of issuing rations to heads of families and individual Indians [instead of to the chiefs]. . . . He

states that they have always been defiant, claimed that they did not enter into the agreement of September 26, 1876 [the Black Hills Treaty], and said that they would remain at the agency as long as they chose, and no longer." *Report of the Commissioner of Indian Affairs, 1878,* p. xxii. For rations issued to the Indians, see ibid., pp. xxii–xxiv, 456–57; Julia B. McGillycuddy, *McGillycuddy Agent: A Biography of Dr. Valentine T. McGillycuddy* (Stanford, Calif.: Stanford University Press, 1941), p. 93; and Powers, "Northern Cheyenne Trek through Western Kansas," pp. 8–9. Indeed, some Northern Cheyennes were so upset at the prospect of moving south that they asked to be merged with the Lakotas. Powers, "Why the Northern Cheyennes Left Indian Territory," p. 74. For discussion of the alarming rations history at Darlington, see Donald J. Berthrong, *The Cheyenne and Arapaho Ordeal: Reservation and Agency Life in the Indian Territory, 1875–1907* (Norman: University of Oklahoma Press, 1976), pp. 8–19. For such difficulties after the northerners arrived, see ibid., pp. 29–31, 34–35. For the perceived food shortages, see especially *Army and Navy Journal*, October 19, 1878, p. 166.

25. Quoted in Helen Hunt Jackson, *A Century of Dishonor: The Early Crusade for Indian Reform* (New York: Harper and Brothers, 1881), p. 100.

26. Senate, *Select Committee Report*, p. 26.

27. Clark to Post Adjutant, Fort Reno, I. T., December 13, 1878, in Cheyenne Outbreak, Microfilm 1495, Roll 6, Special Files, Division of the Missouri, September 1878–February 1879, NA (first quotation); Mackenzie to Pope, September 4, 1877, in Senate, *Select Committee Report*, p. 265 (second quotation).

28. For the significant cultural affiliation issue, see especially Hill, *Webs of Kinship*, pp. 155–89. For the new reality of the Northern Cheyennes' fading home landscape, see Leiker and Powers, *Northern Cheyenne Exodus*, pp. 47–48.

29. Richard N. Ellis, *General Pope and U.S. Indian Policy* (Albuquerque: University of New Mexico Press, 1970), pp. 206–8; Grinnell, *Fighting Cheyennes*, pp. 401–4 (quotations). See also Utley, *Frontier Regulars*, p. 283. On the matter of deficiency of rations and other articles as well as sickness among the Northern Cheyennes at Darlington Agency, see also the reports of First Lieutenant Lawton (undated, but ca. October 1877), in Senate, *Select Committee Report*, pp. 268–76; Agent John D. Miles to Mizner, September 20, 1878, in ibid., pp. 277–78; and Mizner to the AAG, Department of the Missouri, September 19, 1878, in ibid., pp. 279–80, as well as subsequent extensive correspondence on the rations issue from agent Miles, Mizner, and Indian commissioner Ezra A. Hayt as well as medicinal concerns in ibid., pp. 280–301. For General Pope and his background, see Robert M. Utley, *The Commanders: Civil War Generals Who Shaped the American West* (Norman: University of Oklahoma Press, 2018), pp. 151–75.

Chapter 2. Coming Home

1. The total was 92 men, 120 women, 69 boys, and 72 girls. Commissioner of Indian Affairs Ezra A. Hayt to Agent Miles, September 10, 1878, Letters Received by the Office of Indian Affairs, 1824–81, Microfilm Roll 723, copy no. 234 and Red Cloud Agency, 1871–1880, NA. Miles reported that "not one of the chiefs who left this agency September 9, 1878, signed the treaty [of September 26, 1876], and on

more than one occasion one of the chiefs who left informed me in substance that he . . . had only come south on trial and under great pressure, and [they] have continually . . . threatened to return when matters did not go to suit them." Miles to Commissioner of Indian Affairs E. A. Hayt, November 1, 1878, Letters Received and Red Cloud Agency, NA. Mooney, "Cheyenne Indians," p. 398. See also *Report of the Commissioner of Indian Affairs, 1878*, pp. xxii–xxiii, 455–56.

2. See army correspondence regarding efforts to contain the Indians before their departure in *Report of the Secretary of War, 1878*, pp. 44–49. Stolen horses are mentioned in an interview by Walter M. Camp with Little Wolf's son, Buffalo Hump, in 1911. Ellison-Camp Papers, Western History and Genealogy Department, Denver Public Library (hereinafter cited as Ellison-Camp Papers, DPL).

3. Berthrong, *Cheyenne and Arapaho Ordeal*, p. 33; Miles to Hayt, September 10, 1878, and Miles to Hayt, November 1, 1878, Letters Received by the Office of Indian Affairs, 1824–81, Microfilm Roll 723, copy no. 234 and Red Cloud Agency, 1871–1880, NA (quotation); Powell, *Killing of Morning Star's People*, pp. 3–4.

4. Neither Fort Reno nor Darlington Agency accessed the telegraph lines until 1879. Derrick, "Fort Reno," p. 18.

5. *Chicago Tribune*, September 16, 1878.

6. *Record of Engagements with Hostile Indians within the Military Division of the Missouri, from 1868 to 1882* (Washington, D.C.: Government Printing Office, 1882; reprint, Fort Collins, Colo.: Old Army Press, 1972), p. 81. For Pope's background and his role as commander of the Military Department of the Missouri, see Utley, *The Commanders*, pp. 151–75.

7. *We, the Northern Cheyenne People*, pp. 26–28 (quotation); Christina Rose, "Native History: Descendant Tells Father's Story of Fort Robinson Escape," *Indian Country Today*, January 22, 2014, https://newsmaven.io/indiancountrytoday/archive/native-history-descendant-tells-father-s-story-of-fort-robinson-escape-fI-OF2p94EqL2Am-_iGZYw/.

8. "Briefs," in Senate, *Escape of the Cheyenne Indians*, pp. 2–3; *New York Herald*, October 21, 1878; *Army and Navy Journal*, September 28, October 12 and October 18, 1878; *Sidney Telegraph*, September 28, 1878; *New York Times*, September 20 and September 21, 1878; Berthrong, *Cheyenne and Arapaho Ordeal*, p. 34. An important treatment of the Turkey Springs encounter is Bob Rea, "Turkey Springs and Red Hills, September 13–14, 1878," Fort Supply State Historic Site, Fort Supply, Oklahoma. See also George Nellans, "The Great Cheyenne Chase: A Truthful Account by a Dragoon Who Participated in It," copy in the Judge Nellans File, Last Indian Raid in Kansas Museum, Oberlin, Kansas.

9. *New York Herald*, October 21, 1878; Powers, "Northern Cheyenne Trek through Western Kansas," pp. 13–14. For Sand Creek, see *Army and Navy Journal*, October 19, 1878; *Sidney Plaindealer*, October 10, 1878; Nellans, "Great Cheyenne Chase"; and Monnett, *Tell Them We are Going Home*, pp. 61–66. An account by a participating cowman appears in J. W. Berryman, "Early Settlement of Southwest Kansas," *Collections of the Kansas State Historical Society, 1926–1928* 17 (1928): 563–70. Rendlebrock, from Prussia, was appointed as a lieutenant with the Fourth Cavalry in 1862 and received brevets of first lieutenant, captain, and major for his respective services at Franklin, Tennessee; McMinnville, Tennessee; and Selma, Alabama, during the Civil War. Guy V. Henry, *Military Record of Army and Civilian Appointments in the*

United States Army, 2 vols. (New York: D. Van Nostrand, 1873), 2:328; *Army and Navy Journal*, October 26, 1878. For the encounters below the Arkansas River, see also Grinnell, *Fighting Cheyennes*, pp. 405–8. For unknown reasons, Grinnell considered neither the major engagement at Punished Woman's Fork nor the Cheyenne attacks on settlers in northwest Kansas in his treatise.

10. *New York Times*, September 24, 1878. In an interview granted to a correspondent of the *New York Herald* in 1879 at Pine Ridge Agency, Dull Knife alluded to a fight with the soldiers on Crooked Creek (which was perhaps the combat near Sand Creek), calling it the "third fight with the soldiers, in which we had 11 of our people shot," as being the impetus for their determination to fight the soldiers. *New North-West*, May 23, 1879.

11. For the Punished Woman's Fork action, see *New York Times*, September 30, 1878; *Army and Navy Journal*, October 26, 1878; *National Tribune*, July 22, 1920 (a veteran's account); *New York Herald*, October 21, 1878; *Record of Engagements*, p. 80; *Sidney Telegraph*, October 5, 1878; *Sidney Plaindealer*, October 10, 1878; Nellans, "Great Cheyenne Chase"; Monnett, *Tell Them We are Going Home*, pp. 67–74; Powers, "Northern Cheyenne Trek through Western Kansas," pp. 16–17; Vernon R. Maddux and Albert Glenn Maddux, *In Dull Knife's Wake: The True Story of the Northern Cheyenne Exodus of 1878* (Norman, Okla.: Horse Creek Publications, 2003), pp. 79–98. Particulars of the shooting and death of Lewis appear in letters from his adjutant, Second Lieutenant Cornelius Gardener, as well as accompanying medical documents, Records on Diseases and Individual Cases, 1841–1893, F491, Records of the AGO, RG 94, NA. Lewis's obituary is in *Army and Navy Journal*, October 12, 1878. See also "Report of the Surgeon-General, October 1, 1879," in *Report of the Secretary of War, 1879* (Washington, D.C. Government Printing Office, 1879), p. 408; and Greene and Wright, "Chasing Dull Knife," p. 27. First Lieutenant Abram E. Wood, Fourth Cavalry, received the brevet of captain in 1890 for his services fighting at Sand Creek and Punished Woman's Fork, Kansas. *U.S. Army Gallantry and Meritorious Conduct, 1866–1891* (n.p.: Planchet Press, 1986), p. 88. A Northern Cheyenne oral ancestral account passed down to the present appears online: Rose, "Native History: Descendant Tells Father's Story of Fort Robinson Escape," http://Indiancountrytodaymedianetwork.com/2014/01/22/native-history-descendent-tells-fathers-story-fort-robinson-escape-153195.

12. The effective withdrawal of the southern army troops following their somewhat inept performance was not without recrimination. Major Mizner subsequently preferred charges against three officers. Of the three, only Captain Rendlebrock was convicted of misbehavior before the enemy and sentenced to be dismissed from the army. At the urging of Secretary of War George W. McCrary and General Sheridan, however, President Hayes remitted the sentence, allowing Rendlebrock to retire. For specifics, see Stan Hoig, *Perilous Pursuit: The U.S. Cavalry and the Northern Cheyennes* (Niwot: University Press of Colorado, 2002), pp. 211–19.

13. Greene and Wright, "Chasing Dull Knife," p. 27; *Chicago Times*, October 2, 1878. General Pope "did not consider that the present [out]break of the red men would result in anything serious." *Chicago Tribune*, September 16, 1878. Pope believed that "even if they did succeed in crossing the Arkansas river and the Santa Fe railroad without interception they would certainly be turned back before they could cross the Kansas Pacific." Ibid. The Cheyenne animus toward whites in northwestern

Kansas was probably not generated by the 1875 killings of a party of Southern Cheyennes under a headman named Little Bull by soldiers. See John H. Monnett, *Massacre at Cheyenne Hole: Lieutenant Austin Henely and the Sappa Creek Controversy* (Niwot: University Press of Colorado, 1999), especially pp. 99–105.

14. *Daily State Journal* (Lincoln, Nebraska), October 22, 1878.

15. Jerome A. Greene and Peter M. Wright, eds., "Chasing Dull Knife: A Journal of the Cheyenne Campaign of 1878 by Lieutenant George H. Palmer," *Heritage of Kansas* 12 (Winter 1971): 30–31; *Sidney Plaindealer,* October 17, 1878; *Daily State Journal* (Lincoln, Nebraska), October 15, 1878; *New York Herald,* November 3, 1878; *McCook Tribune,* April 29, 1929; Powers, "Northern Cheyenne Trek through Kansas," pp. 18–20 (first quotation) from the *Wellington Press,* November 7, 1878), 31–32n29; *Daily State Journal,* October 22, 1878 (second quotation); *Lincoln Journal,* January 3, 1971; For the Northern Cheyenne depredations in northwest Kansas, see also Nellans, "Great Cheyenne Chase"; *Omaha Bee,* October 7 and October 9, 1878; *Sidney Plaindealer,* October 10, 1878; *Omaha Weekly Republican,* November 22, 1878; *National Tribune,* October 11, 1911; and especially Monnett, *Tell Them We Are Going Home,* pp. 78–101. The latter event is chronicled in Monnett, *Massacre at Cheyenne Hole.* The Cheyenne raids in Kansas became "the subject of discussion" at President Rutherford B. Hayes's cabinet meeting on October 12. *Sidney Plaindealer,* October 17, 1878.

16. See Leiker and Powers, *Northern Cheyenne Exodus,* pp. 59–62.

17. "Iron Teeth, a Cheyenne Old Woman," pp. 20–21. See also the Cheyenne accounts regarding the killing of white citizens in John Stands In Timber and Margot Liberty, *Cheyenne Memories* (New Haven, Conn.: Yale University Press, 1967), pp. 232–34. For further reading on the Northern Cheyennes' movement through Kansas, see "Letters to G. W. Martin, 1905–1906, concerning the route of Cheyenne Indians in crossing Kansas in 1878," in William Elsey Connelley Papers relating to Indian Folklore, MS 1227 Lab 28634 (microfilm), Cheyenne Indian Collection, Kansas State Historical Society, Topeka.

18. *Army and Navy Journal,* November 9, 1878. For more government documents associated with the Kansas raids, see Senate, *Escape of the Cheyenne Indians,* pp. 16–19. For adjudication of the many claims emanating from the raids at both the state and federal levels (most of which went unpaid), see Ramon Powers, "The Kansas Indian Claims Commission of 1879," *Kansas History* 7 (Autumn 1984): 199–211.

19. *Sidney Telegraph,* September 21, 1878.

20. Telegram, AAG Robert Williams to Sheridan, October 4, 1878, in Cheyenne Outbreak, September 1878–February 1879, Microfilm 1495, Roll 6, Special Files, Division of the Missouri, NA (hereinafter cited as Microfilm 1495, Roll 6, NA); Report of First Lieutenant John G. Bourke, October 17, 1878, NA, copy in Fort Robinson Archive, Nebraska State Historical Society (hereinafter cited as NSHS) (quotation); *Sidney Telegraph,* July 11, 1885; *Chicago Times,* September 16, September 21, October 3 and October 4, 1878; *New York Times,* October 5, 1878; *New York Herald,* October 5, 1878; *Chicago Tribune,* October 5, 1878; *Record of Engagements,* 81; Mooney, "Cheyenne Indians," p. 398; Powell, *Killing of Morning Star's People,* p. 5. Berthrong, *Cheyenne and Arapaho Ordeal,* p. 37; Hoig, *Perilous Pursuit,* p. 147. Little Chief's followers did not join the northerners left behind at Darlington until December 1878, when they faced many of the same problems as the followers of Dull Knife

and Little Wolf. Hoig, *Perilous Pursuit*, pp. 37–39. For Sidney Barracks, see *Outline Descriptions of the Posts*, pp. 75–78; Thomas R. Buecker, "Memo: Keep Your Work Straight!" *Periodical* 9 (Winter 1977–78): 3–12; Thomas R. Buecker, "Fort Sidney: Its Role on the Upper Plains," *Periodical* 11 (March 1981): 22–36; Thomas R. Buecker, "The Lingering Death of Old Fort Sidney," *Periodical* 14 (March 1986): 17–30. Sidney Barracks became Fort Sidney in December 1878. Francis Paul Prucha, *A Guide to the Military Posts of the United States, 1789–1895* (Madison: State Historical Society of Wisconsin, 1964), p. 107.

21. "Report of Brig. Gen. George Crook," September 27, 1879, in *Report of the Secretary of War, 1879*, p. 77. The Indians evidently crossed the North Platte River near the mouth of White Tail Creek. Luther North, *Man of the Plains: Recollections of Luther North, 1856–1882*, ed. Donald F. Danker (Lincoln: University of Nebraska Press, 1961), pp. 256–61. For Crook, see Jerome A. Greene, "George Crook," in Paul Andrew Hutton and Durwood Ball, eds., *Soldiers West: Biographies from the Military Frontier*, 2nd ed. (Norman: University of Oklahoma Press, 2009), pp. 246–72. For Crook in the Plains Indian wars, see Paul Magid, *The Gray Fox: George Crook and the Indian Wars* (Norman: University of Oklahoma Press, 2015); for his tenure as department commander in the West (including the Department of the Platte), see especially Utley, *The Commanders*, pp. 35–66, 204–6.

22. *Omaha Bee*, October 16, 1878.

23. Spotted Tail's Brulés had been moved east to the Missouri River in October 1877. *Report of the Commissioner of Indian Affairs, 1878*, p. 38.

24. Carlton to AAG, Department of the Platte, October 16, 1878, with supplement, same date (including map), in Microfilm 1495, Roll 6, NA; "Record of Events," Regimental Return of the Third Cavalry for October 1878, in Microfilm 744, Roll 3, NA; Report of First Lieutenant John G. Bourke, October 17, 1878, NA, copy in Fort Robinson Archive, NSHS; *Army and Navy Journal*, October 9, 1878; *Omaha Bee*, October 9, October 14, and October 16, 1878; *New York Herald*, October 25, 1878; Thomas Thornburgh to AAG, Department of the Platte, October 19, 1878, copy in Fort Robinson Archive, NSHS; *Record of Engagements*, p. 81; Bronson, *Cowboy Life on the Western Plains*, pp. 150–52; Buecker, *Fort Robinson and the American West*, pp. 131–33; James C. Olson, *Red Cloud and the Sioux Problem* (Lincoln: University of Nebraska Press, 1965), p. 262; Robert W. Larson, *Red Cloud: Warrior-Statesman of the Lakota Sioux* (Norman: University of Oklahoma Press, 1997), p. 224. For Camp Sheridan, see *Outline Descriptions of the Posts*, pp. 111, 113. General Crook relayed word from scout and interpreter Ben Clark, with the Cheyennes at Sidney awaiting transit south, that the people with Dull Knife planned to head for the mouth of Tongue River on the Yellowstone if the Sioux did not aid them. Telegram, Crook to Sheridan, October 12, 1878 in Microfilm 1495, Roll 6, NA.

Major Carlton, from Ohio, graduated from West Point in 1859 and rose to command the First Ohio Infantry Regiment during the Civil War, winning brevet appointments of major and lieutenant colonel for service in the Peninsular Campaign and meritorious service in battle at Chickamauga. After the war he was appointed a major in the Third Cavalry in 1876. Carlton retired from the army in 1897. Francis B. Heitman, comp., *Historical Register and Dictionary of the United States Army, 1789–1903*, 2 vols. (Washington, D.C.: Government Printing Office, 1903), 1:282–83.

25. "Iron Teeth, a Cheyenne Old Woman," p. 21. The separation is treated in depth and conclusively in Powell, *Killing of Morning Star's People*, pp. 5–7; Powell, *Cheyennes*, pp. 47–48, 50; Manypenny, *Our Indian Wards*, p. 336; "Proceedings of a Board of Officers," January 25–February 7, 1879, RG 98, Records of the Military Division of the Missouri, Special File 905-M-1879, NA (hereafter cited as "Proceedings of a Board," NA), pp. 16–17. This report suggests that the Indians "split up into several parties" (p. 193). Northern Cheyenne tribal historian John Stands In Timber stated that "Dull Knife had always been more Sioux-like, and he wanted to go to Fort Robinson [Red Cloud Agency] where they had started from. He thought nobody would bother them again." Stands In Timber and Liberty, *Cheyenne Memories*, 235. See also the undated interview with scout Ben Clark regarding the split. Walter M. Camp Papers, Manuscript Department, Lilly Library, Indiana University, Bloomington (hereinafter cited as Camp Papers, Lilly Library, Indiana University). See also Hugh Lenox Scott, *Some Memories of a Soldier* (New York: Century, 1928), p. 98.

26. Quoted in Bronson, *Cowboy Life on the Western Plains*, p. 151.

27. Operations of troops in Dakota Territory (Department of Dakota) during the Northern Cheyenne disturbance are detailed at length in Colonel William H. Wood to AAG, Department of Dakota, October 27, 1878, in Microfilm 1495, Roll 6, NA.

28. Particulars of the exhaustive search for the Cheyennes by Mauck, Thornburgh, and Carlton following the Indians' crossing of the North Platte appear in John G. Bourke, *The Diaries of John Gregory Bourke, Volume 3, June 1, 1878–June 22, 1880*, ed. Charles M. Robinson III, 5 vols. (Denton: University of North Texas Press, 2003–15), pp. 160–72 (Carlton's trail is shown on a period map reproduced on p. 165). See also the report of Captain Peter D. Vroom, Third Cavalry, October 23, 1878, in Senate, *Escape of the Cheyenne Indians*, pp. 15–16; *Record of Engagements*, p. 81; *New York Times*, October 9 and October 11, 1878; Telegram, Crook to Sheridan, October 15, 1878, in Microfilm 1495, Roll 6, NA; *New York Times*, October 15, 1878; Bronson, *Cowboy Life on the Western Plains*, pp. 156–57, 159–60; *Sidney Plaindealer*, October 17, 1878. Crow Butte, adjacent Little Crow Butte, and nearby Crown Butte, along with adjacent spring-fed hills and forested tracts rising in the area of White River, compose the modern Nebraska National Forest and Ponderosa State Wildlife Area. See U.S. Department of the Interior Geological Survey (hereinafter USGS), "Crow Butte, Nebr.," quadrangle, 1980, Sections 8 and 17 and adjoining areas.

29. Red Cloud's people reportedly captured "two men, five women, and three children Cheyennes" and would hold them so that "others may be induced to surrender." Telegram, Colonel John Gibbon to Sheridan, October 20, 1878, in Microfilm 1495, Roll 6, NA. Other scouting activities relative to the Northern Cheyennes are delineated in "Report of Lieutenant-General Sheridan," October 22, 1879, in *Report of the Secretary of War, 1879*, pp. 50–51.

30. "Proceedings of a Board," NA, p. 178.

31. John B. Johnson to Adjutant, Battalion Third Cavalry, October 25, 1878, in Microfilm 1495, Roll 6, NA; Chase to Walter M. Camp, February 24, 1914, copy in the Fort Robinson Archive, NSHS; "Proceedings of a Board," NA, p. 190; U.S. Senate, *Escape of the Cheyenne Indians*, pp. 12–13 (quotations). See also Grinnell, *Fighting Cheyennes*, pp. 414–15.

32. *Army and Navy Journal*, November 9, 1878. Local settler John Farnham reported that Joe Laravie, a scout with Captain John B. Johnson's troops, told Chief

Dull Knife that "if he surrendered he would be sent to Pine Ridge, where he [Dull Knife] wanted to go." The scout himself volunteered this information. Major Carlton, of course, subsequently directed the Cheyennes to Camp Robinson. Camp Papers, Lilly Library, Indiana University, copy in Fort Robinson Archive, NSHS.

33. "Proceedings of a Board," NA, p. 56.

34. Ibid., p. 179; Johnson to Adjutant, Battalion Third Cavalry, October 25, 1878 (quotation), in Microfilm 1495, Roll 6, NA; Crook to Sheridan, October 25, 1878, citing Johnson to AG, Omaha Barracks, October 24, 1878, in ibid.; "Proceedings of a Board," NA, p. 6; *Army and Navy Journal*, November 9, 1878; *New York Times*, October 16, 1878; Carter P. Johnson, "Outbreak of Cheyennes: Interview with Maj. Carter P. Johnson" (hereinafter cited as Johnson, "Outbreak of Cheyennes"), September 19, 1913, Item 2, Ellison-Camp Papers, DPL.

35. Carlton to Assistant Adjutant General, Department of the Platte, October 27, 1878, in Microfilm 1495, Roll 6, NA (quotation); Senate, *Escape of the Cheyenne Indians*, pp. 12–13; *Army and Navy Journal*, November 2 and November 9, 1878; Johnson, "Outbreak of Cheyennes," Ellison-Camp Papers, DPL; "Captain Carter P. Johnson's Statement in Relation to the Cheyenne Outbreak," in Richard E. Jensen, ed., *Voices of the American West, Volume 2: The Settler and Soldier Interviews of Eli S. Ricker, 1903–1919* (Lincoln: University of Nebraska Press, 2005), pp. 230–32; Claim of Price & Jenks for Beef, January 27, 1879, NA, copy in Fort Robinson Archive, NSHS; Powell, *Sweet Medicine*, 1:215–22 (Carter Johnson was a sergeant in Company F of the Third Cavalry and was not present at the surrender, although his account contains several insightful details that most likely occurred); Patricia Y. Stallard, ed., *Fanny Dunbar Corbusier: Recollections of Her Army Life, 1869–1908* (Norman: University of Oklahoma Press, 2003), p. 89; Bronson, *Cowboy Life on the Western Plains*, pp. 163–64; William H. Carter, "History of Fort Robinson," *Northwest Nebraska News*, August 13, 1936; Buecker, *Fort Robinson and the American West*, pp. 134–35; Hoig, *Perilous Pursuit*, pp. 152–54.

36. The long arms were as follows: one Winchester rifle; one Sharp's carbine, caliber .50; one Spencer carbine; one double-barreled shotgun; and nine muzzle-loader rifles of various patterns. The handguns were one Schofield-Smith & Wesson revolver; one Colt's revolver, old pattern; and one horse pistol. *Report of the Chief of Ordnance, 1879* (Washington, D.C.: Government Printing Office, 1879), p. 326. See also Thomas R. Buecker and R. Eli Paul, "Cheyenne Outbreak Firearms," *Museum of the Fur Trade Quarterly* 29 (Summer 1993): 2–12.

37. "Proceedings of a Board," NA, p. 53.

38. Ibid., p. 61. The guns later surrendered to Chase were one Henry rifle, one Sharp's rifle, three muzzle-loading rifles, one Springfield carbine, and two unidentified patterns. *Report of the Chief of Ordnance, 1879*, p. 326.

39. Lieutenant Thompson stated, "The number of arms surrendered was disproportionate to the number I saw before the Indians surrendered, and furthermore no cartridges were given up, and I saw on one Indian[']s waist a belt full of metallic cartridges." "Proceedings of a Board," NA, p. 61.

40. Manuscript vol. 27 (marked "Bourke diary"), copy in Fort Robinson Archive, NSHS. Such evidence also was apparently confiscated from the people after a wagon bearing some of them to Camp Robinson became disabled and was unloaded. The soldiers found initialed linens, a thimble, and a pocket watch, besides napkin rings and an apron bearing dried blood.

41. "Record of Events," in Regimental Returns of the Third Cavalry, October 1878, NA; *Army and Navy Journal*, November 9, 1878; "Proceedings of a Board," NA, pp. 21–22. Carlton commented to Crook: "I regret that the ponies were not shot instead of being brought in here. They were a poor lot, a nuisance and difficult to take care of [in] this weather." Carlton to Crook, October 29, 1878, NA, copy at the Fort Robinson Museum Archive, NSHS.

42. "Proceedings of a Board," p. 181.

43. Ibid., p. 32.

44. "Proceedings of a Board," NA, pp. 21–25, 50 (Johnson quotations), 52–57, 59–60, 180–84, 196; Crook to Sheridan, October 28, 1878, in Microfilm 1495, Roll 6, NA; Senate, *Escape of the Cheyenne Indians*, p. 3; *Army and Navy Journal*, November 9, 1878 (Carlton quotation); *Record of Engagements*, pp. 81–82 (some dates here, however, appear at variance with other reports); Ernest A. Garlington, "The Seventh Cavalry," in Theophilus F. Rodenbough and William L. Haskin, eds., *The Army of the United States: Historical Sketches of Staff and Line with Portraits of Generals-in-Chief* (New York: Maynard, Merrill, 1896) p. 263; Johnson, "Outbreak of Cheyennes," Ellison-Camp Papers, DPL, p. 2; "Captain Carter P. Johnson's Statement in Relation to the Cheyenne Outbreak," copy in the Eli S. Ricker Papers, MS8, Box 26, Folder 14, NSHS Archives; Post Returns, Camp Robinson, Nebraska, September 1878, NA; Post Returns, Camp Robinson, October 31, 1878, NA; Buecker, *Fort Robinson and the American West*, pp. 134–35; Hoig, *Perilous Pursuit*, pp. 153–54; Bronson, *Cowboy Life on the Western Plains*, pp. 164–65; George F. Chase, "Dull Knife & Cheyennes," January 26, 1914, Ellison-Camp Papers, DPL; Alonzo Stringham interview, no date, Microfilm Reel 3, Walter Mason Camp Collection, Manuscripts Division, Harold B. Lee Library, Brigham Young University, Provo, UT; Carlton to AAG, Department of the Platte, October 29, 1878, copy in the Fort Robinson Archive, NSHS. Carlton indicated that the guns taken at Chadron Creek were "muzzle loaders or unserviceable," although he was not present at their taking. He further stated that their breechloaders were taken from them at Camp Robinson, a comment not in line with Captain Johnson's report. See Carlton to Crook, October 29, 1878, NA, copy in the Fort Robinson Archive, NSHS; "Proceedings of a Board, pp. 23–30. Scout and interpreter Louis DeWitt recollected his efforts to induce the Indians to come out peacefully:

> I called to the Indians in dugouts, and after some parleying was admitted into their camp where I remained the rest of the night, hearing the repeated appeals not to return to the assigned [Indian] territory. . . . In the morning, Adjutant Garlington took me to Colonel Carlton's camp, who upon hearing my reported interview commanded me to get Dull Knife and three of his men to talk to them. As a result of my untiring efforts . . . to avoid bloodshed, I gained some assurance, which ended in Colonel Carlton giving them a half hour to surrender or fight, which meant being shelled out.

Winners of the West, May 30, 1930, cited in Jerome A. Greene, ed., *Indian War Veterans: Memories of Army Life and Campaigns in the West, 1864–1898* (New York: Savas Beatie, 2007), pp. 161–62.

45. Johnson, "Interview with Major Carter P. Johnson," Camp Papers, DPL, p. 2; "Captain Carter P. Johnson's Statement in Relation to the Cheyenne Outbreak," NSHS (quotations).

46. "Captain Carter P. Johnson's Statement in Relation to the Cheyenne Outbreak," NSHS. Northern Cheyenne Ted Rising Sun, whose grandmother, Myra Dull Knife Flying, imparted to him the events of 1878, said that "some of their arms, some of the rifles and pistols and other arms were dismantled and hid amongst the persons of the women. And so they were smuggled into the barracks. . . . Later on they were assembled and placed under the floorboards of the barrack." Ted Rising Sun interview, September 9, 1986 (Busby, Montana), Northern Cheyenne Interviews, 3:8, Special Collections and Archives, Oregon State University, Corvallis, Oregon (hereinafter cited as Rising Sun interview, Oregon State University).

47. Scott, *Some Memories of a Soldier*, pp. 98–100 (quotations); "Proceedings of a Board," NA, p. 189. See also R. Eli Paul, ed., *Sign Talker: Hugh Lenox Scott Remembers Indian Country* (Norman: University of Oklahoma Press, 2016), p. 111; Crook to Sheridan, January 22, 1879, in Senate, *Escape of the Cheyenne Indians*, p. 9.

Chapter 3. Time, Place, and the River

1. Buecker, *Fort Robinson and the American West*, pp. 121, 202–3; Edgar B. Robertson, "The Ninth Regiment of Infantry," in Rodenbough and Haskin, *The Army of the United States*, pp. 207, 529, 607; Thomas M. Anderson, "The Fourteenth Regiment of Infantry," in ibid., pp. 607–8; Charles Morton, "The Third Regiment of Cavalry," in ibid., pp. 207–2; *Outline Descriptions of the Posts*, p. 111 (quotation).

2. Harrison Johnson, *Johnson's History of Nebraska* (Omaha: Henry Gibson Herald Printing House, 1880), p. 566. In 1885 present Dawes County, including the land surrounding Fort Robinson, was created by separating from the greater Sioux County. Ibid.

3. Morton, "Third Regiment of Cavalry," in Rodenbough and Haskin, *Army of the United States*, pp. 206–7; "Commissioned Officers, Present and Absent, Accounted for by Name," January and February 1879, in Returns from Military Posts, 1806–1916, Microfilm M617, Records of the Adjutant General's Office, 1780s–1917, RG 94, NA. For these campaigns, see Paul L. Hedren, *Powder River: Disastrous Opening of the Great Sioux War* (Norman: University of Oklahoma Press, 2016); Paul L. Hedren, *Rosebud, June 17, 1876: Prelude to the Little Big Horn* (Norman: University of Oklahoma Press, 2019); Jerome A. Greene, *Slim Buttes, 1876: An Episode of the Great Sioux War* (Norman: University of Oklahoma Press, 1982); and Greene, *Morning Star Dawn*. The Third's officer participants in the Great Sioux War besides Captain Wessells were Captain Joseph Lawson, who had served at Powder River, Rosebud, and Slim Buttes; and Captain Peter D. Vroom; First Lieutenant Emmet Crawford; and Second Lieutenant George F. Chase, who had all served at Rosebud and Slim Buttes.

4. Buecker, *Fort Robinson and the American West*, pp. 115–17, 121. The most thorough telling of Crazy Horse's death appears in Thomas Powers, *The Killing of Crazy Horse* (New York: Alfred A. Knopf, 2010).

5. Chase, "Dull Knife & Cheyennes," January 26, 1914, Camp Papers, DPL; Heitman, *Historical Register and Dictionary*, 1:574; Buecker, *Fort Robinson and the American West*, pp. 130, 198, 203; "Proceedings of a Board," NA, pp. 62, 142–43. Majors Thornburgh and Carlton temporarily occupied Camp Robinson during their efforts to capture the Cheyennes in October 1878. Buecker, *Fort Robinson and the American West*, p. 133.

6. "Record of Medical History of Post [Fort Robinson]: Medical Department U.S.A., 1874," pp. 1–12, copy in Ricker Tablet 31, Microfilm Reel 6, Nebraska Historical Society, Lincoln; Buecker, *Fort Robinson and the American West*, pp. 29–33; Buecker, *Last Days of Red Cloud Agency*, pp. 40–41; Carter, "History of Fort Robinson," p. 12. Camp Robinson was named for First Lieutenant Levi Robinson, killed by an Indian near Laramie Peak, in present Wyoming, on February 8, 1874. Carter, "History of Fort Robinson," p. 9. A one-mile-square military reservation was declared on the site in September 1874 and extended to nine sections in 1876 to forestall private development in the area of the post. Buecker, *Fort Robinson and the American West*, pp. 75–76. See also James B. McCrellis, *Military Reservations, National Military Parks, and National Cemeteries: Title and Jurisdiction* (Washington, D.C.: Government Printing Office, 1898), p. 127.

7. Buecker, *Fort Robinson and the American West*, pp. 33–34, 39, 40, 42, 62; *Outline Descriptions of the Posts*, pp. 111–14; "Record of Medical History of Post [Fort Robinson]," pp. 11–12. Construction of Camp Sheridan, forty-three miles east of Camp Robinson, proceeded in 1875 and was completed the following year. Buecker, *Last Days of Red Cloud Agency*, pp. 43–44; Vance E. Nelson, ed., "Fort Robinson during the 1880s: An Omaha Newspaperman Visits the Post," *Nebraska History* 55 (Summer 1974): 184. Archeological excavation of the ruins of the 1874 cavalry barrack (destroyed by fire in 1898), supervised by state archaeologists Terry Steinacher and Gayle Carlson during the 1980s, disclosed much of the rock undergirding and timber framework of the building's flooring, along with indications that the building was not altogether level. See resulting Archaeological Drawing 25DW51, "1874 Cavalry Barracks, 1987–89," Fort Robinson Archive, NSHS; and James Denney, "Digging into the Past at Fort Robinson," *Sunday World-Herald Magazine of the Midlands* October 4, 1987, p. 11. For the entire post, see also Steven Lissandrello and Sarah J. Pearce, "Fort Robinson and Red Cloud Agency," National Register of Historic Places Inventory—Nomination Form, approved 1984. The combined sites of Fort Robinson and Red Cloud Agency were formally designated as a National Historic Landmark on December 19, 1960 (nps.gov/nhl).

8. "Record of Medical History of Post [Fort Robinson]," pp. 16–18; Buecker, *Fort Robinson and the American West*, p. xxiii; Roger T. Grange Jr., comp., "Treating the Wounded at Fort Robinson," *Nebraska History* 45 (September 1964): 276. A significant stereograph photo of Camp Robinson as it appeared in 1877 shows the largely completed post, including the positions of major structures later referenced here, notably the 1874 cavalry barrack and nearby laundresses' quarters, the guard house, and the adjutant's office, as well as the infantry barracks. Buecker, *Last Days of Red Cloud Agency*, p. 82. The laundresses' quarters also appear on the plan of the post in *Outline Descriptions of the Posts*, p. 112.

9. Senate, *Select Committee Report*, p. 217.

10. Nevin M. Fenneman, *Physiography of Western United States* (New York: McGraw-Hill, 1931), pp. 17–18, 67; Cleophas C. O'Hara, *The White River Badlands* (Rapid City: South Dakota School of Mines, 1920), pp. 19, 38–39, 42–45; Dennis O'Connor Terry, "The White River Group of Northwestern Nebraska: Stratigraphic Revisions, Correlations, and Paleopedology" (1998), University of Nebraska-Lincoln, abstract, AAI9829534, http://digitalcommons.unl.edu/dissertations/AAI9829534.

11. J. S. Kingsley, "The Hat Creek Bad Lands," *American Naturalist* 25 (November 1891): 964, 970–71; Willard B. Robinson, *American Forts: Architectural Form and Function* (Urbana: University of Illinois Press, 1977), pp. 149–50.

12. O'Hara, *White River Badlands*, pp. 144–45; Buecker, *Fort Robinson and the American West*, p. 67; *Lincoln State Journal,* September 27, 1896; M. G. Ferrick, N. D. Mulherin, and D. J. Calkins, "Analysis of the Winter Low-Flow Balance of the Semiarid White River, Nebraska and South Dakota," *Water Resources Research* 31 (August 1995), pp. 1823–2125 (abstract). The broad White River Valley, moreover, would later be conducive to the construction of a railroad to and from the post and provide agricultural settlement potential later in the nineteenth century.

13. Harmon D. Maher Jr., George F. Engelmann, and Robert D. Shuster, *Roadside Geology of Nebraska* (Missoula, Mont.: Mountain Press, 2003), p. 119; USGS, "Crow Butte, Nebr.," quadrangle, 1980, Sections 8 and 17 and adjoining areas.

14. Maher, Engelmann, and Shuster, *Roadside Geology of Nebraska*, p. 118, 120–21; USGS, "Crawford, Nebr.," quadrangle, 1980; USGS, "Smiley Canyon, Nebr.," quadrangle, 1980; Kingsley, "Hat Creek Bad Lands," p. 965–66; John S. Billings, *Circular No. 8: Report on Hygiene of the United States Army with Descriptions of Military Posts* (May 1, 1875) (reprint, New York: Sol Lewis, 1974), pp. 366–67; *Outline Descriptions of the Posts*, pp. 111–12; Federal Writers' Project, *Nebraska: A Guide to the Cornhusker State* (New York: Viking Press, 1939), pp. 322–24; *Nebraska Atlas & Gazetteer* (Freeport, Maine: DeLorme, 2010), pp. 15, 16. The distance between Camp Robinson and Omaha Barracks was computed using contemporary figures as published in *Official Table of Distances for the Guidance of Disbursing Officers of the Army Charged with Payment of Money Allowances for Travel* (Washington, D.C.: Government Printing Office, 1881), pp. 48, 193.

15. Buecker, *Fort Robinson and the American West*, pp. 14, 74, 121.

16. Ibid., p. 50; Douglas C. McChristian, *Fort Laramie, Military Bastion of the High Plains* (Norman: Arthur H. Clark, 2008), p. 367; Agnes Wright Spring, *The Cheyenne and Black Hills Stage and Express Routes* (Glendale, Calif.: Arthur H. Clark, 1949), pp. 122, 159, 295; Jesse Brown and A. M. Willard, *The Black Hills Trails: A History of the Struggles of the Pioneers in the Winning of the Black Hills* (Rapid City, S.Dak.: Rapid City Journal Company, 1924), pp. 47, 48; Edward C. Bryant, *Hat Creek and Hard Times: People and Events in the History of a Wyoming Community* (Fairfax, Va.: Hero Books, 1988), pp. 7, 9, 11; U. S. Congress, House of Representatives, *Executive Document No. 1*, Part 2, 45th Cong., 3rd Sess., Appendix RR, "Annual Report of Captain W. S. Stanton, Corps of Engineers, for the Fiscal Year Ending June 30, 1878," p. 1709 (quotation). The Hat Creek Station historic site and marker are located north of present Lusk, Wyoming, east of U.S. Highway 85. It is described at some length in Federal Writers' Program, *Wyoming: A Guide to Its History, Highways, and People* (New York: Oxford University Press, 1941), p. 223. The line from

Fort Laramie to what was then Fort Robinson eventually fell into disrepair and was replaced by a government line in 1884–85. McChristian, *Fort Laramie*, p. 387.

Chapter 4. Prison House

1. Crook to Sheridan, January 22, 1879, in Senate, *Escape of the Cheyenne Indians*, p. 10.

2. "Record of Events," Regimental Returns of the Third Cavalry for October, November, and December 1878, NA; Buecker, *Fort Robinson and the American West*, pp. xxii, xxiii, 202–3.

3. "Plan of Fort Robinson Showing Line of Retreat of Cheyennes after Their Outbreak Jan. 9, 1879," accompanying "Proceedings of a Board," NA, copy in Fort Robinson Archive, NSHS; *Outline Descriptions of the Posts*, pp. 111–12.

4. Carter P. Johnson, sketch diagram of the interior of the Cheyennes' barrack at Fort Robinson, 1878–79, in Jensen, *Settler and Soldier Interviews*, figure 6, following p. 210 (in this diagram Johnson inexplicably showed the adjoining adjutant's office and guardhouse in reverse order); Johnson, "Outbreak of Cheyennes," September 19, 1913, Ellison-Camp Papers, DPL; Chase, "Dull Knife & Cheyennes," January 26, 1914, Ellison-Camp Papers, DPL; "Plan of Fort Robinson showing Line of Retreat," NA; Post Returns, Camp Robinson, Nebraska, October 1878, NA; Robert S. Ellison, Ellison-Camp Papers, WH1702, item 7, DPL. Regarding the plank fence, Captain Wessells recalled that "the men were never allowed outside of an enclosure about the length of the building & thirty yards wide. This was in rear and surrounded by a slab fence higher than a man's head." Henry W. Wessells IV, "Reminiscences—Wessells H. W.," December 21, 1890, in Henry W. Wessells IV, "Hard Military Service: Two Officers in the 19th Century West," *AB Bookman's Weekly*, October 5, 1998, p. 604. Dull Knife's son, Bull Hump, recalled that "the soldiers had . . . built a fence around [the back of] the house a little way from it and guards were [later?] patrolling outside the fence." "Notes from [Bull] Hump re Dull Knife, Wild Hog etc., at Lame Deer in 1911." Ellison-Camp Papers, DPL. In addition to the single large central heating stove in the barrack proper, documentary evidence indicates that a single small heating stove stood in the guardroom at the northwest corner of the barrack. "Proceedings of a Board," NA, p. 134.

5. "Proceedings of a Board," NA, p. 186. The examining board later concluded that "it was deemed impracticable to separate the men from the women and children as there was not at the post any building except the weak [uninhabited] one in which they were all put, and furthermore as the Indians in their frame of mind required delicate management to keep them quiet, it would have made them suspicious of an intended movement south, to have separated them." Further, "the Commanding Officer desired to use all available troops to try and recapture the other Cheyennes still at large, and could not spare enough men to guard the Indians unless that duty be made easy by keeping them [together] in good disposition." Ibid., pp. 197–98.

6. Sergeant Johnson identified the Lakota scout who discovered the gun as Little Big Man, who had been involved in the events preceding the death of Crazy Horse little more than a year earlier at Camp Robinson. See Johnson's account in Jensen, *Settler and Soldier Interviews*, p. 233.

7. Ibid. (quotation); "Proceedings of a Board," NA, pp. 164–65. One woman was later seen to drop a pistol. Dull Knife retrieved it and delivered it to Lieutenant Chase. Hoig, *Perilous Pursuit*, p. 155. Iron Teeth apparently mentioned this incident too, as well as the hiding of guns beneath the flooring: "we kept five six-shooters, with some cartridges for them. I had one [six-shooter] in my dress. We hid all of these under a loose board of the floor." "Iron Teeth, a Cheyenne Old Woman," p. 76. Major Carlton later believed that the Indians, while "straggling through a snowstorm, and afterwards [when] they had camped on Chadron Creek, . . . had had ample opportunities of secreting their arms." "Proceedings of a Board," NA, p. 187. One report stated that the Indians were allowed to keep a number of bows that were found. *Omaha Herald*, January 22, 1879.

8. Johnson, "Outbreak of Cheyennes," Ellison-Camp Papers, DPL, p. 2 (first quotation). Jensen, *Settler and Soldier Interviews*, p. 233 (second quotation). Johnson further discounted the smuggled guns belief, saying that "this is absolutely false, because there was a guard kept inside the house, walking up and down the centre of the floor, night and day, from the time they were confined until they broke out, and nobody was allowed to enter their buildings without being searched, and it would have been impossible to convey arms to these people after they were confined. I . . . [was] in charge of the guard myself a dozen or more times and I know that it could not have been done." Jensen, *Settler and Soldier Interviews*, p. 233. See also "Proceedings of a Board," NA, pp. 156, 164–65. The "scissors" assertion appears in Major Carlton Horner, "Caleb H. Carlton," copy in Carlton Papers, Box 5, Manuscript Division, Library of Congress, Washington, D.C., copy in Fort Robinson Archive, NSHS. Valentine T. McGillycuddy, who would become agent to the Sioux at their Pine Ridge Agency in 1879, was one who believed that "when the Cheyennes surrendered on Chadron Creek they hid guns there which were later recovered by their Sioux friends and smuggled into the barracks." McGillycuddy Interview, Box 4, f. 3, Envelope 4, Camp Papers, Lilly Library, Indiana University, 225–33.

9. Proceedings of a Board," NA, pp. 26–28 (quotations; see also p. 13). Chase further commented, "I asked Maj. Carlton to make a thorough search of them [the Indians], expressed a desire to remove the Indians from the [barrack] building in which they were confined onto the parade ground and while they should be absent I would go into the building and thoroughly search it. Maj. Carlton disapproved my request to take the Indians out of the building. The Indians were also very strongly opposed to leaving the building." Ibid., p. 51. It was also directed that "the windows were always [to be] kept clear. No persons were allowed to loiter around the windows." Ibid., p. 158.

10. "Proceedings of a Board," NA, pp. 27 (first quotation), 48; Chase, "Dull Knife & Cheyennes," Ellison-Camp Papers, DPL (second and third quotations).

11. "Proceedings of a Board," NA, p. 48; Grinnell, *Fighting Cheyennes*, p. 417 (quotation).

12. "Proceedings of a Board," NA, pp. 134–36. Mixed-blood interpreter James Rowland stated that "the soldiers always treated such Indians kindly. Only the women are afraid of the soldiers, and that at night. I don't know for what reason except they are generally timid." Ibid., p. 151.

13. Ibid., p. 124 (first quotation); Johnson, "Outbreak of Cheyennes," Ellison-Camp Papers, DPL (second and third quotations).

14. Johnson, "Outbreak of Cheyennes," Ellison-Camp Papers, DPL. Lieutenant Chase said that "during the time that I was in charge of the building no person[,] except the three sentinels constantly kept within, was allowed to enter the building with arms, nor was any package or bundle ever allowed to be introduced into the building until first examined by me." Furthermore, Lakotas visiting the prisoners had to leave their arms in Chase's sleeping room. "Proceedings of a Board," NA, p. 49.

15. Mrs. Black Bear interview, George Bird Grinnell Collection, Field Book 348 (1908), Braun Research Library, Southwest Museum, Los Angeles. The *Sidney Telegraph,* November 30, 1878, noted: "The Cheyennes [at Camp Robinson] are closely guarded, and about all the amusement they are granted is an occasional dance with the officers [soldiers?] stationed there. Both the squaws and white gallants get quite enthusiastic." At least two of the Cheyenne women, Red Feather and The Enemy, did not believe that they had been well fed and said that the "coffee was very weak." "Proceedings of a Board," NA, p. 16.

16. "Proceedings of a Board," NA, p. 58.

17. Grinnell, *Fighting Cheyennes*, pp. 417–18; Stands in Timber and Liberty, *Cheyenne Memories*, p. 235; "Proceedings of a Board," NA, pp. 11, 16, 95; *Sidney Telegraph*, November 30, 1878 (quotation); Powell, *Sweet Medicine*, 1:224, 225; Hoig, *Perilous Pursuit*, p. 157. Ted Rising Sun explained that his grandmother, who made the trek, said that "the men were permitted to hunt in the immediately vicinity of the post." Rising Sun interview, 3:6, Oregon State University, p. 8.

18. Grinnell, *Fighting Cheyennes*, p. 417.

19. *We, the Northern Cheyenne People*, p. 28; Powell, *Sweet Medicine*, 1:223; Powell, *Killing of Morning Star's People*, p. 8; Bronson, *Cowboy Life on the Western Plains*, p. 321.

20. "Proceedings of a Board," NA, pp. 109, 157, 201; Johnson, "Outbreak of Cheyennes," pp. 6–7 (quotation), Ellison-Camp Papers, DPL; Powell, *Sweet Medicine*, 1:225.

21. "Proceedings of a Board," NA, p. 136 (first quotation); Crook to Sheridan, October 31, 1878, citing Carlton to Crook on that date (second quotation), Senate, *Escape of the Cheyenne Indians*, p. 2 (third quotation). For a slight variant, see also Crook to AAG, Division of the Missouri, January 22, 1879, Microfilm Publication 1495, Roll 6, NA.

22. Chase, "Dull Knife & Cheyennes," Ellison-Camp Papers, DPL.

23. Untitled document, Box 3, Folder 3, Camp Papers, Lilly Library, Indiana University, copy in Fort Robinson Archive, NSHS.

24. Crook to Sheridan, January 22, 1879, Microfilm 1495, Roll 6, NA (quotations); Senate, *Escape of the Cheyenne Indians*, p. 3.

25. "Proceedings of a Board," NA, pp. 185, 187 (quotation), 200.

26. Crook to Sheridan, November 1, 1878, and Crook to Sheridan, January 22, 1879, in Microfilm 1495, Roll 6, NA; Johnson account in Jensen, *Settler and Soldier Interviews*, p. 234 (quotation); Powell, *Sweet Medicine*, 1:223–24.

27. "Record of Events," Regimental Returns of the Third Cavalry for October, November, and December 1878, NA; Senate, *Select Committee Report,* p. 22; John G. Bourke Diary, vol. 27, page copies in Fort Robinson Archive, NSHS; Johnson, "Outbreak of Cheyennes," Ellison-Camp Papers, DPL, p. 6; Johnson's account in Jensen, *Settler and Soldier Interviews*, p. 234 (quotations; also on the search for Little Wolf's people); Buecker, *Fort Robinson and the American West*, p. 86.

28. Carlton to AAG, Department of the Platte, November 17, 1878, NA, copy in Fort Robinson Archive, NSHS.

29. Ibid. (quotations), Carlton to AAG Robert Williams, November 18, 1878, and Carlton to Williams, November 17, 1878, NA, copy in Fort Robinson Archive, NSHS.

30. Carlton to AAG Williams, November 18, 1878, Carlton to AAG Williams, November 19, 1878, and AAG Williams to Carlton, November 22, 1878, NA, copy in Fort Robinson Archive, NSHS; "Record of Events," Regimental Returns of the Third Cavalry for November 1878, NA.

31. Carlton to AAG, Omaha Barracks, December 10, 1878, and Crook to Sheridan, December 12, 1878 (quotation), both in Microfilm 1495, Roll 6, NA; for Crook's opinion about elusive Cheyennes while the troops were afield, see Crook to AAG, Division of the Missouri, December 12, 1878 (not received at War Department), in "Briefs," in Senate, *Escape of the Cheyenne Indians*, p. 3.

32. Bronson, *Cowboy Life on the Western Plains*, p. 167 (quotations); Powell, *Sweet Medicine*, 1:230–31. As a regional settler Bronson doubtless had a marked interest reflecting his area holdings, although his memories evince considerable sympathy for the Indians' plight. Arriving for the council, Red Cloud and presumably the other Sioux chiefs were diligently searched before being allowed to enter the dormitory. "Proceedings of a Board," NA, p. 158.

33. *Chicago Times*, November 7, 1879.

34. Quoted in Bronson, *Cowboy Life on the Western Plains*, p. 169.

35. *Chicago Times*, November 8, 1878 (first quotation); *Los Angeles Herald*, November 9, 1878 (second quotation).

36. *Los Angeles Herald*, November 9, 1879.

37. Sheridan to AG, Telegram, October 29, 1878 (first two quotations), Sheridan to AG, November 5, 1878 (third and fourth quotations), and Sheridan to AG, Telegram, November 8, 1878 (fifth quotation), all in "Briefs," in Senate, *Escape of the Cheyenne Indians*, pp. 2–3; Schurz to McCrary, November 22, 1878 (sixth quotation), Microfilm 1495, Roll 6, NA.

38. Sheridan to Sherman, Telegram, November 8, 1878, and Anthony to Sheridan, November 11, 1878 (quotations), both in Senate, *Escape of the Cheyenne Indians*, p. 3.

39. Captain Deane Monahan, Third Cavalry, to Agent James Irwin, Red Cloud Agency, November 23, 1878, NA, copy in Fort Robinson Archive, NSHS; "Proceedings of a Board," NA, pp. 78–79 (quotation), 157; Grinnell, *Fighting Cheyennes*, p. 418; Powell, *Sweet Medicine*, 1:228; Stands In Timber and Liberty, *Cheyenne Memories*, p. 235.

Chapter 5. Long Nose

1. Companies C and H of the Third Cavalry stationed at Camp Robinson had previously been stationed at Fort Laramie, Wyoming Territory, where the regimental headquarters remained in 1878–79. Buecker, *Fort Robinson and the American West*, pp. 202–3; Regimental Return of the Third Cavalry, December 1878, Microfilm 744 027–039, 1876–84, NA.

2. William H. Powell, comp., *Records of Living Officers of the United States Army* (Philadelphia: L. R. Hamersly, 1884), p. 113; Heitman, *Historical Register and Dictionary*, 1:1019; Henry, *Military Record of Army and Civilian Appointments*, 1:491;

Wessells, "Hard Military Service," pp. 601–2. For Wessells's participation in the battle of the Red Fork of Powder River on November 25, 1876, see Greene, *Morning Star Dawn,* pp. 103, 111–14, 116. For Northern Cheyenne perspectives on the encounter, see ibid., pp. 127–34, 135–40; and Greene, *Lakota and Cheyenne*, pp. 113–24. For Wessells's father, Henry W. Wessells Sr., see George W. Cullum, *Biographical Register of the Officers and Graduates of the U.S. Military Academy at West Point, N.Y., from Its Establishment, in 1802, to 1890*, vol. 1 (Boston: Houghton, Mifflin, 1891), pp. 560–61.

3. Wessells, "Outbreak of Cheyennes at Ft. Robinson," Ellison-Camp Papers, DPL (quotations); "Proceedings of a Board," NA, pp. 62–63 (last quotation). "Long Nose" in Cheyenne is *tse?eseesehe* (long-nosed one). *English-Cheyenne Student Dictionary* (Lame Deer, Mont.: Language Research Department, Northern Cheyenne Title VII ESEA Bilingual Education Program, 1976), p. 74. The following partial chronology of command at Fort Robinson (including Carlton's occasional presence there) indicates who was designated as being responsible for the Northern Cheyenne prisoners: November 12–23, Major Carlton; November 23–unspecified, First Lieutenant John C. Thompson; November (unspecified)–December 4, Captain John B. Johnson; December 4–December 10, Captain Henry C. Wessells; December 11–December 16, Major Carlton; December 17–January 9, Captain Wessells. "Proceedings of a Board," NA, p. 174.

4. "Proceedings of a Board," NA, pp. 63, 108–9. In another instance Wessells added: The Cheyennes "got excellent bread and meat in my opinion in abundance, coffee twice a day. Potatoes were bought from savings to put in soup and they got more fresh meat than soldiers. I also gave them 4 pounds of tobacco bought with savings." Ibid., p. 73. On Christmas Day the post trader also delivered a box of cigars to them. Ibid., p. 108.

5. Schurz to Sherman, December 5, 1878, referenced in *Senate, Escape of the Cheyenne Indians*, p. 3; copies to and from Crook, Pope, and Governor Anthony cited in ibid.; Telegram, Pope to AAG, Division of the Missouri, December 23, 1878, Microfilm 1495, Roll 6, NA (quotation); Hoig, *Perilous Pursuit*, p. 161; *Frank Leslie's Illustrated Newspaper*, February 15, 1879.

6. "Proceedings of a Board," NA, p. 81 (emphasis added). On the matter of clothing for the Cheyennes, see also the correspondence in *Senate, Escape of the Cheyenne Indians*, pp. 20–22.

7. "Briefs," in *Senate, Escape of the Cheyenne Indians*, p. 4; Carter, "History of Fort Robinson"; Telegram, Crook to AAG, Division of the Missouri, December 20, 1878, and Telegram, Crook to AAG, Division of the Missouri, December 24, 1878 (quotations), both in Microfilm 1495, Roll 6, NA; Crook to AAG, Division of the Missouri, January 22, 1879, in *Senate, Escape of the Cheyenne Indians*, p. 10; Powell, *Sweet Medicine*, 1:227.

8. "Proceedings of a Board," NA, pp. 8, 199; Powell, *Sweet Medicine*, 1:224. The Northern Cheyenne Big Head stated that "the reason the young men had all the say was that Little Wolf who was the leader of the whole band when it left the south had left this portion of it without a head. Dull Knife[,] though formerly a chief, had not been so considered for a long time, except by the whites." "Proceedings of a Board," NA, p. 12. A Cheyenne youth reportedly overheard a reference to guns hidden in the barrack and at least one woman knew that they had been secreted beneath the floor. Ibid., p. 199.

9. "Proceedings of a Board," NA, p. 75.

10. Crook to AAG, Division of the Missouri, January 22, 1879. Microfilm 1495, Roll 6, NA (quotations); Crook to Sheridan, January 22, 1879, in *Senate, Escape of the Cheyenne Indians*, pp. 8–10; Bronson, *Cowboy Life on the Western Plains*, p. 171; Hoig, *Perilous Pursuit*, p. 161.

11. *New York Herald*, January 4, 1879. The change was mandated in General Orders No. 79, Adjutant General's Office, Headquarters of the Army, November 8, 1878, authorizing division commanders "to name and style all posts permanently occupied by troops, or the occupation of which is likely to be permanent, 'Forts.'" *Index of General Orders, Adjutant General's Office, 1878* (Washington, D.C.: Government Printing Office, 1879).

12. Wessells to AAG, Department of the Platte, January 12, 1879, NA, copy in Fort Robinson Archive, NSHS.

13. Crook to Sheridan, January 15, 1879, NA, copy in Fort Robinson Archive, NSHA; "Proceedings of a Board," NA, p. 75; Senate, *Select Committee Report*, p. 11 (Wild Hog quotations); Chase, "Dull Knife & Cheyennes," Ellison-Camp Papers, DPL; Walter S. Schuyler to Crook, January 15, 1879, in Senate, *Escape of the Cheyenne Indians*, p. 24; Crook to AAG, Division of the Missouri, January 22, 1879, Microfilm 1495, Roll 6, NA; Johnson, "Outbreak of Cheyennes," Ellison-Camp Papers, DPL; Grinnell, *Fighting Cheyennes*, p. 418 (Dull Knife quotation); Mooney, "Cheyenne Indians," p. 398; Manypenny, *Our Indian Wards*, p. 337; Carter, "History of Fort Robinson"; Svingen, *Northern Cheyenne Indian Reservation*, p. 20; Hoig, *Perilous Pursuit*, pp. 163–64. See also "Proceedings of a Board," NA, pp. 63, 75, 200.

14. Stands In Timber and Liberty, *Cheyenne Memories*, p. 235 (first quotation); "Proceedings of a Board," NA, pp. 8–9 (second quotation).

15. "Proceedings of a Board," NA, pp. 75–76.

16. Wessells to AAG, Department of the Platte, January 12, 1879, NA, copy in Fort Robinson Archive, NSHS.

17. Johnson to Hare, February 16, 1879, NA copy in Fort Robinson Archives, NSHS (quotations); "Proceedings of a Board," NA, pp. 63–64, 200; Powell, *Sweet Medicine*, 1:231; Powell, *Killing of Morning Star's People*, pp. 8–9. Wessells was further impelled to get the Cheyennes underway quickly, as he was scheduled to begin a four-month leave of absence on January 10, Senate, *Escape of the Cheyenne Indians*, pp. 6–8; Buecker, *Fort Robinson and the American West*, pp. 138–39; Hoig, *Perilous Pursuit*, p. 164. Regarding the discontinuance of the Indians' rations, Wessells later stated that "it was my own idea to cut off their rations and fuel[,] but I notified the Department Commander [Crook] of my action. I thought that by stopping their rations they could be induced to consent to go south knowing as they did they could get rations as soon as they should give up." He further believed that the Indians had saved food and were "preparing for a contingency." "Proceedings of a Board," p. 74. Years later Wessells reflected on his decision: "[I] thought it much better to adopt that course than to knock the building down . . . with the field pieces that were standing only a few yards from the prison." Wessells, "Reminiscences," in Wessels, "Hard Military Service." Wessells did allow that General Crook might countermand his order regarding feeding the people. "Proceedings of a Board," NA, p. 78.

18. Senate, *Select Committee Report*, pp. 11–12 (quotations); Powell, *People of the Sacred Mountain*, 2:1191.

19. Senate, *Select Committee Report*, p. 12.

20. Johnson, "Outbreak of Cheyennes," Ellison-Camp Papers, DPL, p. 7.

21. Ibid., p. 12.

22. Telegram, Wessells to AAG, Department of the Platte, January 5, 1879 (quotations), NA, copy in Fort Robinson Archive, NSHS; "Briefs," in Senate, *Escape of the Cheyenne Indians*; *New York Herald*, January 11, 1879. Two women later testified that "when the officers told them to send their children out to be fed, the women had nothing to say about it, but the young men prevented it." "Proceedings of a Board," NA, p. 15. Lieutenant Charles Johnson's wife wrote: "As they did not want the women and children to suffer, they were asked each day to send them out for food, but the Indian men would not let them come out at all." Letter, Angie Johnson to Abbie Bush, January 15, 1879, copy in Fort Robinson Archive, NSHS. Sergeant Johnson (no relation) elaborated, stating that the men "stoutly refused to permit the women or children to go out, and began to assume an ugly mood. Said they would eat their children and when they were consumed would eat the women. It was no use to try to persuade them—they would all die before they would go back south." Johnson, "Outbreak of Cheyennes," Ellison-Camp Papers, DPL, p. 5; Carter Johnson account in Jensen, *Settler and Soldier Interviews*, p. 236. Johnson reported that "on the morning of the 9th of January the garrison was astonished by the smell of meat cooking in the quarters and the Indians sent out word that they had begun to eat their first baby and were cooking it then. It turned out afterwards that it was nothing but a dog that they had saved for this purpose." Jensen, *Settler and Soldier Interviews*, p. 237. Johnson did not explain how the Indians fueled their cooking fire.

23. "Proceedings of a Board," NA, p. 6; Hoig, *Perilous Pursuit*, p. 164. Women prisoners told Lieutenant Johnson that "the reason that the young men refused to go south was that they had participated in the Kansas outrages and were afraid of being hanged." "Proceedings of a Board," NA, p. 141. Mrs. Angie Johnson, who lived at the post, wrote her sister: "The squaws say . . . that these are the very ones who did the murdering in Kansas and they thought they would be hanged if they were sent back and that was why they were so determined not to go back." Letter, Angie Johnson to Abbie Bush, January 15, 1879, copy in Fort Robinson Archives, NSHS. Lieutenant Johnson further stated that "the squaws admitted after their recapture that these [young men] were the Indians who committed the depredations in Kansas, and that was the reason they were so determined not to go back, fearing punishment." Johnson to Hare, February 16, 1879, copy in Fort Robinson Archives, NSHS.

24. Sheridan to Crook, January 7, 1879, Philip H. Sheridan Papers, General Correspondence, 1853–88, Manuscripts Division, Library of Congress (first two quotations; hereinafter cited as Sheridan Papers, LC); Johnson, "Outbreak of Cheyennes," Ellison-Camp Papers, DPL, p. 5 (third quotation); Johnson account in Jensen, *Settler and Soldier Interviews*, pp. 235–37; Powell, *People of the Sacred Mountain*, 2:1191; Powell, *Sweet Medicine*, 1:232. The directive to move the men to Fort Leavenworth was modified on January 8 so that the adult men would be transferred to Fort Marion at St. Augustine, Florida. *New York Herald*, January 12, 1879; *Frank Leslie's Illustrated Newspaper*, February 15, 1879. *Frank Leslie's* stated that "when this decision was announced to them they became sullen, then silent. They ceased their demands for the long-promised food and clothing." See also *Army and Navy Journal*, January 18, 1879; "Briefs," in Senate, *Escape of the Cheyenne Indians*, p. 4.

25. Post Returns, Fort Robinson, Nebraska, December 1878 and January 1879, NA; Chase, "Dull Knife & Cheyennes," Ellison-Camp Papers, DPL; "Proceedings of a Board," NA, p. 90; First Lieutenant Emmet Crawford to First Lieutenant Charles Morton, January 8, 1879, copy in Fort Robinson Archive, NSHS.

26. Telegram, Crook to Sheridan, January 15, 1879, NA, copy in Fort Robinson Archive, NSHS.

27. Sergeant Johnson's account in Jensen, *Settler and Soldier Interviews,* p. 234; Telegram, Secretary of War George W. McCrary to Secretary of the Interior Carl Schurz, January 10, 1879 (first quotation); Telegram, Sheridan to AG, January 8, 1879. NA, copy in Fort Robinson Archive, NSHS; *Army and Navy Journal,* January 11, 1879; Carter, "History of Fort Robinson"; Powell, *Sweet Medicine,* 1:232–33; "Proceedings of a Board," NA, pp. 164 (second quotation), 134; Monnett, *Tell Them We Are Going Home,* pp. 119–20; Leiker and Powers, *Northern Cheyenne Exodus,* pp. 72–73. The Northern Cheyenne woman Iron Teeth called the barrack "a prison house." Marquis, *Cheyenne and Sioux,* p. 21.

Chapter 6. Commencement

1. Mari Sandoz, *Cheyenne Autumn* (New York: McGraw-Hill, 1953), p. 163. January was also known to them as Hoop-and-Stick Game Moon. Grinnell, *Cheyenne Indians,* 1:71. Judging from evidence recorded along the railroad at North Platte, Nebraska, 243 miles away, the temperature there reached a minimum of –3 degrees (probably recorded during the dark of the morning hours or at night) and a maximum of 30 degrees on January 8. *Report of the Secretary of War, 1879* (part 4, "Report of the Chief Signal Officer"), p. 368; *Official Table of Distances,* p. 162.

2. Wessells to AAG, Department of the Platte, January 12, 1879, NA, copy in Fort Robinson Archive NSHS.

3. Second Lieutenant George W. Baxter (1855–1929) would serve briefly as governor of Wyoming Territory in 1886, appointed by President Grover Cleveland. W. Turrentine Jackson, "The Governorship of Wyoming, 1885–1889: A Study in Territorial Politics," *Pacific Historical Review* 13 (March 1944): 1–11.

4. Ibid.; "Proceedings of a Board," NA, pp. 64, 95; Wessells, "Outbreak of Cheyennes at Fort Robinson," Ellison-Camp Papers, DPL, p. 3 (quotation); letter, Angie Johnson to Abbie Bush, January 15, 1879, Fort Robinson Archive (NSHS); Senate, *Select Committee Report,* p. 12; Chase, "Dull Knife & Cheyennes," Ellison-Camp Papers, DPL, pp. 4–5. Regarding Dull Knife's illness, Sergeant Johnson related that "on several occasions two . . . [soldiers] carried him out naked and rolled him in the snow. He would then lie in the snow a while, naked, and then be carried back. He would not consent to be treated in any other way." Johnson, "Outbreak of Cheyennes," Ellison-Camp Papers, DPL, p. 7.

5. Accounts by Wild Hog and Crow, in Senate, *Select Committee Report,* pp. 12 (quotations), 22–23. James R. O'Beirne, who had arrived from the New Red Cloud Agency, described the scuffle: "Ferguson . . . was wounded by the knife . . . as he [Wild Hog] plunged it with a downward thrust at his breastbone, slightly cutting him. Captain Wessells immediately seized him, and, bearing down on his wrist, broke the blade." *New York Herald,* January 15, 1879 (see also "Proceedings of a

Board," NA, p. 173). Wild Hog's effort "was somewhat weakened by the [chief's] arm being seized," wrote Dr. Edward B. Moseley, but it "made a puncture wound about ¾ inch long and ½ inch deep. The bone was indented to a moderate extent but the cavity of the chest was not opened." Private Ferguson returned to duty ten days later. "Special Report . . . by Asst. Surg. E. B. Moseley," File D-987, Office of the Adjutant General, RG 94, NA. This important document is fully reproduced in Roger T. Grange Jr., comp., "Treating the Wounded at Fort Robinson," *Nebraska History* 45 (September 1964): 278–79. Private Ferguson, from Boston, Massachusetts, was a blacksmith who enlisted in 1874. He was discharged at Fort Fred Steele, Wyoming Territory, late in 1879. U.S. Army Register of Enlistments, 1798–1914, NA. For the Northern Cheyenne perspective on these events, see Powell, *People of the Sacred Mountain*, 2:1195–97.

6. Wessells to AAG, Department of the Platte, January 12, 1879, NA; Senate, *Select Committee Report*, p. 12 (quotation); Johnson, "Outbreak of Cheyennes," September 19, 1913, pp. 4–7; *New York Herald*, January 11, 1879; "Proceedings of a Board," NA, pp. 7, 64, 95–96, 99–100, 173; letter, Angie Johnson to Abbie Bush, January 15, 1879, Fort Robinson Archive (NSHS); Powell, *People of the Sacred Mountain*, 2:1195–96. According to Wessells, while the soldiers struggled with Wild Hog, "one of the Cheyenne women . . . alerted the band, chanting some kind of a song. This seemed to set the prisoners in a great state of uproar and excitement." Wessells, "Hard Military Service," p. 604. Grinnell placed Left Hand at the meeting on January 9, too, but claimed that he somehow fled back to the barrack when the ruckus erupted. Grinnell, *Fighting Cheyennes*, pp. 418–19. Chase also recalled that, in addition to Wild Hog and Old Crow, "Left Hand and one other" were taken to the lower camp. Chase, "Dull Knife & Cheyennes," Ellison-Camp Papers, DPL, p. 5; Powell, *People of the Sacred Mountain*, 2:1197; Powell, *Sweet Medicine*, 1:234–35. Chase claimed that "Wild Hog told me the Cheyennes would break out that night & wanted to get his family out. We [later] took him up in an ambulance & let him talk to the Ind[ian]s thro[ugh] the window. They would not [at first?] permit his family to come out, but he did take back some old people." Chase, "Dull Knife & Cheyennes," Ellison-Camp Papers, DPL, p. 5. Chase also claimed that "I told Wessells this day that the Ind[ian]s would break out that night, but he said he had heard that many times before & seemed to think there was nothing in the report." Ibid. Sergeant Johnson's account of events immediately following the tussle in Wessells's office differed from Chase's in several respects. Ibid., pp. 4–6. Sergeant Johnson stated that at least some of the "Indians rushed out of the quarters heading for the . . . [adjutant's office] but were driven back into their quarters by H troop, which was drawn up in line." Johnson account in Jensen, *Settler and Soldier Interviews*, p. 236; see also Hoig, *Perilous Pursuit*, pp. 165–66. Apparently Chief Tangle Hair was given an opportunity to leave that day too, but his own followers threatened his life if he did so, fearful that he might then direct them to yield. Grinnell, *Fighting Cheyennes*, pp. 425–26. For analysis of this tribal issue, see K. N. Llewellyn, *The Cheyenne Way: Conflict and Case Law in Primitive Jurisprudence* (Norman: University of Oklahoma Press, 1941), pp. 105–6.

7. "Proceedings of a Board," NA, pp. 97, 100, 150, 172, 176; Wessells, "Reminiscences," in Wessells, "Hard Military Service," p. 604.

8. "Proceedings of a Board," NA, pp. 142, 148. Old Crow explained that after his and Wild Hog's experience in Wessells's office the people in the barrack became

scared, "not knowing what . . . might be done to them." At first the young men decided never to leave the barrack and vowed to die there. Later they changed their minds and determined to die fighting. "Then they made their arrangements to escape or die in the attempt." Prior to the incident in Wessells's office, "there was no desire to fight or to break out." Senate, *Special Committee Report*, p. 23.

9. According to the Bureau of Indian Affairs, the number of Cheyenne prisoners, including those subsequently taken to the lower camp, was 148: "forty-nine men, fifty-one women, and forty-eight children." *Report of the Commissioner of Indian Affairs, 1879*, p. xvii. This estimate is based on conclusions presented in "Proceedings of a Board," NA, pp. 165–66. Wild Hog estimated that after he and others were removed to the lower camp about 135 men, women, and children remained in the barrack. Senate, *Select Committee Report*, p. 13. Wessells also later testified that "there were 148 prisoners as near as we could get at it by frequent counts. It was difficult to count them. They were turned over to me as 150." "Proceedings of a Board," NA, p. 74.

10. *Chicago Times*, January 10, 1879 (first quotation); letter, Angie Johnson to Abbie Bush, January 15, 1879 (second quotation), Fort Robinson Archive (NSHS); *Omaha Herald*, January 22, 1879 (third quotation); "Proceedings of a Board," NA, pp. 97, 152. Sergeant Carter Johnson described a much larger confrontation stating that "the Ind[ian]s broke out of the guard house [barrack], seizing sticks and stones and made for Wessells['s] office. Wessells had things ready, however, and they were met by the guard outside and held from coming in. When Hog saw that the guard had the advantage, he called out to them to go back, and after some talking they quieted down and went back [to the barrack]." Johnson, "Outbreak of Cheyennes," Ellison-Camp Papers, DPL, p. 4; Hoig, *Perilous Pursuit*, p. 166.

11. Senate, *Select Committee Report*, p. 13 (first quotation); "Proceedings of a Board," NA, p. 152 (second quotation). See also *New York Herald*, January 11, 1879.

12. Members of the board investigating the breakout concluded that the rifle pits were "to enable the rear guard [of warriors] to control the approaches from the West. The post guard house being near that end of the building, they evidently thought that the guard would fire into the windows of that part when the outbreak should occur." "Proceedings of a Board," NA, p. 193. A news account noted: "Since the [breakout] fight a pit has been found under the prison-house, which was completely carpeted with empty sacks. It is here that the arms were probably hidden, and the question will naturally be asked why was there so incomplete a search?" *New York Herald*, January 16, 1879; see also *Frank Leslie's Illustrated Newspaper*, February 15, 1879; and "Captain Carter P. Johnson's Diagram Showing Outbreak of Cheyennes," MS 8, Eli S. Ricker Collection, Box 28, Folder 91, NSHS Archives; and Archaeological Drawing 25DW51, "1874 Cavalry Barracks," 1987–89, Fort Robinson Archive, NSHS.

13. "Proceedings of a Board," NA, p. 65. The definitive study of the kinds of firearms that the Indians possessed (both those evidently hidden previously beneath the floorboards of the barrack dormitory and those captured by them from troops in the course of their escape) is Buecker and Paul, "Cheyenne Outbreak Firearms."

14. Wessells to AAG, Department of the Platte, January 12, 1879, NA; "Proceedings of a Board," NA, pp. 3, 8; Johnson, "Outbreak of Cheyennes," p. 5 (first quotation), Ellison-Camp Papers, DPL; Telegram, Crook to Sheridan, January 18, 1879. NA, copy in Fort Robinson Archive, NSHS (second quotation); Jensen, *Settler and Soldier Interviews*, p. 236 (third quotation). The presence of rifle pits in the floor, as

well as the trench, is documented in "Report of Brig. Gen. George Crook," September 27, 1879, in *Report of the Secretary of War, 1879*, p. 78, and is further confirmed in Archaeological Drawing 25DW51, "1874 Cavalry Barracks"; Mooney, "Cheyenne Indians," p. 399; Carter, "History of Fort Robinson," p. 15; Bronson, *Cowboy Life on the Western Plains*, pp. 174–75; Powell, *Sweet Medicine*, 1:238; Hoig, *Perilous Pursuit*, pp. 166–67; and Buecker, *Fort Robinson and the American West*, pp. 139–40.

15. A potential schism between some younger warriors and the older men and women was reflected in the councils held by the younger warriors that denied access to the others. Some Indians believed that the warriors refused to keep them informed of decisions regarding the upcoming escape. "Proceedings of a Board," NA, p. 199. Some accounts specified that the women were in bed when the firing started, which seems rather unlikely considering the day's ongoing tumult and preparation. Ibid., p. 15.

16. "Notes from [Bull] Hump re Dull Knife, Wild Hog etc. at Lame Deer in 1911," Ellison-Camp Papers, DPL (first quotation); "Iron Teeth, a Cheyenne Old Woman," p. 22 (second quotation).

17. Powell, *People of the Sacred Mountain*, 2:1197–1201; Powell, *Sweet Medicine*, 1:237; Powell, *Killing of Morning Star's People*, p. 9; "Notes from [Bull] Hump re Dull Knife, Wild Hog etc. at Lame Deer in 1911"; "Iron Teeth, a Cheyenne Old Woman," p. 22 (quotation); Stands In Timber and Liberty, *Cheyenne Memories*, p. 236; "Proceedings of a Board," NA, pp. 9–10, 80.

18. "Proceedings of a Board," NA, pp. 64, 78, 98–99. Regarding the decision not to barricade the windows, interpreter James Rowland later commented: "It is hard to tell what they [the Indians] would have done if the windows had been so barricaded that they could not escape." "Proceedings of a Board," NA, p. 149. The armed cavalry sentries wore standard-issue light blue wool overcoats, kersey-lined and with yellow-lined capes, over their normal fatigue uniforms, probably with sealskin winter caps with flaps pulled down over their ears and tied for warmth, as appropriate. Possibly a few donned buffalo-hide coats, although their issue and distribution by the Quartermaster Department had not become fully standard in the army by 1878–79. On their feet the soldiers would have worn issue buffalo-hide overshoes or rubber-tweed boots called "arctics." Jerome A. Greene, "The U.S. Army Buffalo Overcoat and M1883 Canvas Blanket-Lined Overcoat on the Northern Plains Frontier, 1876–1891," *Military Collector & Historian: Journal of The Company of Military Historians* 44 (Summer 1992): 74; Sidney B. Brinckerhoff, *Boots and Shoes of the Frontier Soldier, 1865–1893*, Museum Monograph No. 7 (Tucson: Arizona Historical Society, 1976), pp. 9–11.

19. "Proceedings of a Board," NA, p. 150.

20. "Proceedings of a Board," NA, pp. 154, 176–77 (first quotation), 202–203; Wessells to AAG, Department of the Platte, January 12, 1879 (second quotation), NA; Bronson, *Cowboy Life on the Western Plains*, p. 175; Douglas C. McChristian, *Regular Army O!: Soldiering on the Western Frontier, 1865–1891* (Norman: University of Oklahoma Press, 2017), pp. 204–5; Hoig, *Perilous Pursuit*, p. 166–67; "Proceedings of a Board," NA, p. 76, 98, 106 (third quotation). Despite his confidence, however, Wessells still believed that a breakout could possibly occur. "Proceedings of a Board," NA, pp. 64–65, 77.

21. First Lieutenant Walter S. Schuyler reported that "although the issue of fuel to the Cheyennes was stopped before their outbreak [that night], they did not [as yet?] suffer from cold as they had some fuel in the prison and had three fires going up to

the time they took down [the] stoves to barricade doors." Schuyler to George Crook, January 16, 1879, "Lt. Schuyler telegrams sent," copy in Fort Robinson Archive, NSHS. Snow depth certainly varied, but an account by John Farnham, who lived at the site of the old agency, placed it at "about a foot deep, so there was no chance [for the Indians] to get away." Camp Papers, p. 281, Lilly Library, Indiana University, copy in Fort Robinson Archive (NSHS). Wessells remembered "about eight inches of snow on the ground." Wessells, "Hard Military Service," p. 604.

22. "Proceedings of a Board," NA, pp. 5, 203; *Chicago Times*, January 11, 1879; McGillycuddy, *McGillycuddy Agent*, p. 97; Hoig, *Perilous Pursuit*, p. 169. For perspective, the rudimentary encompassing time zone was in those days called "Chicago Time," which roughly equates today with the modern Central Time Zone yet included the western part of the state of Nebraska as well. On the matter of time, see William A. Graham, *Abstract of the Official Record of Proceedings of the Reno Court of Inquiry* (Harrisburg, Pa.: Stackpole, 1954), p. 37. Regarding the supposed number of Northern Cheyennes then in the barrack, see note 9 above. Dr. Moseley recorded the temperature about the time of the breakout at 10 degrees. "Record of the Medical History of Post," as cited in Roger T. Grange Jr., "Fort Robinson: Outpost on the Plains," *Nebraska History* 39 (September 1958): 224. (As noted, the low temperature reading at the North Platte Station on January 9 was –1 degree.) "Report of the Chief Signal Officer," in *Report of the Secretary of War, 1879* (part 4), p. 368; Mrs. Black Bear interview, George Bird Grinnell Collection, Southwest Museum, Los Angeles; Grinnell, *Fighting Cheyennes*, pp. 420–21; Powell, *Sweet Medicine*, 1:238–40; Powell, *Killing of Morning Star's People*, pp. 8–9; "Proceedings of a Board," p. 18; Monnett, *Tell Them We Are Going Home*, pp. 122–27. For minute details of the Northern Cheyennes' final preparations, see especially Powell, *People of the Sacred Mountain*, 2:1198–1201. Among the articles carried away was a shield belonging to Red Bird, a young Cheyenne boy wounded during the breakout from Fort Robinson. It was ornamented with grizzly claws, a turtle's tail, and eagle and owl feathers, conveying attributes of those creatures to the possessor. It was believed to have been created in 1780 by Oak, whose son imparted it to his own son, Great Eyes, who gave it to Red Bird while both were interned at Fort Robinson shortly before the breakout. Great Eyes was killed during the escape. See Grinnell, *Cheyenne Indians*, 1:193–94, for more about the shield. See also Leo Killsback, "Crowns of Honor: Sacred Laws of Eagle Feather War Bonnets and Repatriating the Icon of the Great Plains," *Great Plains Quarterly* 33 (Winter 2013): 16.

Chapter 7. Violent Night

1. Johnson to Hare, February 16, 1879, NA, copy in Fort Robinson Archive (NSHS); Bronson, *Cowboy Life on the Western Plains*, pp. 175–76. Most first-person accounts, including Wessells's report, stated that the shooting began "at" or "about" 10 P.M. Wessells to AAG, Department of the Platte, January 12, 1879, NA, copy in Fort Robinson Archive (NSHS). Surgeon Moseley stated that it started at "about 9:45 P.M.," while Crook's aide, First Lieutenant Walter S. Schuyler, who was not present but investigated the affair within days, stated that the first shots came at "ten minutes before 10 o'clock." Schuyler to Crook, January 16, 1879, in "Lt. Schuyler

telegrams sent," copy in Fort Robinson Archive (NSHS) report (hereinafter cited as "Schuyler telegrams"). Edward B. Moseley was appointed assistant surgeon in 1874 and attained the grade of major and surgeon in 1892 and deputy surgeon general in 1902. Grange, "Treating the Wounded," p. 277; Heitman, *Historical Register and Dictionary*, 1:731. A newspaper account (*Chicago Times*, January 11, 1879) stated "the sentinel walking guard on the east side of the prison-room containing the Cheyennes had just cried out, 'Ten o'clock and all's well.' Hardly had the sound of his voice died away on the night breeze when, by a preconcerted signal, the savages burst through two doors and windows which they had previously unfastened." See also *New York Herald*, January 15, 1879; and *Army and Navy Journal*, January 18, 1879, citing the *Chicago Times* story. Various other published accounts state that the action started at 11 P.M. See, for example, *New York Times*, January 11, 1879. The most thorough accounts of the breakout from the Northern Cheyenne perspective appear in Powell, *People of the Sacred Mountain*, 2:1202–4; Powell, *Sweet Medicine*, 1:241–43; Powell, *Killing of Morning Star's People*, pp. 11–17.

2. Private Schmidt had only recently enlisted, on November 12, 1878, at Cincinnati, Ohio, at the age of twenty-four. A native of Bavaria, Germany, Schmidt was a baker in civilian life. He stood 5 feet, 7 inches tall and had gray eyes, light hair, and a fair complexion. U.S. Army Register of Enlistments, 1798–1914, NA; Register of Deaths in the Regular Army, 1860–1889, NA, pp. 212–13.

3. Private Hulse, age twenty-six, from Long Island, New York, had enlisted at Baltimore only recently, on November 23, 1878. He was 5 feet, 9½ inches tall, with brown eyes, dark hair, and a fair complexion. U.S. Army Register of Enlistments, 1798–1914, NA; Register of Deaths in the Regular Army, 1860–1889, NA, pp. 14–15, 88–89.

4. There is no information on Timmany in the U.S. Army Register of Enlistments. 1798–1914. For his wounding, see Grange, "Treating the Wounded," p. 282. Private McHale of Company F, age twenty-three, enlisted in New York City on February 21, 1878. He was 5 feet, 6 inches tall, with gray eyes, brown hair, and a florid complexion. He was discharged at Fort Huachuca, Arizona Territory, on March 1, 1883. U.S. Army Register of Enlistments, 1798–1914, NA; Grange, "Treating the Wounded," p. 282.

5. Private Pulver, from Princeton, Illinois, enlisted August 26, 1876, in Chicago, Illinois, at the age of twenty-two. He had brown eyes, black hair, and a fair complexion and stood 5 feet, 6¾ inches tall. He was discharged April 25, 1879, at Fort McPherson, Nebraska. U.S. Army Register of Enlistments, 1798–1914, NA.

6. *New York Herald*, January 15, 1879; *Army and Navy Journal*, January 18, 1879; "Proceedings of a Board," NA, pp. 9 (quotations), 100–101, 177, 203–4, 152–53; Grange, "Treating the Wounded," pp. 279–83; Hoig, *Perilous Pursuit*, pp. 170–71. The seventh man wounded from the gunfire was Private Edward Glavin of Company E, Third Cavalry, also a sentry, who suffered a bullet wound to his right thumb and returned to duty a few days later. Grange, "Treating the Wounded," p. 283. Glavin, a bricklayer from London, England, enlisted at Indianapolis, Indiana, at age twenty-two. He had gray eyes, dark hair, and a fair complexion and stood 5 feet 6¾ inches tall. Glavin ultimately deserted in August 1879. U.S. Army Register of Enlistments, 1798–1914, NA.

7. "Plan of Fort Robinson, Neb., Showing Line of Retreat of Cheyennes after Their Outbreak, January 9, 1879," NA; "Proceedings of a Board," NA, pp. 17, 141,

and accompanying map, pp. 217–18; Grinnell, *Fighting Cheyennes*, pp. 421–22; Bronson, *Cowboy Life on the Western Plains*, p. 177. Bronson believed that the Indians were headed toward his ranch, only five miles south of Fort Robinson, and abandoned their equipment on realizing that such an effort was futile. Bronson and his cowboys could hear the distant shooting from his ranch. Bronson, *Cowboy Life on the Western Plains*, pp. 179–80. For similar fears among ranchers of the area, see "Dull Knife's Break for Freedom," as related by W. A. Potts, on the reaction at the Ox Yoke Ranch sixteen miles east of the post, in Roy V. Mahlman, *The Weekly Report*, p. 10, copy in Fort Robinson Archive, NSHS. First Lieutenant Schuyler, who investigated the affair for Crook, likened the barrack breakout to a simultaneous rush "through all the windows, the Indians sallying out resolved to kill and be killed, like Malays running amuk [*sic*]." "Schuyler telegrams." The men who initiated the shooting were Tangle Hair, Little Finger Nail, and Gathering His Medicine. Powell, *People of the Sacred Mountain*, 2:1202–3; Powell, *Killing of Morning Star's People*, p. 11.

8. "Proceedings of a Board," NA, pp. 15, 65–66, 100–101, 115, 145, 154 (quotation); Wessells to AAG, Headquarters, Department of the Platte, January 12, 1879, NA.

9. "Proceedings of a Board," NA, pp. 154 (Lanigan quotations), 204; Wessells to AAG, Headquarters, Department of the Platte, January 12, 1879 (Wessells quotation); Wessells, "Reminiscences," in Wessells, "Hard Military Service," p. 604;

10. Stands In Timber and Liberty, *Cheyenne Memories*, p. 236; Camp Papers, Box 2, f. 3, Lilly Library, Indiana University, pp. 280–81; Grinnell, *Fighting Cheyennes*, pp. 420–22; "Iron Teeth, a Cheyenne Old Woman," p. 22 (quotation).

11. Powell, *Sweet Medicine*, 1:243; John Stands In Timber and Margot Liberty, *A Cheyenne Voice: The Complete John Stands In Timber Interviews* (Norman: University of Oklahoma Press, 2013), p. 246; Account of Bull Hump, Ellison-Camp Papers, DPL (quotation); Powell, *People of the Sacred Mountain*, 2:1202–3; Powell, *Sweet Medicine*, 1:241–42; Powell, *Killing of Morning Star's People*, p. 12; Hoig, *Perilous Pursuit*, pp. 173–74.

12. Mrs. Black Bear interview, George Bird Grinnell Collection, Southwest Museum, (first and third quotations); "Schuyler telegrams" (second quotation). Regarding the killing of Northern Cheyenne women and children, former sergeant Carter Johnson recalled years later that there were "only one or two cases in which a woman was killed intentionally or through excitement, and many were killed as they ran through the bushes, [the soldiers] not being able to tell the women from the men." In one instance, he remembered, "thirty or forty . . . were being brought to the guard house by the soldiers when another party of soldiers coming out of Soldier Creek firing at a running Indian stampeded these women. They start[ed] to run and this girl in trying to stop them ran towards the soldiers. They didn't understand her and she was shot dead and the other women then ran into the bushes and this squad of soldiers taking them for bucks fired on them. Otherwise there would have been very few women killed that night." Johnson's account in Jensen, *Settler and Soldier Interviews*, p. 28.

13. Mrs. Black Bear interview (quotations); Bronson, *Cowboy Life on the Western Plains*, pp. 176–77; Powell, *People of the Sacred Mountain*, 2:1203; Powell, *Sweet Medicine*, 1:242–43; Johnson to Hare, February 16, 1879, copy in Fort Robinson Archive (NSHS); "Plan of Fort Robinson, Neb., Showing Line of Retreat of Cheyennes"; account of "Stacy Riggs's mother," in Thomas Benton Williams, *The Soul*

of the Red Man (n.p., 1937), p. 239. Schuyler stated: "No woman or child was intentionally harmed, and in fact many officers and soldiers showed great daring in trying to save them. To take the men prisoners was impossible, as they all refused to surrender, and when exhausted stood at bay. Several soldiers lost their lives in trying to capture such men. No Indian was killed who could have been captured." "Schuyler telegrams."

14. Grinnell, *Fighting Cheyennes*, p. 422; Powell, *People of the Sacred Mountain*, 2:1206–7; Powell, *Sweet Medicine*, 1:246–48. First Lieutenant Charles A. Johnson testified regarding the death of Big Antelope (White Antelope) and his wife. "She said Big Antelope was wounded first and soon after getting to him she was wounded. Then Big Antelope said they might as well die together and he stabbed her and then stabbed himself and so died. She died a few minutes after being brought in here [to Fort Robinson]." "Proceedings of a Board," NA, p. 144 (see also p. 174). White Antelope had taken part in the skirmishing with Crook's soldiers in the Big Horn Mountains a few weeks after the Battle of the Little Bighorn and in the fighting at Dull Knife's village in November 1876. *Chicago Times*, July 26, 1876; Grinnell, *Fighting Cheyennes*, 380–81. For specifics of the army surgeons' treatment of the wounded Indians, many of whom were named, see Powell, *People of the Sacred Mountain*, 2:250–51; and Grange, "Treating the Wounded," pp. 290–92. A listing derived from Grange appears in appendix A.

15. Johnson to Hare, February 16, 1879, NA, copy in Fort Robinson Archive (NSHS) (first quotation); Fort Robinson dispatch, January 14, 1879 (second quotation), in John D. McDermott, Cheyenne Outbreak Notes, Leland D. Case Library, E. Y. Berry Library-Learning Center, Black Hills State University, Spearfish, South Dakota; Bronson, *Cowboy Life on the Western Plains*, pp. 177–78; Powell, *People of the Sacred Mountain*, 2:1203–4; Powell, *Sweet Medicine*, 1:243. Despite the severity of Indian losses on the ground east of White River, surviving warriors were able to unleash volleys of "from six to twelve shots" from "ambush" sites against their pursuers. *Omaha Herald*, January 22, 1879.

16. Angie Johnson to Abbie Bush, January 15, 1879, copy in Fort Robinson Archive (NSHS). "Charlie" was her husband, First Lieutenant Charles A. Johnson, Fourteenth Infantry, the former post commander.

17. Wessells, "Outbreak of Cheyennes at Fort Robinson," Ellison-Camp Papers, DPL, item 13, October 13, 1912 (quotation); "Proceedings of a Board," NA, pp. 15, 65–66, 100–101, 115, 145, 204; Wessells to AAG, Headquarters, Department of the Platte, January 12, 1879, NA; Wessells, "Hard Military Service," p. 604; "Proceedings of a Board," NA, p. 154; *New York Herald*, January 15, 1879. Northern Cheyenne survivors told Grinnell that some of the pursuing troops appeared to be garbed in white, a reference to the long cotton-flannel drawers that they were issued. Grinnell, *Fighting Cheyennes*, p. 421;. Captain Joseph Lawson recalled that the companies "seemed to turn out without any regular formation." "Proceedings of a Board," NA, p. 115. Lieutenant Emmet Crawford, stationed at Fort Laramie, had been on court-martial duty at Fort Robinson and voluntarily joined Wessells in his efforts following the breakout. "Proceedings of a Board," NA, p. 144. For the moments after the breakout, also see Hoig, *Perilous Pursuit*, pp. 172–74. Wessells reported that after mounting his company he moved "at a gallop" to join Vroom at the bluffs. Wessells to AAG, Department of the Platte, January 12, 1879, NA.

18. "Proceedings of a Board," NA, pp. 29, 83–85, 125, 153, 160 (quotation), 204; Powell, *People of the Sacred Mountain*, 2:1203; Powell, *Sweet Medicine*, 1:242–43; Powell, *Killing of Morning Star's People*, p. 12; Hoig, *Perilous Pursuit*, pp. 172–73.

19. "Proceedings of a Board," NA, pp. 174–75.

20. Powell, *People of the Sacred Mountain*, 2:1203; Powell, *Sweet Medicine*, 1:243; Powell, *Killing of Morning Star's People*, pp. 12–13. See also Hoig, *Perilous Pursuit*, p. 173.

21. "Proceedings of a Board," NA, pp. 175–76. The bravery of the Northern Cheyenne warriors drew notice in early news reports of the breakout. Correspondent James R. O'Beirne wrote: "The Indians . . . [fought] like wild beasts even when disarmed, two or three in sheltered positions several times keeping back a squad of soldiers," no doubt referencing their rearguard actions protecting noncombatants outside the barrack and near the bridge as well as elsewhere. *New York Herald*, January 16, 1879.

O'Beirne (1842–1917), representing the *New York Herald*, was on the scene directly following the breakout and subsequent events at Fort Robinson. He had worked as a clerk in the Indian Department in Washington, D.C., and had been assigned by commissioner Ezra Hayt to help manage relocation of the Oglalas from the Missouri River to White Clay Creek in the Pine Ridge country as well as to aid in the construction of agency buildings at White Clay Creek (including movement of materials from the old agency near Camp Robinson to New Red Cloud Agency). O'Beirne initially made his headquarters at Camp Sheridan. Born in Ireland, he graduated from St. John's College (later Fordham University) and during the Civil War led infantry troops at Fair Oaks, Virginia (for which he later received a Medal of Honor) and was badly wounded in the fighting at Chancellorsville. He subsequently served as provost marshal of Washington, D.C., and at the direction of secretary of war Edwin Stanton conducted the pursuit of John Wilkes Booth and other conspirators following President Abraham Lincoln's assassination. O'Beirne years later became deputy U.S. marshal and registrar of wills in Washington, D.C., as well as that city's correspondent for the *New York Herald* and editor of the *Washington Gazette*. In 1890–91 he served as commissioner of immigration, overseeing the station at Ellis Island. During that time, the liberal O'Beirne involved himself in controversy over the purportedly bad treatment of Sioux performers attached to William F. Cody's Wild West Show. For O'Beirne and the Lakotas, see George E. Hyde, *A Sioux Chronicle* (Norman: University of Oklahoma Press, 1956), p. 70; James C. Olson, *Red Cloud and the Sioux Problem* (Lincoln: University of Nebraska Press, 1965), pp. 261–67; and Louis S. Warren, *Buffalo Bill's America: William Cody and the Wild West Show* (New York: Alfred A. Knopf, 2005), pp. 371, 374, 404, 409. See also Fordham University, "James R. O'Beirne," at https://www.fordham.edu/info/26211/hall of_honor/9547/james_r_o_beirne (accessed June 20, 2019).

O'Beirne stated that he represented the *New York Herald* during four Indian campaigns "in which there was fighting." O'Beirne to editor, *Century Magazine*, October 15, 1907, New York Public Library Digital Collections (https://digitalcollections.nypl.org/). O'Beirne's obituary appeared in the *New York Times*, February 18, 1917, stating: "He was for many years Washington correspondent of The New York Herald, and also represented that paper during several of the Indian campaigns that followed the Civil War." While it was unacknowledged at the time, O'Beirne's identity as the *Herald*'s on-site correspondent at Fort Robinson (residing in the quarters of post trader John

W. Dear) is confirmed in the *Army and Navy Journal*, March 1, 1879. There he doubtless composed his dispatches for transmission to the *Herald* following the breakout of the Northern Cheyennes.

22. Powell, *People of the Sacred Mountain*, 2:1204; Powell, *Sweet Medicine*, 1:243–44, 246; Powell, *Killing of Morning Star's People*, pp. 13–14.

23. "Proceedings of a Board," NA, p. 178; Grinnell, *Fighting Cheyennes*, p. 422; *Chicago Times*, January 22, 1879; *Army and Navy Journal*, March 3, 1879; *Chicago Times*, January 11, 1879; Powell, *Sweet Medicine*, 1:243; Powell, *Killing of Morning Star's People*, p. 13. An unnamed retired soldier-participant explained years later that the troops first "struck the Indians . . . where the Chicago & Northwestern Rail Road [now] crosses the [Soldier] creek at the edge of the Fort." This likely refers to the approximate site of Vroom's initial contact with the Cheyennes in Township 31N, Range 52W, Section 17, northwest quarter. See A. N. Keith, "Dull Knife's Cheyenne Raid of 1878," *Nebraska History and Record of Pioneer Days* 7 (October–December 1924): 118; Hoig, *Perilous Pursuit*, pp. 175–76.

24. Chase, "Dull Knife & Cheyennes," Ellison-Camp Papers, DPL.

25. "Proceedings of a Board," NA, pp. 154–55, 159 (quotations). Cramblett's Lake was a spring-fed local pond set in the southern part of Section 23 near the northern part of Section 26, directly south. See Plat No. 2637, Township 31 North, Range 53 West (surveyed 1881–82), Surveyor General's Office, Plattsmouth, Nebraska, 1883; USGS "Smiley Canyon, Nebr.," quadrangle, 1980, shows a slight slough there as of that date. "Cramlet [*sic*] Lake" also appears at that location on a map showing Fort Robinson Military Reservation compiled in the "Office of the Engineer, HQ, Seventh Corps Area, March 1930," copy in Fort Robinson Archive (NSHS).

26. "Proceedings of a Board," NA, pp. 66, 115, 153, 204; *New York Herald*, January 15, 1879 (quotations); *Army and Navy Journal*, January 18, 1879; Fort Robinson medical history, as recorded by Dr. Moseley and cited in Grange, "Fort Robinson," p. 224. Mixed-blood interpreter James Rowland claimed that one Cheyenne woman told him later in the prison barrack that "after she was wounded and down soldiers tried to shoot her in the head but she dodged and they shot her finger off." "Proceedings of a Board," NA, p. 150. Lieutenant James Simpson testified "to my knowledge no woman or child was killed when it could be avoided." "Proceedings of a Board," NA, p. 108.

27. "Proceedings of a Board," NA, p. 115.

28. "Fort Robinson Medical History," as cited in Grange, "Fort Robinson," p. 191; "Proceedings of a Board," NA, 85, 116, 155 (first quotation), 159, 204, 205; *Chicago Times*, January 11, 1879; Johnson's account in Jensen, *Settler and Soldier Interviews*, pp. 236–37; Bronson, *Cowboy Life on the Western Plains*, p. 181 (second quotation); "Plan of Fort Robinson, Neb., Showing Line of Retreat of Cheyennes," in "Proceedings of a Board," pp. 217–18. Among the casualties, Bronson recognized a son of Dull Knife whom he remembered from the barrack council in early November. Initially believed lifeless, the young man suddenly rose up and swiped at Bronson's leg with his knife but missed then fell back dead in the snow. *Cowboy Life on the Western Plains*, pp. 181–82; Powell, *People of the Sacred Mountain*, 2:1207.

29. Powell, *People of the Sacred Mountain*, 2:1205–6; Powell, *Killing of Morning Star's People*, p. 14; "Iron Teeth, a Cheyenne Old Woman," p. 22.

30. Powell, *People of the Sacred Mountain*, 2:1206–7; Powell, *Killing of Morning Star's People*, p. 16.

31. For particulars regarding the collection of the dead, see especially Powell, *People of the Sacred Mountain*, 2:1210–13.

32. "Proceedings of a Board," NA, pp. 29–31, 66–67, 85, 101–2, 161; Grinnell, *Fighting Cheyennes*, p. 4; Account of Black Horse, Camp Papers, Box 2, f. 3, Lilly Library, Indiana University, pp. 280–81; *New York Herald*, January 15, 1879 (including editorial); see also *Army and Navy Journal*, January 18, 1879. Northern Cheyenne traditional accounts supported by on-site archeological research have delineated the principal area of the people's route of ascent from White River into the bluffs. The area lies approximately one mile due south of the modern Smiley Canyon road of Fort Robinson State Park, adjoining modern U.S. 20 on the south. See J. Douglas McDonald, Larry J. Zimmerman, A. L. McDonald, William Tall Bull, and Ted Rising Sun, "The Northern Cheyenne Outbreak of 1879: Using Oral History and Archaeology as Tools of Resistance," in R. H. McGuire and R. Paynter, eds., *The Archaeology of Inequality* (Oxford: Basil Blackwell, 1991), pp. 68–74. The area lies in Township 31 North, Range 53 West, Section 23. USGS, "Smiley Canyon, Nebr.," quadrangle, 1980.

33. Editorial, *Army and Navy Journal*, January 18, 1879, citing *New York Herald*, January 14, 1879 (first quotation); *New York Herald*, January 16, 1879; Bronson, *Cowboy Life on the Western Plains*, pp. 183–84 (second quotation). The massive tan bluffs today border the south side of a six-mile-long east-west paved tour road that leaves and rejoins U.S. 20 and passes through Smiley Canyon. Maher, Engelmann, and Shuster, *Roadside Geology of Nebraska*, pp. 118–21.

34. "Proceedings of a Board," NA, pp. 166–67 (first and second quotations); *Chicago Times*, January 11, 1879; *New York Herald*, January 15, 1879 (third quotation); Wessells, "Outbreak of Cheyennes at Fort Robinson," Camp Papers, DPL; "Proceedings of a Board," NA, p. 138; Grange, "Treating the Wounded," pp. 278–83. According to interpreter Rowland, "I saw them fetch the Indian bodies to the grave and bury them; there were 14 men[,] 9 women[,] and 3 [*sic*] little children, [and] two women and one child died afterwards. The men were mostly old, four or five were young men." "Proceedings of a Board," NA, pp. 150–51; Buecker, *Fort Robinson and the American West*, p. 142. (For background on Dr. Petteys, see Paul L. Hedren, "The Sioux War Adventures of Dr. Charles V. Petteys, Acting Assistant Surgeon," *Journal of the West* 32 (April 1993):29–37.) On the morning of January 10 Chief Old Crow was permitted to view the dead and saw the "bodies of a great many men, women and children." Senate, *Select Committee Report*, p. 23. An area resident at the time named Charles Wells recollected that the dead Northern Cheyennes were buried in the "government saw mill pit" because the ground elsewhere was so badly frozen. Wells further claimed that a local round-up cook desecrated two of the bodies. Paul Frison, *The Apache Slave: Life of Charles Wells* (Worland, Wyo.: Worland Press, 1969), pp. 28–29. Rancher Bronson stated that the dead "—bucks, squaws, and children—lay in a row by the roadside near the sawmill, and there later they were buried in a common trench." *Cowboy Life on the Western Plains*, p. 184. Among the Northern Cheyennes the Fort Robinson breakout is known as Tsexhova'xevose Tsetsehestahese. *We, the Northern Cheyenne People*, p. 28. See also Powell, *Killing of Morning Star's People*, p. 16. For a list of "Cheyenne Names and Relationships" identified by Cheyenne sources regarding the Fort Robinson breakout and its collateral actions, see appendix D.

35. "Proceedings of a Board," NA, p. 206. Former Red Cloud Agency employee Richard C. Stirk further reported that at the sawmill he viewed "two [dead] women . . . lying beside each other with their dresses thrown up over their heads, their naked bodies exposed and sticks run up into them." Jensen, *Settler and Soldier Interviews*, p. 289. For more particulars of this horrendous matter, see "Proceedings of a Board," NA, pp. 77, 116, 132–33, 165, 166–67, 205. Post Adjutant (Second Lieutenant) Cummings stated, "I don't remember how many of [the] bodies this side of [the] bluffs were scalped[,] but all of those in [the] bluffs were scalped." Ibid., p. 167. So far as is known, beyond the references cited and the board summary notation quoted above, no persons were ever charged, arrested, or prosecuted for the desecrations of the Northern Cheyenne bodies, including taking "grown persons' scalps . . . about the size of [a] half dollar." Ibid. The matter was seemingly officially ignored and forgotten. Lieutenant Cummings, who picked up most of the Indian dead, reported that as many as eighteen bodies had been scalped, "one in two places." Ibid. He stated that he met "as many as a dozen citizens with guns in their hands" as he picked up wounded Indians and prisoners in the vicinity. Ibid., p. 169. Civilians identified in the "Proceedings of a Board," NA, as having been seen in the areas where the outrages occurred, in addition to two or three unidentified men in a buckboard (ibid., pp. 112, 133), included John W. Dear, the Indian trader at the old Red Cloud Agency, a man named Henry Clifford, and a man tentatively called "Mr. [Edward] Cook," identified as the "Division Superintendent of the Sidney and Black Hills Stage line." Ibid., pp. 79, 90, 110 (quotation), 167, 169. According to Lieutenant Simpson, Cook claimed to have "shot a wounded squaw through the head with a pistol but that that did not kill her." Ibid., p. 110. In the case of the men in the buckboard, Simpson overheard one of them saying, "I've got a pipe—that's what I've been looking for." This occurred on the top of the bluffs. Simpson claimed that the buckboard was "the one which brings the mail here from the Sidney and Black Hills stage line." Ibid. On the matter of civilian transgressions on the occasion, see also Powell, *Sweet Medicine*, I:248, 252–54. Some bodies had been mutilated by having been shot again after death. Powell, *Killing of Morning Star's People*, p. 17; Buecker, *Fort Robinson and the American West*, p. 152. See also the account in Hoig, *Perilous Pursuit*, pp. 179–80.

36. *New York Herald*, January 16, 1879. The location of the burial pit has apparently been obscured by time and periodic flooding by both Soldier Creek and the White River. Memorandum from former Nebraska State Historical Society curator of the Fort Robinson Museum Vance Nelson to Mrs. Grace Carmody, August 2, 1993, copy in Fort Robinson Archive, NSHS. An unidentified observer cited by former Bureau of Indian Affairs director George W. Manypenny described the burials:

> The soldiers drag out of the army wagons twenty-six frozen bodies. They fall upon the ground like so many frozen hogs. These bodies are pierced by from three to ten bullets each. They are stacked up in piles like cordwood, the scanty clothing of the women being in some instances thrown over their heads. . . . Their heads have been scalped. . . . The officers account for so many shots being fired into the bodies by saying that "whenever the wind stirred a blanket, the soldiers fired again to make sure the Indian was dead."

Quoted in Manypenny, *Our Indian Wards*, p. 339.

37. Telegram, Headquarters Military Division of the Missouri, to Adjutant General, January 10, 1879, copy in Fort Robinson Archive, NSHS (quotation); "Briefs," in Senate, *Escape of the Cheyenne Indians*, p. 23. Concise coverage of the breakout drawn from various government reports appears in *Record of Engagements with Hostile Indians within the Military Division of the Missouri*, pp. 83; and "Report of the Surgeon-General," October 1, 1879, in *Report of the Secretary of War, 1879*, p. 408. See also Carter, "History of Fort Robinson," pp. 15–16. An all-too-brief contemporaneous account, stating that the breakout erupted at 11 P.M., appears in "The Last Indian Fight," *Frank Leslie's Illustrated Newspaper*, February 15, 1879.

38. "Proceedings of a Board," NA, p. 166; Crawford to First Lieutenant Charles Morton, February 26, 1879, copy in Fort Robinson Archive, NSHS (first quotation); Powell, *People of the Sacred Mountain*, 2:1209; *New York Herald*, January 11, 1879 (second quotation). For another contemporary account, see *New York Herald*, January 15, 1879, also reprinted in *Army and Navy Journal*, January 18, 1879.

39. Account of Bull Hump, Ellison-Camp Papers, DPL; Powell, *People of the Sacred Mountain*, 2:1205, 1207; Powell, *Sweet Medicine*, 1:239, 275–76; Powell, *Killing of Morning Star's People*, pp. 14–16. Much of the foregoing military perspective on the events of the breakout is contained or repeated in Telegram, Crook to Sheridan, January 15, 1879, Microfilm 1495, Roll 6, NA.

40. Quoted in Powell, *Killing of Morning Star's People*, p. 17.

Chapter 8. Hat Creek Road

1. *New York Herald*, January 16, 1879. Schuyler delivered a full report to Crook and Sheridan soon after his arrival on January 15. See Crook's report in "Briefs," in Senate, *Escape of the Cheyenne Indians*, pp. 10, 24–25. Schuyler was from New York and graduated from the Military Academy in 1866. He served in the Apache campaigns in the Southwest, during which he earned brevets for gallantry in action in 1872, 1873, and 1874 as well as during Crook's campaign in Wyoming's Big Horn range in 1876. Schuyler was mustered out of service in 1899, after the Spanish-American War. Heitman, *Historical Register and Dictionary*, 1:867.

There may have been an inclination to stifle news in the days immediately following the breakout, in which both officers and enlisted men on the scene were complicit while anticipating direction from the military hierarchy. One correspondent complained: "It is like getting blood out of a turnip to prevail upon soldiers or officers to unseal their lips about the matter." *Sidney Plaindealer*, January 16, 1879. But correspondent O'Beirne reported that Schuyler's role was not to report on "culpability" for the breakout but rather to gather and convey information "to the headquarters of the department so the facts might be known promptly and fully." *New York Herald*, January 18, 1879.

2. Johnson's account in Jensen, *Settler and Soldier Interviews*, p. 239. See also detailed references to Wessells's patrol and others searching for Indians among the bluffs, especially in the immediate aftermath of the breakout on Thursday night into Friday morning, as related in Powell, *Sweet Medicine*, 1:250–55; and Powell, *People of the Sacred Mountain*, 2:1208–15.

3. Wessells later stated that "my plan for the second day (10th) was to send 'L' Company up the Hat Creek road[,] 'A' Company up the Sidney road and through the bluffs just back of post[,] 'C' Company on one of the Indian trails we had seen[,] 'H' to Crow Butte on the right bank of the [White] river, and through the bluffs out to Running Water [Niobrara River] and White River. 'E' Company I sent up White River." "Proceedings of a Board," NA, p. 67.

4. Powell, *People of the Sacred Mountain*, 2:1214–15.

5. Telegram, Crook to Sheridan, January 10, 1879, copy in Fort Robinson Archive, NSHS; Bryant, *Hat Creek and Hard Times*, pp. 7, 9; Spring, *Cheyenne and Black Hills Stage and Express Routes*, pp. 129, 159.

6. "Iron Teeth, a Cheyenne Old Woman," pp. 22–23.

7. Grinnell, *Fighting Cheyennes*, pp. 423–24 (quotations); Powell, *Sweet Medicine*, 1:257–58; Powell, *Killing of Morning Star's People*, p. 18.

8. Powell, *Killing of Morning Star's People*, p. 18.

9. See Nebraska Survey Plats, Township 31N, Range 53W, and Township 31N, Range 54W, surveyed in 1881 and 1882. Surveyor General's Office, Plattsmouth, Nebraska, 1883; USGS, "Smiley Canyon, Nebr.," quadrangle, 1980; USGS, "Andrews, Nebr.," quadrangle, 1980; USGS, "Five Points, Nebr." quadrangle, 1980.

10. "Proceedings of a Board," NA, p. 145.

11. "Proceedings of a Board," NA, pp. 130–31. "The Indian," said Baxter, " . . . seemed determined to kill his man and then die himself." His account includes more details of the encounter, which the lieutenant described as having occurred in the "bluffs south east of the Post." Ibid.; "Report of the Surgeon-General, October 1, 1879," in *Report of the Secretary of War, 1879*, p. 408. Private William Everett of Company H, a Rhode Island native, had enlisted in Chicago, giving his civilian occupation as a teamster. He stood 5 feet, 4 inches tall, with gray eyes, brown hair, and a fair complexion. U.S. Army Register of Enlistments, 1798–1914, NA. See Grange, "Treating the Wounded," pp. 283–84, for specifics of Everett's injury. He died on January 11, 1879. Register of Deaths in the Regular Army, 1860–1889, NA, pp. 14–15, pp. 60–61. Rancher Edgar Bronson's protracted and likely dramatized account of this incident appears in *Cowboy Life on the Western Plains* pp. 187–92. Bronson stated of the man who shot Everett: "The old Cheyenne kept up his rapid fire as long as he could. . . . Suddenly I saw him drop down in the bottom of the washout, limp as an empty sack." Ibid., p. 191. The reporter for the *Chicago Times*, January 13, 1879, speculated that the spacious and naturally fortified site was "a place no doubt well known [to them] and which in years past was used for their camping-ground." A memorial for Everett sponsored by the Columbus Literary Association was held at the post on January 15. *Army and Navy Journal*, January 25, 1879.

Another fatality among the troops on January 11 was Private Bernard Kelley, of Company E, Third Cavalry, who was accidentally shot in his left leg by one of his company members. Placed in the post hospital and later operated upon by Drs. Moseley and Petteys, who amputated his leg, Kelley subsequently "raised his head and shoulders . . . and looked down where his leg had been, then instantly fell back, the eyes rolled up, respiration became irregular and he was dead inside of three minutes." "Proceedings of a Board," NA, p. 118; Grange, "Treating the Wounded," pp. 285–86 (quotation). Kelley died on January 12, 1879. Register of Deaths in the Regular Army, 1860–1889, pp. 14–15. The account of Kelley's medical treatment is replicated in *The Medical and Surgical History of the War of the Rebellion* (part III, vol. 2, Surgical History), second issue (Washington, D.C.: Government Printing Office, 1883), p. 163.

12. "Proceedings of a Board," NA, pp. 170–72. The oldest woman was identified as the wife of Chief Tangle Hair. Powell, *Sweet Medicine*, 1:252; Hoig, *Perilous Pursuit*, pp. 182–83.

13. "Proceedings of a Board," NA, pp. 67, 85–87, 116 (quotations). The "knoll" was said to be located "about 18 miles northwest of the post." Ibid., p. 206. Rancher Bronson, who accompanied the day's pursuit, stated that the Indians had "entrenched themselves" amid "the fallen timber on the crest of this . . . hill." *Cowboy Life on the Western Plains*, pp. 185–86.

14. Telegram, Wessells to AAG, Department of the Platte, January 12, 1879, NA, copy in Fort Robinson Archive, NSHS; Telegram, Crook to Sheridan, January 11, 1879, Microfilm 1495, Roll 6, NA; "Proceedings of a Board," NA, pp. 31–32; Powell, *People of the Sacred Mountain*, 2:1215, 1395; Hoig, *Perilous Pursuit*, pp. 181–82.

15. "Proceedings of a Board," NA, p. 32 (quotation); Grange, "Treating the Wounded," 283. Wessells recalled that he and Vroom "followed the trail till at the base of a large hill we were fired upon. We got under shelter and soon 'A' Company came along. I let 'L' Company return [to the post] and kept 'A' Company. We stayed till after dark with 'A' Company and then went in [to the fort]." "Proceedings of a Board," NA, pp. 67–68; Regimental Return of the Third Cavalry, January 1879, RG 94, NA; Powell, *People of the Sacred Mountain*, p. 2:1215.

16. Bronson, *Cowboy Life on the Western Plains*, pp. 187–91; Grange, "Treating the Wounded," p. 283 (quotations); "Proceedings of a Board," NA, p. 86–87; Powell, *Sweet Medicine*, 1:256–57; Powell, *People of the Sacred Mountain*, 2:1215–16; Hoig, *Perilous Pursuit*, pp. 181–82; Register of Deaths in the Regular Army, 1860–1889, NA, pp. 78–79. A Pennsylvanian, Good had enlisted in 1876 at Pittsburgh at age twenty-two, occupation farmer. He had blue eyes, light hair, and a fair complexion and stood 5 feet, 6½ inches tall. U.S. Army Register of Enlistments, 1798–1914, NA. Good's death reference (ibid.) indicated that he was killed on "Little Bull Creek." The fighting likely occurred in the area of Section 9, Township 32 North, Range 54 West, USGS "Five Points, Nebr.," quadrangle, 1980, about fifteen miles northwest of Fort Robinson. See also Nebraska Survey Plats, Section 9, Township 32N, Range 54W, surveyed 1881 and 1882.

17. "Proceedings of a Board," NA, pp. 68 (quotation), 117.

18. Buecker, *Fort Robinson and the American West*, pp. 142–43; "Briefs," in Senate, *Escape of the Cheyenne Indians*, p. 8; "Proceedings of a Board," NA, pp. 31–33; Bronson, *Cowboy Life on the Western Plains*, p. 192.

19. "Proceedings of a Board," NA, pp. 68, 118, 126–27, 206. Lawson later stated: "I sent a noncommissioned officer and six men to the right of this bluff where the Indians were supposed to be and a noncommissioned officer and six men to the left so as to find the trail in case they had left the bluff, [and] with orders to keep out of range of the bluff. The Indians were still there and fired on one party and killed one of my co. horses." Ibid., p. 117 (quotation); Powell, *People of the Sacred Mountain*, 2:1216–17.

20. Crook to Sheridan, forwarding telegram, Wessells to Crook, January 12, 1879, Microfilm 1495, Roll 6, NA. Based on this information, Sheridan informed the adjutant general that Wessells's comment regarding the Indians' supply of arms and

ammunition suggested that they had been "secreted in the canon where they first made a stand [on January 9]." Sheridan to AG, January 12, 1879, NA, copy in Fort Robinson Archive, NSHS. Crook responded, agreeing with Sheridan, but wished to withhold his "fears upon the subject until the matter has been fully investigated." Crook to Sheridan, January 13, 1879, in Microfilm 1495, Roll 6, NA. At the same time, consideration was given to a notion that the Lakotas had somehow provided guns to the Cheyennes. As one paper surmised, "the Sioux of Red Cloud's band had unreserved access to these captives, with whom they were strongly allied by the association of years and the closest ties of consanguinity." *New York Herald*, January 16, 1879. For this incident regarding Rowland and Wessells (apparently derived from Rowland), see Grinnell, *Fighting Cheyennes*, p. 425.

On January 15 Crook telegraphed Sheridan his views regarding the Indians' armament: "After they had entered the prison [barrack] they having ample time to conceal arms under the floors[,] that place of deposit not being searched[,] the prison has been so guarded that the theory of arms having been introduced subsequently to their incarceration is scarcely tenable[.] Yet events proved that they had at least fifteen guns in addition to the two obtained from the dead sentinels & some few revolvers." Microfilm 1495, Roll 6, NA.

21. "Proceedings of a Board," NA, p. 87; *Chicago Times*, January 3, 1879; *People of the Sacred Mountain*, 2:1216–17; Bronson, *Cowboy Life on the Western Plains*, pp. 179–80. Bronson's Deadman Ranch stood five miles south of Fort Robinson, just two or so miles from where the bluff action occurred the night of the breakout. Bronson, *Cowboy Life on the Western Plains*, p. 178.

22. *Chicago Times*, January 13, 1879. The disparaging term "savages" was often applied to Indian people by the nineteenth-century media. Corporal Henry P. Ore, from New Jersey, enlisted as a private in Philadelphia, Pennsylvania, on September 21, 1876. He stood 5 feet, 7 inches, with light hair, blue eyes, and a fair complexion, and worked as a civilian laborer. U.S. Army Register of Enlistments, 1798–1914, NA. According to army medical records, the carbine ball that struck Ore passed through both his lungs as well as his heart. "On being struck, he fell forward and never moved or uttered a sound." For more particulars, see Grange, "Treating the Wounded," pp. 284–85; and "Proceedings of a Board," NA, p. 159. The mangled bullet that killed Corporal Ore is presently exhibited at the Fort Robinson History Center. See Roger T. Grange Jr., to Colonel Joe M. Blumberg, Armed Forces Institute of Pathology, April 3, 1957; Blumberg to Grange, April 15, 1957; and Grange to Blumberg, April 22, 1957, regarding U.S. Army Medical Museum Specimen MM83, in Fort Robinson Archive, NSHS. Despite Ore's father's request that his son be buried at Fort Robinson, the soldier's remains left Fort Robinson on January 20 for Iowa (for subsequent burial in Illinois). *Cincinnati Daily Star*, January 15, 1879; *Sidney Plaindealer*, January 23, 1879.

23. *Chicago Times*, January 13, 1879; "Proceedings of a Board," NA, pp. 68, 103; "Record of Events," Regimental Return of the Third Cavalry for January 1879, NA. Painter was shot in the left shoulder but lived. Grange, "Treating the Wounded," p. 286. Born in Pennsylvania, Painter enlisted in 1876 in Washington, D.C., civilian occupation butcher. He stood 6 feet tall and was discharged in 1881 at Fort Russell, Wyoming Territory, a soldier of excellent character. U.S. Army Register of Enlistments, 1798–1914, NA. In his comprehensive medical report, assistant surgeon Moseley erroneously reported Painter's wounding as having occurred on January 11 rather

than on the 12th. Hence the date provided in Grange, "Treating the Wounded," p. 286, is also wrong.

24. "Proceedings of a Board," NA, pp. 33–34. Irish-born Sergeant James Taggart enlisted in Chicago, Illinois, on March 8, 1875, civilian occupation carpenter. He had gray eyes, light hair, and a fair complexion and stood 5 feet, 9 inches tall. U.S. Army Register of Enlistments, 1798–1914, NA.

25. "Proceedings of a Board," pp. 33–34. Lieutenant Simpson stated that the men were left "to get Corporal Ore's body, not to allow [the] Indians to mutilate his body or get his carbine." Ibid., p. 103. For an embellished account of how Ore's body was retrieved by Third Cavalry blacksmith John Houk, see former private James E. Snepp, "An Incident of the Fort Robinson Outbreak, 1879," *Winners of the West* (July 1939), reprinted in Jerome A. Greene, ed., *Indian War Veterans: Memories of Army Life and Campaigns in the West, 1864–1898* (New York: Savas Beatie, 2007), p. 163. Sergeant Gottlieb Bigalsky, from Poland, reenlisted in October 1878 at age thirty-three. He was described as having blue eyes, sandy hair, and a fair complexion and being 5 feet, 8 inches tall. Bigalsky was discharged at Fort Thomas, Arizona Territory, in 1883, a man of excellent character. See also Hoig, *Perilous Pursuit*, pp. 183–84.

26. Chase, "Dull Knife & Cheyennes," Ellison-Camp Papers, DPL, p. 7. Chase further explained that the Indians would "take advantage to mix their own trail with every cattle trail in the snow they came across."

27. "Proceedings of a Board," NA, pp. 34–35. Reporter O'Beirne described the Cheyennes' rifle pits as being "on a ridge covered with deep ravines on both flanks and occupying its highest extremity, which broke off abruptly from the surrounding country." *New York Herald*, January 16, 1879. Years later, Chase elaborated on the attack, stating that he was leading his men "among the bluffs and came to a triangular point of a bluff. I had trailed them to this [place] by seeing where a wounded Indian had limped along on a stick, the point of it making a hole in the ground here & there, the ground being frozen & snow gone off as blown off at that place, so that their moccasins did not leave a track." Chase, "Dull Knife & Cheyennes," Ellison-Camp Papers, DPL, p. 7. Lieutenant Simpson stated that the troops "followed the trail north till we got very near the Hat Creek road. . . . I found the track of one Indian who had used sticks to walk with." "Proceedings of a Board," NA, p. 104.

28. As Vroom later reported, "I was ordered to take my company [L] and F Company [and to] take position down the creek the Indians were on, one company to prevent their crossing down the creek bed, and the other to charge them should they attempt to escape across the plains." "Proceedings of a Board," NA, p. 88.

29. Ibid., pp. 36–37. Years later, former Sergeant Carter Johnson stated that "the ground was frozen hard and the shells did no harm. Johnson's account in Jensen, *Settler and Soldier Interviews*, p. 239. Another contemporary description of the landscape for this encounter stated that "the position occupied by the savages was a narrow and deep washout, bordered by almost perpendicular banks, and of a zigzag direction." *Chicago Times*, January 15, 1879. Yet another description termed it "a perfectly flat expanse of country, with a narrow and deep gorge running in a zigzag manner through it." *New York Herald*, January 23, 1879.

30. "Proceedings of a Board," NA, pp. 36–38, 52, 88–89, 105–6 (quotation), 146, 206, 207; Bronson, *Cowboy Life on the Western Plains*, p. 194. Lieutenant Crawford estimated the distance of this engagement from Fort Robinson at "about 23 miles."

"Proceedings of a Board," NA, p. 146. See also *Sidney Plaindealer*, January 16, 1879. The site is calculated to be located in or near Township 33 North, Range 55 West, Section 33, USGS, "Bodarc, Nebr.," quadrangle, 1980 (see also Nebraska Survey Plats, Township 33N, Range 55W, Section 33). It is in a broad, open landscape about ten miles above the head of the middle fork of Soldier Creek where the elevation reaches over 4,000 feet. The salvo proceeded "without effecting the dislodgement of the Indians." See also "Proceedings of a Board," NA, p. 118, which describes the artillery action as having occurred on "Shell Creek." A contemporary assessment of the engagement stated: "It can readily be seen that artillery could not effectively be brought to play in a longitudinal direction; neither could the piece be depressed at the necessary angle which would be required to throw shells into that particular pocket of the washout in which the Indians had entrenched themselves." *Chicago Times*, January 15, 1879.

For estimated mileages reported for the various companies involved, see "Record of Events," Regimental Return of the Third Cavalry for January 1879, NA. Wessells intended to pursue the Indians but returned to the post after learning that a wagon loaded with grain for his horses had upset on the trail. "Proceedings of a Board," NA, p. 89. Vroom commented: "When they escaped they moved up onto the plain and then made for the bluffs. The troops could have been kept in their same positions at night and I think prevented their escape. . . . The companies were near enough for speedy cooperation." "Proceedings of a Board," NA, pp. 88–89. As Lieutenant Crawford recalled, "The troops were so arranged during the day as to completely surround the Indians." Ibid., pp. 146–47.

Lieutenant Simpson remarked about the fusillade: "The companies were placed in position to get the Indians should they attempt to leave the rifle pits they had dug near the ravine. . . . The gun opened on them from three different positions during the day until towards dark, an occasional shot being returned by the Indians, who still held their rifle pits." "Proceedings of a Board," pp. 105–6. See also Powell, *People of the Sacred Mountain*, 2:1218; and Hoig, *Perilous Pursuit*, pp. 184–85.

31. "Proceedings of a Board," NA, pp. 126–27. "We dropped the shell exactly where we were directed to. . . . I was told that the Indians were not where they had been supposed to be, the place where our fire had been directed, but were in rifle pits further up the ravine. I am certain we could have shelled them out had we been properly directed where to fire." Ibid., p. 131. For background on Bullet Proof, see James R. Walker, *Lakota Society*, ed. Raymond J. DeMallie (Lincoln: University of Nebraska Press, 1982), p. 148; Powell, *People of the Sacred Mountain*, 1:584–87, 2:1217; Hoig, *Perilous Pursuit*, p. 185. The site of the engagement on January 13 was said at the time to have occurred on the "North Fork of Indian Creek." *New York Times*, January 17, 1879.

32. Exploding shells in artillery consisted of hollow projectiles filled with black powder, whereas spherical case shot consisted of "a thin shell of cast iron, containing a number of musket-balls, and a charge of powder sufficient to burst it; a fuze is fixed to it as in an ordinary shell, by which the charge is ignited and the shell burst at any particular instant. . . . The spherical case mostly used for field service is the 12-pounder, and contains, when loaded, 90 bullets." Wilhelm, *Military Dictionary and Gazetteer*, pp. 527, 548.

33. Telegram, Wessells to Crook, January 14, 1879 (first quotation), Microfilm 1495, Roll 6, NA; "Proceedings of a Board," NA, pp. 68–69 (second quotation). One

account stated that the troops had been "obliged to make their coffee out of melted snow, hence their return [to Fort Robinson] was imperative." *New York Herald*, January 16, 1879. Powell suggested that the warriors had abandoned their position before the artillery fire opened. *People of the Sacred Mountain* 2:1218. A later examination disclosed that

> the place of defence selected by the Cheyennes was found to be a rifle pit eight feet long and four feet wide, deep enough for their complete concealment, while near them, in the sloping ground, was an oval hole dug out, with the side hollowed so that they could get in under it and be safe from the range of any shot fired at them. This enabled them to keep up a fusillade with deadly effect at close quarters until completely overwhelmed.

New York Herald, January 16, 1879. As for the consideration of potentially storming the position, the *Chicago Times*, January 15, 1879, opined that the Indians would have been "capable of inflicting severe loss upon the number selected for what may be almost termed a forlorn hope."

34. *New York Herald*, January 16, 1879.

35. *Chicago Times*, January 15, 1879.

36. Wessells, "Outbreak of Cheyennes at Fort Robinson," Ellison-Camp Papers, DPL, pp. 6–7.

37. The *Chicago Times* reporter claimed to be

> an eyewitness of the position of the Indians on the evening of Monday [January 14], and saw the chain of sentinels placed about it, forming what seemed a complete guard. In the face of all these precautions, the savages vacated the ravine during the night. They could only have done so by working their way in a snake-like and sinuous manner, and conducting their exit so noiselessly as not to arouse the vigilance of sentinels posted within at least fifty yards of each other.

Chicago Times, January 15, 1879.

38. The approximate distance of the artillery skirmish from Fort Robinson is calculated from a rough average of the reported company distances marched to the post on January 14, as reported in "Record of Events," Regimental Return of the Third Cavalry, January 1879.

39. "Record of Events" (Companies A, C, H, and L), Regimental Return of the Third Cavalry, January 1879, NA; *New York Herald*, January 16, 1879 (quotations); "Proceedings of a Board," NA, pp. 206–207; *New York Times*, January 16, 1879; *Chicago Times*, January 15, 1879; *Sidney Plaindealer*, January 16, 1879. On his return to the post late on January 14, Wessells telegraphed Crook: "My command is utterly worn out but I will try them [the Northern Cheyennes] again with Companies E & H." Microfilm 1495, Roll 6, NA.

40. *New York Herald*, January 16, 1879.

41. Grinnell, *Fighting Cheyennes*, p. 424; Wessells to Crook, January 14, 1879, NA (quotation), copy in Fort Robinson Archive, NSHS. Another view held that if the Indians could obtain horses they would be prone to strike west for the Big Horn Mountains and north to the river of that name. *New York Herald*, January 16, 1879.

New Red Cloud Agency formally became Pine Ridge Agency in December 1878. Olson, *Red Cloud and the Sioux Problem*, p. 283.

42. Sheridan to Pope, January 11, 1879, Sheridan Papers, LC.

43. Telegram, Crook to Sheridan, January 14, 1879 (first quotation) and Telegram, Crook to Sheridan, January 15, 1879, (second quotation), both in Microfilm 1495, Roll 6, NA; *New York Herald*, January 16, 1879; Wessells to Crook, January 14, 1879, NA, copy in Fort Robinson Archive (NSHS); Schuyler to Crook, January 16, 1879 (third and fourth quotations), NA, copy in Fort Robinson Archive, NSHS; *Army and Navy Journal*, January 18, 1879; *New York Herald*, January 16, 1879; *New York Herald*, January 18, 1879; Buecker, *Fort Robinson and the American West*, p. 143.

44. "Record of Events" (Companies E and H), Regimental Return of the Third Cavalry, January 1879, NA; "Proceedings of a Board," NA, pp. 68–69; *New York Herald*, January 18, 1879; *Chicago Times*, January 17 and January 18, 1879; Commissioner of Indian Affairs Edward A. Hayt to Secretary Schurz, January 16, 1879, and Telegram, Crook to Sheridan, January 16, 1879, both NA, copy in Fort Robinson Archive, NSHS; *New York Herald*, January 16, 1879; "Proceedings of a Board," NA, p. 207; *Army and Navy Journal*, January 18, 1879; *Sidney Telegraph*, January 18, 1879; Theophilus F. Rodenbough, *Uncle Sam's Medal of Honor, 1861–1886* (New York: G. P. Putnam's Sons, 1886), p. 322; Powell, *People of the Sacred Mountain*, 2:1219; *New York Herald*, January 18, 1879. Woman's Dress had earlier served as a scout for Crook in 1877. *New York Herald*, January 18, 1879. For the background of Woman's Dress, see Powers, *Killing of Crazy Horse*, pp. 238–39; and James H. Cook, *Fifty Years on the Old Frontier as Cowboy, Hunter, Guide, Scout, and Ranchman* (New Haven, CT: Yale University Press, 1923), pp. 192–93. For the hiring of Shangrau and Woman's Dress, see Shangrau interview in Jensen, *Indian Interviews of Eli S. Ricker*, pp. 264–65. His name is variously spelled in the documents, including Shangreau, Shangreaux, and Shangraw.

45. *New York Herald*, January 16, 1879 (first two quotations); *New York Herald*, January 18, 1879 (third quotation); *New York Times*, January 18, 1879; *Chicago Times*, January 18, 1879. The release of Woman's Dress's relatives was approved by the secretary of the interior. See Special Indian Agent James R. O'Beirne to Commissioner Hayt, January 15, 1879, and Secretary Schurz to Secretary of War, January 18, 1879, both NA, copies in Fort Robinson Archive, NSHS. A fort resident described the damaged barrack as "pretty well battered up, the windows broken out and the floor all torn up and pits dug in the ground." Johnson to Abbie Bush, January 15, 1879, copy in Fort Robinson Archive, NSHS. According to a more detailed accounting,

> at the westernmost end the boards of the floor were torn up. A capital breastwork of earth had been taken from underneath the building and thrown up in lunette form, evidently to defend against an attack through the windows. . . . To the left of this position the door is barricaded by a huge wood stove placed against it. It is supposed that when the flooring was torn up the women and children were to be placed for safety during the fighting between the beams and in the excavations made in the ground. Everything lay in wild confusion. . . . Saddles made out of deer and elk bones, with fastenings of buffalo and deer hide[,] . . . old bows and arrows, torn garments . . . thrown aside as superfluous, attest the wildness and desperation of the bold stroke for liberty.

New York Herald, January 17, 1879. Civilian freighter Richard Stirk viewed the barrack in the aftermath and reported that he "saw the floor torn up and lying there." Stirk said that "he does not credit the statement that they were burning [the wood from] the floor; says fuel might have been withheld for a day. Saw no rifle pits inside and under the floor. He says there were small places digged [*sic*] in the ground where they had things buried; he believes arms [were] buried." Jensen, *Settler and Soldier Interviews*, p. 289.

46. "Proceedings of a Board," NA, pp. 66, 69, 119, 207; *Army and Navy Journal*, January 25, 1879 (first quotation); *New York Herald*, January 18, 1879 (second quotation).

47. *Chicago Times*, January 18 and January 22, 1879 (quotations); *New York Herald*, January 22, 1879; *New York Times*, January 18, 1879; Grange, "Treating the Wounded," pp. 286–87; "Lt. Schuyler telegrams sent," NA, copy in Fort Robinson Archive, NSHS; Powell, *Sweet Medicine*, 1:263; Powell, *People of the Sacred Mountain*, 2:1220; Hoig, *Perilous Pursuit*, pp. 185–86. Barber, age twenty-eight, was from Canada and had recently enlisted at Buffalo, New York, listing his civilian occupation as cabinetmaker. He stood 5 feet, 9¾ inches tall, with gray eyes, dark hair, and a ruddy complexion. U.S. Army Register of Enlistments, 1798–1914, NA. Barber's body was examined at Fort Robinson by Dr. Moseley, who ascertained that he had died from a bullet to the heart. Grange, "Treating the Wounded," pp. 286–87. See also U.S. Register of Deaths in the Regular Army, 1860–1889, NA, pp. 14–15; and "Report of the Surgeon-General, October 1, 1879, in *Report of the Secretary of War, 1879*, pp. 408–9.

48. Red Cloud met with Lieutenant Schuyler on January 18 and gave consent for Lieutenant Dodd to enlist seventeen Oglalas, including several headmen (among them Three Bears, White Bird, Iron Crow, Lone Bear, and No Flesh), and obtain a mountain howitzer from Camp Sheridan. Dodd and the scouts and howitzer would leave Fort Robinson on January 22, apparently too late to join the campaign, as events would play out. *New York Herald*, January 18, January 22, and January 23, 1879; Dodd to AAG, Department of the Platte, February 17, 1879, including muster-in roll of fourteen Oglala scouts, NA, copy in Fort Robinson Archive, NSHS. One of the recruited Oglala scouts, Standing Soldier, stated that "he got over there in time to be in the last part of the last battle." Jensen, *Indian Interviews of Eli S. Ricker*, p. 246. Learning of the effort to recruit scouts, General Sheridan wired Crook (and on down the line to Wessells) that on the advice of interior secretary Chandler, secretary of war McCrary "wishes the Comdg. Officer of Camp [*sic*] Robinson to be instructed in case he uses any of Red Cloud scouts to do so more with the object of securing the surrender of the escaped Cheyennes than for the purpose of fighting them." Telegram, Adjutant General Edward D. Townsend to Sheridan, January 19, 1879, NA.

49. *New York Herald*, January 18, 1879. Such a restrictive directive from any superior command entity has not been identified, however.

50. "Proceedings of a Board," NA, pp. 69–71, 119–20, 207 (first and third quotations); Shangrau interview in Jensen, *Indian Interviews of Eli S. Ricker*, p. 266 (second quotation); *New York Herald*, January 18 and 19, 1879; "Record of Events" (Companies B and D), Regimental Return of the Third Cavalry, January 1879, NA. Bluff Station was also known as Hill Station. Rancher Edgar Beecher Bronson recalled it as "a small, log stage-station on the Cheyenne and Black Hills road." *Cowboy Life on the Western Plains*, p. 322. See also Spring, *Cheyenne and Black Hills Stage and Express Routes*,

pp. 129, 296. Located some twenty-seven miles northwest from Fort Robinson, the site of Bluff Station likely lies in Township 33 North, Range 56 West, Sections 16 and 21, USGS, "Warbonnet Ranch, Nebr.," quadrangle, 1980. It is in the area of modern State Route 29 and approximately 9.5 miles northwest of modern Harrison. Correspondent O'Beirne learned that the Cheyenne entrenchments consisted of "a fort of stone, with logs arranged so as to furnish rests for their rifles. The . . . position commands everything about them." *New York Herald*, January 18, 1879. Shangrau sometimes appears to be a day ahead of events presented in his largely scrambled account. Regarding the recovery of Private Barber's body, he recalled:

> The soldiers found the scalp of the soldier killed . . . lying on a boulder up at the [rifle] pit. John [Shangrau] handed it to Wessel[1]s who thought it was a dog skin . . . [and] threw it away. . . . Wessel[1]s then asked the whereabouts of the soldier's body which, John said, was lying about 100 yards down the hillside. Wessel[1]s ordered that it be taken to the camp. . . . The Indians had taken his clothing and thrown the body over a cliff where it was found. It was carried back on a pack mule.

Shangrau interview in Jensen, *Indian Interviews of Eli S. Ricker*, p. 267.

51. Some writers have assumed that Evans, while augmenting Wessells's force, was in fact to take over the campaign, although that is not borne out in the documents; it was army protocol for a senior officer to assume command whenever he appeared on the scene, which Evans did by joining Wessells on Crook's authority. Wessells, while following Evans's orders, nonetheless maintained a certain suzerainty through subsequent events as they played out and as opportunity afforded, as suggested in Evans's obituary in Cullum, *Biographical Register of the Officers and Graduates of the U.S. Military Academy*, No. 1561, 2:496.

52. "Proceedings of a Board," NA, p. 70; "Record of Events," Regular Army Muster Rolls, Third U.S. Cavalry, Companies A and F, from December 31, 1878, to February 28, 1879, NA; Post Return, Fort Robinson, Nebraska, January, 1879, RG 94, NA; Hoig, *Perilous Pursuit*, pp. 186–87. Evans had received telegraphic dispatches from department headquarters, as well as from Fort Robinson, as events had unfolded. After he left Fort Laramie, couriers carried such notices to him in the field, advising of collateral movements and other information. *New York Herald*, January 18, 1879. A Maryland native and an 1848 graduate of the U.S. Military Academy at West Point, Evans had served in cavalry commands during the Civil War and won brevets for gallantry and meritorious service at Valverde, New Mexico Territory, in 1861 and at Appomattox Court House, Virginia, in 1865. He was breveted colonel after his capture of a Comanche village in the Indian Territory in 1868. Promoted major in the Third Cavalry, Evans served at Tongue River, Rosebud Creek, and Slim Buttes during the Great Sioux War (1876–77) and later served on the Ute Expedition of 1879. He received a brevet for gallantry in action against Apaches at Big Dry Wash, Arizona Territory, in 1882. Promoted lieutenant colonel in the Seventh Cavalry in 1883, Evans retired that year with thirty years of army service. Cullum, *Biographical Register of the Officers and Graduates of the U.S. Military Academy*, 2:495–97. Evans died on April 24, 1906, in Elkton, Maryland. His obituary appears in *The Association of the Graduates of the United States Military Academy* (Saginaw, MI: Seeman and Peters, 1906), Annual Reunion June 11, 1906, pp. 191–92.

53. Evans to Commanding Officer of Companies B and D, 3rd Cav., January 16, 1879, NA, copy in Fort Robinson Archive, NSHS; "Proceedings of a Board," NA, pp. 38, 120–21 (first quotation), 207; "Record of Events," Regimental Returns of the Third Cavalry for January 1879, NA; Shangrau interview in Jensen, *Indian Interviews of Eli S. Ricker*, p. 268 (second quotation). On January 17 Lieutenant Schuyler notified Crook that "Capt. Wessells has found the Cheyennes entrenched on a butte two and one half miles west of the old Hat Creek road. They have about seven guns including one obtained from a soldier [Barber] killed today. They have discended [*sic*] and killed beef in the night and have plenty of snow [for water]. . . . They have only moved twelve miles in three days." Telegram, Schuyler to Crook, January 17, 1879, NA, copy in Fort Robinson Archive, NSHS.

54. This is believed to constitute the broad area in or around Township 33 North, Range 56 W, Sections 1 and 6. USGS, "Bodarc, Nebr."

55. "Proceedings of a Board," NA, pp. 70–71, 207–8 (first two quotations); Evans to Crook, January 22, 1879, in Microfilm 1495, Roll 6, NA (third quotation); *New York Herald*, January 23, 1879; *Chicago Times*, January 23, 1879; *Record of Engagements with Hostile Indians within the Military Division of the Missouri, from 1868 to 1882, Lieutenant General P. H. Sheridan Commanding* (Washington, DC: Government Printing Office; reprint Fort Collins, Colo.: Old Army Press, 1972), p. 84; Buecker, *Fort Robinson and the American West*, p. 145; Powell, *Sweet Medicine*, 1:264–65; Powell, *People of the Sacred Mountain*, 2:1222; Hoig, *Perilous Pursuit*, p. 187. Evans's exchange with the Indians seems to have been light and sporadic, occurring between 1 and 4 P.M. There were no army casualties, although Evans's horse was wounded, as indicated. Shangrau interview in Jensen, *Indian Interviews of Eli S. Ricker*, pp. 268–69; "Record of Events," Regimental Returns of the Third Cavalry for January 1879, NA. Evans's skirmish of January 20 took place in the vicinity of Castle Rock and Coliseum Rock, monolithic landmarks looming above the Warbonnet Creek country northwest of present Harrison in northern Sioux County, Nebraska, and in the western part of the present Gilbert Baker State Wildlife Management Area, about three miles southwest of the site of Bluff Station. Photocopies of three largely imprecise, presumptive, unattributed yet helpful modern penciled maps entitled "Military Operations, Jan. 19–22, 1879," tagged "not to any scale" and "source unknown," in Fort Robinson Archive, NSHS. Sergeant William B. Lewis, Company B, Third Cavalry, subsequently received a Medal of Honor "for conspicuous bravery and personal gallantry" in the direct aftermath of the skirmish. *U.S. Army Gallantry and Meritorious Conduct, 1866–1891*, p. 88; Buecker, *Fort Robinson and the American West*, p. 147; Ralph C. Deibert, *A History of the Third United States Cavalry* (Harrisburg, Pa.: Telegraph Press, n.d.), p. 135. Lewis's voluntary action in the wake of the skirmish is described at length in Rodenbough, *Uncle Sam's Medal of Honor*, pp. 323–25; Hoig, *Perilous Pursuit*, p. 187. See also James E. Potter, "The Medal of Honor in Nebraska, 1864–1879," pp. 11–12, 17–18 (unpublished, undated draft manuscript), copy in Fort Robinson Archive, NSHS. For information gleaned from local inhabitants, see Harrison Community Club, *Sioux County History: First 100 Years, 1886–1986* (Dallas: Curtis Media, 1986), pp. 68–70.

56. "Proceedings of a Board," NA, pp. 38, 70–71 (first quotation), 121; Shangrau interview in Jensen, *Indian Interviews of Eli S. Ricker*, p. 269 (second and third quotations); "Record of Events," Regimental Return of the Third Cavalry for January 1879,

NA; "Record of Events," Regular Army Muster Roll, Third U.S. Cavalry, Company A, RG 94, NA; Powell, *People of the Sacred Mountain*, 2:1222–23. Shangrau had left Evans after dark and camped en route to Wessells's command, joining the captain on the morning of January 21. Shangrau interview in Jensen, *Indian Interviews of Eli S. Ricker*, p. 269.

57. "Proceedings of a Board," NA, pp. 70–71 (quotation); Buecker, *Fort Robinson and the American West*, p. 145. Powell, *Sweet Medicine*, 1:265–66. Powell suggested that soon after the skirmish with Evans the warriors proposed sending the women ahead to Pine Ridge while the men worked to delay the troops, but such an effort did not come to pass. Powell, *People of the Sacred Mountain*, 2:1396n25.

58. "Proceedings of a Board," NA, p. 38–39, 72 (quotation), 121; Powell, *Sweet Medicine*, 1:266–67.

Chapter 9. Mortal End

1. *New York Herald*, January 23, 1879.

2. Grinnell, *Fighting Cheyennes*, p. 424; John Shangrau account in Jensen, *Indian Interviews of Eli S. Ricker*, p. 269; Powell, *People of the Sacred Mountain*, 2:1221–22. It was believed that the Indians would attempt to approach Pine Ridge via the "old Cheyenne trail," which approximated some of the northeastwardly running stage road between Hat Creek and Fort Robinson. *New York Herald*, January 23, 1879. There had been discussions about intercepting the Cheyennes north of the post, but "this cannot be done without leaving the fort and Indian prisoners stripped of sufficient guard." Ibid.

3. Regarding the Northern Cheyennes' likely movements, see also Powell, *People of the Sacred Mountain*, 2:1222–23.

4. Powell understood that the Cheyennes built a fire or fires (apparently seen by the troops) and moved in a formation with a cordon of warriors to safeguard their advance. They still had arms, but their fixed ammunition was limited, although they apparently possessed sufficient lead and powder to reload some previously expended cartridge shells. Ibid.

5. *New York Herald*, January 25, 1879. Late nineteenth and early twentieth century references to the place commonly denote the tributary complex as Indian Creek, a common appellation for other regional streams too. See, for example, former Sergeant Carter Johnson's reference in Jensen, *Settler and Soldier Interviews*, p. 239.

6. The site is in Township 34 North, Range 56 West, Section 12, USGS, "Story, Nebr.," quadrangle, 1980. Jerome A. Greene, *Reconnaissance Survey of Indian-U.S. Army Battlefields of the Northern Plains* (Denver, Colo.: National Park Service Cultural Resources and National Register Program Services, Intermountain Support Office, 1998), pp. 169–74; site diagram sketched June 28, 1997, in author's possession. The site today is on private property approximately twenty-three plus direct line miles from Fort Robinson. Considering the character of the country and the irregular aspects of the Indians' movements to reach that place, however, they had likely traveled at least thirty-five miles since leaving the post. Wessells's troops, including their own marches to and from Bluff Station, probably covered approximately at least the same distance. Captain Lawson stated that the Indians' "pit . . . was about

six feet deep" ("Proceedings of a Board," NA, p. 122), while the board report formally termed it "a hole that they had prepared in the crest of the bluff bank of the creek" (ibid., p. 208). Rancher Bronson, who was not present but who knew the country well and could indeed have visited the site later, described the Cheyennes' position as "a washout about fifty feet long, twelve feet wide, and five feet deep, near the edge of the bluffs." *Cowboy Life on the Western Plains,* p. 195. Yet another contemporary description of the shelter termed it a "buffalo wallow." Spring, *Cheyenne and Black Hills Stage and Express Routes,* p. 296. See also Powell, *Sweet Medicine,* 1:267, and Powell, *Killing of Morning Star's People,* p. 19. For the plan for the women to proceed once darkness settled again, see Powell, *Sweet Medicine,* 1:271; Powell, *People of the Sacred Mountain,* 2:1224. For efforts to confirm the location in 1965, see Gordon Raymond Smith, typed statement, "The Dull Knife Site—Cheyenne Outbreak of 1878–79[,] Fort Robinson, Nebraska," October 22, 1965, copy in Fort Robinson Archive, NSHS. Accompanying this document is a penciled sketch map bearing the notation "High Valley Floor" with a note: "The pit is located on point of flat[-] topped promontory that protrudes out into floodplain and commands a view of bottoms, channel, as well as valley floor." See also Hoig, *Perilous Pursuit,* pp. 189–90.

7. "Proceedings of a Board," NA, pp. 72, 173; *New York Herald,* January 25, 1879 (quotation); John Shangrau account in Jensen, *Indian Interviews of Eli S. Ricker,* p. 269.

8. "Proceedings of a Board," NA, p. 72.

9. Ibid., p. 42. In the aftermath of events, First Sergeant Harry Trebus of Company H, Third Cavalry, was cited for "good judgment in locating the camp of hostile Cheyenne Indians" on January 21 and 22 "and for courage in leading his small party to their camp and thus materially aiding in the capture of the Indians." *U.S. Army Gallantry and Meritorious Conduct, 1866–1891,* p. 89. Trebus, a sailor from Germany, enlisted in 1875 in Boston at age twenty-one. He stood 5 feet 6½ inches tall, with hazel eyes and brown hair. He was discharged at Fort Laramie in 1880. U.S. Army Register of Enlistments, 1798–1914, NA.

10. "Proceedings of a Board," NA, pp. 42–43, 122; *New York Herald,* January 25, 1879; Powell, *Sweet Medicine,* 1:267–68; *People of the Sacred Mountain,* 2:1224–25; Hoig, *Perilous Pursuit,* pp. 188–89. Deblois, a machinist from Massachusetts, enlisted in 1875. He stood 5 feet, 7 inches tall, with gray eyes and brown hair. Subsequent efforts to get Deblois to the post hospital in time fell short, and he died on January 24, two hours before reaching Fort Robinson. (His name has previously been given incorrectly as "DuBlois.") U.S. Army Register of Enlistments, 1798–1914, NA; Grange, "Treating the Wounded," p. 289; Register of Deaths in the Regular Army, 1860–1889, NA, pp. 48–49.

11. *New York Herald,* January 24, 1879 (first quotation); Chase's statement in "Proceedings of a Board," NA, pp. 43–44; Wessells, "Outbreak of Cheyennes at Fort Robinson," Ellison-Camp Papers, DPL, p. 7 (second quotation). Baxter later noted that he received word by courier from Wessells that "the Indians had been found and ordering me to proceed with all haste to the place. Reaching there, Captain Wessells gave me my orders and position on the field. At a preconcerted signal, we all charged and in twenty minutes the fight was over. "Troops were exchanging shot[s] when I arrived on the field." "Proceedings of a Board," NA, p. 129. Many years later Chase stated that "Wessells called out to them for some time to surrender & he would give

them quarter & asked them, at all events, to send their women & children out, but they would only reply with shots." Chase, "Dull Knife & Cheyennes," Ellison-Camp Papers, DPL, p. 9. See also Grinnell, *Fighting Cheyennes*, p. 425; Powell, *Sweet Medicine*, 1:268–69; and Powell, *People of the Sacred Mountain*, 2:1224–25.

12. "Proceedings of a Board," NA, pp. 72, 173; John Shangrau account in Jensen, *Indian Interviews of Eli S. Ricker*, p. 269. Precisely assigned unit strength was as follows: Company A: thirty-five men, one officer; Company E: thirty-eight men, one officer; Company F: forty-six men, one officer; and Company H: twenty-eight men, two officers. "Proceedings of a Board," NA, pp.72, 173; "Record of Events," Regular Army Muster Roll, Third U.S. Cavalry, Company A, Microfilm 744, Roll 31, NA. Because of other duty assignments the companies were generally operating under strength. Within weeks, Wessells stated, "there were four companies present at this time[,] myself in command. There were 20 men of H Company engaged, not more than 2 or 3 holding horses. There were about 100 men [altogether] engaged in the four companies I should think." "Proceedings of a Board," NA, p. 72; see also pp. 208–9; and Regular Army Muster Rolls. Third U.S. Cavalry, Companies A, E, F, and H, from December 31, 1878, to February 28, 1879, NA.

13. "Proceedings of a Board," NA, pp. 43–44 (quotations); *New York Herald*, January 25, 1879. As Shangrau recalled, "the Captain explained that he would divide his men into three parties. One he would send round to come down the creek or channel. One he would send round in an opposite circuit to come up the creek or channel; and the third he would move directly towards the position of the Indians, all concentrating at this point simultaneously." Shangrau account in Jensen, *Indian Interviews of Eli S. Ricker*, p. 270. See also former sergeant Carter P. Johnson's account in Jensen, *Settler and Soldier Interviews*, pp. 239–40. For Companies E and H working together under Wessells, see "Record of Events," Post Returns, Fort Robinson, Nebraska, January 1879, NA; "Proceedings of a Board," NA, p. 38; and Powell, *Sweet Medicine*, 1:268–69. Johnson maintained that at least part of his unit, Company F, "was directed to charge their fire." Johnson account in Jensen, *Settler and Soldier Interviews*, p. 240. In his 1913 interview Carter stated that "My company [F] was the largest of the 4, and we had 19 men in line in the charge." Johnson, "Outbreak of Cheyennes," Camp-Ellison Papers, DPL.

14. *New York Herald*, January 25, 1879; Johnson account in Jensen, *Settler and Soldier Interviews*, p. 240 (quotation).

15. Johnson account in Jensen, *Settler and Soldier Interviews*, p. 240. Sergeant Johnson also referenced this "speech," in which he told the soldiers that the Indians "must now be cleaned up or surrender." Johnson, "Outbreak of Cheyennes," Ellison-Camp Papers, DPL.

16. According to Dr. Moseley's report on Sergeant Taggart, "death was instantaneous." Grange, "Treating the Wounded," p. 288. An Irish immigrant, Taggart had enlisted at Chicago in 1875, his civilian occupation a carpenter. He stood 5 feet, 9 inches tall, with gray eyes and a fair complexion. U.S. Army Register of Enlistments, 1798–1914, NA.

17. "Proceedings of a Board," NA, p. 44. Dr. Moseley's report stated that Farrier Brown of Company A "rushed up to the edge of [the Indians'] entrenchment and discharged his carbine at them and fell instantly, struck by a carbine ball. He uttered several loud screams and made an attempt to throw off his cartridge belt and then

fell back dead inside of two minutes after he was struck." Grange, "Treating the Wounded," p. 288.

18. It was perhaps at this point that Private Marcus Magerlein, reportedly a member of Company K, Third Cavalry, took an early position near the Indians. He was later cited "for bravery in action . . . [for] dashing ahead of the troops under sever[e] fire and being the first to gain a position on the edge of the Indian stronghold, whence he kept up a steady fire, being himself exposed to two fires," for which he later received a Certificate of Merit. *U.S. Army Gallantry and Meritorious Conduct, 1866–1891*, p. 89. (The enlistment of Private Magerlein was not given in U.S. Army Register of Enlistments, 1798–1914, NA).

19. Private George E. Nelson, a Philadelphian, enlisted at age twenty-two in Baltimore in 1876. He was 5 feet, 6½ inches tall, with brown eyes, dark hair, and a fair complexion. U.S. Army Register of Enlistments, 1798–1914, NA. Dr. Moseley recorded that Private Nelson "was shot in the charge Jan. 22, 1879 and fell within 20 ft of the enemy. He was struck by a carbine ball." Grange, "Treating the Wounded," p. 288.

20. The board concluded: "The troops having come up and been placed in position to encircle this rifle pit, charged, and finally, after the Indians had twice been called upon to surrender and refused, placed them *hors du combat*." Ibid., p. 208.

21. "Proceedings of a Board," NA, pp. 44–45 (quotation); Regimental Return of the Third Cavalry, January 1879, NA. Reporter O'Beirne (who was not present but interviewed participants later at the post) gave critical details:

> Company A went up on the north bank of the creek, under the position of the Indians, and Company H, with a part of Company F, were sent below. During this time the pickets were posted so as to keep the Indians down. Company A gave way on the left so as to join Company H, which made the detour around the left of the pit in a westerly direction. Company F, under Lieutenants Hardee [*sic*] and Baxter, took up the position vacated by Company A, while H and F detachments moved up to the east and rear of the besieged. Captain Lawson struck down from the west and rear, swinging out so as to join them in the charge, which was to be signaled by a yell from Lieutenant Chase. Company A moved up too near, and . . . lost in a short time three killed. These were somewhat rashly sacrificed through impatience.

New York Herald, January 25, 1879. (See also O'Beirne's earlier but less detailed account of the Antelope Creek action in *New York Herald*, January 24, 1879, in which he stated that "Companies F and E were in bad positions to accomplish much.") Regarding survivors, Shangrau remembered that "there were 2 women and 3 girl prisoners and one boy was wounded and soon died. One of the girls was Hog's daughter, another was Big Head's daughter." John Shangrau account, Box 2, Folder 3, "Outbreak of Cheyennes," Camp Papers, Lilly Library, Indiana University.

22. Johnson, "Outbreak of Cheyennes," Ellison-Camp Papers, DPL. See also Powell, *Sweet Medicine*, 1:268–69.

23. One account stated that "Lieut. Chase, seeing Capt. Wessells fall, sprang forward and, carrying his superior officer to a small spur of rocks, nearly out of range of the savages' fire, ran back to his company, who were near the edge of

the Indians' entrenchments, and lustily cheered his men forward." *Chicago Times*, January 23, 1879. See also "The Last Indian Fight," *Frank Leslie's Illustrated Weekly*, February 15, 1879.

24. "Proceedings of a Board," NA, pp. 45–46. Dr. Petteys quickly ligated and "sewed up" Wessells's wound. Grange, "Treating the Wounded," p. 289 (quotation); Powell, *People of the Sacred Mountain*, 2:1226. In 1914 Chase described the final moments of the fighting as well as the scene that he witnessed afterward:

> We charged them several times, with guns & revolvers & killed all their men. . . . After the fight had stopped it was a sickening sight. Dead lay across one another[.] Corpses were covered with blood & shot to pieces & human livers and brains lay about. When we came to pull the dead out of the place, which was about 3 ft deep, we got one man still alive but fatally wounded by a shot through the bowels. He begged to go back & die where the dead lay. Likewise a squaw badly wounded requested to go back & die with the dead, so when we left the place that evening we wrapped them in blankets & when we returned the next day [to bury the people] they were dead with the rest.

Chase, "Dull Knife & Cheyennes," Ellison-Camp Papers, DPL, pp. 9–10.

25. "Proceedings of a Board," NA, p. 46.

26. Ibid.

27. Shangrau account in Jensen, *Indian Interviews of Eli S. Ricker*, pp. 270–71; Powell, *Sweet Medicine*, 1:269 (citing Sandoz, *Cheyenne Autumn*, pp. 236–37, who identified the final chargers as Little Finger Nail, Roman Nose, and Bear, pp. 236–37); Powell, *People of the Sacred Mountain*, 2:1226; Powell, *Killing of Morning Star's People*, pp. 19–22; "Proceedings of a Board," NA, p. 46. Wessells's head wound came from "a pistol ball which struck him on the right side of his head on the front of the temporal bone, glanced backwards cutting a wound about three inches long in the temporal muscle and escaped without doing any damage to the bone." The captain "was brought to his knees by the force of the blow and a brisk hemorrhage ensued from the temporal artery which was torn acrost." Dr. Petteys, who was present, treated the injury and stitched the wound closed. Grange, "Treating the Wounded," p. 289; "Record of Events," Regular Army Muster Roll, Third U.S. Cavalry, Company E, NA. Chase also later recalled the shooting of Wessells: "Wessells and I were advancing side by side, with pistols in hand, when Wessells was shot by a glance bullet in the head & the blood from it flew over my coat sleeve. Before this I had been loading my pistol and advancing in a crouching manner & firing. Wessells said, 'I like to see a man walk into battle.' I said, 'all right, I will walk in with you,' & so, side by side, we walked up erect & Wessells was hit, as described." Chase, "Dull Knife & Cheyennes," Ellison-Camp Papers, DPL, p. 10. For Ambrose's wounding and treatment, see Lawson's account in "Proceedings of a Board," NA, p. 122; and Grange, "Treating the Wounded," p. 287. Despite his wound, Wessells recovered sufficiently to take part in the final assault. *Chicago Times*, January 23, 1879. Wessells reportedly regained consciousness soon after several Cheyennes rose in a final death gambit. He "came to the front, and seeing the pits strewn with the dead bodies of the Indians, ordered his men to cease firing with a view of getting the remainder of the savages to surrender, but they heeded him not until one buck only remained

alive." Ibid. See also *Frank Leslie's Illustrated Newspaper*, February 15, 1879. As with its report of the initial breakout, the *New York Herald*'s account of Antelope Creek was also encapsulated in the *Army and Navy Journal*, February 1, 1879. Strangely, despite wide-ranging coverage of the Northern Cheyennes' breakout and the resultant tragedy at Antelope Creek in prominent newspapers throughout the country in 1879, no contemporary mention of the events appeared in *Harper's Weekly*, perhaps the most popular prominent tabloid of the day.

28. John Shangrau account, Box 2, Folder 3, "Outbreak of Cheyennes," Camp Papers, Lilly Library, Indiana University.

29. Lawson's account in "Proceedings of a Board," NA, pp. 122–23.

Chapter 10. Scrutiny

1. The regimental and post returns indicate that Company E returned to the post on January 24 and Companies A, F, and H followed on January 25 and that Evans accompanied the company from Bluff Station as of January 24. Regimental Return of the Third Cavalry, January 1879, NA. See also "Record of Events," Post Returns, Fort Robinson, Nebraska, January 31, 1879, NA. On arrival at Fort Robinson, Companies A, E, F, and L, Third Cavalry, prepared to depart for their home stations early the following week, leaving only Companies C and H at the post. *New York Herald*, January 26, 1879; *Sidney Plaindealer*, January 30, 1879; Buecker, *Fort Robinson and the American West*, p. 203.

2. Buecker, *Fort Robinson and the American West*, p. 203; "Special Report . . . by Asst. Surg. E. B. Moseley," File D-987, Office of the Adjutant General, RG 94, NA,; Grange, "Treating the Wounded," pp. 278–89. On January 26 another soldier, Private George Sproul, Company L, received a gunshot wound in the head, shot by unidentified persons "within five hundred yards of this post" while moving an ambulance in the area of the fort. He died in the post hospital on February 3, 1879. *Army and Navy Journal*, February 1 and February 8, 1879 (quotation); *Sidney Plaindealer*, January 30, 1879. Sproul, aged twenty-four, was a laborer from Boston, Massachusetts, who enlisted on December 15, 1875, in St. Louis, Missouri. He had blue eyes, light brown hair, and a fair complexion and stood 5 feet, 6½ inches tall. U.S. Army Register of Enlistments, 1798–1914, NA. Sproul's remains were removed with the army dead transferred from Fort Robinson to Fort McPherson National Cemetery in 1947, where they repose in Section 7, Grave Number 1167. Moseley recorded in his medical report that "the great proportion of fatal wounds [inflicted by the Northern Cheyennes] is remarkable and their concentration on the trunk of the body shows a deliberation and skill in handling the improved breech-loading arms with which they were liberally supplied, a fact which explains why this particular tribe enjoyed the reputation of being the best warriors on the Plains." Quoted in Grange, "Fort Robinson," p. 224, citing entry by Moseley in "record of the Medical History of Post [Fort Robinson], Medical Department, U.S. Army (Ms. copy), contained in Tablet No. 31, [Eli S. Ricker Collection, NSHS]."

3. "Record of Events," Post Returns, Fort Robinson, Nebraska, January 1879, NA; Regimental Return of the Third Cavalry, January 1879, NA; *Sidney Telegraph*, February 8, 1879; Buecker, *Fort Robinson and the American West*, p. 203.

4. This number is estimated from entries in Grange, "Treating the Wounded," pp. 291–92. See appendix A. The *Chicago Times*, January 28, 1879, commented that "two of the children were also wounded but not dangerously. They [the prisoners] were all searched at the guard house, and two knives only were found in the party."

5. Grange, "Treating the Wounded," p. 292. For aspects of treatment of the wounded at the post, see ibid., pp. 292–93.

6. In 1947–48, following the closure of Fort Robinson, the War Department removed the remains of the army breakout fatalities, along with other cemetery dead, to Fort McPherson National Cemetery, Nebraska. The fatalities from the breakout (with their grave numbers at the national cemetery) are Private Amos J. Barber (1194), Farrier George Brown (1172), Private George Debloise (*sic*: Henry A. Deblois) (1190), Private William W. Everett (1215), Private William H. Good (1212), Private Peter Hulse (1231), Private Bernard Kelley, Section F (1196); Private George E. Nelson (1193), Private Frank Schmidt (1168), and Sergeant James Taggart (1211). Carter, "History of Fort Robinson," p. 8. The remains of Corporal Henry Ore were sent to his family and repose in the Kappa Cemetery, Woodford County, Illinois (per www.FindAGrave.com). The remains of Private Bernard Kelley were initially interred at Fort Robinson (Grave No. 2) before being transferred to the national cemetery.

7. "Proceedings of a Board," pp. 209–10 (first quotation); Grinnell, *Fighting Cheyennes*, p. 426 (second quotation); Powell, *Sweet Medicine*, 1:270n20; See also appendix A for Northern Cheyenne wounded.

8. *Army and Navy Journal*, March 8, 1879 (quotations on soldiers); "Report of Brig. Gen. George Crook," September 27, 1879, in *Report of the Secretary of War, 1879*, p. 77 (quotation on Cheyennes).

9. *Report of the Secretary of War, 1881* (Washington, D.C.: Government Printing Office, 1881), p. 84.

10. "Iron Teeth, a Cheyenne Old Woman," p. 23.

11. Ibid., pp. 23–24.

12. "Letter from 'Red Cloud' to General Crook," January 3, 1879, as rendered by Irwin, NA, copy in Fort Robinson Archive, NSHS. Red Cloud's reference to the "young men who have all gone north" was presumably in regard to those who followed Little Wolf.

13. Telegram, Schuyler to Crook, January 17, 1879, NA, copy in Fort Robinson Archive, NSHS; Telegram, Schuyler to Crook, January 17, 1879 (second telegram), NA, copy in Fort Robinson Archive, NSHS (quotation).

14. "Briefs," in Senate, *Escape of the Cheyenne Indians*, p. 29; Telegram, Schuyler to Crook, January 24, 1879, NA, copy in Fort Robinson Archive, NSHS (quotation). The directive evidently was understood to include all of the Northern Cheyenne prisoners except those noted below.

15. *New York Herald*, January 29, 1879.

16. Telegram, Adjutant General Edward D. Townsend to Sheridan, January 28, 1879, NA, https://commons.wikimedia.org/wiki/File:Adjutant_General_E.D._Townsend_to_Lieutenant_General_Sheridan._-_NARA_-_284987.tif.

17. *New York Herald*, January 31, 1879 (quotations); *Omaha World-Herald*, February 1, 1879; *Sidney Telegraph*, February 8, 1879; *Army and Navy Journal*, February 8, 1879; Grange, "Treating the Wounded," p. 290; Powell, *Sweet Medicine*, 1:273–74. On February 3 Captain Vroom, then in command, urged that all of the remaining

Northern Cheyennes be permitted to go to Pine Ridge "if they so desire," a recommendation concurred with by Crook and Sheridan. Telegram, Sheridan to Adjutant General Edward D. Townsend, February 3, 1879, NA, copy in Fort Robinson Archive, NSHS; see also Powell, *Sweet Medicine*, 1:273–74. Grinnell stated that "about fifty-eight were sent to Pine Ridge." *Fighting Cheyennes*, p. 426.

18. Actually there were four, all female.

19. *New York Herald*, February 1, 1879.

20. Ibid. (first quotation); Corbusier, "Camp Sheridan, Nebraska," p. 42 (second and third quotations). Corbusier opined: "What a glorious victory over a handful of helpless people, all in the name of progress!" Ibid.

21. Charles P. Jordan, Red Cloud Manuscript, MS 71, NA, copy in Fort Robinson Archive, NSHS. A briefer reminiscence by Jordan appeared in the *Omaha World-Herald*, January 21, 1906, in which he stated: "The scene was pathetic in the extreme. These survivors were made up of the remnants of large families and in some instances one boy or girl or woman was the only one left from the fight. These people were [ultimately] distributed throughout the Sioux tribe."

22. Susan Bordeaux Bettelyoun and Josephine Waggoner, *With My Own Eyes: A Lakota Woman Tells Her People's History*, ed. Emily Levine (Lincoln: University of Nebraska Press, 1998), p. 4.

23. *New York Herald*, February 11, 1879; *Army and Navy Journal*, February 15, 1879; Telegram, Crook to Sheridan, January 16, 1879, re: Schuyler to Crook, January 16, 1879 (quotations), NA, copy in Fort Robinson Archive, NSHS. See also Telegram, Crook to Sheridan, January 23, 1879, in Microfilm 1495, Roll 6, NA.

24. *Omaha Herald*, February 11, 1879 (first two quotations); *New York Herald*, February 11, 1879 (third and fourth quotations).

25. *New York Herald*, February 11, 1879; *Sidney Plaindealer*, February 13, 1879; *Omaha Herald*, February 9 and February 11, 1879; *New York Times*, February 9, 1879; *Army and Navy Journal*, February 15, 1879; Manypenny, *Our Indian Wards*, pp. 339–40; *New York Herald*, February 11, 1879 (quotations), which contains a very descriptive account of the Indians' arrival and departure from Fort Sidney.

26. *Leavenworth Weekly Times*, February 20, 1879; *Omaha Herald*, February 15, 1879; *Omaha Republican*, February 15 1879. The delegation was headed by Sheriff William B. ("Bat") Masterson. *New York Times*, February 15, 1879; Powers, "Northern Cheyenne Trek through Western Kansas," pp. 21–22; Leiker and Powers, *Northern Cheyenne Exodus*, p. 91. The seven prisoners, as named in the *Dodge City Times*, February 22, 1879, were "Crow, Wild Hog, Tall Man, Old Man, Run Fast, Young Man, and Frizzle Head." The names are more properly recorded as Wild Hog, Old Crow, Porcupine, Tangle Hair, Blacksmith, Noisy Walker (aka Old Man), and Left Hand (aka Strong Left Hand). Leiker and Powers, *Northern Cheyenne Exodus*, p. 91; Powell, *Sweet Medicine*, 1:274. Because of Wild Hog's recent injury in dismounting from a wagon in Dodge City, he used "a long piece of board [as a crutch] for support." *Dodge City Times*, February 22, 1879.

27. Agent Miles convinced the judge that the elderly and genial Old Crow had neither participated in nor condoned the raids and killings and, moreover, had loyally served the army as a scout in 1876. Old Crow was conducted back to Darlington Agency, where he remained until his death during the 1920s. Low and Powers, "Northern Cheyenne Warrior Ledger Art," pp. 20–21.

28. For the Indians' historically and culturally significant ledger art, as well as other drawings rendered by them while jailed in Dodge City over several months, see ibid., pp. 2–25. The artwork has been primarily attributed to Wild Hog and Porcupine. Ibid., pp. 19–20.

29. *Atchison Champion*, June 29, 1879, as quoted in Powers, "Northern Cheyenne Trek through Western Kansas," p. 24; see also Leiker and Powers, *Northern Cheyenne Exodus*, pp. 92–95; and Monnett, *Tell Them We Are Going Home*, pp. 177–82. Various committees and commissions examined and estimated the claims for damages caused by the attacks of September 1878. In 1882 the federal government deducted $9,870.10 from Northern Cheyenne treaty funds to reimburse the damage claims in part. Powers, "Northern Cheyenne Trek through Western Kansas," p. 26; Monnett, *Tell Them We Are Going Home*, pp. 184–86. During the interim between the Dodge City and Lawrence proceedings, members of the U.S. Senate Select Committee on the Removal of the Northern Cheyennes interviewed several of the Indians regarding their tenure at Darlington as well as their outbreak from the Indian Territory and the subsequent Fort Robinson breakout. Leiker and Powers, *Northern Cheyenne Exodus*, p. 87; Senate, *Select Committee Report*, pp. 3–14.

30. *Emporia News*, October 24, 1879 (quotation); *Report of the Commissioner of Indian Affairs, 1879*, p. xvii.

31. For further details of the return of Wild Hog and the other Indians to Fort Reno, see Berthrong, *Cheyenne and Arapaho Ordeal*, pp. 40–41.

32. Motivated by Congress, Sherman urged Sheridan to "have the matter of Camp [*sic*] Robinson thoroughly investigated and reported as soon as you think it can be done without injustice as I know the President is disturbed by reports of unnecessary cruelty by army officers." Telegram, Sherman to Sheridan, January 21, 1879, in Microfilm 1495, Roll 6, NA (in response to Senator William B. Allison, Committee on Indian Affairs, U.S. Senate, to Secretary of War George B. McCrary, January 17, 1879, in ibid.).

33. "Board of Officers. A number of officers assembled by military authority for the transaction of business." Wilhelm, *Military Dictionary and Gazetteer*, p. 64. (The "board of officers," both at the time and since, has been erroneously called a "Court of Inquiry," which suggests an imputation against an officer or soldier: ibid., p. 119.)

34. "Briefs," in Senate, *Escape of the Cheyenne Indians*, p. 30 (quotations); "Proceedings of a Board," p. 1; *Army and Navy Journal*, February 1, 1879. The genesis of the board appears in AG to Sheridan, January 18, 1879, NA, copy in Fort Robinson Archive, NSHS.

35. Captain Johnson and Lieutenant Thompson had to be summoned "without delay" from Fort Laramie on January 27. Colonel Carlton did not arrive at Fort Robinson until February 5, two days before the proceedings adjourned. "Lt. Schuyler telegrams sent," NA, copy in Fort Robinson Archive, NSHS.

36. Much of the information contained in this singularly essential "Proceedings of a Board" document has been incorporated, as appropriate, throughout the present study. On January 28, while the board was already in session, General Crook wired, suggesting topical guidelines for gathering the data from the Indians: "It would be well in examining the prisoners to get their reasons for leaving the agency and coming north[,] why they surrendered to Captain Johnson[,] What understanding they had among themselves as to their disarmament, Whether an attempt to get their

concealed arms previous to the order for them to go south would have brought on a fight, In short to get their complete history from commencement to end of this affair." Crook to Evans, January 28, 1879, NA, copy in Fort Robinson Archive, NSHS.

37. "Proceedings of a Board," NA, p. 14.

38. "Proceedings of a Board," NA, pp. 2–17; Powell, *Sweet Medicine*, 1:271–72.

39. "Proceedings of a Board," NA, pp. 3–4; *Report of the Chief of Ordnance, 1879*, pp. 326–27 (quotations and list). See appendix F for a complete list of known Northern Cheyenne weaponry surrendered or captured. For routine correspondence pertaining to the Indian ordnance surrendered during the breakout, see Major Andrew W. Evans, Third Cavalry, to AAG Department of the Platte, February 18, 1879, together with accompanying subordinate letters, NA, copies in Fort Robinson Archive, NSHS. One of the recovered Springfield carbines was identified as having been taken by the Northern Cheyennes from Private Frank Schmidt, killed during the breakout of January 9. Second Lieutenant George F. Chase, Company A, Third Cavalry, to Post Adjutant, Fort Laramie, February 12, 1879, NA, copies in Fort Robinson Archive, NSHS.

40. "Proceedings of a Board," NA, pp. 52–61, 140–41. The fact that so much evidence for the Kansas raids had recently been found among Dull Knife's people following their surrender dispels any notion that that chief's followers had not been complicit in those events.

41. Ibid., pp. 83–113.

42. Ibid., pp. 20–52, 113–23, 130–31.

43. Ibid., pp. 132–38, 144–48, 165–74.

44. These included Private Julius P. Janzohn, Company F; Sergeant Michael Lanigan, Company C; Sergeant George W. Allen, Company A; Sergeant Gottlieb Bigalsky, Company A; Sergeant John Mitchell, Company C; Private John Corbett, Company C; Private James W. Payne, Company C; and Private Arthur G. Ross, Company A. Ibid., pp. 152–60, 174–78.

45. Ibid., pp. 160–65.

46. Ibid., pp. 148–51.

47. Ibid., p. 178 (quotation), 183, 188, 191.

48. Ibid., p. 192.

49. Ibid., pp. 193 (first and second quotation), 197–98 (third quotation), 298 (fourth quotation).

50. Ibid., pp. 198–99 (first and second quotations), 200–202 (third quotation).

51. Ibid., pp. 203–7.

52. Ibid., p. 92.

53. Ibid., pp. 209–10.

54. Ibid., pp. 210–15. See also *New York Herald*, March 11, 1879; and *Army and Navy Journal*, March 15, 1879 (quotations below), which quoted the conclusions. A condensed report of the proceedings was ostensibly prepared in Sheridan's offices by mid-March 1879 and transmitted through General Sherman, who approved it, to the secretary of war. Sherman commented that the earlier full report, with its accompanying materials, "gives a clear and perfect history of the whole affair from beginning to end—and leaves no room for further comment." He further stated that in his judgment "the events are fairly accounted for and were incident to the desperate nature of the captive Indians." Some aspects of the newspaper coverage of the

proceedings were deemed erroneous by Major Evans in a missive of March 21, 1879, included among typed copies of Fort Laramie correspondence, January–February 1879, in Fort Robinson Archive, NSHS.

55. Telegrams, Sheridan to Crook, March 5, 1879; Sheridan to Terry, March 9, 1879; and Sheridan to Sherman, March 22, 1879, Sheridan Papers, LC.

Chapter 11. Pine Ridge Interlude

1. *New York Herald*, February 14, 1879: "None of the leading chiefs would acknowledge that they had any information where the noted refugee was." See also *New York Herald*, February 13, 1879; Powell, *Sweet Medicine*, 1:275–76; Powell, *People of the Sacred Mountain*, 2:1242–43; Powell, *Killing of Morning Star's People*, pp. 23–24. The arrival of Dull Knife at Red Cloud Agency likely occurred between February 2 and 7, 1879. On February 10 agent Irwin notified the military authorities that Dull Knife and his family were among the Sioux. One week later General Crook wired Irwin that "'Dull Knife' and family will be allowed to remain at the agency until instructions of the Lt[.] General Comd'g the Division . . . are received." Telegram, AAG to Irwin, February 17, 1879, NA, copy in Fort Robinson Archive, NSHS. Post gossip at the time held that "'Old Dull Knife' with his wife & one child . . . were taken from near the post to Red Cloud Agency by a half breed Cheyenne in a wagon [unbeknownst] to the officers at this post." Emmet Crawford to Charles Morton, February 26, 1879, NA, copy in Fort Robinson Archive, NSHS. See also *We, the Northern Cheyenne People*, p. 30.

2. "Dull Knife," *New North-West*, May 23, 1879.

3. Ibid.

4. Ibid.

Chapter 12. Denouement

1. Telegram, Sheridan to Sherman, January 22, 1879, Sheridan Papers, LC.

2. Paul Andrew Hutton, *Phil Sheridan and His Army* (Lincoln: University of Nebraska Press, 1986), p. 337; Telegram, Sheridan to Sherman, January 22, 1879, Sheridan Papers, LC (quotations). Sheridan is referring to the disarming and dismounting of the Lakotas at Standing Rock and Cheyenne River agencies along the Missouri River in the late fall of 1876 by troops of General Alfred H. Terry's command. See Greene, *Indian War Veterans*, pp. 147–54; and especially Paul L. Hedren, *Great Sioux War Orders of Battle: How the United States Army Waged War on the Northern Plains, 1876–1877* (Norman: Arthur H. Clark, 2011), pp. 132–37. Fort Robinson was located perhaps forty miles west of the approximate edge of the Sand Hills area, though about eighty miles from their interior core zone.

3. Telegram, Sheridan to Sherman, January 22, 1879, Sheridan Papers, LC (quotations); William T. Sherman Papers, 1837–1891, LC.

4. Probably in Little Cherry or Chokecherry Valley in modern Sheridan County, Nebraska, immediately east of the Cherry County line and some thirty miles southwest of present Merriman.

5. Powell, *People of the Sacred Mountain*, 2:1245–49 (which gives further details). The area is a short distance below the upper Snake River and contains numerous small lakes. See *Nebraska Atlas & Gazetteer*, pp. 18–19. The specific lake has been identified as Lost Chokecherry Lake. Marquis, *Cheyennes of Montana*, p. 78; Powell, *Killing of Morning Star's People*, pp. 24–25; John D. McDermott Files, Cheyenne Outbreak Notes, Leland D. Case Library, Black Hills State University, Spearfish, South Dakota. See also the area represented in Township 30N, Range 41 West, Section 36, USGS, "Gordon, SE, Nebr.," quadrangle, 1969. Information about the Moorehead and Ashbaugh killings appear in a March 19, 1924, U.S. Forest Service memorandum filed by Nebraska National Forest supervisor Jay Higgins, copy in Fort Robinson Archive, NSHS.

6. Powell, *People of the Sacred Mountain*, 2:1249–50. The raid and the deaths of the cowboys are documented in *Omaha Daily Herald*, February 6 *and* February 7, 1879 (which specified the date); *Omaha Daily Bee*, February 11, 1879; *Omaha Weekly Bee*, February 19, 1879; *Army and Navy Journal*, February 15, 1879 (date of the Weatherell raid); *Sidney Plaindealer*, February 13, 1879; *New York Herald*, February 8, February 10, February 11, and February 13, 1879; *New York Times*, February 11, 1879 (quotation). Reports of the Weatherell train raid suggested that the Cheyennes involved were all men and that "no travois lodge poles nor baggage accompanied them." "No squaws were seen in the party," and the men were well armed. Furthermore, it was reported that a Sioux man saw the Northern Cheyenne party in the vicinity of Pass Creek, suggesting that both the Oglalas and the Brulés were aware of their presence in the area. *New York Herald*, February 10, 1879.

7. Powell, *The Killing of Morning Star's People*, p. 25; Powell, *People of the Sacred Mountain*, 2:1252–54.

8. *Sidney Plaindealer*, January 23, 1879; Regimental Returns of the Fifth Cavalry, January and February 1879, Microfilm 744, NA; *New York Herald*, February 13, 1879 (quotation); Telegram, Crook to Sheridan, January 18, 1879, Microfilm 1495, Roll 6, NA; *New York Herald*, January 26 and February 17, 1879; *Army and Navy Journal*, January 25, February 1, and February 22, 1879; Eli S. Ricker, interview with Jacob A. Augur, undated, in Jensen, *Settler and Soldier Interviews of Eli S. Ricker*, p. 301 (Auger as a colonel commanded Fort Robinson, 1902–1907). Captain Samuel P. Ferris graduated from West Point in 1857 and served with the Eighth Infantry into the Civil War, becoming colonel of the Twenty-Eighth Connecticut Infantry in 1862. He received brevet appointments for his service at Port Hudson, Louisiana, and Hatcher's Run, Virginia. In the postwar army Ferris joined the Fourth Infantry in 1869 and was on detached duty with the Fifth Cavalry in early 1879. He died in 1882. Heitman, *Historical Register and Dictionary*, 1:417–18.

On February 10 Sheridan reported recent word from Camp Sheridan that Little Wolf's people had crossed the road to Fort Randall, about forty miles east of New Red Cloud Agency at Pine Ridge. Crook to Sheridan, February 10, 1879. Sheridan Papers, LC. On February 18 the general apparently inflated the size of Little Wolf's assemblage, notifying Washington that his band of seventy-five to eighty warriors "superbly mounted and well armed, with plenty of ammunition" had passed between "Spotted Tail Agency and the Missouri river." Sheridan Papers, LC.

9. *New York Herald*, February 13, 1879 (quotations); *Army and Navy Journal*, February 22, 1879.

10. Correspondent O'Beirne commented that "the troops probably will not pursue the escaped Cheyennes across the reservation of the Sioux, which is the route they have shrewdly taken. It is thought that such action would provoke hostilities from the young bucks in Spotted Tail's band [to the east at his agency] and furnish them a good excuse . . . for assuming a warlike attitude." *New York Herald*, February 13, 1879. An editorial in the *Army and Navy Journal* on February 22, 1879, condemned Ferris's effort as a "wild-goose chase . . . with the thermometer at 30 degrees below zero. . . . That no trace was found of the Indians is not surprising—the snows took care of the trails."

11. *New York Herald*, February 14, 1879. These troops were further sent to quell "a disturbance south of the Spotted Tail Agency along the northern line of Nebraska." Telegram, Sheridan to Adjutant General, February 20, 1879, Sheridan Papers, LC.

12. Powell, *Killing of Morning Star's People*, p. 25; Powell, *People of the Sacred Mountain*, 2:1254–55 (which also contains details of the four-day stopover at Bear Butte). For a comprehensive history of Fort Meade, see Bob Lee, *Fort Meade and the Black Hills* (Lincoln: University of Nebraska Press, 1991).

13. Powell, *Killing of Morning Star's People*, pp. 24–25; Powell, *People of the Sacred Mountain*, 2:1255–56. Despite apparent solidity during their trek, the Northern Cheyennes experienced occasional social discord en route. A major quarrel resulting in the death of Chief Black Crane happened as the people moved into Montana Territory and is fully described in *People of the Sacred Mountain*. To follow the areas of Little Wolf's probable 1879 course through northern Nebraska into South Dakota and Montana, see the DeLorme atlas and gazetteer series compilations for the respective states and areas: *Nebraska Atlas & Gazetteer* (2010), pp. 19, 32, 33, 46, 47; *South Dakota Atlas & Gazetteer* (2017), pp. 24–25; *Wyoming Atlas & Gazetteer* (2017), p. 71; and *Montana Atlas & Gazetteer* (2017), pp. 34–35 (all published Freeport, Maine: DeLorme). The route approximated stretches along today's U.S. Highway 212 running from Belle Fourche, South Dakota, through extreme northeastern Wyoming and into Montana.

14. *Army and Navy Journal*, March 1, 1879; *New York Herald*, February 28, 1879 (quotations).

15. *Army and Navy Journal*, March 1, 1879; *New York Herald*, February 28, 1879 (quotations); "Report of Lieutenant-General Sheridan, October 22, 1879," in *Report of the Secretary of War, 1879*, p. 52; *New York Times*, February 11, 1879; Hoig, *Perilous Pursuit*, p. 196; Buecker, *Fort Robinson and the American West*, p. 152. For these and other attacks on stage stations and freight wagons in the northern Black Hills and along the Bismarck trail surmised to have been committed by Indians, see *New York Herald*, February 25 and February 26, 1879; and *New York Times*, February 26, 1879. See also First Lieutenant William P. Clark to AG, Department of Dakota, April 6, 1879, forwarding "Supplemental Report," in Microfilm 1495, Roll 6, NA.

16. The crisis and exile of Black Coyote had been at least partly motivated by his interest in Black Crane's young wife, as deftly chronicled in Powell, *People of the Sacred Mountain*, 2:1255–56, 1399n18. For an alternative take, see Stands In Timber and Liberty, *Cheyenne Memories*, pp. 45–47. An altogether different view of the matter appears in Thomas B. Marquis, *A Warrior Who Fought Custer* (Minneapolis, Minn.: Midwest, 1931), pp. 328–30.

17. *Report of the Secretary of War, 1879*, p. 52; Powell, *People of the Sacred Mountain*, 2:1256. Miles was in Washington, D.C., serving on an equipment board during the

winter of 1878–79. Virginia W. Johnson, *The Unregimented General: A Biography of Nelson A. Miles* (Boston: Houghton Mifflin, 1962), p. 215. Whistler, a Wisconsin native, graduated from the U.S. Military Academy at West Point, New York, in 1842 and served as a lieutenant during the Mexican-American War and a colonel with the New York artillery during the Civil War. He held brevets for meritorious service in both conflicts, including that of brigadier general. After the war Whistler became a major in the Twenty-Second U.S. Infantry and was promoted lieutenant colonel, Fifth Infantry, in 1874 (in which capacity he served as commanding officer in Miles's absences). Whistler retired in 1886 as colonel of the Fifteenth Infantry. Heitman, *Historical Register and Dictionary*, 1:1026. William Philo Clark, from New York, graduated from West Point in 1868 and was appointed a second lieutenant in the Second Cavalry. Clark was promoted to first lieutenant in 1869 and was regimental adjutant until 1876. Considered an exceptional officer, he served as assistant aide-de-camp to General Crook, 1876–78, during which time he took part in several engagements of the Great Sioux War. Clark was promoted captain in 1881 and died suddenly in September 1884, while on staff duty in Washington, D.C. Powell, *Records of Living Officers of the United States Army*, p. 108; Heitman, *Historical Register and Dictionary*, 1:306. See especially Mark J. Nelson, *White Hat: The Military Career of Captain William Philo Clark* (Norman: University of Oklahoma Press, 2018). Clark researched and authored the significant book *The Indian Sign Language* (Philadelphia: L. R. Hamersly, 1885), which goes well beyond that important topic and should be required reading for students of nineteenth-century Plains Indian life and history. See also Buecker, *Fort Robinson and the American West*, p. 92; Greene, *Morning Star Dawn;* Hoig, *Perilous Pursuit*, p. 196. Lieutenant Kingsbury had graduated from West Point in 1870. Heitman, *Historical Register and Dictionary*, 1:601.

18. "Report of Brigadier-General Alfred H. Terry, October 1, 1879," in *Report of the Secretary of War, 1879* (hereinafter Clark report), pp. 52, 55–56. Clark's report was reprinted in Senate, *Select Committee Report*, pp. 246–50, while a handwritten version is found in Microfilm 1495, Roll 6, NA. The Northern Cheyenne scouts were Brave Wolf, Young Two Moon, Young Spotted Wolf, White Horse, and Wolf Voice (a Gros Ventre married to a Northern Cheyenne). Hump, a prominent Miniconjou Lakota, also accompanied them. Powell, *People of the Sacred Mountain*, 2:1256. For Seminole, see Paul L. Hedren, ed., *Ho! For the Black Hills: Captain Jack Crawford Reports the Black Hills Gold Rush and Great Sioux War* (Pierre: South Dakota Historical Society Press, 2012), pp. 106–7.

19. Clark report, p. 56. Clark further wrote: "I desired a perfect understanding with these scouts, as I felt they would be the means through which I must, in any event, at first communicate with the hostiles to secure a surrender either before or after a fight, and I hoped to secure a victory without loss of life, keenly appreciating the fact, however, that a victory gained at the expense of deception would indeed be dearly bought." See also Powell, *People of the Sacred Mountain*, 2:1256–57.

20. Grinnell identified the two scouts as Red War Bonnet and George Farley, a mixed-blood, and stated that "Little Wolf saw that they had soldier's guns, and clothing and horses, and was not deceived." *Fighting Cheyennes*, p. 410 (quotation); Powell, *People of the Sacred Mountain*, 2:1257. One of the Lakota scouts was Billy Jackson, who recounted his capture and escape from Little Wolf's people in "Billy Jackson's Capture by the Cheyennes," *Forest and Stream* 49 (August 7, 1897): 102–3.

21. *New York Times*, March 31, 1879; Hoig, *Perilous Pursuit*, pp. 199–200.

22. Charcoal Butte was apparently known among the Northern Cheyennes as Strong Point. *Army and Navy Journal*, May 3, 1879.

23. Clark report, p. 57 (quotation); see also Powell, *People of the Sacred Mountain*, 2:1258; Grinnell, *Fighting Cheyennes*, pp. 410–11; and John W. Bailey, *Pacifying the Plains: General Alfred Terry and the Decline of the Sioux, 1866–1890* (Westport, Conn.: Greenwood Press, 1979), p. 185. According to Grinnell's informants, Clark instead sent scouts Young Spotted Wolf, White Horse, Little Horse, Hump, and Wolf Voice to Little Wolf's camp bearing a message. It was Wolf Voice who located the camp. *Fighting Cheyennes*, pp. 411–12.

24. Clark report, p. 57. Although Little Wolf was his brother-in-law, the scout Brave Wolf explained that during his two years at Fort Keogh he "had found the white man true to his word and . . . would go on with the white chief and do all he could to make Little Wolf surrender." *Army and Navy Journal*, May 3, 1879.

25. Clark report, p. 57. A slightly variant yet fully compatible rendering of the events preceding Little Wolf's surrender appears in Powell, *People of the Sacred Mountain*, 2:1258–59.

26. Clark report, p. 57. Grinnell gave the following account, based on his Cheyenne sources:

> The next morning the Cheyennes started on, Little Wolf riding ahead, and soon two men were seen coming, and presently one called out: "I am White Hat"—Lieutenant W.P. Clark's Indian name. Behind Clark were soldiers all drawn up in line—two troops—and Clark with the interpreter sat on his horse in front of them. . . . Clark said: "I have prayed to God that I might find my friend Little Wolf, and now I have done so." The two shook hands, and then Clark moved into Little Wolf's camp, and that night they gave rations to the Cheyennes.

Fighting Cheyennes, p. 412. See also Powell, *People of the Sacred Mountain*, 2:1260; Stands In Timber and Liberty, *Cheyenne Memories*, pp. 236–37; and Nelson, *White Hat*, pp. 137–46.

27. Clark report, p. 57. A somewhat variant account from the *Pioneer Press* (St. Paul, Minnesota) appeared in the *Army and Navy Journal*, May 3, 1879. Powell's account detailed Little Wolf's appearance and dress: he was on horseback, with his hair adorned with a single eagle feather, wearing a simple cloth shirt, breechcloth, and cloth leggings and carrying his chief's accessories, notably the Sweet Medicine Chief's bundle. *People of the Sacred Mountain*, 2:1259.

28. Clark report, pp. 57–58 (quotations); Sheridan to Adjutant General Edward D. Townsend, April 2, 1879, Sheridan Papers, LC.

29. Telegram, Lieutenant Colonel Joseph N. G. Whistler to AAG, Department of Dakota, March 31, 1879, and Telegram, Brigadier General Alfred H. Terry to AG, Division of the Missouri, April 2, 1879, both in Microfilm 1495, Roll 6, NA; Clark report, pp. 57–58 (quotation); Powell, *People of the Sacred Mountain*, 2:1261.

30. Clark report, p. 58.

31. Ibid. (quotation); *Army and Navy Journal*, April 26, 1879; Telegram, Colonel John Gibbon to Sheridan, March 29, 1879, in Microfilm 1495, Roll 6, NA; *Record of Engagements with Hostile Indians within the Military Division of the Missouri*, p. 84

(salient parts of Clark's report also appear in Rodenbough, *Uncle Sam's Medal of Honor*, pp. 328–31). On April 2, 1879, General Terry via telegram announced the formal surrender to Sheridan: "The terms of surrender were simply to give up arms and ponies, no promises were made." Microfilm 1495, Roll 6, NA. See also Powell, *People of the Sacred Mountain*, 2:1261; and Hoig, *Perilous Pursuit*, pp. 196–201.

32. Major George Gibson to AAG, Department of Dakota, April 6, 1879, in *Report of the Secretary of War, 1879*, pp. 58–59 (quotation); *Army and Navy Journal*, April 5, 1879.

33. Telegram, Whistler to AAG, Department of Dakota, April 2, 1879, forwarded with Terry's supplemental endorsement, in Microfilm 1495, Roll 6, NA.

34. Telegram, Whistler to AAG, Department of Dakota, April 2, 1879, forwarded with Terry's supplemental endorsement (first quotation), and Sheridan's response (second quotation), in Microfilm 1495, Roll 6, NA. Sheridan's further response directed attention to *Revised Statutes of the United States*, which indicated that Clark's proposed action would be in violation of the statute, a copy of which was appended in ibid.

35. Cited in *Army and Navy Journal*, May 3, 1879.

36. *Army and Navy Journal*, May 17, 1879.

37. Dennis M. Kennedy, an Irish immigrant, enlisted in Philadelphia in 1876. He later served with the Third Cavalry and was discharged in 1881 at Fort McKinney, Wyoming Territory. White, *Index to Pension Applications*, p. 453; U.S. Army Register of Enlistments, 1798–1914, NA. The private killed was Leo Baader, Company E, Second Cavalry, an enlistee from Germany. Ibid.; Register of Deaths in the Regular Army, 1860–1889, NA, pp. 16–17.

38. Details of the Mizpah Creek skirmish and Glover's subsequent pursuit were summarized as follows:

> Private [Leo] Baader, Company E, 2nd Cavalry, while acting in the capacity of guide to Signal Sergeant Kennedy, U.S.A., from Powder River telegraph station [en route] to Fort Keogh, M.T., was killed by hostile Cheyennes, April 5, 1879, on Mizpah Creek, and Signal Sergeant Kennedy dangerously wounded. The Signal Sergeant and Private Baader had stopped at noon, April 5th, at the post where the Deadwood telegraph line crosses Mizpah Creek, about forty-five (45) miles distant from this post. Suddenly they were fired upon by six ambushed Indians, the first fire killing the private. The sergeant endeavored to reach his horse, and was wounded, but hid himself away in the brush. The Indians disappeared, but returned at night without finding him, but succeeded in securing the scalp of the private they had killed, and the government horses ridden by the sergeant and private, and a revolver belonging to the former. A party from Deadwood en route to Keogh the next day fortunately appeared, and brought the wounded sergeant in to Keogh. Immediately on learning of the above Indian murder, I dispatched three separate detachments; one to follow on the back trail of the Cheyennes captured by Lieutenant Clark, 2nd Cavalry; another to scout up Tongue River for sixty miles in the hopes of heading the Indians off; and the third detachment to hasten to the scene of the outrage, take up the trail and follow it. I felt most anxious to secure these Indians, for the salutary effect it might have on the captive Indians at this post—in exhibiting to them the power of the Government to

> punish evil. The detachment moved out with celerity, and [on] April 12th the hostile Cheyennes were brought captive to Keogh, having surrendered to Sergeant Glover, Company B[,] 2nd Cavalry. They numbered eight persons—three bucks, four squaws, one child. The horses ridden and [the] revolver worn by the sergeant who was wounded were recovered.

Whistler to AAG, Department of Dakota, April 17, 1879, in Microfilm Publication 1495, Roll 6, NA. See also Glover's own report, April 15, 1879, signed "Thomas B. Glover," in ibid. Glover was from New York City, where he enlisted on March 20, 1876, at age twenty-four. A civilian teamster, he had gray eyes and brown hair and stood 5 feet, 8 inches in height. He was discharged at Fort Keogh on March 19, 1881. U.S. Army Register of Enlistments, 1798–1914, NA. Private Baader's scalp and horse were discovered by Glover's party in the possession of the Indians. *New York Times*, April 14, 1879. Sergeant Glover received a citation for gallantry on February 4, 1880, and further received the Medal of Honor on November 20, 1897. *U.S. Army Gallantry and Meritorious Conduct*, p. 100; *Medal of Honor of the United States Army* (Washington, D.C.: Government Printing Office, 1948), 231. See also Glover's later personal account (in which he is identified as Thaddeus B. Glover), in W. F. Beyer and O. F. Keydel, eds., *Deeds of Valor*, 2 vols. (Detroit: Perrien-Keydel, 1907), 2:260–64.

It was further stated that the initial attack on Sergeant Kennedy and Private Baader occurred while they were eating lunch and that Kennedy, shot in the hip, used his pistol to fend off the warriors from under cover until help arrived. Sergeant Glover's action occurred on April 10, some forty-five miles east of Fort Keogh, near where the Deadwood telegraph line crossed Mizpah Creek. *Army and Navy Journal*, April 19, 1879.

39. Stands In Timber and Liberty, *Cheyenne Memories*, p. 241.

40. Quoted in Whistler to AAG, Department of Dakota, April 17, 1879, in Microfilm 1495, Roll 6, NA.

41. Telegram, Whistler to AAG, Department of Dakota, June 14, 1879, in Microfilm 1495, Roll 6, NA.

42. Little Chief was half Northern Cheyenne and half Lakota. Powell, *People of the Sacred Mountain*, 2:923 (which also provides information on his background); and Hoig, *Peace Chiefs of the Cheyennes*, pp. 137–41.

43. Within months of Little Chief's arrival at Darlington, General Sheridan urged that Little Wolf's people as well as "all Northern Cheyennes now at Ft. Keogh" be sent to join them there, because "those now there will probably be discontented until all their people are either required to join them or they [Little Chief's followers] are permitted to return to the North." Sheridan to Adjutant General, April 21, 1879. Sheridan Papers, LC.

44. *New York Times*, May 16, 1879; *Army and Navy Journal*, March 22 and May 24, 1879; *Army and Navy Journal*, December 10, 1881; *Report of the Commissioner of Indian Affairs, 1879*, p. xix; Senate, *Select Committee Report*, pp. 142–43; Robert M. Utley, *Frontier Regulars: The United States Army and the Indian, 1866–1890* (New York: Macmillan, 1973), p. 294; Greene, *Yellowstone Command*, pp. 194, 196, 288; Hill, *Webs of Kinship*, p. 212; Berthrong, *Cheyenne and Arapaho Ordeal*, pp. 36–45; *Army and Navy Journal*, December 10, 1881 (quotation). Overall, approximately 315

Northern Cheyennes were transferred from Oklahoma to the Pine Ridge Reservation in 1881; about 345 followed two years later, with 330 remaining in Oklahoma because of intermarriage with Southern Cheyennes and other tribal- or family-related matters. See Berthrong, *Cheyenne and Arapaho Ordeal*, pp. 46–47; and Marquis, *A Warrior Who Fought Custer*, pp. 324–25. On the Pine Ridge Reservation, Little Chief became an important spokesman for the Northern Cheyenne population. He and Chief Standing Elk departed from Pine Ridge for Montana in 1891 with approximately 400 people with government approval, and other Northern Cheyennes followed thereafter. Greene, *American Carnage*, pp. 35, 333; Svingen, *Northern Cheyenne Indian Reservation*, pp. 21–22, 43–44. Northern Cheyenne population figures for Pine Ridge Reservation in 1890 appear in *Report of the Commissioner of Indian Affairs, 1891* (Washington, D.C.: Government Printing Office, 1891), p. 50. For the important role of cultural affinity as it affected the saga of Little Chief and his followers, see especially Hill, *Webs of Kinship*, pp. 202–35.

The Northern Cheyenne reservation was established by the Executive Order of November 26, 1884, to include 371,200 acres; it was expanded by the Executive Order of March 19, 1900, to include approximately 460,000 acres. Stands In Timber and Liberty, *Cheyenne Memories*, p. 240n; Svingen, *Northern Cheyenne Indian Reservation*, pp. 44, 146.

45. Svingen, *Northern Cheyenne Indian Reservation*, pp. 94–95.

46. For explication, see Robert M. Pringle, "The Northern Cheyenne Indians in the Reservation Period" (B.A. thesis, Harvard College, 1958). See also *We, the Northern Cheyenne People*, pp. 47–61.

Chapter 13. Reflections

1. *Chicago Times*, January 13 (first quotation; emphasis added) and January 28, 1879 (second quotation).

2. "Report of Brig. Gen. George Crook," September 27, 1879, in *Report of the Secretary of War, 1879*, pp. 77 (first quotation; emphasis added), 78 (second quotation).

3. *Frank Leslie's Illustrated Weekly*, February 15, 1879.

4. *Army and Navy Journal*, January 25, 1879.

5. *Chicago Times*, January 28, 1879.

6. *New York Herald*, January 17, 1879.

7. Ibid.

8. Ibid.

9. *New York Times*, September 29, 1879.

10. Ibid.

11. *New York Herald*, January 18, 1879. See also Rising Sun interview, Oregon State University, p. 8. One view held that arms and ammunition were spirited into the barrack by the women "sewed up in their clothing." *New York Times*, September 28, 1879.

12. *New York Herald*, January 18, 1879. Dr. Valentine T. McGillycuddy, appointed agent to the Oglalas at New Red Cloud Agency in March 1879, believed that "when the Cheyennes surrendered on Chadron Creek they hid guns there which were later recovered by their Sioux friends and smuggled into the barracks at Ft. Robinson by

squaws." McGillycuddy Interview, Camp Papers, Lilly Library, Indiana University, p. 281.

13. *New York Herald*, January 23, 1879 (quotation); *New York Times*, September 28, 1879.

14. Letter, Wessells to retired Colonel Homer W. Wheeler, January 16, 1924, as quoted in Earl A. Brininstool, *Dull Knife (A Cheyenne Napoleon)* (Hollywood, Calif.: Privately published, 1935), p. 23 (later reprinted in Earl A. Brininstool, *Fighting Indian Warriors: True Tales of the Wild Frontiers* [Harrisburg, Pa.: Stackpole, 1953], p. 144).

15. *New York Times*, September 28, 1879; *New York Herald*, January 25, 1879 (quotations).

16. *New York Herald*, January 25, 1879.

17. Ibid.

18. Ibid.

19. *New York Herald*, January 24, 1879. For the incarceration of Southern Cheyenne prisoners at Fort Marion, St. Augustine, Florida, 1875–78, see Brad D. Lookingbill, *War Dance at Fort Marion: Plains Indian War Prisoners* (Norman: University of Oklahoma Press, 2006).

20. *New York Herald*, January 17, 1879.

21. The historian Loring Benson Priest wrote:

> The task of arousing interest in Indian affairs would have been considerably easier if the Negro and Indian problems had been connected in the public mind. . . . When Congress conferred citizenship on the Negroes in 1866, however, any mention of the Indians was omitted. Many Americans argued that the Indians were included by implication, but the absence of specific reference to the race prevented reformers from treating the Negro and Indian problems as a unit.

Uncle Sam's Stepchildren: The Reformation of United States Indian Policy, 1865–1887 (New Brunswick, N.J.: Rutgers University Press, 1942), p. 58. In regard to education, however, the federal government attempted to integrate Indian people into the cultural mainstream through boarding schools established for freed black people; as well as others created solely for Indian children. See Henry E. Fritz, *Movement for Indian Assimilation, 1860–1890* (Philadelphia: University of Pennsylvania Press, 1963), pp. 164–66; William T. Hagan, *American Indians* (Chicago: University of Chicago Press, 1961), pp. 135–37.

22. *New York Herald*, January 18, 1879.

23. The terms "monstrous" and "butchery" were used editorially in *Frank Leslie's Illustrated Newspaper*, February 1, 1879, in encouraging congressional investigation. "By all means," stated the paper, "let Congress probe this shameful affair to the very bottom."

24. Manypenny, *Our Indian Wards*, p. 341. See also Jackson, *Century of Dishonor*, p. 99.

25. Jackson, *Century of Dishonor*, p. 99.

26. *Army and Navy Journal*, January 31, 1880. See also Senate, *Select Committee Report.*

27. *New York Herald*, January 25, 1879. The controversy stemming from treatment of the Northern Cheyennes at Darlington was only one of several that resulted in

Hayt's dismissal from office in early 1880. For details, see Robert M. Kvasnicka and Herman J. Viola, eds., *The Commissioners of Indian Affairs, 1824–1977* (Lincoln: University of Nebraska Press, 1979), pp. 155–66.

28. *New York Herald*, January 25, 1879.

29. For the Ponca situation, see James H. Howard, *The Ponca Tribe* (Lincoln: University of Nebraska Press, 1995); Joe Starita, *"I Am a Man": Chief Standing Bear's Journey for Justice* (New York: St. Martin's Press, 2009); and Jackson, *Century of Dishonor*, pp. 186–217; for the Utes, see Robert Emmitt, *The Last War Trail: The Utes and the Settlement of Colorado* (Norman: University of Oklahoma Press, 1954); and Mark E. Miller, *Hollow Victory: The White River Expedition of 1879 and the Battle of Milk Creek* (Niwot: University Press of Colorado, 1997).

30. *Lincoln State Journal*, September 27, 1896 (quotation); Fort Robinson State Park curator Vance Nelson to Grace Carmody, August 2, 1993, copy in Fort Robinson Archive, NSHS.

31. *Lincoln State Journal*, September 27, 1896.

32. "Proceedings of a Board," NA, 166–67 (emphasis added).

33. Wells, *Apache Slaves*, pp. 28–29.

34. Alice C. Fletcher to Professor Putnam, February 4, 1882, attributed to Peabody Museum Papers, UAV 677.38 (Box 4) C-G, copy in Fort Robinson Archive, NSHS. It is not known whether this apparent academic impulse was actually indulged at or around Fort Robinson. See also the contextual period background on Fletcher in annotated introduction to Alice C. Fletcher, *Life among the Indians: First Fieldwork among the Sioux and Omahas*, ed. and ann. Joanna C. Scherer and Raymond J. DeMallie (Lincoln: University of Nebraska Press, 2013), pp. 65, 69, 70.

35. *Crawford Tribune* (special souvenir edition), June 26, 1903; *Alliance Herald*, April 8, 1904.

36. One area resident in the 1920s or 1930s recalled seeing a monument bearing the words "Indian woman and child, Unknown" at the possible site of the mass burial. Vance Nelson, Weekly Administrative Report for Fort Robinson State Park, July 13–18, 1966 (hereinafter cited as Nelson, Weekly Report), copy in Fort Robinson Archive, NSHS. The place of interment appears to have been near the junction of Sections 17 and 18, Township 31 North, Range 52 West, USGS, "Crawford, Nebr.," quadrangle, 1980.

37. Vance Nelson to Grace Carmody, August 2, 1993, copy in Fort Robinson Archive, NSHS; *Omaha World-Herald*, June 28, 1993.

38. Nelson, Weekly Report, July 13–18, July 19–25, August 2–8, and August 9–15, 1966, copy at Fort Robinson Archive, NSHS. The aged Stands In Timber did not make the trip. For efforts in the 1990s to organize a coordinated search for the grave through the Mari Sandoz Heritage Society at Chadron State College and the Nebraska State Historical Society, see Weekly Report, August 9–15, 1966. Citizens from the area who helped search for the grave included Crawfordites Arthur P. Howe, a druggist; Howard Dodd, a sheepherder; and townsman Roy Moss. Information provided by Vance and Karen Nelson. A search conducted by the staff of the National Archives reportedly at the request of U.S. senator Roman L. Hruska found no documentation to pinpoint the remains of the Northern Cheyenne dead in the area of the sawmill. Nelson, Weekly Report, August 9–15, 1966.

39. Lawrence Sommer to Dale Kennedy, September 16, 2002, copy in Fort Robinson Archive, NSHS.

40. Carlos Carvallo to Commanding Officer, May 18, 1880, Records of U.S. Army Continental Commands, 1784–1921, Endorsements, Fort Laramie, vol. 1, p. 331, RG 98, NA, copy in the files of Fort Laramie National Historic Site. Dr. Carvallo, a native of South America, was appointed assistant surgeon in the U.S. Army from the District of Columbia in May 1867. He served at the Kalorama Hospital and at Sedgwick Barracks in Washington, D.C., to December 1868 before being assigned as post surgeon to Fort Richardson, Texas, in March 1868, prior to serving at Fort Laramie. Carvallo died on July 23, 1882. Henry, *Military Record of Army and Civilian Appointments*, 1:63; Heitman, *Historical Register and Dictionary*, 1:288.

41. Private Ruby apparently did not accompany the approved project. He had been a Prussian soldier and as an immigrant joined the U.S. Army in 1878 at Washington, D.C., at age thirty-five. He was described as having brown hair and eyes and a dark complexion and standing 5 feet, 6½ inches tall. Ruby was discharged at Fort Robinson in 1883, a soldier of excellent character. U.S. Army Register of Enlistments, 1798–1914, NA.

42. Assistant surgeon Major George A. Otis, from Massachusetts, had served with that state's forces through most of the Civil War. Discharged in 1864, he finished the war as an assistant surgeon of volunteers, earning a brevet for faithful and meritorious service. He became an assistant surgeon, U.S. Army, in 1866, and was breveted lieutenant colonel. Otis died in 1881. Heitman, *Historical Register and Dictionary*, 1:762.

43. Extracts from "Medical History of Fort Laramie," September 1880 and October 1880, Fort Laramie National Historic Site library, copies enclosed in correspondence, Fort Laramie National Historic Site superintendent Charles C. Sharp to Captain Elgin C. Cowart Jr., curator, Medical Museum, Armed Forces Institute of Pathology, Washington, D.C., January 17, 1966. For details, see Anatomical Section IV Logbook (MM8762), National Institute of Health and Medicine, Armed Forces Institute of Pathology, Army Medical Museum Collection, Washington, D.C., entries 2090, 2091, 2092, 2093, 2094, 2095, 2096, and 2097 (AnatomicalSection4LogbookAnatomicalSectionas1344–2171mm8762: https://archive.org/details/AnatomicalSection4LogbookAnatomicalSectionas1344-2171mm8762/page/n1). The long bones said to have been collected by assistant surgeon Carvallo and shipped to the Army Medical Museum were not identified in the logbook. (In April 1880 a skeleton and three crania described as "Sioux" were sent from Fort Robinson to the museum by assistant surgeon William B. Brewster, who also forwarded five more bones and crania in June and July 1880. Ibid. The origin of these remains was not indicated.)

44. Ranger Steven Fulmer, Fort Laramie National Historic Site, to the author, July 16, 2017.

Epilogue

1. Leiker and Powers, *Northern Cheyenne Exodus*, p. 125.

2. Ibid., p. 186. The White River also bisects the Pine Ridge Reservation, where many of the Fort Robinson breakout survivors later lived. For discussion and critique of Sandoz's book, see ibid., pp. 152–56; Powell, *Killing of Morning Star's People*, pp.

39–40; and Liza Rae Lindell, "Visionaries of the American West: Mari Sandoz and Her Four Plains Protagonists" (M.A. thesis, South Dakota State University, Brookings, 1993), pp. 44, 48. For a synopsis of Ford's cinematic effort, see Leiker and Powers, *Northern Cheyenne Exodus*, 159–71.

3. Joe Starita, *The Dull Knifes of Pine Ridge: A Lakota Odyssey* (New York: Putnam, 1995), p. 75. Dull Knife's remains were eventually interred in the cemetery in Lame Deer, Montana, where they repose in a grave adjoining that of Little Wolf, who died in 1906. Many descendants of Dull Knife's family continued living at Pine Ridge, where they reside today. Ibid., p. 70; Greene, *Morning Star Dawn*, p. 194. For the anguished last years of Little Wolf, see Grinnell, *Cheyenne Indians*, 1:89; Powell, *Sweet Medicine*, 1:281–94; and Gary L. Roberts, "The Shame of Little Wolf," *Montana The Magazine of Western History* 28 (Summer 1978): 37–47.

4. Bird Wild Hog to Walter M. Camp, March 31, 1914, Ellison-Camp Papers, DPL; Camp Papers, Lilly Library, Indiana University; *Chadron Democrat*, August 15, 1889.

5. Monnett, *Tell Them We Are Going Home*, pp. 206–8; Marquis, *Cheyennes of Montana*, p. 52n1.

6. *Cheyenne Daily Leader*, January 30, February 1, and February 17, 1881.

7. Heitman, *Historical Register and Dictionary*, 1:1019; Wessells, "Hard Military Service," p. 602; Caspar Whitney, "The Santiago Campaign," *Harper's Magazine* (October 1898): 795–802; "San Juan Hill Order of Battle," p. 3 (September 7, 2018), https://en.wikipedia.org/wiki/San_Juan_Hill_order_of_battle.

8. Wessells to Walter M. Camp, October 19, 1918, Ellison-Camp Papers, DPL. Born in Germany, Schurz (1829–1906) emigrated to the United States in 1852, became a lawyer and diplomat, and served as a general officer during the Civil War. After the war he resumed his law practice and became a news correspondent and editor, while also championing civil service reform. Schurz supported Ulysses S. Grant for the presidency and was appointed U.S. senator from Missouri. As indicated, he served as secretary of the interior in 1877–81 during the Hayes administration. *Harper's Encyclopaedia of United States History*, 10 vols. (New York: Harper and Brothers, 1902), 8:87–88.

9. Wessells, "Outbreak of Cheyennes at Ft. Robinson," Ellison-Camp Papers, DPL.

10. Jensen, *Settler and Soldier Interviews*, p. 242; Heitman, *Historical Register and Dictionary*, 1:574; Thomas R. Buecker, *Fort Robinson and the American Century, 1900–1948* (Lincoln: Nebraska State Historical Society, 2002), pp. 21, 159, 160.

11. For an example of an 1878 outbreak event manifesting the Northern Cheyennes' dedication to their past, see Powers and Leiker, "Remembering the Battle of Punished Woman's Fork."

12. *We, the Northern Cheyenne People*, p. 32; Leiker and Powers, *Northern Cheyenne Exodus*, pp. 186–88ff.; *Big Horn County News*, December 14, 1988; *Native Sun News*, January 14, 2014; *Indian Country Today*, January 22, 2014; Senate Commemoration 17, State of South Dakota, Ninetieth Session, Legislative Assembly (2015), http://sdlegislature.gov/docs/legsession/2015/Bills/SC17P.htm; Nebraska State Historical Society flyer: *The Cheyenne Outbreak Barracks, Dedication, June 7, 2003*.

13. *Kansas City Star*, January 16, 1994 (first quotation); *Indian Country Today*, October 14, 1993 (second and third quotations).

14. 25 USC Ch. 32: Native American Graves Protection and Repatriation Act (NAGPRA); Francis P. McManamon, "The Native American Graves Protection and Repatriation Act (NAGPRA)," in *Archaeological Method and Theory: An Encyclopedia* (New York: Garland, 2000), ed. Linda Ellis, accessed at https://www.nps.gov/archeology/tools/laws/nagpra.htm; *Rapid City Journal*, October 4, 1993; *Indian Country Today*, October 14, 1993 (first quotation); *New York Times*, October 10, 1993; *Omaha World-Herald*, October 18, 1993; *Kansas City Star*, January 16, 1994 (second quotation). Since 2014 Northern Cheyenne youths in Montana have also taken part in a local two-day Reservation Run to honor their ancestors. The 2014 inaugural event also acknowledged the significant role of tribal elders in having facilitated the return of the remains in 1993. *Native Sun News*, January 24, 2014. In 2017 the remains of two more Northern Cheyenne men were found in the bluffs west of Fort Robinson and were likewise interred on a knoll overlooking Busby in August of that year. *Billings Gazette*, August 27, 2017.

15. *Native Sun News*, January 16, 2014; *Omaha World-Herald*, September 7, 2014. Over the course of its construction, donations came from a variety of contributory entities, including individuals and foundations, under the purview of the Northern Cheyenne Breakout Legacy Fund and administered by the Nebraska Community Foundation, Lincoln, Nebraska.

16. *Omaha World-Herald*, September 7, 2014, and July 16, 2016; *Rapid City Journal*, July 19, 2016; *Billings Gazette*, July 19, 2016; *Soaring Eagle Signals*, Fall 2016.

Bibliography

Manuscript Materials and Collections

Black Hills State University. Leland D. Case Library. E. Y. Berry Library-Learning Center. Spearfish, South Dakota

John D. McDermott Files, Cheyenne Outbreak Notes.

Brigham Young University, Manuscripts Collection, Harold B. Lee Library. Provo, UT

Walter Mason Camp Collection.

Denver Public Library. Western History and Genealogy Department. Denver

Ellison-Camp Papers

Chase, George F. "Dull Knife & Cheyennes." January 26, 1914.

Johnson, Carter P. "Outbreak of Cheyennes: Interview with Maj. Carter P. Johnson, 9/19/[19]13."

"Notes from [Bull] Hump re Dull Knife, Wild Hog, etc. at Lame Deer in 1911."

Fort Laramie National Historic Site. Fort Laramie, Wyoming

Correspondence, Superintendent to Curator, Medical Museum, Armed Forces Institute of Pathology.

Fort Laramie indorsements.

"Medical History of Fort Laramie."

Fort Supply State Historic Site. Fort Supply, Oklahoma

Rea, Bob. "Turkey Springs and Red Hills, September 13–14, 1878."

Indiana University. Manuscript Department. Lilly Library. Bloomington, Indiana

Walter M. Camp Papers.

Kansas State Historical Society. Cheyenne Indian Collection. Topeka

"Letters to G. W. Martin, 1905–1906, concerning the route of Cheyenne Indians in crossing Kansas in 1878." William Elsey Connelley Papers relating to Indian Folklore, MS 1227 Lab #28634 (microfilm).

Last Indian Raid in Kansas Museum. Oberlin, Kansas

Judge Nellans File: "The Great Cheyenne Chase: A Truthful Account by a Dragoon Who Participated in It."

Library of Congress. Manuscripts Division. Washington, D.C.
Philip H. Sheridan Papers. General Correspondence, 1853–1888.
William T. Sherman Papers. General Correspondence, 1837–1891.
National Archives. Washington, D.C.
Cheyenne Outbreak, September 1878–February 1879. Special Files, Division of the Missouri. Microfilm 1495, Roll 6.
Letters Received by the Office of Indian Affairs, 1824–81. Microfilm, Roll 723.
Record Group 94. Records of the Adjutant General's Office (some accessed at Ancestry.com)
Moseley, Edward B. "Special Report of twenty-one (21) cases of wounds and operations during the 'Cheyenne outbreak,' January 1879."
Post Returns, Camp Robinson and Fort Robinson, Nebraska, 1878–1879.
"Proceedings of a Board of Officers," January 25–February 7, 1879. Records of the Military Division of the Missouri, Special File 905-M-1879.
"Record of Medical History of Post [Fort Robinson]: Medical Department U.S.A., 1874." Copy in Ricker Tablet 31, Microfilm Reel 6, Nebraska Historical Society, Lincoln.
Records of U.S. Army Continental Commands, 1784–1921. RG 98. Endorsements, Fort Laramie. Copy in files of Fort Laramie National Historic Site, Wyoming.
Records on Diseases and Individual Cases, 1841–1893. File D-987.
Red Cloud Agency, 1871–80.
Regimental Returns of the Third Cavalry, 1878, 1879.
Regimental Returns of the Fifth Cavalry, 1879. Microfilm 744.
Register of Deaths in the Regular Army, 1860–1889. ARC ID: 1226156. Records of the Adjutant General's Office.
Regular Army Muster Rolls. Third U.S. Cavalry. Microfilm 744.
Returns from Military Posts, 1806–1916. Microfilm 617, 1,550 rolls. Records of the Adjutant General's Office, 1780s–1917.
Sioux War Papers. National Archives Microfilm M666, Reel 281.
U.S. Army Register of Enlistments, 1798–1914. Records of the Adjutant General's Office. 1780s–1917.
National Institute of Health and Medicine. Armed Forces Institute of Pathology.
Army Medical Museum Collection. Washington, D.C.
Anatomical Section IV Logbook. MM8762.
Nebraska State Historical Society (NSHS). Lincoln
Eli S. Ricker Papers.
Fort Robinson Archive.
"Record of Medical History of Post [Fort Robinson]. Medical Department U.S.A., 1874."
John G. Bourke Diary. Manuscript vol. 27.
Oregon State University. Special Collections and Archives. Corvallis, Oregon
Northern Cheyenne Interviews.
Southwest Museum. Braun Research Library. Los Angeles, California
George Bird Grinnell Collection.

Bibliography

Government Publications

Billings, John S. *Circular No. 8: Report on Hygiene of the United States Army with Descriptions of Military Posts* (May 1, 1875). Reprint, New York: Sol Lewis, 1974.

The Clash of Cultures Trails Project: Assessing the National Significance of Trails Associated with U.S. Army/American Indian Campaigns in the Trans-Mississippi West. Denver: National Park Service, 2002.

Greene, Jerome A. *Reconnaissance Survey of Indian-U.S. Army Battlefields of the Northern Plains.* Denver: National Park Service Cultural Resources and National Register Program Services, Intermountain Support Office, 1998.

Heitman, Francis B., comp. *Historical Register and Dictionary of the United States Army, 1789–1903.* 2 vols. Washington, D.C.: Government Printing Office, 1903.

Index of General Orders, Adjutant General's Office, 1878. Washington, D.C.: Government Printing Office, 1879.

Kappler, Charles J., comp. and ed. *Indian Affairs: Laws and Treaties.* 2 vols. Washington, D.C. Government Printing Office, 1904.

Lissandrello, Steven, and Sarah J. Pearce. "Fort Robinson and Red Cloud Agency." Dawes County, Nebraska. National Register of Historic Places Inventory—Nomination Form. National Park Service. U.S. Department of the Interior, Washington, D.C.

"Map of Reconnaissances of Routes in and Leading from the Department of the Platte by Captain W. S. Stanton, Corps of Engineers, 1875–76 & 77, Drawn by R. E. Koehneman." In U.S. Congress, House of Representatives, "Annual Report of Captain W. S. Stanton, Corps of Engineers, 1875–76 & 77." *Executive Document No. 1*, part 2. 45th Cong., 3rd Sess. Appendix RR, following p. 1747.

"Map of the Yellowstone and Missouri Rivers and Their Tributaries, Explored by Capt. W.F. Raynolds, Topl. Engrs, and 1st Lieut. H. E. Maynadier, 10th Infy. Assistant, 1859–60, Revised and Enlarged by Major G. L. Gillespie, U.S. Engr's; Bvt. Lt. Col. U.S.A. Chief Engr. Military Division of the Missouri. 1876." Reproduction. Denver: Clason Map Company, ca. 1930.

McCrellis, James B. *Military Reservations, National Military Parks, and National Cemeteries: Title and Jurisdiction.* Washington, D.C.: Government Printing Office, 1898.

The Medal of Honor of the United States Army. Washington, D.C.: Government Printing Office, 1948.

The Medical and Surgical History of the War of the Rebellion (Part III, vol. 2: Surgical History). 2nd issue. Washington, D.C.: Government Printing Office, 1883.

Native American Graves Protection and Repatriation Act. 25 U.S.C. Ch. 32: Native American Graves Protection and Repatriation Act. http://uscode.house.gov/view.xhtml?path=/prelim@title25/chapter32&edition=prelim.

Nebraska Survey Plats (1881 and 1882). Surveyor General's Office, 1883. Plattsmouth, Nebr. https://sso.nebraska.gov/maps/glo.asp.

Official Table of Distances for the Guidance of Disbursing Officers of the Army Charged with Payment of Money Allowances for Travel. Washington, D.C.: Government Printing Office, 1881.

Outline Descriptions of the Posts in the Military Division of the Missouri. Chicago: Headquarters Military Division of the Missouri, 1876; reprint, Bellevue, Nebr.: Old Army Press, 1969.

Record of Engagements with Hostile Indians within the Military Division of the Missouri, from 1868 to 1882. Washington, D.C.: Government Printing Office, 1882; reprint, Fort Collins, Colo.: Old Army Press, 1972.

Report of the Chief of Ordnance, 1879. Washington, D.C.: Government Printing Office, 1879.

Report of the Commissioner of Indian Affairs, 1878. Washington, D.C.: Government Printing Office, 1878.

Report of the Commissioner of Indian Affairs, 1879. Washington, D.C.: Government Printing Office, 1879.

Report of the Commissioner of Indian Affairs, 1891. Washington, D.C.: Government Printing Office, 1891.

Report of the Secretary of War, 1878. Washington, D.C.: Government Printing Office, 1878.

Report of the Secretary of War, 1879. Washington, D.C.: Government Printing Office, 1879.

Report of the Secretary of War, 1881. Washington, D.C.: Government Printing Office, 1881.

Senate Commemoration 17. S.C. 17. State of South Dakota. Ninetieth Session, Legislative Assembly (2015). http://sdlegislature.gov/docs/legsession/2015/Bills/SC17P.htm.

Table of Distances and Itineraries of Routes between the Military Posts in, and to Certain Points Contiguous to, the Department of the Platte. Omaha, Nebr.: Engineer Office, Headquarters Department of the Platte, 1877.

U.S. Congress, House of Representatives. "Annual Report of Captain W.S. Stanton, Corps of Engineers, for the Fiscal Year Ending June 30, 1878." In *Executive Document No. 1*, part 2. 45th Cong., 3rd Sess., 1879. Appendix RR.

U.S. Congress, Senate. *Letter from the Secretary of War, to the Chairman of the Committee on Indian Affairs, Communicating Information in Relation to the Escape of the Cheyenne Indians from Fort Robinson.* Misc. Doc. No. 64, 45th Cong., 3rd sess., 1879. Contains briefs of dispatches.

———. *Report of the Select Committee to Examine into the Circumstances Connected with the Removal of the Northern Cheyennes from the Sioux Reservation to the Indian Territory.* Senate Report No. 708, 46th Cong., 2nd Sess., 1880.

Books, Articles, Dissertations, and Pamphlets

Abrams, Marc H., comp. and ed. *Newspaper Chronicle of the Indian Wars, Including a Comprehensive Account of the Sioux War of 1876.* Vols. 10–11. Brooklyn, N.Y.: Abrams, 2010.

Anderson, Harry H. "Cheyennes at the Little Big Horn: A Study of Statistics." *North Dakota History* 27 (Spring 1960): 3–15.

Anderson, Thomas M. "The Fourteenth Regiment of Infantry." In Theophilus F. Rodenbough and William L. Haskin, eds., *The Army of the United States:*

Historical Sketches of Staff and Line with Portraits of Generals-in-Chief, 586–609. New York: Maynard, Merrill, 1896.
Bailey, John W. *Pacifying the Plains: General Alfred Terry and the Decline of the Sioux, 1866–1890*. Westport, Conn.: Greenwood Press, 1979.
Berryman, J. W. "Early Settlement of Southwest Kansas." *Collections of the Kansas State Historical Society, 1926–1928*. 17 (1928): 563–70.
Berthrong, Donald J. *The Cheyenne and Arapaho Ordeal: Reservation and Agency Life in the Indian Territory, 1875–1907*. Norman: University of Oklahoma Press, 1976.
Bettelyoun, Susan Bordeaux, and Josephine Waggoner. *With My Own Eyes: A Lakota Woman Tells Her People's History*. Ed. Emily Levine. Lincoln: University of Nebraska Press, 1998.
Beyer, W. F., and O. F. Keydel, eds. *Deeds of Valor*. 2 vols. Detroit: Perrien-Keydel, 1907.
"Billy Jackson's Capture by the Cheyennes." *Forest and Stream* 49 (August 7, 1897): 102–3.
Bourke, John G. *The Diaries of John Gregory Bourke, Volume 3, June 1, 1878-June 22, 1880*. Ed. Charles M. Robinson III. Denton: University of North Texas Press, 2007.
Boye, Alan. *Holding Stone Hands: On the Trail of the Cheyenne Exodus*. Lincoln: University of Nebraska Press, 1999.
Brinckerhoff, Sidney B. *Boots and Shoes of the Frontier Soldier, 1865–1893*. Museum Monograph No. 7. Tucson: Arizona Historical Society, 1976.
Brininstool, Earl A. *Dull Knife (A Cheyenne Napoleon)*. Hollywood, Calif.: Privately published, 1935.
———. *Fighting Indian Warriors: True Tales of the Wild Frontiers*. Harrisburg, Pa.: Stackpole, 1953.
Bronson, Edgar Beecher. *Cowboy Life on the Western Plains: The Reminiscences of a Ranchman*. New York: Grosset and Dunlap, 1910.
Brown, Jesse, and A. M. Willard. *The Black Hills Trails: A History of the Struggles of the Pioneers in the Winning of the Black Hills*. Rapid City, S.Dak.: Rapid City Journal Company, 1924.
Bryant, Edward C. *Hat Creek and Hard Times: People and Events in the History of a Wyoming Community*. Fairfax, Va.: Hero Books, 1988.
Buecker, Thomas R. *Fort Robinson and the American Century, 1900–1948*. Lincoln: Nebraska State Historical Society, 2002.
———. *Fort Robinson and the American West, 1874–1899*. Lincoln: Nebraska State Historical Society, 1999.
———. "Fort Sidney: Its Role on the Upper Plains." *Periodical* 11 (March 1981): 22–36.
———. *Last Days of Red Cloud Agency: Peter T. Buckley's Photograph Collection, 1876–1877*. Lincoln: Nebraska Historical Society, 2016.
———. "The Lingering Death of Old Fort Sidney." *Periodical* 14 (March 1986): 17–30.
———. "Memo: Keep Your Work Straight!" *Periodical* 9 (Winter 1977–78): 3-12.
Buecker, Thomas R., and R. Eli Paul. "Cheyenne Outbreak Firearms." *Museum of the Fur Trade Quarterly* 29 (Summer 1993): 2–12.

Buecker, Thomas R., and R. Eli Paul, eds. *The Crazy Horse Surrender Ledger.* Lincoln: Nebraska Historical Society, 1994.

Carter, William H. "History of Fort Robinson." *Northwest Nebraska News*, August 13, 1936.

Clark, William P. *The Indian Sign Language.* Philadelphia: L. R. Hamersly, 1885.

Cook, James H. *Fifty Years on the Old Frontier as Cowboy, Hunter, Guide, Scout, and Ranchman.* New Haven, CT: Yale University Press, 1923.

Corbusier, William T. "Camp Sheridan, Nebraska." *Nebraska History* 42 (March 1961): 29–53.

Cullum, George W. *Biographical Register of the Officers and Graduates of the U.S. Military Academy at West Point, N.Y., from Its Establishment, in 1802, to 1890.* 2 vols. Boston: Houghton Mifflin, 1891.

Deibert, Ralph C. *A History of the Third United States Cavalry.* Harrisburg, Pa.: Telegraph Press, n.d.

Denney, James. "Digging into the Past at Fort Robinson." *Sunday World-Herald Magazine of the Midlands* (October 4, 1987): 9–11.

Derrick, W. Edwin. "Fort Reno, Indian Territory: Frontier Guardian." *Periodical, Journal of the Council on Abandoned Military Posts* 10 (Winter 1978–79): 14–17.

Dickson, Ephriam D. III, *Fort Robinson.* Chicago: Arcadia, 2010.

Donovan, James. *A Terrible Glory: Custer and the Little Bighorn—The Last Great Battle of the American West.* Boston: Little, Brown, 2008.

Eastman, Charles A. *Indian Heroes and Great Chieftains.* Boston: Little, Brown, and House, 1929.

Ellis, Richard N. *General Pope and U.S. Indian Policy.* Albuquerque: University of New Mexico Press, 1970.

Emmitt, Robert. *The Last War Trail: The Utes and the Settlement of Colorado.* Norman: University of Oklahoma Press, 1954.

Federal Writers' Program, *Wyoming: A Guide to Its History, Highways, and People.* New York: Oxford University Press, 1941.

Federal Writers' Project. *Nebraska: A Guide to the Cornhusker State.* New York: Viking Press, 1939.

Fenneman, Nevin M. *Physiography of Western United States.* New York: McGraw-Hill, 1931.

Ferrick, M. G., N. D. Mulherin, and D. J. Calkins, "Analysis of the Winter Low-Flow Balance of the Semiarid White River, Nebraska and South Dakota." *Water Resources Research* 31 (August 1995): 1823–2125 (abstract).

Ferris, Robert G., ed. *Soldier and Brave: Historic Places Associated with Indian Affairs in the Trans-Mississippi West.* Washington, D.C.: National Park Service, 1971.

Fletcher, Alice C. *Life among the Indians: First Fieldwork among the Sioux and Omahas.* Edited and annotated by Joanna C. Scherer and Raymond J. DeMallie. Lincoln: University of Nebraska Press, 2013.

Frazer, Robert W. *Forts of the West: Military Forts and Presidios and Posts Commonly Called Forts West of the Mississippi River.* Norman: University of Oklahoma Press, 1965.

Frison, Paul. *The Apache Slave: Life of Charles Wells.* Worland, Wyo.: Worland Press, 1969.

Fritz, Henry E. *The Movement for Indian Assimilation, 1860–1890*. Philadelphia: University of Pennsylvania Press, 1963.

Graham, William A. *Abstract of the Official Record of Proceedings of the Reno Court of Inquiry*. Harrisburg, Pa.: Stackpole, 1954.

Grange, Roger T., Jr. "Fort Robinson: Outpost on the Plains," *Nebraska History* 39 (September 1958): 191–241.

———, comp. "Treating the Wounded at Fort Robinson." *Nebraska History* 45 (September 1964): 273–94.

Greene, Jerome A. *American Carnage: Wounded Knee, 1890*. Norman: University of Oklahoma Press, 2014.

———, comp. *Battles and Skirmishes of the Great Sioux War, 1876–1877: The Military View*. Norman: University of Oklahoma Press, 1993.

———. *Beyond Bear's Paw: The Nez Perce Indians in Canada*. Norman: University of Oklahoma Press, 2010.

———. "The Crawford Affair: International Implications of the Geronimo Campaign." *Journal of the West* 11 (January 1972): 143–53.

———. "George Crook." In Paul Andrew Hutton and Durwood Ball, eds., *Soldiers West: Biographies from the Military Frontier*, 246–72. 2nd ed. Norman: University of Oklahoma Press, 2009.

———. *Indian War Veterans: Memories of Army Life and Campaigns in the West, 1864–1898*. New York: Savas Beatie, 2007.

———, comp. *Lakota and Cheyenne: Indian Views of the Great Sioux War, 1876–1877*. Norman: University of Oklahoma Press, 1994.

———. *Morning Star Dawn: The Powder River Expedition and the Northern Cheyennes, 1876*. Norman: University of Oklahoma Press, 2003.

———. *Slim Buttes, 1876: An Episode of the Great Sioux War*. Norman: University of Oklahoma Press, 1982.

———. "The U.S. Army Buffalo Overcoat and M1883 Canvas Blanket-Lined Overcoat on the Northern Plains Frontier, 1876–1891." *Military Collector & Historian: Journal of the Company of Military Historians* 44 (Summer 1992): 73–79.

———. *Washita: The U.S. Army and the Southern Cheyennes, 1867–1869*. Norman: University of Oklahoma Press, 2004.

———. *Yellowstone Command: Colonel Nelson A. Miles and the Great Sioux War, 1876–1877*. Norman: University of Oklahoma Press, 2006.

Greene, Jerome A., and Peter M. Wright, eds. "Chasing Dull Knife: A Journal of the Cheyenne Campaign of 1878 by Lieutenant George H. Palmer." *Heritage of Kansas* 12 (Winter 1971): 25–36.

Grinnell, George Bird. *The Cheyenne Indians: Their History and Ways of Life*. 2 vols. New Haven, Conn.: Yale University Press, 1923.

———. *The Fighting Cheyennes*. Norman: University of Oklahoma Press, 1956.

Hagan, William T. *American Indians*. Chicago: University of Chicago Press, 1961.

Harper's Encyclopaedia of United States History. 10 vols. New York: Harper and Brothers, 1902.

Harrison Community Club. *Sioux County History: First 100 Years, 1886–1986*. Dallas: Curtis Media, 1986.

Hedren, Paul L. *After Custer: Loss and Transformation in Sioux Country*. Norman: University of Oklahoma Press, 2011.

———. *Great Sioux War Orders of Battle: How the United States Army Waged War on the Northern Plains, 1876–1877*. Norman: Arthur H. Clark, 2011.

———. *Ho! For the Black Hills: Captain Jack Crawford Reports the Black Hills Gold Rush and Great Sioux War*. Pierre: South Dakota Historical Society Press, 2012.

———. *Powder River: Disastrous Opening of the Great Sioux War*. Norman: University of Oklahoma Press, 2016.

———. *Rosebud, June 17, 1876: Prelude to the Little Big Horn*. Norman: University of Oklahoma Press, 2019.

———. "The Sioux War Adventures of Dr. Charles V. Petteys, Acting Assistant Surgeon." *Journal of the West* 32 (April 1993): 29–37.

———. *Traveler's Guide to the Great Sioux War*. Helena: Montana Historical Society Press, 1996.

Henry, Guy V. *Military Record of Army and Civilian Appointments in the United States Army.* 2 vols. New York: D. Van Nostrand, 1873.

Hill, Christina Gish. *Webs of Kinship: Family in Northern Cheyenne Nationhood*. Norman: University of Oklahoma Press, 2017.

Hoig, Stan. *The Peace Chiefs of the Cheyennes*. Norman: University of Oklahoma Press, 1980.

———. *Perilous Pursuit: The U.S. Cavalry and the Northern Cheyennes*. Niwot: University Press of Colorado, 2002.

Howard, James H. *The Ponca Tribe*. Lincoln: University of Nebraska Press, 1995.

Hutton, Paul Andrew. *Phil Sheridan and His Army*. Lincoln: University of Nebraska Press, 1985.

Hyde, George E. *A Sioux Chronicle*. Norman: University of Oklahoma Press, 1956.

"Iron Teeth, a Cheyenne Old Woman." In Thomas B. Marquis, *Cheyenne and Sioux: The Reminiscences of Four Indians and a White Soldier*, edited by Ronald H. Limbaugh, pp. 4–26. Stockton, Calif.: Pacific Center for Western Historical Studies, University of the Pacific, 1973.

Jackson, Helen Hunt. *A Century of Dishonor: The Early Crusade for Indian Reform.* New York: Harper and Brothers, 1881.

Jackson, W. Turrentine. "The Governorship of Wyoming, 1885–1889: A Study in Territorial Politics." *Pacific Historical Review* 13 (March 1944): 1–11.

Jensen, Richard E., ed. *Voices of the American West, Volume 1: The Indian Interviews of Eli S. Ricker, 1903–1919*. Lincoln: University of Nebraska Press, 2005.

———, ed. *Voices of the American West, Volume 2: The Settler and Soldier Interviews of Eli S. Ricker, 1903–1919*. Lincoln: University of Nebraska Press, 2005.

Johnson, Harrison. *Johnson's History of Nebraska*. Omaha: Henry Gibson Herald Printing House, 1880.

Johnson, Virginia W. *The Unregimented General: A Biography of Nelson A. Miles*. Boston: Houghton Mifflin, 1962.

Keith, A. N. "Dull Knife's Cheyenne Raid of 1878." *Nebraska History and Record of Pioneer Days* 7 (October–December 1924): 116–18.

Killsback, Leo. "Crowns of Honor: Sacred Laws of Eagle Feather War Bonnets and Repatriating the Icon of the Great Plains." *Great Plains Quarterly* 33 (Winter 2013): 1–23.

———. "Morning Star Rises: Peace, Power, and Righteousness in the Face of Colonization." *Wicaso Sa Review* (Spring 2018): 5–37.

———. "Morning Star, Violence, and the Rights of Indigenous Peoples." In "Remembering the Battle of Punished Woman's Fork: The 2013 Scott City Symposium." *Kansas History: A Journal of the Central Plains* 38 (Winter 2015–16): 239–42.

Kingsley, J. S. "The Hat Creek Bad Lands." *American Naturalist* 25 (November 1891): 964, 970–71.

Kooser, Ted. *Flying at Night: Poems 1965–1985*. Pittsburgh: University of Pittsburgh Press, 2005.

Kvasnicka, Robert M., and Herman J. Viola, eds. *The Commissioners of Indian Affairs, 1824–1977*. Lincoln: University of Nebraska Press, 1979.

Larson, Robert W. *Red Cloud: Warrior-Statesman of the Lakota Sioux*. Norman: University of Oklahoma Press, 1997.

Lee, Bob. *Fort Meade and the Black Hills*. Lincoln: University of Nebraska Press, 1991.

Leiker, James N., and Ramon Powers. *The Northern Cheyenne Exodus in History and Memory*. Norman: University of Oklahoma Press, 2011.

Liberty, Margot. "Cheyenne Primacy: New Perspectives on a Great Plains Tribe." *Plains Anthropologist* 56, no. 218 (2011): 155–74.

Lindell, Liza Rae. "Visionaries of the American West: Mari Sandoz and Her Four Plains Protagonists." M.A. thesis, South Dakota State University, Brookings, 1993.

Llewellyn, K. N.. *The Cheyenne Way: Conflict and Case Law in Primitive Jurisprudence*. Norman: University of Oklahoma Press, 1941.

Lookingbill, Brad D. *War Dance at Fort Marion: Plains Indian War Prisoners*. Norman: University of Oklahoma Press, 2006.

Low, Denise, and Ramon Powers. "Northern Cheyenne Warrior Ledger Art: Captivity Narratives of Northern Cheyenne Prisoners in 1879 Dodge City." *Kansas History: A Journal of the Central Plains* 35 (Spring 2012): 3–25.

Maddux, Vernon R., and Albert Glenn Maddux. *In Dull Knife's Wake: The True Story of the Northern Cheyenne Exodus of 1878*. Norman, OK: Horse Creek Publications, 2003.

Magid, Paul. *The Gray Fox: George Crook and the Indian Wars*. Norman: University of Oklahoma Press, 2015.

Maher, Harmon D., Jr., George F. Engelmann, and Robert D. Shuster. *Roadside Geology of Nebraska*. Missoula, Mont.: Mountain Press, 2003.

Manypenny, George W. *Our Indian Wards*. Cincinnati: Robert Clarke, 1880.

Marquis, Thomas B. *Cheyenne and Sioux: The Reminiscences of Four Indians and a White Soldier*. Edited by Ronald H. Limbaugh. Stockton, Calif.: Pacific Center for Western Historical Studies, University of the Pacific, 1973.

———. *The Cheyennes of Montana*. Edited by Thomas D. Weist. Algonac, Mich.: Reference Publications, 1978.

———. "Red Ripe's Squaw: Recollections of a Long Life Interpreted by Thomas B. Marquis." *Century Magazine* 118 (June 1929): 201–9.

———. *A Warrior Who Fought Custer*. Minneapolis: Midwest, 1931.

McChristian, Douglas C. *Fort Laramie, Military Bastion of the High Plains*. Norman: Arthur H. Clark, 2008.

———. *Regular Army O!: Soldiering on the Western Frontier, 1865-1891*. Norman: University of Oklahoma Press, 2017.

McDermott, John D., R. Eli Paul, and Sandra J. Lowry, eds. *All Because of A Mormon Cow: Historical Accounts of the Grattan Massacre, 1854–1855*. Norman: University of Oklahoma Press, 2018.

McDonald, J. Douglas, Larry J. Zimmerman, A. L. McDonald, William Tall Bull, and Ted Rising Sun. "The Northern Cheyenne Outbreak of 1879: Using Oral History and Archaeology as Tools of Resistance." In R. H. McGuire and R. Paynter, eds., *The Archaeology of Inequality*, 68–74. Oxford: Basil Blackwell, 1991.

McGillycuddy, Julia B. *McGillycuddy Agent: A Biography of Dr. Valentine T. McGillycuddy*. Stanford, Calif.: Stanford University Press, 1941.

McManamon, Francis P. "The Native American Graves Protection and Repatriation Act (NAGPRA)." In Linda Ellis, ed., *Archaeological Method and Theory: An Encyclopedia*. New York: Garland, 2000. Accessed at https://www.nps.gov/archeology/tools/laws/nagpra.htm.

Miller, Mark E. *Hollow Victory: The White River Expedition of 1879 and the Battle of Milk Creek*. Niwot: University Press of Colorado, 1997.

Monnett, John H. *Massacre at Cheyenne Hole: Lieutenant Austin Henely and the Sappa Creek Controversy*. Niwot: University Press of Colorado, 1999.

———. "'My heart now has become changed to softer feelings': A Northern Cheyenne Woman and Her Family Remember the Long Journey Home." *Montana The Magazine of Western History* 59 (Summer 2009): 45–61.

———. *Tell Them We Are Going Home: The Odyssey of the Northern Cheyennes*. Norman: University of Oklahoma Press, 2001.

Mooney, James. "The Cheyenne Indians." *Memoirs of the American Anthropological Association* 1 (September 1907): 357–442.

Moore, John H. *The Cheyenne*. Cambridge, Mass.: Blackwell Publishers, 1996.

———. *The Cheyenne Nation*. Lincoln: University of Nebraska Press, 1987.

Moore, John H., Margot P. Liberty, and A. Terry Straus. "Cheyenne." In Raymond J. DeMallie, ed., *Plains*, in William C. Sturtevant (gen. ed.), *Handbook of North American Indians*, vol. 13, part 2, 863–85. Washington, D.C.: Smithsonian Institution, 2001.

Moulton, Candy. *Valentine T. McGillycuddy: Army Surgeon, Agent to the Sioux*. Norman, Okla.: Arthur H. Clark, 2011.

Nebraska State Historical Society (NSHS). *The Cheyenne Outbreak Barracks, Dedication, June 7, 2003*. Lincoln: NSHS, 1903.

Nelson, Mark J. *White Hat: The Military Career of Captain William Philo Clark*. Norman: University of Oklahoma Press, 2018.

Nelson, Vance E., ed. "Fort Robinson during the 1880s: An Omaha Newspaperman Visits the Post." *Nebraska History* 55 (Summer 1974): 181–202.

North, Luther. *Man of the Plains: Recollections of Luther North, 1856–1882*. Edited by Donald F. Danker. Lincoln: University of Nebraska Press, 1961.

O'Hara, Cleophas C. *The White River Badlands*. Rapid City, South Dakota School of Mines, 1920.

Olson, James C. *Red Cloud and the Sioux Problem*. Lincoln: University of Nebraska Press, 1965.

Paul, R. Eli. *Blue Water Creek and the First Sioux War* (1956). Norman: University of Oklahoma Press, 2004.

———, ed. *Sign Talker: Hugh Lenox Scott Remembers Indian Country*. Norman: University of Oklahoma Press, 2016.

Potter, James E., ed. *From Our Special Correspondent: Dispatches from the 1875 Black Hills Council at Red Cloud Agency, Nebraska*. Lincoln: Nebraska State Historical Society, 2016.

Powell, Peter J. *The Cheyennes, Ma̍heoo̍'s People: A Critical Bibliography*. Bloomington: Indiana University Press, 1980.

———. *The Killing of Morning Star's People*. Chadron, Nebr.: Mari Sandoz Heritage Society, 1994.

———. *People of the Sacred Mountain: A History of the Northern Cheyenne Chiefs and Warrior Societies, 1830–1879, with an Epilogue, 1969–1974*. 2 vols. San Francisco: Harper and Row, 1981.

———. *Sweet Medicine: The Continuing Role of the Sacred Arrows, the Sun Dance, and the Sacred Buffalo Hat in Northern Cheyenne History*. 2 vols. Norman: University of Oklahoma Press, 1979.

Powell, William H., comp. *Records of Living Officers of the United States Army*. Philadelphia: L. R. Hamersly, 1884.

———. *Records of Living Officers of the United States Army*. Philadelphia: L. R. Hamersly, 1890.

Powers, Ramon. "The Dull Knife Raid of 1878: A Story of the Frontier." M.A. thesis, Fort Hays Kansas State College.

———. "The Kansas Indian Claims Commission of 1879." *Kansas History* 7 (Autumn 1984): 199–211.

———. "The Northern Cheyenne Trek through Western Kansas in 1878: Frontiersmen, Indians and Cultural Conflict." *Trail Guide* 17, nos. 3–4 (entire issue).

———. "Why the Northern Cheyennes Left Indian Territory in 1878: A Cultural Analysis." *Kansas Quarterly* 3 (Fall 1971): 72–81.

Powers, Ramon, and James Leiker, eds. "Remembering the Battle of Punished Woman's Fork: The 2013 Scott City Symposium." *Kansas History: A Journal of the Central Plains* 38 (Winter 2015–16): 218–49.

Powers, Thomas. *The Killing of Crazy Horse*. New York: Alfred A. Knopf, 2010.

Preston, Douglas J. "Little Finger Nail's Ledger Book." *Natural History* 89 (October 1980): 82–87.

Priest, Loring Benson. *Uncle Sam's Stepchildren: The Reformation of United States Indian Policy, 1865–1887*. New Brunswick, N.J.: Rutgers University Press, 1942.

Pringle, Robert M. "The Northern Cheyenne Indians in the Reservation Period." B.A. thesis, Harvard College, 1958.

Prucha, Francis Paul. *A Guide to the Military Posts of the United States, 1789–1895*. Madison: State Historical Society of Wisconsin, 1964.

Remington, Frederic. *Crooked Trails*. New York: Harper and Brothers, 1998.

———. "A Sergeant of the Orphan Troop." *Harper's New Monthly Magazine* 95 (August 1897): 441–50.

Roberts, Gary L. *Massacre at Sand Creek: How Methodists Were Involved in an American Tragedy*. Nashville, Tenn.: Abingdon Press, 2016.

———. "The Shame of Little Wolf." *Montana The Magazine of Western History* 28 (Summer 1978): 37–47.

Robinson, Willard B. *American Forts: Architectural Form and Function*. Urbana: University of Illinois Press, 1977.

Rodenbough, Theophilus F. *Uncle Sam's Medal of Honor, 1861–1886*. New York: G. P. Putnam's Sons, 1886.

Rodenbough, Theophilus F., and William L. Haskin, eds. *The Army of the United States: Historical Sketches of Staff and Line with Portraits of Generals-in-Chief*. New York: Maynard, Merrill, 1896.

Rose, Christina. "Native History: Descendant Tells Father's Story of Fort Robinson Escape." *Indian Country Today*, January 22, 2014. https://newsmaven.io/indiancountrytoday/archive/native-history-descendant-tells-father-s-story-of-fort-robinson-escape-fI-OF2p94EqL2Am-_iGZYw/.

Sandoz, Mari. *Cheyenne Autumn*. New York: McGraw-Hill, 1953.

"San Juan Hill Order of Battle" (September 7, 2018). https://en.wikipedia.org/wiki/San_Juan_Hill_order_of_battle.

Scott, Hugh Lenox. *Some Memories of a Soldier*. New York: Century, 1928.

Sooktis, Rubie. "Surviving the Odds: People of Dull Knife and Little Wolf." In "Remembering the Battle of Punished Woman's Fork: The 2013 Scott City Symposium." *Kansas History: A Journal of the Central Plains* 38 (Winter 2015): 236.

Spring, Agnes Wright. *The Cheyenne and Black Hills Stage and Express Routes*. Glendale, Calif.: Arthur H. Clark, 1949.

Stallard, Patricia Y., ed. *Fanny Dunbar Corbusier: Recollections of Her Army Life, 1869–1908*. Norman: University of Oklahoma Press, 2003.

Stands In Timber, John, and Margot Liberty. *Cheyenne Memories*. New Haven, Conn.: Yale University Press, 1967.

———. *A Cheyenne Voice: The Complete John Stands In Timber Interviews*. Norman: University of Oklahoma Press, 2013.

Starita, Joe. *The Dull Knifes of Pine Ridge: A Lakota Odyssey*. New York: Putnam, 1995.

———. *"I Am a Man": Chief Standing Bear's Journey for Justice*. New York: St. Martin's Press, 2009.

Svingen, Orlan J. *The Northern Cheyenne Indian Reservation, 1877–1900*. Niwot: University Press of Colorado, 1993.

Terry, Dennis O'Connor. "The White River Group of Northwestern Nebraska: Stratigraphic Revisions, Correlations, and Paleopedology" (1998). University of Nebraska–Lincoln, abstract. AAI9829534. Accessed at http://digitalcommons.unl.edu/dissertations/AAI9829534.

Trefousse, Hans L. *Rutherford B. Hayes*. New York: Henry Holt, 2002.

U.S. Army Gallantry and Meritorious Conduct, 1866–1891. N.p.: Planchet Press, 1986.

Utley, Robert M. *The Commanders: Civil War Generals Who Shaped the American West*. Norman: University of Oklahoma Press, 2018.

———. *Frontier Regulars: The United States Army and the Indian, 1866-1890*. New York: Macmillan, 1973.

———. *Frontiersmen in Blue: The United States Army and the Indian, 1848–1865*. New York: Macmillan, 1967.

Walker, James R. *Lakota Society*. Ed. Raymond J. DeMallie. Lincoln: University of Nebraska Press, 1982.

Warren, Louis S. *Buffalo Bill's America: William Cody and the Wild West Show*. New York: Alfred A. Knopf, 2005.
Weist, Tom. *A History of the Cheyenne People*. Billings: Montana Council for Indian Education, 1977.
Wessells, Henry W., IV. "Hard Military Service: Two Officers in the 19th Century West." *AB Bookman's Weekly*, October 5, 1998, pp. 601–605.
West, Elliott. "Called Out People: The Cheyennes and the Central Plains." *Montana The Magazine of Western History* 48 (Summer 1998): 2–15.
We, the Northern Cheyenne People: Our Land, Our History, Our Culture. Lame Deer, Mont.: Chief Dull Knife College, 2008.
White, Virgil D., comp. *Index to Pension Applications for Indian Wars Service between 1817 and 1898*. Waynesboro, Tenn.: National Historical Publishing Company, 1997.
Whitney, Caspar. "The Santiago Campaign." *Harper's Magazine* (October 1898): 795–802.
Wilhelm, Thomas. *A Military Dictionary and Gazetteer*. Philadelphia: L. R. Hamersly, 1881.
Williams, Thomas Benton. *The Soul of the Red Man*. N.p., 1937.
Woodward, George A. "Some Experiences with the Cheyennes." *United Service* 1 (April 1879): 188–91.

Newspapers and Periodicals

Army and Navy Journal (Washington, D.C.). 1878, 1879.
Atchison Champion (Kansas). 1879.
Big Horn County News (Hardin, Montana). 1988.
Billings Gazette (Montana). 2016, 2017.
Cecil Whig (cecildaily.com) (Elkton, Maryland). 2017.
Cheyenne Daily Leader (Wyoming). 1881.
Chicago Times. 1876, 1878, 1879.
Chicago Tribune. 1878.
Cincinnati Daily Star (Ohio). 1879.
Daily State Journal (Lincoln, Nebraska). 1878.
Dodge City Times (Kansas). 1879.
Emporia News (Kansas). 1879.
Frank Leslie's Illustrated Newspaper (New York). 1879.
Harper's Weekly (New York). 1879.
Indian Country Today (Washington, D.C.). 1993, 2014.
Iola Daily Record (Kansas). 1905.
Kansas City Star. 1994.
Leavenworth Weekly Times (Kansas). 1879.
Lincoln Journal (Nebraska). 1971.
Lincoln State Journal (Nebraska). 1896.
McCook Tribune (Nebraska). 1929.
National Tribune (Washington, D.C.). 1911, 1920.

Native Sun News (Rapid City, South Dakota). 2014.
New North-West (Portland, Oregon). 1879.
New York Herald. 1878, 1879.
New York Times. 1878, 1879, 1993.
Omaha Bee (Nebraska). 1878, 1879.
Omaha Herald (Nebraska). 1879.
Omaha Weekly Republican (Nebraska). 1878.
Omaha World-Herald (Nebraska). 1906, 1993, 1994, 2016.
Rapid City Journal (South Dakota). 1993, 2016.
Sidney Plaindealer (Nebraska). 1878, 1879.
Sidney Telegraph (Nebraska). 1878, 1885.
Soaring Eagle Signals (Billings, Montana). 2016.
Wellington Press (Kansas). 1878.
Winners of the West (St. Joseph, Missouri). 1939.

Historical Maps and Atlases

Archaeological Drawing 25DW51, "1874 Cavalry Barracks." 1987–88. Fort Robinson Archive, Nebraska State Historical Society, Lincoln.

"Captain Carter P. Johnson's Diagram Showing Outbreak of Cheyennes." Nebraska State Historical Society Archives, MS 8, Eli S. Ricker Collection, Box 28, Folder 91.

"Military Operations, Jan. 19–22, 1879." Set of three modern penciled maps, unattributed and without scale, labeled "source unknown." Fort Robinson Archive, Nebraska State Historical Society.

Montana Atlas & Gazetteer. Freeport, Maine: DeLorme, 2017.

Nebraska Atlas & Gazetteer. Freeport, Maine: DeLorme, 2010.

"Plan of Fort Robinson Showing Line of retreat [*sic*], of Cheyennes after Their outbreak Jan. 9, 1879," accompanying "Proceedings of a Board." National Archives, copy in Fort Robinson Archive, Nebraska State Historical Society.

"Plat of Sioux County. County Ownership Plats." Series 4140. South Sioux City, Nebr.: Western Cartographers, n.d.

South Dakota Atlas & Gazetteer. Freeport, Maine: DeLorme, 2017.

U.S. Department of the Interior Geological Survey (USGS). "Andrews, Nebr." Quadrangle, 1980. Washington, D.C.: U.S. Department of the Interior.

———. "Bodarc, Nebr." Quadrangle, 1980. Washington, D.C.: U.S. Department of the Interior.

———. "Crawford, Nebr." Quadrangle, 1980. Washington, D.C.: U.S. Department of the Interior.

———. "Crow Butte, Nebr." Quadrangle, 1980. Washington, D.C.: U.S. Department of the Interior.

———. "Five Points, Nebr." Quadrangle, 1980. Washington, D.C.: U.S. Department of the Interior.

———. "Gordon, SE, Nebr." Quadrangle, 1969. Washington, D.C.: U.S. Department of the Interior.

———. "Harrison West, Nebr." Quadrangle, 1978. Washington, D.C.: U.S. Department of the Interior.

———. "Smiley Canyon, Nebr." Quadrangle, 1980. Washington, D.C.: U.S. Department of the Interior.

———. "Story, Nebr." Quadrangle, 1980. Washington, D.C.: U.S. Department of the Interior.

———. "Warbonnet Ranch, Nebr." Quadrangle, 1980. Washington, D.C.: U.S. Department of the Interior.

Wyoming Atlas & Gazetteer. Freeport, Maine: DeLorme, 2017.

Index